THE ALCOHOLIC SOCIETY

THE ALCOHOLIC SOCIETY: ADDICTION & RECOVERY OF THE SELF

Norman K. Denzin

With a new introduction by the author and a foreword by John M. Johnson

Routledge
Taylor & Francis Group
New York London

Originally published in 1987 by Sage Publications, Inc.

Published 1993 by Transaction Publishers

Published 2017 by Routledge
711 Third Avenue, New York, NY 10017, USA
2 Park Square, Milton Park, Abingdon, Oxon OX14 4RN

First issued in hardback 2017

Routledge is an imprint of the Taylor & Francis Group, an informa business

Library of Congress Catalog Number: 92-35675

Library of Congress Cataloging-in-Publication Data

Denzin, Norman K.

The alcoholic society: addiction and recovery of the self/Norman K. Denzin; with a new introduction by the author and a foreword by John M. Johnson.

p. cm.

Combined ed. of: The alcoholic self; and, The recovering alcoholic.

Includes bibliographical references and index.

ISBN 978-1-56000-669-5

1. Alcoholics-Rehabilitation-United States. 2. Alcoholism-Treatment-United States. 3. Alcoholism-Psychological aspects. I. Johnson, John M. II. Denzin, Norman K. The alcoholic self. III. Denzin, Norman K. The recovering alcoholic. IV. Title.

HV5279.D43 1993
616.86'1'0019-dc20

92-35675 CIP

ISBN 13: 978-1-5600-0669-5 (pbk)
ISBN 13: 978-1-1385-3417-9 (hbk)

Contents

Part IV A.A. and the Social Worlds of Recovery

Introduction to the Transaction Edition

Since the *Alcoholic Self* and its companion, *The Recovering Alcoholic* were written, a number of important changes surrounding alcoholism and its treatment have occurred in American culture.[1] As these changes occurred, some things remained the same. I will briefly address each.

This society continues to encourage drinking as a valued form of self-expression. We live, as David Maines says, in a drinking society. Freedom from self and daily life are set in the time-out periods our culture associates with drinking. A sense of self-worth arises from the effects alcohol produces. Drinking is basic to the American way of life.

Our culture has not succeeded, as other cultures have, in the ritual control of alcohol consumption. In the United States novice drinkers teach one another how to drink. This drinking occurs within a larger popular culture with particular norms or rules concerning "drunken comportment" and "time-out experiences." This culture connects being an adult with drinking and sexuality. These two acts are joined in the drinking situation, the bar or party scene.

Drinking in America is structured around two basic myths. The first, the myth of "wine and roses," asserts the belief that an intimate, loving, sexual self can only come into existence in a setting that joins wine and roses. (Of course wine and roses are metaphors, for any alcoholic beverage or symbol of love.) This myth argues that members of the opposite sex have the greatest chance of finding love, romance, and intimacy in those settings where alcoholic beverages are served.

The second myth is called the alcoholism alibi. In its various forms this myth argues that in any culture only a small number of drinkers have, or will have a problem with alcohol. This myth allows a culture to have its drunks, alcoholics, and problem drinkers concurrently with social drinking. Such cultures deserve the alcohol problems they get, for by engaging in the alibi they engage in a form of denial or bad faith that shifts responsibility away from the culture and its various institutions—school, college, family, or workplace—to the shoulders of the individual drinker. These two myths work in conjunction. They are repeated daily in the mass media. Together they serve to produce the kinds of alcoholic selves analyzed in this book.

AN ADDICTION CULTURE?

The decade of the 1990s is a time of renewed public concern about drinking and the problems of alcohol consumption in American society. A new temperance movement, paralleling the outbreak of a national war on drugs is one manifestation of this concern.[2] Other indicators can be seen in the many new recovery groups that have appeared in the last decade, including the Adult Children of Alcoholics (ACOA) and the Co-Dependency (CODA) movements.[3] As these new groups appear, old arguments concerning alcoholism as a disease reappear. These developments carry important implications for the alcoholic self and its recovery. CODA and ACOA groups have now become integral parts of the institutional treatment of alcoholism. Alcoholics and their family members are now placed in these two groups, as they learn the languages and ideologies of Alcoholics Anonymous.

Adult Children of Alcoholics and Their Offspring

The major figures in the ACOA and CODA movements, which have been intensively studied by David Rudy (1991) and John Steadman Rice (1992), include R. S. Ackerman, Claudia Black, Janet Woitiz, Sharon Wegscheider, John Bradshaw, and Melody Beattie. There are currently over 1,000 ACOA and CODA groups in the United States. Over 100 volumes on the movements have been published, and over twenty national conferences have been held. At least two national magazines, *Changes* and *Focus*, are devoted to the movements and their members. *People* and *Newsweek* carried cover stories on ACOA in 1988. Over one million copies of Janet Woitiz's *Adult Children of Alcoholics* (1983) have been sold. The 1992 Democratic candidate for president publicly announced his status as an adult child of an alcoholic parent.

The Movement Literatures

The literatures of these two movements bring together three dominant discourses in American culture: those on addiction, therapy, and family. The increasing medicalization of illness in American culture has spread the disease model to the alcoholic family. The ACOA and CODA ideologies thus merge the disease concept of alcoholism with the treatment ideology of the medical model. The expansion of the treatment industry has encouraged the development and interdependence of these movements, for now ACOAs and CODAs (like alcoholics) are in need of medical and psychotherapeutic treatment.

These movements reflect the patriarchal biases of the culture. Their primary participants are women, who have now been assigned the new disease of codependency. The codependency label can be read, in part, as a masculine label attached to women masking issues of gender inequality in this culture. At the same time, these twin movements fit well, as Rudy argues, with the renewed interest in genetic theories of alcoholism, for the diseases of the ACOA and the CODA are regarded as generational phenomena. (This formulation absolves the individual of responsiblity for his condition.)

These two literatures share certain central characteristics. They are influenced by the languages and literatures of the 12-Step groups (A.A. and Al-Anon, and Alateen). They accept the disease concept of alcoholism and now generalize that concept to the lived experiences of nonalcoholics; that is, adult children of alcoholic parents have the *disease of codependency*. These literatures focus on the new disease, its forms, meanings, and consequences.

Codependency, it is argued, is a process addiction, an addiction to a way of life, to be distinguished from a chemical or ingestive addiction, which is an addiction to a substance. Process addictions now appear alongside substance addictions. (In this literature an addiction is anything persons feel they have to lie about.) Process addictions put people out of touch with their feelings. They mask a dependence on any mood-altering experience that has life-damaging consequences. Codependents are dependent on others for their own happiness; they let another person's behavior affect their sense of who they are. Such individuals are obsessed with controlling the other person's behavior. This disease is chronic, progressive (CODAs want and need to be around sick people), habitual, and self-destructive. It includes a variety of disorders such as alcoholism, drug addition, eating disorders, obsessive gambling, and sexual compulsions.

CODAs are drawn into relationships with alcoholics, drug addicts, or chronically ill individuals, and irresponsible people. CODAs have low self-worth, repress their emotions, are obsessive, controlling, filled with denial, are poor communicators, don't trust others, are filled with anger, often have problems with their sexual identities, and are failures in intimate relationships. CODAs and ACOAs play out the identities of family mascot, hero, scapegoat, and lost child.

CODAs and ACOAs hold to four myths: (a) I caused my parent's alcoholism; (b) I am unique; (c) I have to be in control; (d) Mr. or Ms. Right will come along and make my life happy. They adhere to the silence rules: don't talk about your emotions; don't express your true feelings; don't communicate directly. ACOAs and CODAs are afraid of authority figures, seek approval from others, fear angry people and criticisms, become overly responsible, feel guilt when they stand up for themselves, are addicted to excitement, confuse love with pity, loving those they pity, and pitying those they love, inflate their feelings, judge themselves harshly, develop dependent personalities, become reactors, not actors, are rigid perfectionists, abandoned and shamed, as a result of their alcoholic childhoods, they adopt the lost child syndrome.

The New American Family

The ACOA and CODA literatures expand the potential audience for psychotherapy. They create new cultural subjects, or new identities for adult men and women in American culture, namely being ACOAs, or CODAs. They offer trenchant criticisms of the American family system. They propose a new therapy of liberation.

These texts teach that what happened to you as a child is happening to you now, for your childhood in a dysfunctional family has not equipped you to build healthy, normal, warm, intimate relationships with others, including your children. ACOAs and CODAs come from dysfunctional families, where they never learned true love, or how to express their emotions. They learned shame and guilt, feeling that their failures caused the failures in their alcoholic parents. Lacking a "carefree childhood" ACOAs and CODAs became young adults at an early age. They never learned how to be normal. They thought (and think) that a chaotic life is normal, while believing in "Brady Bunch" images of the ideal American family. Trapped in a cycle, CODAs and ACOAs now reproduce their distorted, dysfunctional childhoods in their adult relationships. The problems they experience today are directly related, then, to their alcoholic childhood. This means they must learn how to redefine their past, so that they can get free of it.

This literature creates a very specific picture of the dysfunctional family, the alcoholic who was brutal and destructive and the adult child who suffers from the disorders outlined above. It appeals to people who suffer problems of daily living and to people who have repressed their experiences as children of alcoholics, including sexual abuse and violence.

John Bradshaw argues that 95 percent of all American families are dysfunctional. Such families teach a poisonous pedagogy that translates into psychological abandonment of children, the instilling of guilt and shame, and the denial of emotions. This produces false selves, selves that hide behind codependency masks. The sickness of the American family is thus a symptom of society at large, which is also sick, for we live in a codependent culture. The family transmits this illness through repressive rules that are carried over into our schools, churches, and government. society then becomes the ultimate dysfunctional family system. The key repressive institutions of the society (family, school, church, state), repress emotions and teach us to obey others, control all our actions, become rigid perfectionists, blame ourselves for our failures, and keep silent about our feelings. This poisonous pedagogy reproduces feelings of abandonment that creates a shame-based, codependent inner self.

Codependency theorists make codependency an addictive process that requires therapy and treatment. This process addiction, they argue, should become a personality disorder listed in the APA's *Diagnostic and Statistical Manual: Third Edition* and treated as an emotional disease. Treatment and recovery include the use of psychotherapy, 12-Step groups, goal setting, and recovery of the inner, childlike self that was lost in childhood. A new form of family therapy is required, one that uncovers the repressive rules that structure childhood in this culture. This therapy would teach self love.

ACOA AND CODA IDEOLOGY

These are liberationist ideologies, purporting to free the self from itself. As rationalist ideologies they argue the irrationality of remaining in unhealthy relationships. Their emotionalism appeals to cultural stereotypes about ideal family histories and ideal, childhood experiences. Their anti-institutional, and anti-family bias is directed against the major institutions of American society. Although medically based and presuming the disease model of illness, they rest on populist, everyday ideologies of treatment. Their assumption that everyone is sick threatens to trivialize the usual concepts of illness and disease. They presume that changes from within the family can change history; to this end they treat the family as the basic institution in society. Everyone, they claim, has been emotionally abused, and only the individual can be the judge of the nature and extent of this abuse. We are, as Bradshaw argues, "The stories we tell about our childhoods."

Based on weak, anecdotal cases, this literature creates blanks that anyone can fill in, for who can't remember something unhappy about their childhood? These literatures have, in a sense, created a national epidemic; everyone, if they are honest, today suffers from a process addiction. This amorphous disease now generates millions, even billions of dollars. What were once bad habits have become signs of illness; Americans seem to have become obsessed with disease and recovery. The ACOA/CODA literatures offer steps for recovery for anyone who can read.

Some argue that these movements are reactions to the "selfish" seventies, where people attempted to get whatever they could of life. The cognitive therapies of the seventies (*I'm O.K., You're O.K.*) and the popular religious therapies of the 1950s (Norman Vincent Peale's *The Power of Positive Thinking*) emphasized the individual's ability and power to heal himself. Faith and rational thinking could produce happiness. Like Mary Baker Eddy's Christian Science movement, the self-help movements of the fifties, sixties, and seventies emphasized faith and will power.

The new self-help movements are different. They shift attention away from the self and place it on the sick society. They encourage a kind of collective fantasy about recovery and freedom from the sick family.

These new literatures idealize ideal family life. They feminize illness and promote masculine images of health and recovery. They subscribe to a form of the *genetic fallacy* (a criticism lodged against psychoanalysis) arguing that the problems of the present are produced by problems in childhood, that the last event in a series of events is determined by the first event in the chain. This literature punishes the alcoholic at the same time that it empowers previously oppressed people (the sexually abused). In creating new destigmatized images of addiction, this literature in a certain sense de-medicalizes illness by returning therapy to lay-12-Step groups. Like psychoanalysis, it argues that the repressed emotions are the key to recovery, that things are always symbols of other things and nothing is without symbolic meaning. Everybody needs help.

A Feminine Disease? The New Alcoholic Spouse

Prior to the 1980s alcoholics and their family members were associated with two groups, A.A. and Al-Anon (see Jacqueline P. Wiseman, *The Other Half: Wives of Alcoholics and Their Social Psychological Situation.* Aldine de Gruyter, 1991). The ACOA and CODA movements have changed all of this. From Al-Anon women learned that they were not responsible for their husbands' alcoholism. From the codependency movement, however, they learn that they have been co-alcoholics, dependent on their husband's alcoholism for their own sense of well-being.

These two belief systems redefine the condition of the alcoholic's wife in two ways. First, she suffers from the disease of codependency and must seek treatment. Second, she cannot cure her husband; that is his job.

Ramona M. Asher (*Women With Alcoholic Husbands: Ambivalence and the Trap of Codependency.* University of North Carolina Press, 1992) has extensively examined the negative consequences of this self-transformation. Codependency fosters a new negative identity for women, asking them to assume a new form of illness with ambiguous psychological and behavioral dimensions. This process of medicalization then contributes to an ideology that recommends a lifelong process of recovery. For many women this is a no-exit model; they may remain trapped inside Al-Anon, CODA, or other recovery groups. For others there may be a progressive commitment to a transcendent perspective that constantly seeks new forms of self-development. And some may stand still in the recovery process, endlessly echoing its ideology. Some women may become trapped inside a lifetime search for a new self that can never be found, seeking without direction new recovery identities. These individuals may experience a sense of marginalization from the dominant culture and view themselves as perpetual outsiders.

As particular types of deviance become middle-class problems, the probability of medicalization increases in direct relationship to a new problem's economic profitability. Wives of alcoholics are caught in this situation, and may continue to find themselves pulled into the codependency programs Asher describes. There is an additional dimension to this medicalization process. Historically women in this culture have had second-class citizenship. Codependency, some argue, reproduces this process. It is women, not men, who are commonly defined as codependent. If women had more power in this culture, would they be defined as codependents?

This is the negative side of the codependency movement. On the positive side this movement signals a new direction for American women and their relationships to the family system. In the 1950s and 1960s women did not see themselves as suffering from a disease or illness. They were quite content to get on with the business of raising and running a family. Their fulfillment came from within the family itself.

Asher's (and Wiseman's) wives strike out on their own, break free of their husbands' control, create and discover new careers outside the family, and look back critically on the family system that produced them. These women no longer seek fulfillment entirely within the family. This is what the ideology of codependency and recovery gives them. In this movement lie kernels of radical social change. If women are being taught to break free from the family, and to seek their identities outside the patriarchal-marital bond, then husbands too may be free to no longer reproduce the patriarchal structures they think they have to enact.

In this, as usual, women lead the way, even as they are stigmatized for doing so. Thus the terms and slogans of recovery from alcoholism (denial, discovery, codependency, "No pain, no gain," "Good coming from bad") transcend the specifics of alcoholism. They refer back to something deeper, namely the gendered selves and intimate relationships between men and women that this culture promotes.

CONTROLLED DRINKING FOR THE ALCOHOLIC: IS ALCOHOLISM A DISEASE?

As these movements gain force social scientists debate whether or not alcoholism is a disease. This debate has merged with the "controlled drinking controversy," which refers to the ability or inability of an alcoholic who has exhibited uncontrolled or out-of-control drinking patterns, to return to normal controlled alcohol consumption. This term is typically applied to an alcoholic in the advanced stages of alcoholism. The literature on this concept is complex and contradictory. It is coterminous with arguments concerning whether or not alcoholism is a unitary disease, with symptoms of increased severity, building on one another, and finally producing a full-blown disease defined, in part, by loss of control over drinking. The history of the concept of controlled drinking has moved through five key phases, each defined by conflicting arguments concerning whether or not alcoholism is a disease. Many of the alcoholics I studied were caught in this controversy or lived through each of its phases.

Phase One: 1935-1960 From the creation of Alcoholics Anonymous (A. A.) in 1935 through 1960, the unitary disease concept of alcoholism defined research, treatment, and public policy. Led by E. M. Jellinek, Mark Keller, and others, social scientists posited a progressive, four-stage medical model of alcoholism. Alcoholics, they argued, moved from the presymptomatic stage (drinking to reduce anxiety and stress), to the prodomal (onset of secret drinking, blackouts), crucial, and then chronic stages of addiction. In the crucial stage the alcoholic lost control over alcohol consumption. such individuals could never again go back to controlled, normal social drinking.

This model defined four distinct types of alcoholics: *alpha, beta, gamma,* and *delta* alcoholics. According to Jellinek, the gamma alcoholic was the prevailing type of alcoholic in the United States, and the one most likely to become a member of A.A. This medical model held until the early 1960s. The alcoholics I studied, while never using Jellinek's term, defined themselves as having lost control over their drinking. Jellinek's model divided any population of drinkers, as many have argued (e.g., Stockwell and Clement), into two categories: a large group of harm-free, normal social drinkers, and a tragic minority of uncontrolled alcoholic drinkers.

Phase Two: 1960-1970 In 1962 D. L. Davies argued (based on his own and others' research), that many formerly heavy drinkers had become adjusted social drinkers, rather than abstainers. The Davies's report challenged the medical-disease model, and questioned the loss of control concept. This report was quickly supported by a series of national surveys (Cahalan) indicating that individuals move in and out of problem-drinking situations. At the same time behavioral researchers (Mendelson and Mello, Miller, Marlatt, Schaefer), influenced by Bandura's social learning theory, reported findings indicating that the drinking patterns of gamma alcoholics, including loss of control and craving, could be manipulated in the laboratory.

In this new literature alcoholism was transformed from a unitary disease, into a multidimensional illness, with drinkers classified along a continuum, from occasional problem drinker, to problem drinker, to a person in the acute stages of alcohol dependency. Abstinence now became only one among several treatment goals.

Phase Three: 1970-1980 Phase Three was defined by controversy over the behavioral-learning theory models. The mid-1970s Sobell and Sobell study of gamma alcoholics who were taught to drink socially aroused considerable controversy, for many of their subjects, in a follow-up, were found to still be drinking in an out-of-control manner.

During this same decade the Comprehensive Alcohol Abuse and Alcoholism Prevention, Treatment, and Rehabilitation Act was passed and revised. This act mandated federal support for the treatment of alcoholism, and required that insurance companies be prepared to pay part of the cost of treatment for alcoholism. By 1990 there were over 5000 alcoholism, or substance abuse treatment centers in the United States, treating over one million individuals a year, at an annual cost of over 20 billion dollars. The prevailing form of treatment drew upon the medical-disease-A.A. conception of alcoholism. This was a paradox, for the dominant social science theories refuted the disease model.

Phase Four: 1980-1990 Community-based treatment methods developed in Great Britain, based on the bahavioral, multidimensional views gained favor. New treatment goals were developed, in an attempt to match alcohol dependency (various degrees of harmful drinking) with varying degrees of abstinence, or controlled drinking. The disease concept was called a myth (Fingarette). This myth not only supported the treatment industry, but it also prolonged the problem drinking careers of many, while absolving them of responsibility over their drinking. At the same time it mandated a single treatment goal (abstinence), and treatment modality (A.A.). Critics of the myth argued that no form of treatment was better than any other. Multivariant treatment models, rejecting the traditional concept of a unitary syndrome of alcoholism, were developed. At the same time the

Federal Drug-Free Work Place Act was passed, giving employers the power to test their workers for drug (including alcohol) use. The disease model underwrote this legislation.

Phase Five: 1990-Present The present decade is defined, in part by what David Pittman calls The New Temperance Movement. This movement builds on the War On Drugs of the 1980s. Various consumer and public interest groups are attempting to reduce the per capita consumption of alcoholic beverages, arguing that there are enormous health risks associated with drinking alcohol. Paradoxically, the medical-disease model is still very much alive in the publications of CODA and ACOA, even as it continues to be attacked in the social science and public health literature.

Discourse in this field appears to have returned to where it was in 1935 when alcoholics were called weak-willed, and alcoholism was defined as a moral illness, or failure of self. Jellinek's attempts to formulate a multidimensional, progressive conception of the illness persists, even in the multivariant models of the behavioral researchers. At the same time, membership in recovery groups continues to expand. The American population and the social science community persist in debating whether or not alcoholism is a disease defined by loss of control over drinking. The population is still divided into two groups, normal social drinkers and alcoholics, and A.A. remains the most popular form of treatment for this "disease."

The controversy over this "disease" will endure, as alternative, community-based and institutional forms of treatment organized under the multivariant label proliferate. Learning theory treatment models will still be blended with abstinence programs. Controlled drinking will remain a problematic, but limited topic of interest in the social science community. Yet the disease model, with its goal of abstinence, will still be foremost in the public mind, even as all forms of addiction continue to be viewed as failures of will-power.

We have come a long way from the lonely, self-destructive alcoholic of the 1940s. Today's alcoholic wreaks havoc upon everyone and causes new forms of illness. These new diseases create new cultural subjects who suffer, in their way, from this disease called alcoholism.

THE FUTURE

The alcoholic in the 1990s, unlike the cultural subjects I studied in the early and mid-1980s, now suffers from a double illness. He or she is first and foremost an alcoholic with a substance addiction. But underneath this substance addiction lurks an all-pervasive cultural illness, the disease of codependency. The alcoholic of the 1990s now requires at least two forms of treatment: A.A. for alcoholism, and ACOA and CODA groups for the disease of codependency. At the same time this figure is caught in the public (and scientific) discourse over controlled drinking, and whether or not alcoholism really is a disease.

If the culture decides that alcoholism is not a disease, then it removes the category of the sick alcoholic from its cultural descriptions of problem drinkers. If alcoholism is a disease, then the sick alcoholic remains. Clearly enormous policy implications follow, depending on how alcoholism is defined. If it is not an illness, then problem drinkers can be taught to drink in socially responsible ways. If it is an illness, then enormous primary intervention programs to stop alcoholism before it gets started are unnecessary, because problem drinkers will become alcoholics once they start to drink. There is no stopping them. If alcoholism is not a disease, then intervention and prevention strategies are warranted, for persons who might have problems with alcohol can (and must) be identified and taught how to be safe social drinkers. If alcoholism is not a disease, then a war on drugs is not necessary. If it is a disease, then educational programs which educate against drug and alcohol abuse are warranted; but not wars!

A culture which respects the drug alcohol would undertake careful means to integrate that drug into its daily patterns of ritual and routine. It would not leave instructions on drug use up to novices; it would have the older, more mature members of the culture teach the novice drinkers how to drink. Such a culture would be wary of the evidence about the genetic foundations of alcoholism. (If it took that evidence seriously then it would routinely inform cultural members that if you come from an alcoholic home, and if you drink, the odds are better than even that you too will become an alcohol abuser.) It would thus make abstinence from the drinking act an acceptable cultural identity.

Such a culture would seriously address the myths it has brought to the drinking act, including the myths of the normal social drinker, the alcoholism alibi, and the myth of wine and roses. It would clearly state to its members that alcohol is an addictive drug, period, and that it alone will not bring love, intimacy or personal happiness.

It remains to be determined how far the ACOA and CODA movements will go. It is clear that large numbers of cultural members no longer accept things as they once were. The American family is under attack from within. Some of these attacks are probably good, especially those which expose the violent underside of family violence and family sexual abuse. What is clear is this. America's attitudes toward drinking and alcoholism have moved to a new level of social awareness. The medicalization of alcoholism has now medicalized the American family and made it the site of multiple illnesses. It is not clear how far this medical metaphor will be taken.

Finally, it is necessary to locate this study (and its participants) in their historical moment. The men and women I studied were (on average), in their late 20s, middle 30s or early 40s. Many had been married (on average) for at least two decades, and lived with their drinking problem from 10 to 20 years (again on average). Working backward, many of these men and women were born in the 1940s (and 1950s), and married in the 1960s (or early 1970s). The alcoholism they shared with their significant others (1960-1985) overlaps with the Vietnam War, the women's movement, a world-wide economic depression, the rise of multi-national corporate capitalism, the defeated ERA moment in the U.S., the political conservatism of the 1980s, the AIDS crisis, an anti-drug decade, the return (worldwide) to a new traditionalism emphasizing a new politics of family, health, and sexuality, and the rise to power of two new social movements (CODA and ACOA).

The alcoholics I studied lived through and embodied this historical moment. Like their counterparts in the 1940s and 1950s, these men and women were struggling to make sense of their selves, their marriages, their jobs, and their places in society. They turned to alcohol as a way of easing the pain. In that turn they lost control of the alcohol and turned their marriages (and other intimate relationships) into nightmares of suffering. Each of the alcoholics I studied became an universal singular, epitomizing in their singularity individual attempts to make sense of this senseless moment, universalizing in their gestures and actions the epoch to which they belonged.

And even as this happened, these men and women find that their shared and individual histories are being rewritten by a new generation born from their alcoholic marriages. This new generation, the adult children of these alcoholic parents, are finding new ways to make sense of their own situations, just as their mothers (and fathers) did. As they do this they rewrite their cultural understandings of alcoholism, the alcoholic, the alcoholic family and its marriages and its meanings, and thereby create a new cultural text for their own children to inherit. And life goes on. Meaning of course that the interpretations applied to the foregoing terms have changed dramatically.

So what we have here in the present book is a historical picture, an incomplete glimpse, hopefully better than what we had before, dated, yes, but a testimony, like its subjects, to its historical moment.[4] For this book, like its men and women, has one step in the modernist past, and another in Mills's postmodern epoch where everything changed, and nobody knew quite how to make sense out of anything. So these alcoholics turned to the time-worn methods of drink and alcohol to do the work for them.

A new age is upon us, demanding new methods, rethinking old ways of doing sociology. But as we move forward, we will still need (hopefully) ethnographies like *The Alcoholic Society*, to show us just how far we need to go.

Norman K. Denzin

Notes

1. I record here my debt to Irving Louis Horowitz for suggesting the merger of the two texts into one, and for giving them a title which better represents the intent of my original project, (which I did not understand at the time). I also thank John M. Johnson for allowing me to reprint here his original forewords to *The Alcoholic Self* and *The Recovering Alcoholic*. I also want to thank Linda Detman for her assistance with the proof reading of the manuscript and the production of the list of references and indexes.
2. As David Pittman observes, for the third time in the twentieth century the United States is in the midst of a war on drugs. The first war occurred during those years bounded by Prohibition, 1914-1933, the second overlapped with the Vietnam War years, 1965-1972, and the third has just begun.
3. While the majority of American substance abuse treatment centers employ a version of A.A. in their treatment programs, the theory has not been without its critics. During the mid-1980s a new treatment movement emerged and defined itself against A.A. Led by the therapist Albert Ellis, this movement goes by various names, including Alcoholics for Rational Recovery. The group rejects A.A.'s spiritual program, and feels that the religious emphasis is counterproductive for recovery. Another counter-A.A. group is "Women for Sobriety."
4. Elsewhere ("Researching Alcoholics and Alcoholism in American Society," *Studies in Symbolic Interaction*, II:81-101, 1990), I have described in fuller detail the incomplete nature of my methods, and their relationship to what now passes as postmodern ethnography.

REFERENCES

Cahalan, Don. 1987. *Understanding America's Drinking Problem*. San Francisco: Jossey-Bass.

Fingarette, Herbert. 1988. *Heavy Drinking: The Myth of Alcoholism as a Disease*. Berkeley: University of California Press.

Rice, John Steadman. 1992. "Discursive Formations, Life Stories, and the Emergency of 'Co-Dependency': 'Power/Knowledge' and the Search for Identity." *Sociological Quarterly*, 33:337-364.

Rudy, David. R. 1991. "The Adult Children of Alcoholics Movement: A Social Constructionist Perspectives." Pp. 716-732 in David J. Pittman and Helene Raskin White (eds.), *Society, Culture, and Drinking Patterns Reexamined*. New Brunswick: Rutgers Center for Alcohol Studies.

Sournia, Jean-Charles. 1990. *A History of Alcoholism*. London: Basil Blackwell.

Foreword

Who could have anticipated that a study of drunks could have produced such a profound analysis of American white male culture, and what it means to be alive in America in the latter part of the twentieth century? What we are about to read in the following pages of Norman K. Denzin's book is an extraordinary analysis of alcoholism and alcoholics, one that is grounded in the recognition of the truth of each alcoholic's life. But it is also much more than that. It is a statement about white male culture and American social structure. In its pages, one finds the evidence of vast social and spiritual poverty as well as hopefulness about the possibilities for regeneration. In its pages, one will find the stories of how Denzin joined with many others in a search for their souls, and how one comes to recognize the existence of a spiritual power that transcends the individual. There is much more than this, too. But this book, like all other books, will gain its meaning for the reader based perhaps not so much on what Denzin says in its pages, but on how the life experiences of the reader have led to a certain stage of growth and development that allows for one, rather than another, interpretation of its contents. This is as it should be.

That we should find grand things in small and unexpected places is a noble part of the sociological tradition. So in this respect, Denzin's book stands shoulder to shoulder with some of our classics. In Emile Durkheim's *Suicide*, we learned how the seemingly most individual and private act of taking of one's life told us much about the nature of social cohesion and group integration. Max Weber's studies told us how the other worldly asceticism of Calvinism created the ethic for material accumulation, so prevalent in Western societies. Robert Merton has told us about how the seemingly most obscure acts of rule violation tell us about the goals of American culture. From Kingsley Davis, we learn how the history of prostitution tells us much about the stability and integration of family life. From the works of Jack Douglas, we have learned about the interdependencies of deviance and respectability, and how the creation of social rules contains the seeks and possibilities of their violations for social actors. In the works of Erving Goffman, we were surprised to learn how mental hospitals and other total institutions could enlighten us about normality and the taken-for-granted and unseen rules by which it is presented and seen by others. These works, as well as many others in the social science traditions, began in small places, but partly transcended their space and time because they bridged the gap between the lived experiences of individuals and the social contexts in which they search for their truth. Denzin's book creates such a bridge, and from its edifice even those of us who do not drink will be much enlightened about what it means to be alive in our time.

The Alcoholic Society can be read in many ways. The most straightforward way, perhaps, is to learn about the substance of alcoholism, alcoholic experience, the alcoholic self, and the seeds of its regeneration. In this way, Denzin's book has much to say to us. This is a phenomenological analysis, which stems from the fact that many individuals shared their lives with Denzin in his search for truth. His goal is to articulate the inner structure and the inner experience of alcoholism. He recognizes each alcoholic as a universal singular, and the truth contained in each individual's experience with alcohol. Using alcohol is part of the experience of being a normal American at this point in time, and is associated by individuals with their selfhood, freedom, and locations in the status order. The story of alcoholism, then, is a story about a relationship between individuals and social structure. From Denzin's view, this relationship involves a disease of time, a disease of self, and disease of emotionality for those who experience it in daily life. Alcoholics use alcohol in an attempt to make peace with their sense of the relationships between past, present, and future. The alcoholics' path is a mistaken one, but their problem is one that concerns all of the rest of us, too, and so in their search we may all learn more about our own path, to the extent that our own individual experiences have led us to recognize the problem. Alcoholism involves, for alcoholic subjects, a disease of emotionality. Alcoholics use alcohol to make some peace with their negative emotions, guilts, fears, and resentments. They seek to control these, as do most of the rest of us. They are mistaken in their path, but in their search we learn more about our own guilts and fears, and how it is that, in recognizing them for what they are, we recognize more about the divine essence of life itself. Alcoholism involves a disease of self, and experienced separation between the alcoholic subject and the place of alcohol in the social and spiritual order. Alcoholics use alcohol to gain, recognize, and assert their power in the world, their attempt to live an authentic existence with others. Alcoholics seek self-control. Each believes that he or she is in control of the world that surrounds the self, and in this control is experienced a sense of pride by the alcoholic subject, which leads him or her to take the next drink, even when the individual knows that he or she will probable lose control of self. It is this pride in self that ties the alcoholic to a competitive relationship with alcohol. The path is a mistaken one, but from the alcoholic's search, we learn more about our own, and our universal concerns to grapple with these questions. Finally, we find in Denzin's book the story about how the spiritual poverty of alcoholism contains the seeds for its own recovery, which begins with an alcoholic's surrender to his or her self-pride, bad faith, and imaginary ideals. In this surrender, we learn about how alcoholics achieve a more true and authentic sense of their rightful and legitimate power as individuals, and their rightful place in the social and spiritual world.

Another way this book can be read is as a statement about American male culture in the latter part of the twentieth century. The values of alcoholics, whether they be men or women, are those that are found to be ingrained in white male culture. We all know, recognize, and value them: individuality, control, responsibility, identification with one's social roles, and the power to achieve social success as defined in this culture at this point in time. Denzin's focus is the alcoholic subject and the experience of alcoholism, but in this focus we find illuminated these larger structures and the processes of male culture. In this respect, the book is at once phenomenological and structural, thus bridging the frequently observed gap between different layers of social understanding Denzin writes:

> To study the active alcoholic, then, is to hold a mirror up to one side of society; that side which is taken-for-granted and driven deep inside the selves of ordinary men and women. To study recovery is to examine another side of society; that side which makes problematic what others take-for-granted. This is what the recovering alcoholic accomplishes. In his or her actions, the alcoholic subject reveals to the rest of us how we might become something other than we now are. In studying the alcoholic we study ourselves.

A final way to read this book is as a story about how Denzin joined with many others in a search for their souls. Western rationality guides individuals to separate the knowing subject from the objects of its knowledge, and denies to individuals a recognition of their divine and universal being in self. All of our speech in daily life is animated by our confusions in making this recognition. All readers of this book share this animus with Denzin and his alcoholic subjects. We read this book because we are still trying to use our rationality and our intellect to understand that which cannot be understood solely through rationality and intellect. We read it because we all desire to be in better touch with the deep wellsprings of our desires and our emotions.

Parts I and II of *The Alcoholic Society* detail the inner structures of alcoholic experience.

In Parts III and IV Denzin tells us how individuals join with others to recover from their disease. Whereas the study of active alcoholism reveals what is taken for granted and driven deep inside the consciousness of ordinary Americans, the study of the recovery process makes problematic what other cultural members take for granted in their daily lives. The social and spiritual poverty of alcoholism contains the seeds for its own recovery. The process begins with the alcoholic's surrender to his or her self-pride, bad faith, and imaginary ideals. The recovery process is a group process, and through participation in Alcoholics Anonymous (A.A.) we learn how participation in the storytelling rituals and traditions of A.A. produces a new definition and sense of self that flows from the group structures of the A.A. collective. The treatment process is predicated on the assumption that the pretreatment style of sobriety drove the alcoholic to drink, and from this provides a reinterpretation of the alcoholic's taken-for-granted ideas concerning self, emotionality, temporality, others, alcohol, and alcoholism. A.A. members are similar to others who undergo a group socialization process, such as mental patients, military recruits, prisoners, and college students. They socialize one another, and collectively develop adaptive strategies for dealing with problematic situations. They develop their own meanings for the cultural problematics they are presented with. They develop a "medicalization" or "treatmentization" of their worldview. A.A. members teach and support each other in the development of a new sense of self-pride, one founded on a recognition of their alcoholism, and their personal achievement of recovery. This book details how all this occurs in the daily lives of alcoholic subjects. It shows how A.A. gets inside the self of the alcoholic, and how spiritual regeneration occurs as a collective accomplishment.

Although formally open to all alcoholics regardless of social rank, status, or position, the recovery processes outlined by Denzin are implicitly structured by gender and race. The pretreatment style of sobriety that drove the alcoholic to drink is one that is, for the most part, grounded in the values of a culture dominated by whites and males, even for women and minority alcoholics. The rituals of talking and story-telling that occur in A.A. groups involve a shift from male to female emotionality and emotional expression, and so perhaps it is not surprising to learn that seven of ten A.A. participants will experience one or more "slips" or relapses into alcoholism as they undergo the treatment process. Members of minority groups show an even greater tendency to relapse, and Denzin's work shows how this tendency is tied to the group ideology and processes. Slips and relapses are at the heart of the recovery process, and are related to the identity the alcoholic forms about himself or herself as an alcoholic.

American society is secular, democratic, and competitive. At no institutional level is there a formal ontology, theory, or perspective on the self and its rightful place in the social and spiritual order. This produces for many individuals a subject-object dualism, an experienced separation between the active, knowing, sentient subject and his or her social experiences within this culture at this point in time. Recovering alcoholics seek a more authentic, truer sense of this relationship, and so this book may be read as a story of their spiritual search and success.

John M. Johnson
Arizona State University, Tempe

Preface

This book is about the alcoholic society, the alcoholic self, and its recovery. It is an analysis of the lived experiences of ordinary men and women who pursue to the extreme the cultural injunction to drink and have a good time. Many of the stories that are told in the following pages are filled with hope, for many alcoholics do recover from alcoholism. But not all do, and tragedies are recorded here.

A society, MacAndrew and Edgerton remind us, gets the kinds of alcoholics and drunks it deserves. American society is a drug-oriented society, an addiction society, a society preoccupied with drugs, alcohol, their consumption and social control. Two-faced in its attitudes, American society encourages alcohol consumption, but does not want alcoholics. Hence the enormous pressures on problem drinkers in this culture to seek help for their condition.

THE ALCOHOLIC SELF AND ITS RECOVERY

The alcoholic self is divided against itself, trapped within the negative emotions that alcoholism produces. The rather enormous literature on alcoholism does not contain any seriously sustained consideration of the lived experiences of the active alcoholic who lives an alcoholic self on a daily basis. This book, represents an attempt to fill this void.

My point of departure is the active, problem drinker who comes to be defined as "alcoholic." Throughout this study I employ the lay definition of alcoholism. An alcoholic is a person who defines himself or herself as an alcoholic. To this definition I add two features. First, the alcoholic has lost control over drinking. Once an alcoholic starts drinking he or she is unable to stop and will continue drinking until intoxicated. Second, the alcoholic is unable to abstain from drinking. These two criteria were present in the life stories of every alcoholic I observed in this investigation. They are the same criteria employed by Jellinek (1960).

I understand alcoholism to be a disease of conduct that is emotional, interactional, temporal, and relational. Alcoholism is rooted in the self-definitions and self-feelings of the alcoholic. The term *alcoholism* references, then, a twofold phenomenon. First, excessive, addictive drinking is at the heart of alcoholism. Second, drinking masks underlying interactional processes embedded in the self of the drinker. These processes structure the lived experiences of the alcoholic. Alcohol is used as an anesthetic to escape from deep problematics of self, including a basic uneasiness with living in the world without the aid of a drug. For alcoholics these underlying processes become distorted as alcoholism takes over their lives. The alcoholic is trapped in a vicious circle of addictive drinking. The self the alcoholic drank to escape remains buried inside the lived experiences that alcoholism produces. Alcohol has produced an alcoholically divided self.

This book reflects a dissatisfaction with current behavioral, cognitive, structural, and psychoanalytic theories of alcoholism. The literature concerned with these theories offers very few insights into the phenomenon of alcoholism as a form of lived experience that traps the individual in a self-destructive cycle of existence. My intentions are to present the inner side of alcoholism, as seen from the point of view of the active, drinking alcoholic.

The alcoholic subject is a mirror to the larger society. This individuality compresses into a single lifetime the tensions, the contradictions, and the conflicts that flow through the "social bodies" of a drinking culture. American culture, alternatively permissive and then prohibitive in its attitudes toward alcohol and drinking, "scripts" subjectivity and selfhood in the consumption of alcohol and other drugs. Nearly crushed and destroyed by alcohol consumption, the alcoholic suffers that disease of conduct modern society chooses to call "alcoholism."

The alcoholic, recovering or still drinking, sheds light on the structures of everyday life that are taken for granted. This individual brings into vivid focus what it means to be a "normal" interactant in everyday situations. The alcoholic takes to the point of near self-destruction commonplace assumptions regarding alcohol, drinking, selfhood, emotionality, altered states of consciousness, and social relations with others.

The recovering alcoholic, who I define as a once-active alcoholic who no longer drinks, undergoes radical transformations in identity as the drinking self of the past is let go of. In the 1990s recovery from alcoholism involves socialization processes that often begin in treatment centers and then move to Alcoholics Anonymous. In these contexts, which I call the social worlds of recovery, the alcoholic discovers a new, nondrinking self that may find its place in a preexisting society of recovering selves. The recovering self, like the alcoholic self, is a group and interactional phenomenon.

The rather large literature on treatment for alcoholism does not contain any sustained, in-depth analysis of the lived experiences of the recovering alcoholic self. The second part of this book begins where the first part ends. That is, with the alcoholic who has surrendered, however superficially, to alcoholism. This individual is pushed and sometimes pulled either directly into a treatment center for alcoholism, or into Alcoholics Anonymous. He may find that he has no true desire to stop drinking, or to recover, yet others force these options upon him. Whether he likes it or not he is asked to recover from alcoholism. Hence he finds himself moved along a trajectory of experience that includes treatment and then participation in A.A. This twin trajectory of social experience constitutes the focus of my analysis. The following question structures my inquiry: "How is the recovering self of the alcoholic lived into existence?" This is an interactional and phenomenological study of the institutional and group socialization practices that create and shape the recovering alcoholic self.

My research sites are twofold: substance abuse or alcoholism treatment centers and Alcoholics Anonymous. My methods are interpretive and ethnographic. I do not study, except incidentally, the recovery process that occurs outside these socialization contexts. I am mindful, however, that alcoholics do recover—that is, stop drinking—in ways other than those that I study in this work. Some seek counseling. Some join self-help and therapy groups that are not based on Alcoholics Anonymous's 12 Steps. Others recover with spouses or significant others. Others just stop drinking. Some enter spiritual programs, or related 12 Step programs (for example, Emotions Anonymous, Grow, Narcotics Anonymous, Women for Sobriety), and so on (see Wholey, 1984). The recovery experiences of such persons are not well understood.

This work may be controversial or problematic for certain experts in the field of alcoholism studies. It is, in a sense, "pro-Alcoholics Anonymous." I am of the opinion that one's biases should be immediately placed in front of the reader. I have seen A.A. work and I have seen individuals die from "alcoholism" after they were taught how to become normal social drinkers.

The recovering alcoholic is an individual who (1) incorporates the identity of recovering alcoholic into his or her self-conception; (2) having once been an active, drinking alcoholic, becomes a nondrinker, and (3) for the purpose of this study calls himself or herself a member of Alcoholics Anonymous.

The recovering alcoholic self undergoes transformations in experience that produce situational and long-term commitments to the identity of "recovering alcoholic." This new identity will include central components of the A.A. program of recovery, that is, if the alcoholic commits himself to A.A. This means he will become an A.A. member. It is this individual that I study in this work.

The recovering alcoholic is, in a sense, an outsider to the broader drinking culture of American society. Previously a drinking member in the public and private situations of that culture, the alcoholic was nearly destroyed by alcohol. In the pursuit of a desired self that was to be given in the drinking act, alcoholics found that their drunken comportment produced the label of alcoholic. They became failed drinkers; stigmatized deviants who had lost control over themselves and over alcohol. As recovering alcoholics, ex-drinkers thus look somewhat askance at the society that defined them as alcoholic. Some even feel betrayed, for they pursued a prescribed mode of valued self-expression that nearly killed them.

Having once internalized society's commonsense reasons for drinking, the recovering alcoholic now learns an interpretive theory that makes the drinking of alcohol a tabooed, or forbidden, self-act. The recovering alcoholic, once a deviant drinker, carries the history of this past self within a new selfhood that allows for the appearance of "being normal" within a society of other "normals." By studying the recovering alcoholic self we gain insight, then, into another side of being normal, but deviant at the same time.

The Alcoholic Society addresses a behaviorist bias in much of the current literature on alcoholism and the recovery process. That literature is often preoccupied with behavior modification techniques that are intended to transform the alcoholic into a social drinker. It does not offer an interpretation of the phenomenon of recovery as lived from the inside by the alcoholic self. My intentions are to present the inner side of this process as seen from the point of view of the recovering alcoholic self.

This work is an elaboration of my earlier study, *On Understanding Emotion* (Jossey-Bass, 1984) which offered a phenomenological analysis of emotionality as a facet of lived experience. This volume applies that perspective to the experiences of the active and recovering alcoholic. I assume that alcoholism is a form of self-experience in which negative emotions divide the self into warring inner factions that are fueled and distorted by alcohol and intoxication.

At the same time this book, in its expanded new edition, anticipated and inserts itself into the analysis developed in my subsequent study, *Hollywood Shot by Shot: Alcoholism in American Cinema* (Aldine de Gruyter, 1991). In *Hollywood Shot by Shot* I show how mainstream American cinema, from 1932-1989, articulated and developed particular "diseased" conceptions of the male and female alcoholic and the alcoholic family. Arguing that films typify social experience, I examined how cultural representations, as given in movies, shape lived experiences, asking also how lived experiences shape their own cultural representations.

The present book is both background and foreground for *Hollywood Shot by Shot*. (*The Alcoholic Society* should also be read alongside *Treating Alcoholism* [Sage, 1987], which develops an approach to treatment based on the concepts contained herein.)

This book is directed to four audiences. First, it is addressed to those social theorists who are concerned with the vanishing subject in modern, postcapitalist society. The recovering alcoholic is a universal instance of a subjectivity that refuses to be obliterated by the forces of the postmodern world. Second, this work is addressed to social psychologists, sociologists, psychologists, anthropologists, medical scientists, and other practitioners who are concerned with alcoholism and the recovery process. Third, it is aimed at practitioners in the field who confront the problematics of recovery on a routine, regular basis. It is also intended for alcoholics who are recovering from alcoholism.

CONTENTS AND ORGANIZATION

This work is divided into fourteen chapters. In Chapter 1, I discuss alcohol use and drinking in American society, situate my study within the alcoholism literature, present the Six Theses of Alcoholism, and discuss my empirical materials. Chapter 2 critically examines current scientific theories of alcoholism and alcoholics. I give special attention to Gregory Bateson's theory of alcoholism, which he calls "cybernetics of self." Chapter 2 presents what I hope is a definitive critique of radical behavioral approaches to alcoholism and its treatment.

Chapter 3 is a study of the theory of alcoholism and alcoholics that Alcoholics Anonymous offers to the active (and recovering) alcoholic. Chapter 4 presents a phenomenological analysis of the lay theory of drinking, problem drinking, alcoholism, and alcoholics. It examines the arguments the problem drinker constructs so as to continue drinking.

Chapter 5 sets out in detail the Six Theses of Alcoholism. These are interpretive positions that examine, from different angles, the inner structures of experience surrounding alcoholism. I focus on temporality, social relationships, emotionality, bad faith or denial, self-control, and the process of surrender. Chapter 6, the "Alcoholically Divided Self," studies the alcoholic self as a structure of negative experience. I examine the negative emotions—anger, fear, hate, resentment—that characterize the alcoholic situation. I also devote considerable attention to the relationship between alcohol and violence. Finally, I take the alcoholic through the stages of self-collapse and surrender that accompany the final stages of active, alcoholic drinking.

Chapter 7 speaks in compressed detail because the topic is elaborated at length in Parts III and IV, to the recovering alcoholic self. I examine the main structures of experience that must be confronted if recovery is to occur.

Chapters 8 and 9 deal with the treatment experiences of alcoholics who become residents or clients in substance abuse treatment centers. Chapters 10, 11, and 12 deal with the social worlds of recovery as experienced in Alcoholics Anonymous. In order they take up the A.A. group, slips and relapses, and the restructuring of self that occurs once the individual becomes committed to building a "recovering alcoholic self." Chapters 13 and 14 offer a set of reflections on alcoholism, recovery and American society. I suggest that in studying the alcoholics we study ourselves. Active or recovering, the alcoholic reveals to each of us how we might become more than we currently are, or considerably less than we now take for granted.

Throughout this book, I have tried to use nonsexist language. At times, however, the multiple use of "he or she" and "his or her" in a sentence has resulted in awkwardness. Therefore, at times the male or female pronouns and possessives are used exclusively in a passage. I have tried to use them equally often in order to convey the existence of alcoholism in both women and men.

Norman K. Denzin

ACKNOWLEDGMENTS

I would like to thank Carl Kingery for suggesting this project, Katherine Ryan-Denzin for her insights and support throughout, my father, step-mother, and children for their patience, John Johnson and C. Wesley Mayfield for their assistance and aid in conceptualizing this volume, Mitchel Allen for giving it an early life, and Irving Louis Horowitz and the people at Transaction books for keeping it alive.

Self-consciousness withdrawn into the inmost retreats of its being. . . . Doubled, divided and at variance with itself. . . . It lives in dread of action and existence . . . it is a hollow object which it fills with the feeling of emptiness [Hegel, 1931:251].

Alcohol:	a colorless volatile flammable liquid, C_2H_5OH, synthesized or obtained by fermentation of sugars and starches, and widely used, either pure or denatured, as a solvent, in drugs, cleaning solutions, explosives, and intoxicating beverages.
Alcoholic:	a person who drinks alcoholic liquors habitually and to excess, or who suffers from alcoholism.
Alcoholism:	a chronic pathological condition, chiefly of the nervous and gastroenteric systems, caused by habitual excessive alcoholic consumption . . . temporary mental disturbance, muscular incoordination, and paresis caused by excessive alcoholic consumption. [American Heritage Dictionary of the English Language.]
Disease:	*(dis-ease)* uneasiness (in this sense often written dis-ease); a disorder or want in health or body; an ailment: cause of pain—to make uneasy. [*Chambers 20th Century Dictionary*, 1983: 356].
Anonymous Alcoholic:	"When I drink I can't predict my behavior."
Recovery:	Act of recovering. The regaining of something lost or taken away. To regain the strength, composure, balance, etc., of (oneself). Time required for recovery [*American College Dictionary*].
Recovering Alcoholic:	An alcoholic who has stopped drinking and regained a sense of self previously lost to alcohol.

1

INTRODUCTION:
Studying Alcoholism, Interpreting Recovery

> Hell is our natural home. We have lost everything. We live in fear of living. Alcohol was our only friend. We found ourselves in alcohol and then it turned against us and tried to kill us. No other friend would do that to you. But we kept on drinking because we had to [Female alcoholic, 58 years old, sobriety date unknown].

> I used to have to drink every day. Now I don't have to. I'm an alcoholic, sure, but I'm a recovering alcoholic [Recovering alcoholic, sober 8 years, male, 35 years old occupation, lawyer].

In this study I examine a basic question: How do ordinary men and women live and experience the alcoholic self active alcoholism produces? I understand alcoholism to be a self-destructive form of activity in which the drinker compulsively drinks beyond the point where he or she can stop drinking for any extended period of time, even if he or she wants to. I adopt the point of view of those self-defined alcoholics who bring their lived experiences to the tables and meeting rooms of Alcoholics Anonymous. I assume that each alcoholic is a universal singular, epitomizing in his or her lifetime the experiences of all alcoholics (see Sartre, 1981: vi).

Alcoholism has, since 1955, been designated as a form of physical, as well as mental, illness by the American Medical Association. An inquiry into alcoholism is also a study in mental illness, but into a form of mental illness to which alcoholics give special meaning. The practicing alcoholic may be said to live an emotionally divided self (James, 1961; Denzin, 1984a). This, then, is a phenomenological study in biography and society, for it joins the private problems of alcoholics with the public discourse and the public experience that surrounds alcoholism's presence in American society (Bertaux, 1981; Gusfield, 1981; Mills, 1959; Beauchamp, 1980; Madsen, 1974).

Alcohol is the most abused chemical substance in the world (Royce, 1981). According to a recent psychiatric, epidemiological survey, 13.6% of Americans at some time in their lives have suffered from alcohol abuse and alcohol dependence (*New York Times*, 1983). In the United States some 9 million people are estimated to be alcoholics and a recent Gallup poll estimates that one-third of Americans have a drinking problem. The "mental illness" associated with alcohol abuse is thought to rank second to depression as the most prevalent mental disorder in American society. The human and economic costs of alcoholism are incalculable, and are barely reflected in the statistical facts that record alcoholic-related suicides, broken marriages and families, loss of work productivity, ruined lives, personal degradation, and the loss of self, income, sanity, and physical health (Cockerham, 1981: 169). Alcoholism, alcohol, and alcoholics touch the lives of one out of seven Americans at some point in their lifetimes.

ALCOHOL USE IN THE UNITED STATES

It is estimated that 7 out of 10 Americans drink, at least occasionally (Royce, 1981: 3). In a survey of the incidence of problem drinking in the United States conducted in 1967, Cahalan found that 43% of the men and 21% of the women who drank had experienced serious problems directly related to the drinking of alcohol at some time in their lives (Johnson, 1973: 183; Cahalan, 1970). Having, or having had, problems related to alcohol use is, then, if not a personal experience of the individual who drinks, at least a problem he or she is aware that others have had.

A social text has been written that positions the problem or alcoholic drinker squarely within a matrix of medical, social, scientific, personal, economic, and ideological beliefs that performs two symbolic moves simultaneously (see Johnson, 1973). First, alcohol use is part of the experience of being a normal American, male or female, during the first two-thirds of the twentieth century. Second, alcohol abuse, although associated with selfhood, freedom, and the status symbolism of the new middle class (Johnson, 1973), must be dissociated from the self of the abuser. Alcoholism, being a disease or an illness, is not the responsibility of the drinker. Yet, the ethos of self-responsibility and self-control that permeates American culture makes alcoholism the personal responsibility of the drinker who abuses alcohol. This subtle interpretation of alcoholism as an illness, which has the self at its center, escapes general public understanding. Hence, although the popularization of the disease or medical conception of alcoholism has spread throughout American society, it remains an illness that is not like other illnesses or diseases (diabetes, cancer) the individual may incur. It is not a purely medical or biological problem. This understanding remains in place, despite the efforts by the American Medical Association, the National Council on Alcoholism, the World Health Organization, the National Institution on Alcoholism and Alcohol Abuse, and Alcoholics Anonymous to persuade the public otherwise (Beauchamp, 1980: 22-48; A.A. 1957: 235-251; see also Blane, 1968; Chafetez and Yoerg, 1977).

This vicious ambiguity that surrounds the American attitude toward the self and the disease called alcoholism is revealed in the Mulford and Miller survey of 1964 in which they asked a random sample of respondents to give their personal views of the alcoholic. Of the sample, 65% said the alcoholic was sick. There were 60% who said the alcoholic was weak willed, and 31% who said alcoholics were morally weak. Only 24% said the alcoholic was sick, without using any of the other labels (Johnson, 1973: 146; Mulford and Miller, 1964). Being weak willed and morally weak are two meanings directly associated with strength of self and with self-will or willpower. Vaillant's (1983: 1-11) most recent review of the meanings surrounding the disease concept of alcoholism confirm the Mulford and Miller (1964) and Mulford (1970) findings.

The American alcoholic, then, at least since the 1960s, has been perceived as being sick, as suffering from an illness or a disease, but lacking willpower and self-will. The disease or illness conception of alcoholism has not succeeded in removing the *stigma of self* from the conduct of the alcoholic who has alcoholism (see Beauchamp, 1980: 68; Kurtz, 1979: 199-230; Levine, 1978: 160).

The alcoholic typically has been contrasted with the normal social drinker (Beauchamp, 1980). The normal social drinker apparently possesses skills, powers, and immunities that allow him or her to drink within the range of normal conduct that our culture prescribes. That is, the normal social drinker does not have socially defined problems with alcohol. These problems do not exist because of attributes he or she possesses. These abilities are in the individual and in the terminology that culture and science use to describe his or her use of alcohol. Locating the ability to control or not to control alcohol in the individual shifts attention away from the culture, the social groups, and the historical social structures the person inherits from society. By positioning the normal social drinker midway between the problem, alcoholic drinker and the person who abstains, American society has driven its obsession with self-control into the mind of every man and woman who comes in contact with alcohol. That is, control is a personal phenomenon that can be manipulated by willpower and the methods of modern behavioral science. The mythical social drinker who drinks normally thus epitomizes America's relationship with alcohol, alcoholism, and the alcoholic.

SITUATING THIS STUDY

The "alcoholism" that the alcoholic confronts on a daily basis is experienced as a relationship with the world. Consequently, it must be studied interactionally and interpretively as a structure of experience that is produced and reproduced, over and over again, in the lived experiences of the "alcoholic" man or woman.

As a study in lived experience, this investigation necessarily becomes an examination of temporality, emotionality, and interaction. That is, the alcoholic's being in the world is temporal. Alcohol alters his or her inner stream of emotional, temporal experiences. The alcoholic's interactional experiences with others are woven through an alcoholically altered inner stream of consciousness. The alcoholic confronts "reality" from the vantage point of the social world of alcohol, which, like the world of emotionality, is a separate province of reality (Denzin, 1984a: 95). Although embedded in the everyday life world, the world of alcohol stands distinct from that world. Yet when in the world that alcohol gives him or her, the drinker takes that world everywhere. The alcoholic cannot just walk away from it, as one might walk away from the work or family worlds one also occupies. Like the world of emotion, the world of alcohol shatters the taken-for-granted assumptions of the everyday world, rendering its assumptions and presuppositions meaningless and irrelevant.

Alcoholism and alcohol cut through every structure of the subject's life, leaving nothing in his or her world untouched. Consequently, a study of the self of the recovering or practicing alcoholic becomes an inquiry into the meaning of existence as existence is lived by the man or woman who places alcohol between himself or herself and the world of others. This investigation is an extended essay on the understanding of what I term "alcoholic existence." By disclosing the meanings of existence as seen from the point of view of the recovering alcoholic, I hope to shed light on what it means to live at this moment in the twentieth century. The active alcoholic is a person who, for some extended period of his or her life, approaches the world through an altered state of consciousness.

Alcoholic subjects find themselves, as Marx might say, inserted into a mode of existence and into a moment in history over which they have no control. Alcoholics find that history is going on behind their backs. Alcoholics drink in an attempt to control their relationship to these events that are occurring in front of and behind them. They find that they are the victims of their own actions and that their lives have lost meaning for them. They experience divided selves and hate themselves and everyone who surrounds them. As they alter their consciousness in order to change their beings and presences in the world, they find that the world destructively acts back on them.

"Normal" Time and Emotion

The alcoholic lives a *dis-ease* of time and emotion that is experienced as an uneasiness with self. This uneasiness is dealt with through alcoholic drinking. Alcohol obliterates or neutralizes the alcoholic's fear of time and self. Fearful of time, the alcoholic dwells in the negative emotions of the past. Such self-feelings undercut and undermine the alcoholic's ability to confront the present and the future in a straightforward manner.

In contrast to alcoholic time and emotion stands "normal" time and feeling. "Normal" temporality and "normal" emotionality conceptualize these processes in a reflective, purposive fashion. This allows the person to incorporate self-feelings and temporal experiences into ongoing action in a nondisruptive, non-self-destructive way. Normal emotionality does not dwell in the negativity of the past. It is not fearful of the present and the future. Normal emotionality does not undercut the self-structures of the person. Alcoholic emotionality does. Alcoholic temporality turns away from the present and leads to the production of negative emotional experiences, which further locate the alcoholic in the addictive cycle of drinking alcoholism turns upon.

An understanding of the alcoholic requires an interpretation of "normal" time and emotion, for the alcoholic attempts to achieve a state of "normalness" through the drinking act. Afraid of not being normal, the alcoholic drinks alcoholically so as to cover up this fear. The alcoholic hopes that the next drink will allow him or her to experience time and self-feeling in the way that normals do.

THE SIX THESES OF ALCOHOLISM

Six theses, or interpretive positions, structure my understanding of alcoholism (see Chapter 5 for an extended discussion of each). The first is the "Thesis of the Temporality of Self." This thesis assumes that the alcoholic lives his or her experiences in the world primarily through the altered temporal consciousness that alcohol produces. This means that the alcoholic is always out of temporal synchronization with fellow interactants. Thought and emotional processes are dulled or sped up as a result of the alcohol consumed. Alcoholism is a dis-ease of time.

The second thesis concerns the relational structures of the alcoholic's self. It assumes that the alcoholic lives within alcohol-centered social relationships that have been distorted and twisted by the effects of alcohol on the alcoholic's self. In contrast to more normal social relationships in which affection and love may bond two individuals, in the alcohol-centered relationship, alcohol becomes the object that joins interactants in a combative, competitive, negative, hostile relationship. The emotionality of self is the third thesis. As indicated above, alcoholism is a dis-ease of emotionality and self-feeling. The alcoholic experiences negative, painful emotions on a daily basis. Alcohol blunts the ability to feel emotionality. Feelings are always filtered through the altered temporal consciousness alcohol creates.

The fourth thesis is the "Thesis of Bad Faith." I suggest that alcoholics and their significant others attempt to escape alcoholism by denying its existence. Structures of denial, self-deception, lying, and bad faith thus lie at the heart of the alcoholic's alcoholism (see Sartre, 1956, on bad faith).

The fifth thesis is the "Thesis of Self-Control." This thesis, following from the fourth, asserts that alcoholics believe they are in control of themselves and the world that surrounds them. As Bateson (1972a: 312) has argued, the alcoholic's self-pride leads him or her to risk taking a drink, even when knowing that self-control will be lost. Pride in self ties the alcoholic into a competitive relationship with alcohol. The alcoholic drinks in order to prove self-control.

The sixth thesis is the "Thesis of Self-Surrender." This interpretation argues that the alcoholic's recovery begins when he or she surrenders to false self-pride, breaks through the systems of bad faith, and comes to accept his or her alcoholism. Until such surrender, recovery cannot begin. In this volume I take the alcoholic up to and through surrender. In the next volume in this series, I examine the recovery process that follows from surrender.

The Alcoholic Self

A basic premise organizes the Six Theses. Every alcoholic I observed drank to escape an inner emptiness of self. This emptiness, often traced to early family experiences of death, parental loss, sexual abuse, drug abuse, or alcoholism, was manifested in terms of a fundamental instability of self. In this regard the alcoholic grotesquely displays the inner narcissicism and tendency toward madness that Lacan (1977), Lasch (1983, 1985), and Kohut (1984) have located at the core of human existence. The self-other experiences, the self-ideals, and the ideal selves that the alcoholic pursues are largely imaginary and out of touch with the world of the real. Alcohol sustains these imaginary ideals. The alcoholic lives in the realm of the imaginary and this may be a troubled world of sexual and emotional relations that reflect the alcoholic's unstable inner self. As a result of living in the realm of the imaginary, the alcoholic is unable to take the attitude of the other, to use Mead's (1934) phrase. He or she is unable to enter into and find a place in a society of preexisting selves. His or her imaginary life will not permit this. Intense preoccupations with self shut the alcoholic off from others. Because alcohol's psychological and physiological effects cannot be shared emotionally, the alcoholic's self is cut off from the world of normal interaction with others (see Tiebout, 1954).

These six theses, and the basic premise that organizes them, are drawn from three sources. They are based on my reading of the scientific literature on alcoholism. They are contained, in different form, in Alcoholics Anonymous's theory of alcoholism (see Chapter 3). Most important, they are grounded in my empirical materials.

EMPIRICAL MATERIALS

I examine the stories of self that active and recovering alcoholics bring to Alcoholics Anonymous, a worldwide organization of recovering alcoholics whose estimated membership in 1985 was over 1 million in over 58,000 groups in 110 countries. My materials are drawn from a five-year period of study, primarily in a medium-sized community of 150,000 in the eastern part of the United States. I have observed the workings of A.A. in over 2,000 open and closed meetings. I have gathered observations from substance abuse treatment centers and detoxification programs. I have had discussions and interviews with active and recovering alcoholics and their family members who belong to Al-Anon and Alateen. I also have had conversations with treatment personnel, physicians, psychiatrists, social workers, hospital emergency room nurses, and alcoholism counselors who make it their business to work with alcoholics. I have firsthand experience with alcoholism in my own family.

In addition to these sources, I have examined the literature of Alcoholics Anonymous including *The Big Book,* or *Alcoholics Anonymous* (1976). Other sources include *Twelve Steps and Twelve Traditions* (1953), *As Bill Sees It* (1967), *Came to Believe* (1973), *Living Sober* (1975), *Dr. Bob and the Good Oldtimers: A Biography, with Recollections of Early A.A. in the Midwest* (1980), *"Pass It On": The Story of Bill Wilson and How the A.A. Message Reached the World* (1984), *Lois Remembers* (1977), *The Grapevine* (the international monthly journal of Alcoholics Anonymous), *Twenty-Four Hours a Day* (Hazelton, 1975; this book is not authorized by A.A.), and numerous materials printed and distributed by the World Services Office of A.A.

The community or social world of alcoholics I observed numbered over 200 regular members who maintained near or continuous sobriety (as determined by self-report) by attending one or more meetings a week. Within this number there were 5 distinct groupings of recovering alcoholics. There was a core number of members (15) who had been sober over 10 years—one for 22 years—and the remainder averaging 14 years. These members were the "old-timers" in the A.A. community. There was a second group, with 50 members, who had been sober 5 to 10 years. The third group, numbering 40, had been sober from 2 to 5 years. The fifth group of 80 members had been sober less than a year, 45 for 6 months or more, 30 for 6 months or less. The most "slips" (returns to drinking) occurred within this group.

Within this broad fivefold structure there were other segments or smaller groupings. There were two women's groups, one gay and lesbian group, one young people's group, and seven Narcotics Anonymous groups that drew largely from the younger A.A. pool. I observed over 700 individuals who came and went or visited A.A. meetings during this period of time and defined themselves as alcoholics in meetings. A large proportion of this pool of individuals were patients in the two treatment centers in the community.

Traditionally, "two or more alcoholics meeting together for purposes of sobriety may consider themselves an A.A. group, provided that, as a group they are self-supporting and have no outside affiliation" (A.A., 1985: ii). Because two persons constitute a group for A.A.'s purposes, and therefore can have a meeting, and because the A.A. community I studied regularly saw the participation of "old-timers" in meetings, it would not be uncommon at any meeting to have members whose sobriety spanned the time frame of less than a day to over 15 years.

However, chronological age and sobriety date (days, months, years of continuous sobriety) often are widely divergent within A.A. Interactional age (Denzin, 1977: 162) or A.A. experience may bear little relationship to the individual's real age, sobriety date, A.A. age, or birthday. Thus in the community of recovering alcoholics I studied there were 2 individuals under the age of 25 with 4 years of sobriety, and 2 members under the age of 18 with 2 years sobriety each. There were numerous members over 45 who had less than 6 months of sobriety. Similarly, at least 5 members had over 10 years A.A. experience, but not one of them had succeeded in gaining over 9 months of sobriety. Slips, discontinuities in sobriety, and age at the time of the first serious encounter with A.A. disrupt and distort the relationship among these 3 age or temporal structures.

These temporal discrepancies potentially are present in every encounter that occurs between A.A. members. The gaps and distortions that arise among these 3 temporal structures (chronological age, length of continuous sobriety, and interactional experience with A.A.) support and underwrite the A.A. position that it is a 24-hour, one-day-at-a-time program that its members practice. The often-heard statement at A.A. meetings, "Whoever got up earliest this morning has the most sobriety at this meeting," is a pivotal point of departure for every recovering alcoholic—just as it is for every A.A. member who slips and comes back.

I observed fewer open meetings than closed meetings. An *open meeting* is open to any individual who has an interest in alcoholism. He or she need not be an alcoholic to attend. A *closed A.A. meeting* is attended only by individuals who have a desire to stop drinking and who may call themselves alcoholics, as the only requirement for A.A. membership is a desire to stop drinking. Persons who attend closed A.A. meetings typically identify themselves as alcoholic during the meeting when their turn to speak comes: "My name is Bill and I'm an alcoholic."

In the community I studied the number of meetings had increased to at least 4 closed A.A. meetings every day. In total there were 2 open meetings, 37 closed meetings, and 5 Al-Anon (meetings for spouses, friends, or relatives of alcoholics) meetings weekly. There were two alcohol treatment centers in the community, and six others within a fifty-mile radius of the city. There was a social club for alcoholics and the members of their families. There was no intergroup organization that connected the groups, as there typically is in communities over 150,000. The organization, or network, that existed between groups was coordinated by a small group of individuals who had an average of 14 years of continuous sobriety. A 24-hour answering service was maintained by the groups, however. The oldest meeting in the community dated from 1960.

Treatment Centers

I studied three treatment centers that employed a multimethod approach to the treatment of alcoholism (Kissin, 1977:44-46). Each of these centers utilized, in varying degrees, the following treatment modalities: (1) detoxification units; (2) inpatient, residential treatment of three to four weeks; (3) aftercare programs; (4) family counseling; (5) outpatient counseling; (6) ongoing group therapy, drawing upon a variety of human relations, group dynamic treatment approaches, including psychodrama, confrontational therapy Re-evaluation Counseling (Scheff, 1979), Reality Therapy (Glasser, 1965), group lectures, and the use of recovering alcoholics as therapists and group leaders; (7) individual psychiatric counseling; (8) pastoral counseling; (9) nutritional therapy; (10) recreational therapy; (11) occupational rehabilitation services; and (12) A.A. lectures and A.A. meetings.

All three centers also utilized, in varying degrees, the Twelve Steps of A.A. In each center the patient (client or resident) was taken through the first five Steps of A.A. The termination of treatment often coincided with Family Week and with the alcoholic having done a Fourth and Fifth Step (see Glossary).

These three centers offer a program of treatment that is typical of alcoholism treatment centers in the United States at this time (Kissin, 1977; Merryman, 1984). They did not, however, utilize the aversive therapy programs and the Individual Behavior Modification programs that attempt to resocialize alcoholics into becoming social drinkers (see Mello, 1983; Sobell and Sobell, 1978; Wholey, 1984).

I give these treatment centers the names *Westside Lodge*, *Northern Center*, and *Eastern*. They were all located within the eastern part of the United States in medium-to-large metropolitan areas. Westside had facilities for 20 patients. Northern could treat 60 patients at a time. Eastern had a 30-bed capacity. All three dealt with alcohol and drug abuse and all three treated males and females. Each had approximately a 3:1 staff-client ratio.

I have observed the workings of Westside and Eastern for four years. At Northern I followed a cohort of patients through a four-week treatment cycle. In all three centers I employed the previously outlined methods.

This work may be read as a case study of the lives of those men and women who were drinking and recovering during the period of my fieldwork (1980-1985). While I present no life in its entirety, I present slices of life-stories, or stories of self that are given around the "tables" of A.A. At the same time I present accounts of self that were given in the treatment centers that I studied. My methods are ethnographic, involving participant observation, open-ended interviewing, triangulation, and the study of biographical and autobiographical accounts of the recovery process (see Berryman, 1973; Merryman, 1984).

In the interpretive analysis that follows I intend to remain as close as possible to the actual lived experiences of recovery. The center of consciousness that I work outward from is that of the alcoholic who goes through treatment and then becomes a regular member of A.A. I present an "ideal typical" (Weber, 1946) version of this experience, seeking to find the universal, or generic structures of recovery. Hence, it is a process, not individual experience, that I seek to understand. However, that process can only be captured by studying individuals and the interactions they confront. Because these events occur within institutional and group settings my study is necessarily sociological, as well as interpretive, phenomenological, and interactionist (Blumer, 1969).

As with my investigation of the alcoholic self and the existence that self lives (Denzin, 1986a), this inquiry should be evaluated by the following criteria. First, do my interpretations illuminate and reveal recovery as a lived experience? Second, are the interpretations based on thickly contextualized materials that are temporally, historically, and biographically grounded? Third, do the interpretations engulf and incorporate previous understandings of the recovery process? Fourth, do the interpretations cohere into a meaningful totality that produces understanding, however provisional and incomplete? If these criteria are met, I shall be pleased.

Part I

DIFFERING VIEWS OF ALCOHOLISM

2

SCIENCE AND ALCOHOLISM

Consider the following account given by a 53-year-old printer at his second A.A. meeting after a 6-month absence. He has been attempting to stop drinking on his own for 2 years.

> I can't get off the damned stuff by myself. When dad died he made me promise that I'd quit. I promised him, but I can't. I just can't seem to get to where I was when Dad died. The old man drank a quart of Old Fitzgerald everyday for 30 years, then he quit cold when the doctor told him to. My sister's an alcoholic, she can't quit either. The boss says Frank you've got to quit. I try, but you know I get those shakes in the morning on the way to work. I stop and get a half-pint of Peppermint Schnapps, so they can't smell it on my breath, and I drink it and then I quiet down, start to smile, and feel good. It starts to wear off about the middle of the morning. That's why I keep the cold beer in the ice chest in the trunk of the car. I go out for a smoke and sneak a beer. That gets me through to noon. Then I take lunch at Buddies and have a couple shots of Schnapps, with the beer that everybody else has. I can make it through the afternoon. Then I stop after work and really hit it. I get so shook up about not being able to stop that I seem to drink more. I keep drinkin till I pass out every night. The wife understands, and when I mark the days off on the calendar when I ain't had a drink she's so proud of me. I just think I ought to be able to do this thing by myself. The old man did. But I can't. I guess I'll just have to keep coming back to you people. My body's starting to show the effects now. The Doc says the liver can't take too much more of this. I don't know, when I take that drink these problems all go away. But they're there when the drink wears off.

This drinker displays the three criteria of alcoholism that are employed in this investigation. He calls himself an alcoholic. He cannot abstain from drinking for any sustained period of time and once he starts drinking he cannot stop. He qualifies as an alcoholic subject, the topic of this chapter. He is, in short, a gamma alcoholic, an example of the predominating species of alcoholism in the United States. He is the type of alcoholic most likely to come to Alcoholics Anonymous (Jellinek, 1960: 33).

My intentions are to review critically the classic and contemporary theories of alcoholism, to lay bare the underlying assumptions that structure current scientific understandings of this phenomemon as it currently presents itself to American society. A single thesis organizes my discussion. The scientific literature on alcoholism has, with the exception of the works of Jellinek, Madsen, and Bateson, produced an image of the alcoholic subject that is disconnected from the lived experiences of persons who live alcoholism on a daily basis.

I will treat the following topics: (1) the picture of the alcoholic subject as given in the anthropological, sociological, psychological, and psychiatric literature; (2) scientific theories of alcoholism, including genetic, learning theory, sociocultural, and interactionist formulations; and (3) an evaluation of these theories from a social phenomenological point of view. In discussing the scientific theories of alcoholism, I will give special attention to radical behaviorism. I will examine in detail the concepts of "craving" and "loss of control." I also will apply Lindesmith's (1968, 1974, 1975, 1977) theories of opiate addiction to the "addiction" experiences of the alcoholic.

THE ALCOHOLIC SUBJECT

The alcoholic subject, the subject of the classical and recent scientific literature on alcoholism, comes in several varieties: Skid Row (Wiseman, 1970; Spradley, 1970), chronic (Straus, 1974), alpha, beta, delta, gamma, epsilon (Jellinek, 1960); asymptomatic drinker, alcohol abuser, alcohol dependent (Vaillant, 1983); blue collar or college educated (Vaillant, 1983); primary-secondary (Madsen, 1974; Fox, 1957); American Indian (MacAndrew and Edgerton, 1969); black (Watts and Wright, 1983); female (Gomberg, 1976); gay and lesbian (Schuckit and Duby, 1983), a winner of the Nobel Prize for literature (Vaillant, 1983; Duhman, 1984); upper class or middle class, old and young (Royce, 1981); rural and urban, Finnish and Swedish (Room, 1983). There are, in short, no typical alcoholic subjects, only individuals who have been identified as alcoholic or as having problems with alcohol.

Nor is there an agreed-upon alcoholic or prealcoholic personality type (Solomon, 1983; Barnes, 1983), although some (Menninger, 1938; Knight, 1937) have spoken of an alcoholic personality. This conception persists in the literature, as does the search for such a type (Williams, 1976: 243-250). Catanzaro (1967: 38-40) suggests that the following characteristics, in various combinations, may "have formed the seed bed in which alcoholism grew": (1) high levels of anxiety in interpersonal relations; (2) emotional immaturity; (3) ambivalance toward authority; (4) low tolerance of frustration; (5) low self-esteem; (6) feelings of isolation; (7) perfectionism; (8) guilt; (9) compulsiveness; (10) angry overdependency; (11) sex-role confusion; and (12) an inability to express angry feelings adequately (see Madsen, 1974; MacAndrew and Edgerton, 1969, for criticisms of such formulations). Narcissism (Tiebout, 1954; Zwerling and Rosenbaum, 1959) also has been associated with the alcoholic personality (see Roebuck and Kessler, 1972: 96), as have defiance, grandiosity, and resentment (Tiebout, 1949).

To speak of an alcoholic personality type is to appeal to an objectively definable alcoholic or prealcoholic human nature that underlies and structures the problem drinker's actions in the world. Such an appeal presumes an essential structure to alcoholic human nature that precedes alcoholic existence. The explanatory recourse to a fixed, innate, or semi-impermeable personality structure that precedes alcoholic experience, or apparently calls out alcoholic conduct, is wholly incorrect and inappropriate. The fact that a "normal" personality type has never been identified also undercuts the attempt to locate an alcoholic or prealcoholic personality type.

However, the literature remains preoccupied with *who* this subject is, *when* he or she became an alcoholic, *why* this occurred, and whether or not he or she can be taught or *resocialized* so as to no longer be a problem drinker. Accordingly, this literature can be interpreted as offering a series of answers or hypotheses to causal questions concerning the etiology and natural history of alcoholism, although few natural history investigations have been undertaken, the majority being cross-sectional, sample surveys (Vaillant, 1983). The alcoholic subject is both the *effect* of causal agents that play upon him or her as alcohol is and is not consumed, as well as the *cause* of the effects that are experienced as a result of these factors, including continuing to drink. A circular model of causation that revolves around the alcoholic subject thus organizes this scientific literature.

The Alcoholic Experience

The individual whom science identifies as being alcoholic typically is assumed to have passed through the *prealcoholic* and *prodomal* phases of alcoholism. He or she is in either the *crucial* or *chronic* phase of the illness (Jellinek, 1962: 359-366). This alcoholic subject will have moved from socially motivated drinking to being a drinker who experiences "rewarding relief in the drinking situation" (Jellinek, 1962: 359). He or she soon "becomes aware of the contingency between relief and drinking" (Jellinek, 1962: 361). In this early, prealcoholic stage of drinking the subject will move between occasional and constant relief drinking. In the *prodomal* phases of drinking the subject will experience the onset of "blackouts." His or her drinking behaviors will indicate that beer, wine, and spirits have ceased to be beverages—they have become drugs the drinker needs. In this phase the drinker will begin to drink surreptitiously, will gulp drinks, feel guilt about doing so, and display a general preoccupation with alcohol. Alcohol consumption will be heavy, although overt intoxication is infrequent. This phase may last from 6 months to 4 or 5 years. It ends with the onset of "loss of control, which is the critical symptom of alcohol addiction" (Jellinek, 1962: 363).

Loss of control, Jellinek argues, means that any drinking of alcohol starts a chain reaction that "is felt by the drinker as a physical demand for alcohol." Once a drink is taken the "gamma" alcoholic may drink until intoxication, or until he or she is too sick to ingest any more alcohol. Loss of control develops gradually, and does not occur every time the subject drinks (Jellinek, 1960: 145).

After recovery from intoxication "it is not the loss of control—that is, the physical demand, apparent or real—which leads to a new bout after several days or weeks. The renewal of drinking is set off by the original psychological conflicts or by a simple social situation which involves drinking" (Jellinek, 1962: 363). Once the alcoholic drinks again he or she displays an inability to control the quantity drunk. It is still possible to control whether or not he or she will drink on any given occasion. The problem drinker will be drawn back to drinking when tensions arise, for a drink has become the remedy for reducing tension and anxiety. An alcoholic drinks to prove that he is the "master of his will" (Jellinek, 1962: 363). The drinker does not know that he or she has undergone a process that no longer makes it possible for him or her to control the amount of alcohol he or she drinks.

With the periodic loss of control emerge complex rationalizations the drinker gives him- or herself for drinking. The drinker locates explanations that "prove" that control has not been lost. Grandiose behaviors followed by periods of abstinence, a marked loss of self-esteem, signs of aggressive behavior, and changes in drinking patterns appear in this, the crucial phase of alcoholism. At this point, the subject's life has become totally "alcohol centered."

> The "physical demand" involved in the loss of control results in continual rather than continuous drinking. Particularly the "matutinal drink"...shows the continual pattern. The first drink at rising, let us say at 7 a.m., is followed by another drink at 10 or 11 a.m., and another drink around 1 p.m., while the more intensive drinking hardly starts before 5 p.m. [Jellinek, 1962: 365].

The *chronic phase* sees alcohol dominating the subject's daily round of activity. He or she suffers a loss of tolerance for alcohol. "Half of the previously required amount of alcohol may be sufficient to bring about a stuporous state" (Jellinek, 1962: 366). Trapped within a drinking cycle, in which the craving for a drink appears at regular four-hour intervals, the alcoholic finds that guilt and remorse have become reasons to continue drinking. The addict drinks to relieve the stresses created by excessive drinking. He or she craves the expected effect of relief from the withdrawal effects being felt (Jellinek, 1960: 146).

Although these reactions to excessive drinking give the appearance of an "alcoholic personality," they are but secondary behaviors superimposed over "a large variety of personality types which have a few traits in common, in particular a low capacity for coping with tensions" (Jellinek, 1962: 367).

The alcoholic subject (in the crucial and chronic phases of alcoholism) displays the following characteristics: polydrug use, experiences with hospitals and emergency rooms for alcohol-related illnesses (comas, gastritis, hepatic disease, peripheral neuropathy, nutritional deficiencies, cirrhosis, internal bleeding, convulsive disorders, alcohol psychoses, hallucinosis, acute withdrawal reactions, rationalization, resentments, sexual impotency, loss of efficiency at work, geographic moves, changes in friends and family, changes in drinking places, emotional and physical violence, traffic accidents, and feelings of guilt about drinking (Jellinek, 1960, 1962; Vaillant, 1983: 25-31; Keller and McCormick, 1968: 14; Guze et al., 1963). This individual will live from inside an alcoholic body. The vital organs of the body will be affected by alcohol intake. Vitamin B and C deficiencies, fractures and other bone injuries, heavy and frequent bruising, dermatitis, a weakening of the body muscles, subdural hematoma, hypothermia or loss of body heat, and adrenal failure are all common.

Alcohol routinely alters the drinker's consciousness of self and relations with others. It is a drug that quickly establishes its presence in the world, the body, and the consciousness of the heavy drinker. Psychological and physiological dependency upon it therefore is not surprising, for it produces all the classic symptoms of addiction: changes in tolerance, cellular adaptation or tissue change, and withdrawal. Chemically it is a sedative, a hypnotic, a tranquilizer, a narcotic, a depressant, and, sometimes, a hallucinogenic, as well as an anesthetic. It is like most barbituates in these respects, except that it is both a stimulant and a depressant, is socially acceptable as a respectable addiction to millions, and is selective in its addictive effects, leading 1 in 7 drinkers (some estimates say 1 in 12) to become addicted to it (Royce, 1981: 7-8).

Alcoholic Interactions

Layered, or woven, through the above-mentioned physiological effects of alcohol upon the body and consciousness of the alcoholic will be the interactional effects of alcoholism upon his or her comportment. The interactional style of the alcoholic carries over into all of his or her dealings with others. This will include the alcoholic's mode of self-presentation, the manner in which he or she manages emotion, stress, frustration, dealings with others, making jokes, accomplishing daily routines, following rituals and commands, taking turns in conversation, deferring to others, listening; how he or she sleeps, eats, drinks, drives an automobile, makes love, shows affection to his or her children, pays bills, keeps appointments, plays golf, and reads the newspaper. Alcoholism's effects are thus integral parts of the alcoholic's self-presence in the world of others.

The public symptoms or signs of alcoholism are twofold: physiological, in terms of effects on the body, and interactional, in terms of interactional style, mode and manner of speaking, and so on (see Goffman, 1967: 137-148, on the mental symptoms of mental illness and the public order). The alcoholic's situational improprieties and forms of public misconduct lead others to define him or her as a threat to the normal interactional orders of home, work, and public places more generally understood. His or her misconduct is taken as a symptom of an underlying disorder that may or may not be defined as alcoholic, psychotic, insane, violent, or just plain unacceptable. (On the mental illness labels that are applied to alcoholics, see Solomon, 1983: 670-712.)

SCIENTIFIC THEORIES OF ALCOHOLISM

Scientific theories cluster into three broad groupings, depending upon the predisposing factors to alcoholism that are emphasized. These groupings are (1) biological-genetic-medical, (2) psychological-psychoanalytic, and (3) anthropological-sociological (Kissen, 1977: 1; Biegel and Ghertner, 1977; Vaillant, 1983: 2-11). I will take up each of these groupings in turn.

Genetic Theories of Alcoholism

Goodwin (1976, 1979), Goodwin and Guze (1974: 37-52), Madsen (1974: 44-64), McClearn (1983), and Grove and Cadoret (1983) have summarized the basic findings on the genetic antecedents to alcoholism. Goodwin (1979) suggests several innate variations in the response to alcohol that could predispose a subject to abuse or avoid the use of alcohol. These factors include (1) adverse reactions to alcohol, including the "flushing" response observed in Japanese subjects, which could lead to an intolerance to alcohol; (2) innate factors that allow large quantities of alcohol to be ingested; and (3) innate differences in the way alcohol affects the brain, leading to more euphoria for some subjects than for others. After a thorough review of family, twin, adoption, genetic marker, and animal studies, Goodwin and Guze (1974: 49) conclude, "While a genetic factor cannot be ruled out, conceivably it can be ruled in."

Recent work by Schuckit and Duby (1983) also has shown a possible familial factor in the metabolism of alcohol. Nonalcoholic "male relatives of alcoholics were found to produce higher levels of blood acetaldehyde to a standard oral dose of alcohol when compared to an age- and sex-matched control group" (Grove and Cadoret, 1983: 51). A biological predisposition to alcoholism or to alcohol abuse may, then, be inherited, just as learning how to drink, how to abuse alcohol, when, and for what reasons surely is grounded in part in one's family experiences (Goodwin, 1976: 48-49). Certainly conceptions of excessive alcohol use and abuse are learned in the family context, as well as in the broader fields of social experience that encompass the subject (Goodwin, 1976: 48; Jessor et al., 1968; McCord, McCord, and Mendelson 1960; Vaillant, 1983).

These observations suggest that although there is no genetic or hereditary theory of alcoholism per se, the weight of the evidence warrants sensitivity to genetic, biological, and biochemical factors, as well as to factors learned and transmitted in the family context (but see MacAndrew and Edgerton, 1969: 83-90). Recent arguments suggest an interactional and dialectical relationship between hereditary and environmental factors (Lewontin et al., 1984) in the genesis of alcoholism.

The *integration hypothesis* of Ullman (1958: 48-54) would suggest that a family, work, religious, or ethnic group will have lower rates of alcohol problems when it has clear rules surrounding how alcohol is to be used. When members of the culture are exposed to alcohol at an early age and are given appropriate adult models who drink in moderation socially and who discourage intoxication, then rates of problem drinking or alcoholism will be low. The Italians and the American Jewish community have been identified as two cultures that have integrated alcohol use successfully into their group structure (Bales, 1946; Beauchamp, 1980: 43), but not the Irish (Stivers, 1976), American black (Kane, 1981; Watts and Wright, 1983), or Hispanic communities (Kane, 1981). The American teenage culture has not integrated alcohol use successfully either (Mandell and Ginzburg, 1976: 167-204).

The integration hypothesis would mediate the genetic predisposition argument concerning the etiology of alcoholism, but it will not explain how certain members of "alcohol-integrated" cultures come to be defined as alcoholic. Clearly, however, genetic predispositions are mediated by cultural, or group, effects, for "experiences in groups produce alcoholics" (Rubington, 1977: 382).

BEHAVIORAL SCIENCE THEORIES OF ALCOHOLISM

Being "an alcoholic is a symbolic interaction process" (Mulford, 1969: 122). Drinking alcohol is a social act that has inner, covert and outer, overt phases that merge in the stream of experience of the drinker. Attached to the world through a circuit of selfness, the drinker's inner and outer worlds of experience are mediated and interpreted through interior self-conversations and self-indications. The self mediates the drinking act. The physical act of grasping a drink and drinking it is mediated and preceded by inner, covert actions, making it difficult, if not often impossible, to delineate firmly the line between inner and outer experiences; that is, between thinking a drink and taking a drink. The self of the drinker is always ahead of her in experiences yet to be taken, or just behind her in actions that are still being completed and felt.

The major behavioral science theories of alcoholism are causal. They seek to locate anterior and inner psychological states that precede the actual taking of a drink. They seek, too, to locate in the drinker's social, psychological, and cultural environment factors or forces that would condition or shape the psychological predisposition to drink (Madsen, 1974: 103-109). Three psychological-psychoanalytic theories—the simple *tension-reduction model* of alcoholism of Horton (1943) and Bacon et al. (1965), which has been elaborated and incorporated into the "learning theory" of alcoholism; the *power theory* of McClelland and associates (1972); and the *dependency theory* of McCord et al. (1960), Blane (1968), Knight (1937), Lisansky (1960), and White (1956)—compete with one another. Three anthropological-sociological theories—the "time-out" theory of MacAndrew and Edgerton (1969), Bateson's (1972a) "Cybernetics of self theory of alcoholics," and Madsen's (1974) "Anxious American Model"—locate the sources of problem drinking in cultural ambiguities in American society. (See also Jessor et al.'s, 1968, multivariate theory.)

I will take up each of these theoretical formulations in turn, understanding that no one of them accounts for the full range of drinking patterns observed in alcoholics.

Tension-Reduction Theory

The *tension-reduction*, or *anxiety-reduction*, model assumes that drinking is a learned means of reducing conditioned anxiety that is present in the psychological and social environments of the drinker (Conger, 1951, 1956; Horton, 1943; Ludwig, 1983). An initial dependency on alcohol is assumed to become established in predisposed individuals who learn to use alcohol to achieve states of euphoria and to reduce feelings of anxiety or tension. Because alcohol is its own reinforcer, producing reduction in unpleasant cognitive and emotional states, its continued use persists even in the face of negative stimuli and social reactions (Mello, 1983: 136). An "addiction-memory" sustains its continued consumption (Mello, 1972: 221). Alcoholism is thus regarded as learned behavior (Mello, 1983; Vogel-Sprott, 1972: 504) and should be understandable in terms of learning or reinforcement theory (Mello, 1983).

Ludwig (1983) has extended the "opponent-process" theory of motivation of Solomon (1983) to the question "Why do alcoholics drink?" His is perhaps the most elaborate tension-reduction learning theory model. He assumes that early alcohol use yields positive affective, or euphoric, states that are greater than the mild dysphoria associated with withdrawal from the drug. Because withdrawal represents an opponent of euphoria, the best way to remove this effect is to use the substance that produces the positive effect. This strengthens the opponent process of withdrawal, which requires an increased consumption of alcohol. Over time, individuals drink more to feel normal. The secondary conditioning of neutral stimuli within drinking situations brings the start of drinking behavior more and more under the control of conditioned stimuli. These conditioned stimuli elicit a subclinical "withdrawal syndrome which. . . is associated with craving. . . that directs the alcoholic to an effective source of relief from dysphoria" (Ludwig, 1983: 210). In those conducive drinking settings where craving is likely to occur, the first couple of drinks heighten craving and consumption of alcohol. A chain-conditioning process "in the absence of psychological, physical, or situational determinants, ensures that alcoholics will continue to drink until they reach their hypothetical pharmacological ceilings" (Ludwig, 1983: 211). Loss of control is thus located in this chain-conditioning sequence, which produces a relative inability to regulate or control alcohol intake. After the end of a drinking bout a relapse to drinking may occur through the ability of these conditioned stimuli to elicit the subclinical withdrawal syndrome and the related automatic craving experience (Ludwig, 1983: 211). A vicious circle of addictive behavior (Kissen, 1977: 5) is set in motion, and the behavior continues to produce the negative effects that are not sought, yet in order to remove the negative effects the act that produced the effects must be engaged in. Withdrawal becomes a conditioned stimulus for the conditioned response of drinking. Craving, withdrawal, and loss of control, familiar symptomatic behaviors of the alcoholic, are thus located in the addictive cycle wherein alcohol becomes both the stimulus and the response to the very conditions its use is intended to remove or alleviate.

A causal circularity is embedded in the tension-reduction, behavioral learning theory model. This point, which will be taken up next, has not impeded the implementation of variants on the tension-reduction social learning model in treatment centers. The assumption since Davies's (1962) article, "Normal Drinking in Recovered Alcoholics," has been that at least certain types of alcoholics could be resocialized to drink normally again (see Davies, 1960; Pattison, 1966; Pattison et al., 1968, 1977; but see Pendery et al., 1982). A resurgence in behavioral learning, tension-reduction, and social learning theories has appeared with the recent advent of increased federal funding for alcoholism research (see Madsen, 1974). It is to these theories that I now turn.

Learning Theories of Alcoholism

The most recent, influential, and controversial versions of the learning theory of alcoholism are given in Mello (1972, 1983) and Sobell and Sobell (1978). Building upon Skinner's operant theory of learning, the behavioral theory of alcoholism and alcoholics is not a theory of alcoholism. Rather, it represents an attempt to apply operant methods of conditioning to either determine the alcoholic's preferred pattern of drinking (Mello, 1972: 224) or attempts to modify the alcoholic's "alcoholic" drinking style, so as to produce a normal pattern of social drinking (Sobell and Sobell, 1978: 33).

Drinking, as with Ludwig's (1983) formulations, is hypothesized as being learned, acquired, and maintained "as a function of its consequences...the consumption of alcohol is preceded by certain events (antecedents), internal and/or external, followed by various short- and long-term consequences" (Sobell and Sobell, 1978: 33). Drinking behavior is defined as a discriminated operant response. The atheoretical structure of the Mello and Sobell and Sobell formulations makes no determination of the nature of the motivation, the intentionality, the self-conceptions, or the relations with others that might involve the alcoholic in the drinking act. In short, these models do not consider alcoholic drinking from a symbolic interactionist or interpretive point of view. Consistent with Skinnerian behaviorism (Skinner, 1953), these models make no assumption about hypothetical constructs that might intervene between events and behavior in alcoholic drinking (Mello, 1983: 137).

The basic concepts in these behavioral formulations are (1) the complex of discriminating stimuli that are present for any person at any time; (2) behavioral options (operants), which include appropriate and inappropriate drinking responses in an experimentally controlled environment; (3) reinforcement, which is any event that maintains behavior or increases the probability of the recurrence of that behavior; and (4) punishment, which is any event that decreases the rate of emission of a behavior. The behavioral effects of stimulus events and reinforcement and punishment schedules thus increase or decrease the likelihood of any unit of behavior being emitted, that is, drinking or drinking inappropriately. This behavioral model focuses on the consequences of behavior. There is no analysis of the inherent properties of the stimulus or reinforcing event; their properties are determined behaviorally. The Mello and Sobell studies offer, then, behavioral analyses of the reinforcing *effects* of alcohol (Mello) and adversive conditioning sessions on drinking behavior (Sobell and Sobell).

The Mello studies involved four reinforcement schedules: fixed interval, extinction of one minute, differential reinforcement of zero response and random sequencing, or multiple-chain scheduling of reinforcement. The Sobell and Sobell Individualized Behavior Therapy (IBT) sessions occurred in a simulated bar setting in a hospital. A variable-ratio electric shock avoidance schedule was employed when inappropriate drinking behaviors (as defined by the subject's treatment goal) were emitted. Videotapes showing the drinker intoxicated also were employed by the Sobells. Mello's studies involved the uses of individual operant conditioning booths and a modified driving machine. In both situations the "alcoholic" could work to earn money to buy alcohol that was dispensed automatically by the machine. The subjects in the Mello studies were, "for the most part, homeless men with a history of repeated incarceration for public drunkenness" (Mello, 1972: 224). The subjects in the Sobell study were gamma alcoholics who had "voluntarily admitted themselves to Patton State Hospital for treatment of alcoholism" (Sobell and Sobell, 1978: 82).

The conclusions from the studies reported by Mello (1972, 1983) and Sobell and Sobell (1978) may be summarized as follows. Sobell and Sobell reported success for their experiment. They concluded that they had succeeded in "shaping" the behaviors of the gamma subjects in their study so that they could practice controlled social drinking upon discharge from treatment. Their experimental group was reported to have been functioning significantly better throughout a two-year follow-up than were subjects in a control group who had been treated with the traditional methods of abstinence. An additional third year of follow-up by Caddy et al. confirmed Sobell and Sobell's conclusions (Pendery et al., 1982: 170). The effect of the Sobell study was to put before the American public and the scientific community of alcoholism researchers the proposals that gamma alcoholics could be returned, through IBT, to normal social drinking. This conclusion contradicts the earlier position of Jellinek (1962) and Alcoholics Anonymous (1976).

The Mello studies and others summarized by her (1983: 254, 259-260) lead to the conclusions that (1) subjects did not display loss of control in free drinking programs; (2) subjects never consumed all of the alcohol supply that was in front of them; (3) subjects could initiate periods of abstinence and could control the amount they drank; (4) the amount subjects drank could be manipulated by a work reinforcement schedule; (5) abstinence could be bought; (6) alcoholics will taper off and control their drinking; (7) some alcoholics can drink socially; (8) alcoholics do not display craving and loss of control, as these two phenomena have been conceptualized historically in the literature; and (9) alcoholics will continue to drink, even after alcohol produces negative, dysphoric effects for them.

Observations

Midway through her first experiment with alcoholics in the individual operant conditioning booths, Mello (1972: 228) observed that "it became apparent that neither subject's performance was coming under stimulus control as would be expected in the usual performance on a multiple chain schedule from a sophisticated pigeon." If Mello's subjects did not perform like sophisticated pigeons, they did display control over their drinking conduct in ways that permitted the above-listed conclusions to be drawn.

The Sobell subjects did not have the same experiences as those in the Mello experiments. The Pendery et al. (1982) follow-up of 18 of the 20 subjects in the controlled drinking experiment revealed that (1) of the first 16 admitted into the study, 13 were rehospitalized for alcoholism treatment approximately one year after discharge (this was contrary to the Sobell statements that their controlled subjects were functioning well in each of the follow-up periods for year 1 and year 2); (2) of the subjects studied in Caddy et al.'s (1978) third-year follow-up, 6 performed well 100% of the days, but Pendery et al. found that 4 of the 6 had engaged in excessive drinking during the third year (1 of the 2 who was rated as doing well had been hospitalized three times since discharge from the Sobell experiment for alcoholism); (3) the long-term drinking histories of the 20 subjects throughout a ten-year period (until the end of 1981) revealed that the one drinker who had been controlling his drinking after the end of the first year was still doing so, 8 controlled drinking subjects were still drinking excessively and regularly, and 6 were abstaining at the end of the follow-up, but only after multiple hospitalizations for alcoholism. "Four of the controlled drinking subjects eventually died alcohol-related deaths" (Pendery et al., 1982: 174). One was found floating face up in a lake, another died of a massive myocardial infarction (alcohol induced), another of respiratory failure, and another committed suicide, jumping from a pier into the bay.

These findings led Pendery et al. (1982: 174) to conclude that there is no evidence "that *gamma* alcoholics (in the Sobell study) had acquired the ability to engage in controlled drinking safely after being treated in the experimental program" (italics in original). These findings are an indictment of the behaviorial therapy employed by Sobell and Sobell, and it is an indictment of the learning theory that underlies their model. I shall take up a critique of this model in a moment, but first it is necessary to reflect on Mello's conclusions that her experiments (and those of others) demolish the twofold belief in the literature concerning the alcoholic's loss of control over drinking once the first drink is taken and the related belief of "the fatalistic craving" of alcohol (Mello, 1972: 282). Because these two phenomena are so closely interrelated, I shall treat them together in my discussion.

Craving and Loss of Control

Mello (1972: 259) states:

> The disease concept of alcoholism has long been encumbered by the notions of "need" and "craving" which are frequently advanced to account for addictive drinking. Craving has been defined as a loss of control over drinking and it implies that "every time the subject starts drinking, he is compelled to continue until he reaches a state of severe intoxication (Mardones, 1963: p. 146). The circularity inherent in this reasoning is evident. The lack of experimental data about drinking patterns has led to an implicit reification of concepts like "need" and "craving" which are defined by the behavior that they are invoked to explain. . . .
>
> No empirical support has been provided for the notion of "craving" by direct observation of alcoholics subjects in a situation where they can choose to drink alcohol in any volume at any time by working at a simple task. Although most subjects have consistently consumed enough alcohol on the first day of the experiment to raise their blood alcohol above 150 mg/100 ml, subsequent drinking patterns have been highly variable.

Mello (1972: 259-260) then concludes that no subject allowed to program his or her drinking freely has shown "loss of control" or a tendency to drink to oblivion. She suggests that these findings (1) argue against the validity of the general construct "craving" and (2) may lead to "more rational therapeutic approaches to problem drinking which acknowledge individual differences in potential capacity for controlled drinking." She does indicate, however, that these findings do not explain the problem of "readdiction," or the return to drinking by alcoholic as compared to "problem drinkers" (Mello, 1972: 261).

It must be noted that her criticisms of the craving and loss of control concepts fail to take account of Jellinek's (1960: 42-43, 139-146, 153-154) careful analysis of these phenomena as they occur in the latter stages of alcoholism, in particular Jellinek's point that loss of control does not occur 100% of the time (Jellinek, 1960: 145), and craving typically is set off "only in the presence of withdrawal symptoms" and these are late developments in gamma and delta alcoholism (Jellinek, 1960: 43).

Mello's arguments lend support to the IBT program of the Sobells, yet her inability to account for the phenomenon of "readdiction," or the return to noncontrolled alcoholic drinking, undermines her basic thesis that alcoholics can be taught to control their drinking. Indeed, the problem of readdiction restates the issue of "craving" and "loss of control." Readdiction pinpoints the failure of experimental studies of controlled alcoholic drinking. Mello (1972: 261) states the problem ironically: "The fact that the alcoholic is vulnerable to readdiction upon reexposure to the agent [alcohol] is one constraint on social drinking."

Mello (1972: 261) fails to establish her point that the concept of craving is a "logically and empirically inadequate explanatory concept to account for addictive drinking." That is, alcoholics who return to drinking reexperience the "craving for a drink" phenomenon, and once taking the first drink they set in motion an addictive cycle of drinking that is not unlike the cycle they broke when they became abstinent (or dry) for a period of time.

It is necessary to examine Mello's argument and her experimental findings in detail. I will begin with the Multiple Chain Schedule of Reinforcement experiment, in which alcoholics were given free access to alcohol on a 24-hour basis. Mello argues that her alcoholics drank enough alcohol on the first day to raise their blood alcohol level to a stable level, after which time they consumed an estimated 12 to 18 ounces of alcohol per day (half bottle). On the basis of this finding she argues that alcoholics can control their drinking and not drink to complete intoxication each time they take a drink.

A second experiment saw 13 of 18 subjects drinking 32 ounces of alcohol within a 24-hour period (Mello, 1972: 239). Prior to the cessation of this experiment, when alcohol would be withdrawn from the alcoholics, 5 of 23 subjects increased their intake, 9 decreased their intake slightly, and 6 "increased their blood alcohol levels in the 24-hour period immediately prior to cessation of drinking" (Mello, 1972: 241).

Three points may be taken from these findings. First, Mello's alcoholics were consuming large amounts of alcohol on a regular basis. Second, once they reached a stable level of blood alcohol, they stabilized their drinking at a high plateau, so as to avoid withdrawal symptoms. Third, in anticipation of withdrawal, rather than lowering their intake, they increased it, revealing anticipated craving upon cessation. Loss of control, or drinking to excess, thus occurs when the alcoholic believes his or her supply is about to be ended. *When he has a stable, regular drinking supply, the alcoholic in fact stabilizes his drinking at a high, alcoholic, addictive level.* Mello misunderstands the phenomenology of alcoholic drinking behavior and the craving process as it is experienced and anticipated by alcoholics. Her studies thus fail to offer a test of the craving and loss of control hypotheses.

Lindesmith on Addiction and Craving

Alfred Lindesmith (1947, 1968, 1975; Lindesmith et al., 1975, 1977) has examined the addiction process with narcotic users in great detail. His work illuminates the phenomenon of alcoholic craving and loss of control. By drawing upon it I am not suggesting that alcohol addiction is exactly like narcotic addiction. There are, however, important parallels. He suggests that withdrawal effects appear 4 hours (approximately) after the addict takes the last injection. (See Jellinek's remarks, above, on the alcoholic's 4-hour drinking cycle in the critical phase of addiction.) If no further drugs are taken withdrawal symptoms increase in intensity for about 72 hours and the most noticeable effects of the drug disappear after 2 weeks. An injection of the drug during withdrawal causes the withdrawal effects to disappear within minutes. This reaction is biological.

With full addiction (as evidenced with Mello's subjects) regular drug use produces a tolerance for the drug, or a drug balance in the body. The main effect of the drug is to maintain this balance, to prevent withdrawal symptoms, and to cause the addict to feel normal. The user may experience a "kick" when he or she shoots up, but during the several hours between injections it is difficult to determine if the person is under the effects of the drug or not.

According to Lindesmith et al. (1975: 227), the initial experience with heroin often is perceived as unpleasant. Alcoholics report similar statements when they discuss the first time they ever drank. They give accounts of vomiting, painful hangovers, and headaches the next day. Even when the first experience is pleasurable, the attitude it produces is not the same attitude that is expressed after addiction. This means that the "falling in love" with heroin or alcohol that pleasure theorists espouse cannot be considered a causal factor because causes must precede effects, rather than follow them.

In the initial period of drug use radical changes occur that reverse the drug's effects for the user. The original depressing effects of the drug vanish and are replaced by stimulating ones. However, euphoria or the positive effects of beginning drug use soon vanish. They are replaced by the negative effects of relieving the withdrawal distress and achieving normality. Tolerance builds up for the drug, for more and more of it is needed in order to relieve the distress effects of withdrawal.

Craving for the drug is located in the experience of taking the drug for the relief of withdrawal symptoms. "It is the repetition of the experience of using drugs to alleviate withdrawal distress (when the latter is recognized and properly identified) that appears to lead rapidly to the changed orientation toward the drug and to the other behavior that constitutes addiction" (Lindesmith et al., 1975: 226). Addicts, Lindesmith et al. (1975: 226) argue, do not get hooked on the pleasures of the drug (for example, as with opium), but on the experiences "of relief that occur immediately after a shot in a matter of five or ten minutes." Addiction is established in the experiences that occur immediately after each injection, and not in the way the user feels during the remaining time between shots.

The beginning drug user, like the gamma alcoholic in the critical phase, takes a shot every 4 hours. Addiction is established in this injection experience. It occurs approximately 10 minutes after each shot and not by how the user feels the other 230 minutes in each 4-hour interval. Those who think of drugs use in terms of being high, as being a euphoric or solely pleasurable experience, focus on the 230 minutes and not on the 10 minutes that follow the injection. They think of addiction as an ecstatic pleasure that extends throughout the intervals between shots, to be renewed by the next shot. But addicts report that they feel normal between injections, and they are the final authority on this, as alcoholics are authorities on alcohol use (Lindesmith et al., 1977: 518).

The addict (and the alcoholic) situation may be illustrated as shown in Figure 2.1. The rhythm of regular "fixes," injections, or drinks of the drug moves into the center of the subject's life, as he or she becomes addicted, "falls in love" with, or learns to crave the drug (Lindesmith et al., 1975: 228). All other activities are drawn progressively into the orbit of the drug rhythm, organized around it, and subordinated to it. The drug has taken control of the user's life.

Normal subjects report that they are unable to understand how anyone could become addicted to heroin or alcohol (see Lindesmith, 1975: 151; Beecher, 1959: 334). The same attitude characterizes the beginning drinker or drug user, who has no intention of becoming an addict or alcoholic when he or she first uses or takes a drink. However, as Lindesmith (1975: 151) notes in regard to the heroin addict, this self-confidence begins to fade when the user has his or her first experience with withdrawal, which is likely to be met with surprise and perhaps fear. The taking of a drink or the injection of a shot to

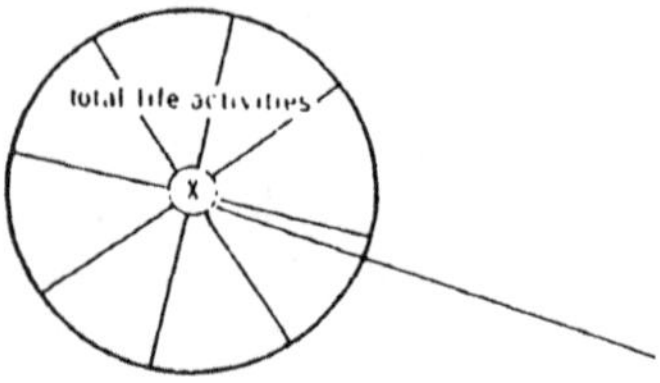

Figure 2.1: The Addict and the Alcoholic Situation.

remove the withdrawal effects quickly establishes in the user's or drinker's mind the connection between the drug and the feeling of withdrawal, however.

The addict, or alcoholic, soon moves to an injection, or drinking, schedule that locates drug intake at the center of his or her life. To return to Figure 2.1, the heroin or alcohol rhythm becomes the temporal structure that organizes every other activity (and perhaps thought) in the user's life.

It must be noted, however, that the addiction to alcohol that the alcoholic experiences takes several years to establish, although addiction to heroin and other narcotics can be established relatively quickly. Furthermore, the fact that alcohol consumption is regarded as a normal social practice in our culture makes for an entirely different set of attitudes toward the drug at the outset. Once addiction to alcohol has been established (Jellinck's prodomal, critical and crucial phases of alcoholism) the processes that Lindesmith describes for the narcotic addict appear to fit the alcoholic experience (see Jellinek, 1960: 115-121).

The Pleasure Theory

Those investigators who explain addiction in terms of the pleasure theory (McAuliffe and Gordon, 1974; Ludwig, 1983; Mello, 1983) presume that the drug must produce intense pleasure to be as powerfully addicting as it is. Even the opponent-process theory of Ludwig

(1983; see discussion above) must argue that the pleasurable effects of alcohol overcome the negative, dysphoric effects of withdrawal, hangovers, alcohol-related illness, high financial costs, self-degradation, the threat of arrest, DUIs, loss of family, and so on. Such theorists persist, however, in attempting to explain addiction in terms of the "high" that is experienced when the drug is taken.

There are two problems with this explanation. The first has been suggested. This is the absence of pleasure, as reported by alcoholics and addicts, in the time that intervenes between injections or drinks. Except in the few moments that follow the drug injection, the addict is, according to Lindesmith et al. (1975: 228), "one of the most miserable, unhappy types in our society." A similar description can be given to the alcoholic in the critical and chronic phases of alcoholism. The second problem with the euphoria theory lies in its tautological structure. The high that is the supposed key to addiction is part of the phenomenon of addiction. In this case the condition that is said to explain addiction is "simply part of it" (Lindesmith et al., 1975: 227). To equate the high with the cause of addiction is equivalent to saying that the cause of a person's illness is the high fever he or she is experiencing.

The alcoholic's or addict's statement that he likes the high that alcohol or heroin gives him is simply proclaiming that he is addicted to the drug (Jellinek, 1960: 64). These statements do not explain how he acquired this attitude or definition in relationship to the drug in question.

Euphoria, following Lindesmith's (1975: 149) metaphor, may be thought of as the bait that lures the user into a trap. The pleasure theorists seem to view addiction not as a trap, but as the rational pursuit of pleasure (Lindesmith, 1975: 149). Lindesmith suggests that they are so preoccupied with the euphoric bait on the addiction hook that they fail to see the hook—the painful and unpleasant effects of addiction. The key to addiction lies not in euphoria, but in the experience of taking the drug to relieve withdrawal symptoms.

Craving and Relapse

Addicts who relapse (Lindesmith, 1975: 147) do not do so out of a desire to avoid withdrawal effects, for they have passed through this stage when they stopped using. Nor do addicts return to drug use out of a desire animated by the pleasure principle, for, as Lindesmith has shown, the pleasures that are felt in the addiction arise only after the addiction has been established. The pleasure theory again confuses effects with causes. The crucial etiological question in the case of craving for drugs (or alcohol) and readdiction is to explain how the craving is contracted, learned, and brought into existence. Craving arises in conjunction with the use of the drug after physical dependence has been established (Lindesmith, 1975: 150). It is at this point that the compulsive and irrational aspects of the addict's behavior come into existence. A preoccupation with the supply, the fear of not having a fix when it is needed, and the hiding of the supply occur at this point in the addictive cycle. At the same time the ecstatic praise that the addict extols upon the drug appear in this phase, for this euphoric pleasure has become a motive for the continuation of drug use. Alcoholics, in a parallel fashion, will extol and speak eloquently of the effects of the first drink of the day, or of the drink that removes the shakes and the trembling feelings that they are experiencing.

The Two Forms of Craving

Mello (1972) fails to distinguished between the two forms of craving suggested by Jellinek (1960: 141), Isbell (1955), Ludwig (1983: 201), and Lindesmith (1975: 147). *Physiological* (or nonsymbolic) craving is located in the withdrawal effects felt as the drug leaves the subject's body. *Psychological, symbolic,* or *phenomenological* craving arises when the subject feels a compelling need, or desire, to drink or use, irrespective of (and often in the absence of) any withdrawal symptom. In phenomenological craving the subject's consciousness centers on the drug and on the effects she imagines will be produced were she to drink or use. As she imagines herself drinking or using she may produce shadow physiological effects that simulate the "real" effects of the drug in the body.

The following two statements from alcoholics who returned to drinking after lengthy periods of abstinence speak to phenomenological craving. The first speaker had been sober for four and a half years.

> I could imagine the taste of that stuff in my throat. I could feel my mind clear of the fear I felt. I imagined those feelings for two months. Finally, one Saturday morning I went to Walgreens and bought a half-pint. I told myself I'd drink half of it and throw the rest away. I took one drink, drank the half-pint, drank it, bought another, drank it, then bought a fifth, drank part of it, went to work drunk, walked through the front door, out the back, drove cross town, hid my car, checked into a motel and kept this up for three days. Then I went back to work, drinking a fifth every day. This lasted two months, until I ended up on the mental ward again, right back where I was four and a half years

> ago, drunk, insane and out of my mind. I came back to A.A. after that. I accepted the fact that I was an alcoholic [field conversation, July 5, 1981, recovering male alcoholic, 75 years old, retired, 10 years sober].

The next speaker had been sober three months, having gone through a treatment center three months earlier:

> It was a Sunday afternoon, mid-July. Everybody was gone. I'd been cleaning out my garage. I think I was angry at something. Suddenly the thought came over me that a drink would taste good. A straight shot of gin, warm and sweet. I knew my wife had thrown a bottle of wine behind the wood pile last spring. Least I thought she had. All I could think about was that bottle. I moved every stick of wood in that pile and the bottle wasn't there. Then I checked the neighbor's garden cause she'd thrown a bottle in there. No bottle. I gave up. I didn't drink that day, but the next Friday I went out and bought a bottle of that new 110 proof Irish whiskey and drank three shots. Put it back, got another, said I'd save it for a week, next day I finished it. I was off, then, on a four and one-half month binge that had me drinking everyday. I finally came back to you people in late November and accepted that I was an alcoholic. [field conversation, August 4, 1982, male alcoholic, 54 years old, academic, 4 years sober].

These two alcoholics began their relapses when they experienced phenomenological cravings for alcohol. Physiological craving was not present in terms of withdrawal symptoms, although each imagined the taste and effects of alcohol. Once each subject went back to drinking a loss of control was experienced. Hence their relapse sequence was as follows: (1) phenomenological craving, (2) imagined physiological craving, (3) actual drinking, and (4) loss of control, followed by attempts to control drinking, but drinking at an alcoholic level throughout the relapse.

Relapse occurs because the user has failed to replace the heroin or alcohol rhythmic center of his or her life with an alternative structure of experiences that do not involve drug ingestion. He or she remains psychologically addicted to the phenomenological, interactional, social, and cultural experiences (that is, lifestyle) that addiction brings.

Alcoholic Craving and Readdiction

Lindesmith suggests, then, that relapse or readdiction occurs because the user previously has been changed by the drug-using experience. The user has acquired new conceptions and attitudes as well as new knowledge of his or her body and its capabilities and the effects of the drug on the body. This is not an experience that can be altered easily or let loose of. The user's changed conceptions of self (produced by the drug) remain after he or she has stopped using or drinking. Similarly, an alcoholic drinker who controls his or her drinking will still drink to obtain the effects of total obliteration that complete intoxication has produced in the past. In short, Lindesmith's arguments suggest that alcoholics are addicted to and crave the experience that alcohol produces, independent of alcohol's addictive effects on their bodies. Further, his position suggests that "craving" is neither constant nor always present. It is only physiologically present when the effects of withdrawal are felt. It is felt at the moment when the drug is taken to relieve withdrawal symptoms. Loss of control will not occur if the alcoholic has stabilized his or her blood alcohol level at a level at which withdrawal symptoms are no longer felt. This is the state that Mello's subjects quickly tried to obtain and then maintained throughout her experiments.

Loss of control occurs—that is, the alcoholic drinks to oblivion—when the subject desires to maintain the high that previously was experienced in the early stages of drinking, but finds that the high can no longer be obtained or sustained. Having drunk past the point where the high would be felt, the subject continues drinking, not because of a loss of control, but in an attempt to prove that he can control his drinking and experience the feelings he once felt (see Bateson, 1972a, and the discussion below).

Reflections on Mello

These remarks suggest that the concepts "craving" and "loss of control" are necessary constructs in the explanation of alcoholic drinking. They reference opposite sides of the addictive process. When alcoholics are in control of their drinking, their behavior is being controlled by the alcohol in their bodies. No longer feeling withdrawal symptoms, they have drunk themselves into a steady-state where they feel normal. This is the state they desire, not euphoria; although they may define feeling normal in euphoric terms. They will drink and experience the negative effects of the drug so as to achieve this normal state. Hence the phenomenology of their drinking turns on the cognitive and emotional definitions of self they attach to the drinking experience and to the effects alcohol brings to their lived bodies. They are addicted to the experience of being normal, but they can be normal only by drinking alcoholically. Mello's studies fail to capture this pivotal feature of the alcoholic's drinking.

A similar set of reflections can be directed to the Sobell studies. They apparently succeeded in controlling at a socially acceptable level the drinking behaviors of their alcoholic subjects while in treatment. In fact, they succeeded in bringing their subjects' blood alcohol levels up to normal, so that withdrawal symptoms were not felt while in treatment. However, their subjects were addicted to the experience of addiction, and to the experience of controlling for themselves their drinking patterns. Once they left treatment they attempted to take control over their own drinking. They quickly returned to a level of readdictive drinking that required more than a few ounces of alcohol a day to relieve the withdrawal symptoms that were felt. This interpretation is supported by the fact that 13 of the first 16 subjects in the experiment were readmitted for alcoholism treatment within a year of discharge.

The Self and Addiction

A theory of addiction (and relapse) cannot explain addiction or relapse solely in terms of the effects that the drug in question produces for the user. Not only are such explanations tautological, and hence untestable, but they fail to locate the key factor in addiction, which is the user's symbolic and interactional relationship with the drug. The self of the user lies at the core of the addiction process. This self, in its many forms, structures and defines the user's relationship to heroin or alcohol. As Jellinek (1962) and Bateson (1972a) argue, self-pride and denial lie at the core of the alcoholic's relationship to alcohol, drinking, and alcoholism. Alcoholics believe that they can control their use of the drug. They also deny that they have problems when they drink. Self-pride and denial thus lock them in the drinking cycle that constitutes addictive, alcoholic drinking. Addiction can be explained only by going outside the presumed causal effects of the drug in question. Three "causal" agents thus lie at the core of alcohol and drug addiction: the self of the user, his or her physiological and lived body, and the drug in question. I turn now to a critique of the radical behavioral learning theory that underlies the research discussed above.

BEHAVIORISM, LEARNING THEORY, AND ALCOHOLISM

The empirical evidence from the Pendery et al. follow-up of the Sobell experiment and the results reported by Mello effectively refute the key features of behavioral learning theory as it has been applied to the drinking practices of alcoholics. That is, gamma alcoholics, as conditioned by Sobell and Sobell, were not able to sustain a socially controlled, nonalcoholic drinking program. Mello's subjects continued to drink at alcoholic levels throughout her experiments. Her data thus support, rather than refute, the centrality of "craving" and "loss of control" as key elements in the gamma alcoholic's drinking patterns. Both of these bodies of research lend support to Lindesmith's argument that addiction occurs when the alcoholic learns to drink so as to remove the negative effect of withdrawal symptoms.

These studies effectively undercut the ability of learning theory to account for or control alcoholic drinking. This is so because, consistent with Skinner (1953), these researchers refuse to deal with the cognitive, emotional, interactional, and self-reflective foundations of alcoholic drinking. Their arguments are premised, first, on Thorndike's (1913) Law of Effect (a behavior is maintained by it consequences, "a reward or reinforcement strengthens either the response it follows, or the connection between that response and a stimulus"; Zurriff, 1985: 188). Second, they assume the simple principles of classical and operant conditioning (an unconditioned stimulus can be replaced by a conditioned stimulus that will elicit the same response previously associated with the unconditioned stimulus). Alcoholics refuse to conform to Thorndike's Law of Effect. They will not submit to Skinner's theory of operant conditioning and they will not model their behaviors in terms of simple Pavlovian theories of aversive stimuli. The alcoholic's denial system, self-concept, and concept of "pride in drinking" lead him or her to drink over and over again, even in the face of disaster and failure. Contrary to Thorndike or Skinner, the alcoholic denies the Law of Effect as it supposedly applies to his or her behavior. (see Tiebout, 1949, 1953, 1954, for a discussion of the "ego" factor in alcoholism).

Problems with Behaviorism

As a theory and a method in the field of alcoholism research, radical behaviorism (1) is anti-introspective; (2) is against the use of mentalistic constructs such as meaning, motive, intention, or self; (3) makes no presumption about causal factors that lie outside the immediate behavioral field of the alcoholic; (4) rejects cognitive or emotional interpretations of alcoholic learning; (5) attempts to remove a theory of the alcoholic subject from the phenomenon of alcoholism; (6) rejects first-person accounts by alcoholics as being of any use in the understanding of alcoholism; and (7) aims, following Watson (1913) and Skinner (1953), to be a purely objective, experimental branch of natural science.

These seven features of behaviorism make it particularly unsuited for the interpretation and understanding of alcoholism. This is so for the following reasons. First, the very factors that behaviorism excludes (meaning, intentionality, self, language, first-person accounts) stand at the center of alcoholism, for the alcoholic actively produces and defines her alcoholism as she becomes progressively addicted to alcohol. Second, behaviorism ignores the lived-body of the alcoholic, as that body and its withdrawal symptoms are defined and given meaning by the alcoholic. Third, behaviorism's search for causal factors ignores the fact that physical causality (as given in stimuli and reinforcement schedules) do not operate at the level of lived experience for the alcoholic. (See Merleau-Ponty, 1967; Sartre, 1956: 477). Fourth, because the alcoholic's self-system stands at the center of her alcoholism, any theory that attempts to explain alcoholism by ignoring the self is doomed to failure.

Fifth, a learning theory's concept of learning is unable to deal with the complex forms of learning that involve self-mediating processes (Bateson, 1972b) that are based on language and verbal interaction (Chomsky, 1959). Sixth, learning theory appears to be unable to reverse the negative, self-destructive behaviors that stand at the core of alcoholism. Seventh, behaviorists have been unable to locate a functional law that would connect some property of drinking with some property of a reinforcement schedule that would produce invariant control over drinking behavior.

Eighth, the temporal structure of behaviorism teleologically confounds effect with cause. Reinforcement schedules are presumed antecedent causes which supposedly affect rates of drinking behavior, when in fact drinking (the effect) becomes the cause for following or not following the reinforcement schedule. Because the subject mediates and defines stimuli and reinforcement schedules, any system that stands outside the subject's definitional system is flawed from the beginning. There are, that is, no stimuli, responses, or reinforcement schedules that stand independent of the subject's definitional field of experience. The start-stop, static model of conduct that behaviorists assume is unable to account for the creative, novel drinking behavior of the alcoholic.

Ninth, the reverse anthropomorphism of behaviorism (Kuhn and Hickman, 1956: 18-20), as applied to alcoholics, only recognizes those characteristics of man that have been found in nonhumans. By Mello's own admission, her early experiments failed to produce alcoholic subjects who would respond like "sophisticated pigeons." Such a failure would be otherwise benign in its effects, were it not for the fact that behaviorism, as employed in the Sobell studies, was used as a tool that destroyed human lives. It is necessary to call a moratorium on radical behaviorism as it currently is utilized in the field of alcoholism research. (See Redd et al., 1979: 8-10, for a critical reading of radical behaviorism as applied to the complex forms of behavior that alcoholism represents.)

PSYCHOANALYTIC THEORIES

The following two theories develop psychoanalytic themes of sexuality and childhood experiences as central components of alcoholism in adulthood. They are variations on personality theories of alcoholism, for they seek to locate the motivation for alcoholism in the personality makeup of the drinker.

Power Theory

McClelland et al.'s (1972) *power theory of drinking* refutes the tension, or anxiety reduction, theory that argues that men drink primarily to reduce their anxiety. They suggest that in cultures in which high amounts of anxiety are contained in folk tales, less drinking, rather than more, occurs. They also suggest that at the individual level small amounts of alcohol have no or little effect on anxious thoughts. Some experimental studies (Nathan et al., 1970; Cappell and Herman, 1972: 59) have indicated that anxiety increases during drinking.

McClelland's power theory argues that men who have accentuated needs for personal, not social, power drink excessively. Such men have power fantasies while drinking that express aggressiveness, thrill-seeking, and antisocial activities. Doubts about sexual potency and feelings of weakness are suppressed. A desire for personal dominance over others, a desire to gain power, glory, and influence is expressed in the fantasies of heavy drinkers when they drink. These fantasies reflect a world that is a competitive arena for males who must establish their dominance over one another. Personalized power fantasies increase as the level of alcohol consumption increases. Drinking is viewed as a means for the male to feel stronger. Men with exaggerated needs for personalized power receive direct gratification from these powerful fantasies that alcohol fuels. They want power but feel weak. They drink in order to feel powerful.

This formulation, which has not been well developed for women who are heavy drinkers or alcohol abusers (Williams, 1976: 278), does not offer a convincing argument for those males who have the need for personal power but do not become heavy drinkers (McClelland, 1972: 335). Nor does it account for those heavy drinkers who do not have power fantasies. It is not at all clear how McClelland's theory would deal with MacAndrew's and Edgerton's (1969) and Lemert's (1958, 1964, 1967) argument that the behaviors and thoughts that are felt when under the influence of alcohol are patterned and learned culturally. It is not the effects of alcohol that fuels the power fantasies or the aggressive actions of the drinker, but the culture. That is, power fantasies are part of being male in patriarchal cultures. McClelland's findings are therefore the artifacts of those cultures that are alcohol ambivalent, permissive, and overly permissive (Pittman, 1967: 6-12). Abstinent cultures (Islam, Hindu, ascetic Protestant) should, and do, present problematic materials for McClelland's theory (see McClelland et al., 1972: 249-250). Similarly, the type of drinker described by Spradley (1970: 252-262), the one who has no desire for personal power but drinks to excess, appears troublesome for the power theory.

Dependency Theory

McClelland goes to great lengths to refute dependency theory, which contends that heightened masculinity is a reaction formation against underlying dependency needs felt by the male (Williams: 1976, 254-256). Psychoanalytic in orientation, this theory assumes that the prealcoholic has a permanently unfulfilled desire or need for dependency, but is ashamed of this need. The prealcoholic male desires maternal care and attention, yet wants to be free of this care. This produces a dependency conflict, the origins of which are to be found in childhood. A facade of self-reliant manhood is developed to mask this dependency need. Because drinking is a masculine activity it helps the alcoholic to maintain an image of independence and self-reliance. Drinking satisfies dependency needs by providing feelings of warmth, comfort, and omnipotence. Drinking recreates the maternal caring situation. Accordingly, the motivation for drinking lies in the desire to satisfy dependency needs—not to feel powerful. Concerns for power are surface representations shielding or hiding underlying dependency strivings. Dependency, not the search for power, is the main cause or feature of alcoholism.

Both the power and the dependency theories assume that alcoholics have an inadequate masculine identity. Each, in this sense, returns to a psychoanalytic theme regarding sexuality, anxiety, neuroses, and maladaptive adult behavior, all traceable to childhood family experiences. Power theory locates this lack in a need-conflict culture. Dependency locates it in the early childhood experiences of the drinker. Power theory assumes that alcoholics act in a powerful way because they are concerned with power, not with underlying dependency needs. Both theories, then, take the same action patterns as a point of departure—heavy drinking, and masculine aggressiveness—but reach different conclusions concerning the cause or motivational reasons for alcoholism. It is probably the case that alcoholic males seek not only power, but also desire warm relationships with their mothers or with other women; just as women probably seek power and warm relationships with their mothers, their fathers, and with other males and females. The same criticisms that were applied to the power theory can be applied to the dependency theory.

ANTHROPOLOGICAL THEORIES OF ALCOHOLISM

I will now review the three major anthropological theories of alcoholism.

Time-Out Theory

MacAndrew and Edgerton's (1969) *"time-out" theory* of drunken comportment is both a critique of the alcoholism literature that seeks to locate invariant personal psychological effects in alcohol consumption and a cultural-anthropological argument for the thesis that all societies create time-out periods when their members are not held accountable for their actions. Alcohol is ingested during those time periods. Hence, drunken comportment is culturally patterned behavior and has very little to do with the psychological needs of the drinker, or the biochemical effects of alcohol on and in the drinker's body.

They marshall considerable evidence to support the following points: (1) There are societies in which drunken comportment does not display the "disinhibited" effects commonly ascribed to alcohol; (2) There are societies in which drunken comportment has undergone historical transformation; (3) There are societies in which drunken comportment varies from one situation to another (MacAndrew and Edgerton, 1969: 61). They argue that drunken comportment is learned behavior. The presence of alcohol in the body does not necessarily produce disinhibition. Over the course of socialization people learn from their societies how to be drunk and how to comport themselves when they have consumed alcohol. Because all societies appear to have "time-out" periods and because many, if not most, societies prescribe and permit the use of alcohol, drunken comportment will vary from one society to another, as will, presumably, the effects of alcohol consumption on the drinker's personal and social worlds.

Strictly speaking, MacAndrew and Edgerton's thesis is not a theory of alcoholism. It is, however, a powerful anecdote to much of the prevailing literature that argues for the near universal effects of alcohol upon human consciousness (McClelland et al., 1972: 2). Still, continued, prolonged use of alcohol has negative effects upon the human body and these effects apparently transcend cultural definition and interpretation. The MacAndrew and Edgerton argument can be read as closely supporting the position of Madsen (1974), who suggests that the American alcoholic lives in a culture that places a high value on the kinds of experiences that join alcohol consumption with adventure, thrill-seeking, and the quest for another "reality," other than the ordinary taken for granted world (Madsen, 1974: 107-108).

The Anxious American Thesis

Madsen's Thesis extends the cultural-anthropological position by locating American varieties of alcoholism within the shifting values of American society. Focusing primarily on two subspecies of gamma alcoholism, primary and secondary alcoholism (Fox, 1957), and consolidating the evidence on the genetic, hereditary, and learned components of heavy alcohol use and abuse, Madsen offers a multicausal model of alcoholism. He proposes that is there not only an ambivalence about alcohol use in American culture, but that the American ambivalence surrounding freedom and the escape from it places the person who is prone to become alcoholic in a position in which she is drawn to alcohol as a means of escaping the anxiety that surrounds her. Because alcohol has been given the cultural meanings of being both an anxiety reducer and the producer of euphoria, it is turned to in moments of high anxiety. The alcoholic mind is a product of the environmental stresses that reflect the generalized American anxiety regarding freedom, control, achievement, success, pleasure, adventure, love, nurturing, warmth, power, and caring. Conflicting values radiate throughout the society and these conflicts are lived and experienced in most prominent form in the lives of alcoholics who withdraw from society through alcohol in order to find a measure of comfort, security, and self-worth. Eschewing mono-causal motivational theories of why alcoholics drink, Madsen, drawing on his own observations with alcoholics in treatment centers and in Alcoholics Anonymous, suggests that alcoholics and heavy drinkers drink for such reasons as the following: death, oblivion, self cure, to escape from undefined pain, to fill a need, because they are addicted, for purposes of aggression, for fantasy purposes, because they are dependent on others, because they have no one to be dependent upon, because they cannot stop, because they do not want to stop, because they think they can drink normally, because they are happy, because they are depressed, because a loved one is ill or has died, because someone has offered them a drink, and so on. In short, heavy drinkers drink because they drink. Madsen's work has the value of being closely in touch with the lived experiences of alcoholic drinkers and recovering alcoholics. His inquiry attempts to position the understanding of alcoholism within American culture and American history in a way that other theories fail to do. He notes, with insight, that the alcoholic man or woman is a reflection of the society, the history, and the culture of which he or she is a member. Certain alcoholics perhaps take too far that American charge to "take time-out" from the everyday, mundane world of ordinary life. He or she, perhaps because of genetic and hereditary predispositions, as well as because of patterns of behavior learned in the family context, is drawn to alcohol in a way that other drinkers are not. And, he or she becomes a living victim of the value conflicts that endorse the use of alcohol as a means of escaping from conflict, ambiguity, loneliness, and alienation. Although Madsen does not draw upon the work of Gregory Bateson, he might well have, for Bateson's views on alcoholism anticipate and develop to a higher level Madsen's observations on the alcoholic's dilemma.

BATESON'S THEORY

Bateson's "Cybernetics of Self" theory of alcoholism (1972a) is the most advanced of any theory thus far offered in the field. It may be outlined in terms of the following arguments:

(1) The sober world and life of the alcoholic lead him or her to drink. In his or her drinking the alcoholic denies the insane premises of that world. Intoxication is a subjective corrective to the insane, sober world the alcoholic finds himself or herself in.

(2) "Pride" coupled with risk-taking lead the alcoholic to drink and attempt not to get drunk. The alcoholic's pride is mobilized behind the proposition "I can stay sober... [and] I can do something where success is improbable and failure would be disastrous." (Bateson, 1972a: 322)
(3) The alcoholic is involved in a relationship with alcohol and his or her significant others that is schmismogenic (given to self-destructive divisions and conflicts), competitive, symmetrical, and complementary. This network of social interactions leads the alcoholic to competitively drink in an attempt to prove self-control.
(4) Hence, even though the alcoholic knows he has lost control over alcohol and even though significant others call him alcoholic, he continues to drink in an attempt to prove self-control. Pride-in-self and risk-taking thus tie the alcoholic to a self-destructive drinking cycle that threatens to produce insanity and the loss of everything he values.
(5) Drinking represents a step out of sobriety and a symmetrical struggle with the bottle, in which the alcoholic has stopped drinking (in order to prove self-control), into a complimentary drinking relationship with alcohol. This move, Bateson hypothesizes, signals the alcoholic's desire for a complementary, sociable relation with himself or herself and with others.
(6) Each time the alcoholic drinks and fails to maintain control over her drinking, she produces an occasion to drink again, so as to prove to herself and to others that self-control has not been lost.

Observations

Bateson's theory attempts to analyze the alcoholic's inner phenomenological dialogues with self, yet structurally it locates the alcoholic in a materialistic society that is seen as promoting the use of alcohol as a means of dealing with emotionality, failure, success, and competition. Bateson's theory locates alcoholism, not in the alcoholic, but in his relationship to himself, to alcohol, and with others.

However, the major thesis that drinking represents a step from symmetrical struggle into a desire for complimentarity in social relations must remain problematic. The "step into complimentarity argument" does not deal well with those alcoholics I observed who sought to be alone when they drank. It is not a relation with others that is sought, so much as it is a desire to be at one with one's self, away from the gaze and the criticism of others.

Consider one of the passages from Lowry's *Under the Volcano* (1971, pp. 128-129) in which the Consul has been drinking alone, on the porch of his house. Finding a bottle of tequila hidden in his garden, he drinks from it. Careless of being observed, he finds that his neighbor has been watching him. He states: "He wanted...an opportunity to be brilliant . . . to be admired . . . to be loved." The loneliness, paranoia, and guilt of compulsive, alcoholic drinking are evident in Lowry's account. Hidden bottles, people looking over her shoulder, the desire for a quiet drink alone, the abrupt decision to be with others, the longing for love; these behaviors and thoughts are commonplace in the double-bind structures that trap the alcoholic drinker. Drawn to others yet fearful of them, drinking so as to overcome that fear; in these thoughts and others like them, the alcoholic displays the complexities, contradictions, and negations that characterize his total existence in the world—both with himself and with others.

These points are not developed sufficiently by Bateson (see Faulkner, 1981: 435-448, for a case that initially confirms, and then disconfirms, Bateson's thesis). That is, alcoholic drinking, which begins in the biography of the drinker as a symmetrical, competitive social act with others that permits moments of shared complimentarity or sociality, turns into an antisocial act that promotes separateness from others. As a social act it contains both structures of experience within itself. It permits the alcoholic in the later stages of his drinking career to escape from the maddening presence of others. The isolated alcoholic, bitter and alone, believes that if he drinks and does as others do he can for a moment become like and with them; even though as the alcoholic drinks he knows that he desires to be separate from them. The alcoholic is caught in the double bind of symmetrical and complementary structures of experience—desiring neither and wanting both at the same time. The symmetrical struggle is with the self, not with others. Because Bateson does not position firmly a double-bind relationship between symmetry and complimentarity, the dialectics of the alcoholic's inner and outer experiences with himself, alcohol, and others are not fully grasped.

AN INTERPRETATION OF SCIENTIFIC THEORIES OF ALCOHOLISM AND THE ALCOHOLIC

A complex and variegated view of alcoholism and the alcoholic is suggested in the theories just reviewed. A common theme or thread unites these views and this may be termed the *objective thesis* of alcoholism, alcohol, and the alcoholic. This thesis, which does not apply to Bateson, Jellinek, or Madsen, assumes that the mind and the body of the alcoholic may be studied objectively as a thing, independent of lived experience. Just as the objective, measurable effects of alcohol on the body may be studied, so too may the behaviors, the intentions, and the personality of the alcoholic. Such a view generates discussions of the symptoms that do or do not define who an alcoholic is. In each case alcoholism is not studied from within as lived experience. The objectivist thesis suffers from the following flaws or problematics.

First, objective science, behavioral, pharmacological, psychological, sociological, and epidemiological, orients itself to the phenomenon of alcoholism from a position that is at once controlling, rational, and normative. That is, these inquiries, taken as a totality, aim to control the uses and abuses of alcohol within human society. They do so from a rational, normative point of view that accepts drinking as normal and socially integrating, not understanding that alcoholics presume the antithesis of these standards. It is only in this view that the recent behavioral controversy within the alcoholism literature can be understood (Pendery et al., 1982).

Second, the objective point of view seldom admits within its scientific paradigm history the sexuality of the drinker (to any significant degree), the economic-political-social context wherein the experience of becoming an alcoholic appears, or the materialist world that structures and furnishes the technology that produces the alcohol in the first place (Denzin, 1977a, 1978). In short, the modern scientific view of alcohol, the alcoholic, and alcoholism is ahistorical, sexist, normative, and biopolitical in bias (compare to Foucault, 1982). It reflects the increasing thrust in American society to control the mind and the body of modern individuals by science and technological means.

Third, this literature, with the exceptions of Jellinek, Madsen, and Bateson, has not dealt with nor conceptualized alcohol as a means of dealing with the frightening demands of freedom and being in the world at this moment in the twentieth century. The attempt to investigate and interrogate scientifically the structures of alcohol-induced experience from the objectivist standpoint confronts and flies in the face of the alcoholic experience itself, which is an attempt to deny the control that the world of external, rational, scientific structures exerts over the daily existence of the alcoholic.

Fourth, because of the anterior focus of alcoholism research on forces that cause the alcoholic to drink or not drink, the temporality of the present and the future goes unnoted.

An essential part of the alcoholic's existence lies in the alcoholic's ability to change temporal consciousness. This allows the alcoholic to alter her relationship with herself and the surrounding world. These essential temporal features of alcoholism have escaped notice in the recent scientific literature. Failing to grasp the facticity of the alcoholic's situation, failing to understand that each situation for the alcoholic is different and unique, the literature has lost itself in the search for necessary and sufficient causes when such causes apparently do not operate in the alcoholic's life-world.

CONCLUSIONS

I have reviewed the dominating genetic, psychological, psychoanalytic, anthropological, sociological, and interactional theories of alcoholism. Each theory has been found wanting in one degree or another. Motivational, personality, and learning theories of alcoholism have been criticized. Recurring problems include how to account adequately for the dynamics of addiction, readdiction or relapse, craving, loss of control, the centrality of the self in the alcoholism process, and the actual lived experiences of the practicing alcoholic. A less than complete picture of the alcoholic subject has thus been produced by the theories of alcoholism that have been reviewed. Until the alcoholic self in located firmly in the center of the alcoholic experience, science will continue to remain out of touch with alcoholism.

I turn next to Alcoholics Anonymous and its theory of alcoholism and the alcoholic. This theory, contrary to scientific theories, has been written by alcoholics. It does, however, selectively rest upon the arguments of a small number of medical practitioners concerning the so-called "allergy and craving" theories of alcoholism. A.A.'s theory is a theory of the alcoholic self.

3

ALCOHOLICS ANONYMOUS AND ALCOHOLISM

I turn in this chapter to Alcoholics Anonymous's theory of alcoholism and alcoholics. I will consider the following three topics: (1) Alcoholics Anonymous, science, and religion; (2) Alcoholics Anonymous's alcoholism; and (3) the alcoholic of Alcoholics Anonymous.

The alcoholic self who comes to A.A. finds an existing society of recovering alcoholic selves. In G. H. Mead's (1934) terms, Alcoholics Anonymous is an emergent society of preexisting alcoholic selves organized around the principles of recovery contained in the texts of A.A. Recovery involves learning how to take the attitude of the selves in this preexisting structure so that their attitudes can be applied to the individuals own experiences with alcoholism.

The problematic drinker will confront A.A.'s views at some point in his or her drinking career, usually as a result of a court order or the pressure of friends, family, employers, physician, psychiatrist, or psychologist, or because he or she has gone through a treatment center (Leach and Norris, 1977: 481). On rare occasions drinkers will come to A.A. claiming no outside influence or pressure. They will find a theory of alcoholism and an interpretive structure fitted to the experiences of problem drinkers that is likely to match their own. If they do not like what they find, they are told:

> Try to drink and stop abruptly. Try it more than once. It will not take long for you to decide, if you are honest with yourself about it. . . though

> you may yet be a potential alcoholic. We think few to whom this book will appeal can stay dry for anything like a year [A.A., 1976, pp. 31-32, 34].

ALCOHOLICS ANONYMOUS, SCIENCE, AND RELIGION

Individuals who come to A.A. with problems with drinking bring a conception of alcohol, alcoholics, and alcoholism that has been differentially influenced by the "scientific-objective" theories just discussed. And, they will bring a personal "lay theory" of their problems that somehow must be fitted to the scientific and A.A. views of their problems.

If science in the traditional sense (Durkheim, 1973: 220-223) is understood to embody the principle that proposals for action in the world can only be made when rigorous, verifiable, causal knowledge has been obtained, then A.A. is scientific. It builds upon the following taken-for-granted assumption that is simple and causal: "If a man does not take the first drink he cannot get drunk." Yet A.A. does not inquire into the etiology, the causes, or the neurophysiology of alcoholism. It does not, as does science, ask causal questions, nor does it deal in absolutes or probabilities. As such, A.A. is an action-oriented, pragmatically structured set of experiences that combines elements of religion (James, 1904), depth and analytic psychiatry, medicine, existential philosophy, sociology, and social psychology (Bateson, 1972a: 331-335; Kurtz, 1979).

Alcoholics Anonymous presents itself to the problem drinker in simple, direct, ordinary language (see Maxwell, 1984; Rudy, 1986). In their meetings, A.A. members dissect, over and over again, the meanings of such ordinary words as power, control, resentment, emotion, sobriety, dry, fear, patience, anger, surrender, serenity, peace, love, and powerlessness. In the above senses, Alcoholics Anonymous is both scientific and not scientific. It is a blend of all of the above points of view into a workable lay theory of recovery from alcoholism. But unlike the personal theory of his or her problems the problem drinker develops (see Chapter 4), A.A.'s theory is grounded in a group perspective. It is a group, lay theory of alcoholism that finds authority in its spoken words and in the formal texts of A.A., including *Alcoholics Anonymous* and *The Twelve and Twelve*. The group and collective foundations of A.A. transcend the personal, lay theories of any given individual, drinking or not drinking.

Alcoholics Anonymous, however, is unlike science in the following critical respects. First, the essential structures of the A.A. traditions exist and are passed on through an oral tradition; that is, through the A.A. meetings. A.A. does not rely as exclusively upon the printed page for the transmission of its knowledge as science does. It is primarily an oral tradition.

Second, unlike science, which Durkheim asserted (1973: 220-223) can affirm nothing that it denies (that is, if it cannot be proven, it does not exist) and deny nothing that it affirms, A.A. affirms what it denies proof to, although denying what it rigorously affirms. That is, although arguing that a scientific proof for the existence of God can never be given, A.A. proposes a belief in a power greater than the individual (A.A., 1976: 48-49). It asks individuals to make a leap of faith and come to believe in a power greater than themselves. This Durkheimian power is collective. It is in the group and not in the group, or in the individual. It transcends the individual (Bateson, 1972a: 333). Yet it is defined individually. Although this power's existence cannot be directly nor even indirectly proven, its influence is involved daily in the group prayer collectively recited at the end of each meeting.

Similarly, doubting, but not denying that recovery from alcoholism can occur if the 12 steps are not taken, A.A. strongly urges each individual to follow its suggested steps to recovery. Hence A.A. affirms what it says cannot be proven, although denying, or at least rigorously doubting, the possibility of what it affirms. As a consequence, third, unlike science, which can establish nothing that is not based directly or indirectly on these two principles, A.A. moves forward, without records, regularly kept statistics, or information on whether or not its methods and assumptions do in fact work. (See Leach and Norris, 1977: 470-507, for a review of the first three A.A. sobriety surveys.) It directs its members, instead, to read the 44 life stories of recovery given in the *Big Book,* and A.A. regularly reports the recovery experiences of its members in its international monthly journal, *The Grapevine.*

Fourth, much of modern behavioral science (Bateson, 1972a: 336) builds upon the Cartesian dualism that posits an objective world that can be studied, interpreted, and controlled by the methods of modern inquiry. Alcoholics Anonymous denies this dualism. It denies also an objective view of the world, locating the alcoholic subject, instead, in a world that is intersubjective, noncausal, spiritual, collective, and distinctly oriental, as opposed to western and occidental.

Fifth, because of its traditional notions of alcoholism as a disease (see below), because it does not keep records on its members, and because it conducts its primary work within "closed" meetings, A.A. is regarded by many as being antiscientific and not amenable to scientific inquiry (Maisto and McCollum, 1980: 18-19). That is, A.A. is regarded as having closed its doors to science (Sagarin, 1969). This belief is challenged by A.A.'s Eighth Tradition, which welcomes the findings of science as they contribute to a better understanding of alcoholism. The antiscientific belief persists in the scientific literature on A.A., this despite the fact that *The Grapevine* regularly reports research findings on alcoholism.

Sixth, A.A.'s emphasis on a power greater than the individual places a wedge between this belief system and the rationality of modern science that in most forms is atheistic if not agnostic. A.A.'s religious spirituality and its pragmatic program of action, which in Weber's terms (1946: 153) is a practical ethic to action, speaks to man's ills in ways that no modern behavioral science can. Alcoholics Anonymous's elective affinities (Weber, 1946) with the pragmatic (James, 1955; Dewey, 1922; Mead, 1964), existential themes of religion, psychology, and psychiatry make it a practical, secular, scientific, and spiritual ethic. It blends, then, science, religion, and common sense in ethical and practical ways that no one of these points of view alone can do. And, because its simple focus is on alcoholism and the drinking act, it is not drawn off into unrelated areas of scientific, religious, political, and cultural concerns in which its local knowledge (Geertz, 1983) on alcoholism would prove to be unworkable or divisive.

Seventh, because A.A. accepts the disease conception of alcoholism, it is at least on the side of those alcoholism researchers (Jellinek, 1960; Keller, 1978) who regard it as a disease. Yet within the alcoholism literature the controversy over whether or not alcoholism is or is not a disease, and, if so, is it a unitary disease (Maisto and McCollam, 1980: 20-25), rages on. A.A.'s incontrovertible position on this matter also can be seen as placing it outside the realm of modern behavioral science as that science studies alcoholism (Sobell et al., 1980).

Eighth, and closely related to point seven, is A.A.'s position, taken from the physician William Silkworth, that abstinence from alcohol is mandatory if recovery is to be achieved (A.A., 1976: xxviii). Many behavioral researchers call for alternatives to abstinence, arguing that abstinence may, for some drinkers, be dysfunctional to social and psychological functioning (Sobell and Sobell, 1978: 29; Maisto and McCollam, 1980: 19). Such researchers call for individualized behavior therapy programs fitted to the drinking patterns of each individual, assuming that nonproblem drinking may be an alternative for many "alcoholic" drinkers. These programs are designed to bypass the "severe social stigma of being an alcoholic on this continent" (Sobell and Sobell, 1978: 28). They attempt to resocialize the problem drinker into nonproblem, controlled drinking patterns.

The abstinence versus controlled drinking controversy aligns A.A. with the nondrinking position, suggesting that its stance is detrimental to the recovery of certain types of drinkers. It is argued also that A.A.'s position produces or contributes to the large population of "hidden ex-alcoholics" (Sobell and Sobell, 1978: 28; Beauchamp, 1980: 49-66). A.A.'s humanistic desire to offer a path to recovery for the "alcoholic" drinker is thus countered by the behavioral scientist's desire to control the effects of alcohol on the problem drinker.

In the above senses Alcoholics Anonymous constitutes a structure of beliefs and assumptions that stand to the side of modern behavioral science as it approaches the alcoholism problem in the modern post-industrial society. The essential ethical and philosophical stance of A.A., which is anti-Cartesian and antiscientific control, places it fundamentally at odds with much of modern science as well. As Bateson (1972a: 33) forcefully argues:

> If we continue to operate in terms of a Cartesian dualism of mind versus matter, we shall probably also continue to see the world in terms of God versus man; elite versus people; chosen race versus others; nation versus nation; and man versus environment. It is doubtful whether a species having *both* an advanced technology *and* this strange way of looking at its world can endure.

A.A., Bateson contends, offers a way out of this dilemma, and it is a dilemma when it is first confronted by the problem drinker who has been taught by science and religion to be in control of himself or herself and drinking.

ALCOHOLICS ANONYMOUS'S ALCOHOLISM

A.A. defines the alcoholic as a sick person, suffering from an obsession, a fatal malady, a progressive illness that is physical, mental, spiritual, emotional, and self-destructive (A.A., 1976: xiii, 18, 30, 92; A.A., 1953: 22-23, 32-33, 107). The illness that alcoholics have is alcoholism. This illness is placed in remission only through death or abstinence from alcohol. It is treated by A.A. and A.A. meetings. The illness, alcoholism, and the sick person—the alcoholic—are thereby located within an interpretive circle that for A.A. remains forever closed and forward moving. It is nearly impossible, in this respect, to separate A.A.'s conception of the alcoholic from its conception of alcoholism. The two are intimately interwoven in what for A.A. is a life or death matter. "To drink is to die" (A.A., 1976: 66). This is A.A.'s reasoning and this is the circle in which it places its members.

A.A. believes, and quotes the physician William Silkworth, that "real alcoholics" have an allergy to alcohol. Silkworth states:

> We believe, and so suggested a few years ago, that the action of alcohol on these chronic alcoholics is a manifestation of an allergy; that the phenomenon of craving is limited to this class and never occurs in the average temperate drinker. These allergic types can never safely use alcohol in any form at all . . . this phenomenon, as we have suggested, may be the manifestation of an allergy which differentiates these people, and sets them apart as a distinct entity. . . . The only relief we have to suggest is entire abstinence [A.A., 1976: xxxiv-xxvi].

Bill Wilson, the cofounder of A.A., described Silkworth's position in a letter to the psychoanalyst C. G. Jung in June of 1961:

> It was his theory [Silkworth's] that alcoholism had two components—an obsession that compelled the sufferer to drink against his will and interest, and some sort of metabolism difficulty which he then called an allergy. The alcoholic's compulsion guaranteed that the alcoholic's drinking would go on, and the "allergy" made sure that the sufferer would finally deteriorate, go insane, or die [A.A., 1963].

Elsewhere in his letter to Jung, Wilson speaks of reading William James's *Varieties of Religious Experience* while being hospitalized for his last bout with active alcoholism. He discusses his realization that the conversion experiences James analyzed involved ego collapse. Jung, in reply to Wilson, suggested that the alcoholic craves a spiritual wholeness that is contradicted by drinking: *"spiritus conta spiritum"* (Leach and Norris, 1977: 455, italics in original).

Several salient factors must be extracted from the above quotations and statements from Silkworth, Wilson, and Jung. The first is the allergy theory of alcoholism. As Jellinek (1960) noted, the conception of alcoholism as an allergy had been set forth as early as 1896. It did not originate with Silkworth. Second, although the notion has been discredited scientifically (Leach and Norris, 1977: 454), it continues to be used by A.A. members. As Jellinek (1960: 87) notes, the figurative use of the term "alcoholism as an allergy is as good as or better than anything else for their purposes, as long as they do not wish to foist it upon students of alcoholism." Third, Silkworth's formulations isolate a particular class or type of drinker who suffers from this allergy. Fourth, he locates the phenomenon of craving at the core of the allergy. Fifth, he advocates abstinence and the experiencing of an entire psychic change in the life of the drinker.

Wilson's letter to Carl Jung takes the allergy formulation to its most severe extreme: death, insanity, or institutionalization. Sixth, he positions the drinker's self centrally in the process of alcoholism, noting that the drinker often drinks against his or her own will and interest. Seventh, he builds upon Silkworth's position that an entire psychic change is required, noting that he was prepared for a conversion experience. Connecting this experience to William James's *Varieties of Religious Experience* has permanently located James, along with Jung, in the annals of A.A. (A.A., 1976: 26, 28, 569-570). Wilson notes the importance of the appearance of his friend Edwin T. at that moment in his life when he was most desperate and ready for a conversion experience. In Edwin T. he found another person with whom he could communicate. Eighth, Wilson notes that the ego or self of the alcoholic must be shattered. Silkworth's presentation of the allergy formulation thus entered Wilson's life at or during a time period when he was most ready to receive it.

Ninth, Carl Jung's remarks to Wilson elaborate the pivotal point that the conversion that occurs must be spiritual. It reveals a thirst or desire for wholeness. The alcoholic experiences, as James had remarked in *Varieties of Religious Experience* (1961: 150), a divided self (Denzin, 1984a). That self cannot be united or joined, James and Jung argued, without a conversion experience. More important, Jung argued that alcohol stands in the way of the spiritual experience.

This position is developed in A.A. as an individual, yet collective, version of spirituality is discovered. (See A.A., 1973.) Indeed, A.A.'s *Twelve Steps* are described as "a group of principles, spiritual in nature, which if practiced as a way of life, can expel the obsession to drink and enable the sufferer to become happily and usefully whole" (A.A., 1953: 15).

The disease or illness that alcoholics in A.A. believe they have is, then, spiritual, mental, and physical. Before the mental and spiritual sides of the illness can be treated, however, the alcoholic often must receive physical treatment, the object of which is "to thoroughly clear the mind and the body of the effects of alcohol" (A.A., 1976: 143). As noted earlier the alcoholic will, in all likelihood, suffer from vitamin deficiencies and any number of alcohol-related disorders including cirrhosis, diabetes, internal bleeding, pancreatitis, and jaundice.

THE ALCOHOLIC OF ALCOHOLICS ANONYMOUS

A.A. distinguishes four types of alcoholics or problem drinkers. These four types of heavy drinkers are all regarded by A.A. as candidates for their program. They correspond in varying degrees to Jellinek's alpha, beta, gamma, and delta alcoholics (Jellinek, 1960: 38-39). However, Jellinek argues, as indicated in Chapter 2, the gamma alcoholic is probably the type most likely to come to A.A. (Jellinek, 1960: 38). A.A.'s four types of drinkers have passed through the prealcoholic and prodomal phases of alcoholism and are in or near the crucial or chronic phases of the illness as described by Jellinek.

A.A.'s Typology of Alcoholics

The primary alcoholic that Alcoholics Anonymous directs its program to is the individual who has "lost the power of choice in drink" (A.A., 1976: 24). This is the drinker who is unable to not take the first drink, this in spite of the suffering and humiliation he or she may have suffered "even a week or a month ago" when he or she last drank (A.A., 1976: 24). Called the *real alcoholic,* this individual is described as follows:

> But what about the real alcoholic? He may start off as a moderate drinker; he may or may not become a continuous hard drinker; but at some stage of his drinking career he begins to lose all control of his liquor consumption, once he starts to drink.
>
> Here is the fellow who has been puzzling you, especially in his lack of control. He does absurd, incredible, tragic things while drinking.

A.A. (1976: 21-22) gives the following additional characteristics to the "real" alcoholic. He or she (1) is almost always insanely drunk; (2) becomes antisocial; (3) gets drunk at the wrong time; (4) is dishonest about alcohol; (5) goes on drinking sprees; (6) goes to bed intoxicated, yet reaches for a drink the first thing in the morning; (7) hides alcohol; (8) uses medications for sleeping purposes, mixing these with alcohol; and (9) visits physicians, hospitals, and sanitariums because of alcohol-related problems.

A.A. (A.A.: 110) compares the "real alcoholic"—the drinker who has been placed in one institution after another, who has been violent, and insane while drinking, who drinks on the way home from the hospital, and who has had delirium tremens—with three other types of heavy drinkers. The *first type* drinks heavily, sometimes continually. He spends a great deal of money on alcohol, and the mental and physical effects of alcohol may be showing, but he does not see them.

This type of alcoholic may be an embarrassment to his family and friends when he drinks too much, which is often. He may be certain that it is possible to control his intake of alcohol, and is insulted if told he is an alcoholic. A.A. states that "this world is full of people like him. Some will moderate or stop altogether, and some will not. Of those who keep on, a good number will become true alcoholics after awhile" (A.A., 1976: 109).

The *second type* of heavy drinker has the following characteristics: (1) he shows a lack of control over his drinking; (2) he gets violent when he drinks; (3) he tries to stop, or go on the wagon, and fails; (4) he has started to lose friends and his work suffers; (5) he drinks in the morning to control nervousness; (6) he is remorseful after a heavy drinking spree; and (7) he thinks drinking moderately is possible. Of this drinker A.A. states: "We think this person is in danger. These are the earmarks of a real alcoholic. Perhaps he can still tend to business fairly well. He has by no means ruined everything. As we say among ourselves, *He wants to stop*" (A.A., 1976: 109, italics in original).

The *third type* of drinker has gone further than the second type. Friends are lost and homes nearly destroyed. This individual cannot work, or hold a job, and has begun to make the rounds of emergency rooms, hospitals, detoxification centers, and treatment centers. This type admits he or she cannot drink like other people. He or she does not know why and may want to stop, but cannot (A.A., 1976: 110).

Having isolated the "real" alcoholic and compared his or her career to the trajectory of other types of heavy drinkers, A.A. further characterizes this alcoholic as a person who has led a double life. Like a stage actor, she attempts to maintain a certain reputation of being in control of her drinking and career. Yet she is haunted by the guilt that was produced by the last drinking spree, and is fearful that others may have seen her when she was drunk. She attempts to push these memories to the side, believing that the next time she drinks such an event will not occur again. The real alcoholic is "under constant fear and tension—that makes for more drinking" (A.A., 1976: 73).

This drinker will have attempted any of the following methods to control her drinking: (1) drinking only beer, (2) limiting the number of drinks, (3) marking the bottle and not drinking below that line, (4) never drinking alone, (5) never drinking in the morning, (6) keeping alcohol out of the house, (7) going on the "wagon" or "taking the pledge," (8) never drinking during business hours, (9) drinking only at social gatherings and parties, (10) switching from bourbon to vodka because it is odorless, (11) drinking only natural wines, (12) agreeing to resign from work if she ever gets drunk on the job again, (13) taking a trip, (14) not taking a trip and always staying at home, (15) engaging in a rigorous exercise program and joining a health club, (16) seeing a psychiatrist, (17) reading inspirational religious books, (18) accepting voluntary commitment to treatment centers, (19) taking antabuse, (20) joining a church, (21) taking the geographical cure by moving from one city or part of the country to another, and (22) changing wives, husbands, or lovers (A.A., 1976: 31). This list could be extended indefinitely, for the alcoholic who has yet to come to A.A. will have tried any or all of these methods and others as well in an effort to control her drinking.

However, these methods are doomed to failure for, according to A.A., "no real alcoholic *ever* recovers control" over alcohol (A.A., 1976: 30). The actual or potential alcoholic "with hardly an exception, will be *absolutely unable to stop drinking on the basis of self-knowledge*" (A.A., 1976: 39, italics in original).

The double life the "real" alcoholic leads will have left no area of his or her life untouched. Work, sexuality, family, relations with friends, personal health, the desire for wealth, power, material possessions and finances, lifetime goals and ambitions; these pivotal points and others of the same magnitude will have been touched, altered, and perhaps destroyed by the alcoholic's illness and by his or her behavior patterns (A.A., 1953: 42-43). Not only is alcoholism a family illness, but it is an illness, A.A. argues, that cuts to the core of the self of every individual who is involved with the alcoholic, whether wife, child, close friend, father, mother, or employer (A.A., 1976: 104-150). A.A.'s alcoholism and A.A.'s alcoholic are relational phenomena.

THE ALCOHOLIC SELF

The excessive, addictive use of alcohol by the alcoholic is traced by A.A. to the self of the drinker. A.A. states, "self, manifested in various ways, was what had defeated us" (1976: 64), and, alcohol or "liquor was but a symptom" of the illness the alcoholic manifested while drinking (1976: 64). The causes and conditions of that illness are located, as just indicated, in self and in the emotions of self—chiefly resentment, guilt, anger, and fear. These emotions are rooted in the alcoholic's past, the wreckage of which he or she is told to "clear away" and to "Give freely of what you find and join us. . . . We realize we know only a little... The answers will come, if your own house is in order.... God...will show you how to create the fellowship you crave" (A.A., 1976: 164).

Thus A.A.'s alcoholism is transformed into an emotional illness, into an illness of self, emotionality, and being in the world. The alcoholic is an emotionally ill individual. The alcoholic's illness is rooted in the emotions she attaches to herself and to the past she has constructed while drinking. A.A. believes that while drinking she was insane, defining sanity as "soundness of mind." A.A. states that "some will be willing to term themselves 'problem drinkers,' but many cannot endure the suggestion that they are in fact mentally ill" (A.A., 1953: 33). Continuing this line of interpretation, A.A. argues that "no alcoholic, soberly analyzing his destructive behavior, whether the destruction fell on the dining-room furniture, or his own moral fiber, can claim soundness of mind for himself" (A.A.'s 1953: 33).

A double structure thereby is embedded in A.A. conception of alcoholism and the alcoholic. Connected to self, emotionality, unsound thinking, a past that cannot be let loose of, and the excessive, addictive, craving, allergenic use of alcohol, alcoholism becomes a disease, or illness of living in the world. Alcohol becomes but a symptom of A.A.'s illness. A.A.'s double structure, then, addresses how not to take the first drink, so as to keep the symptom of the illness out of the alcoholic's mind and body. But second, it addresses the emotional and mental illness, or complex of "unsound thinking structures," that have been built up around the alcoholic's self and relationship to the world of others. At the second level, A.A. becomes a structure of group interactions whose primary purpose is to help each alcoholic stay sober today so as to be able to maintain emotional balance and emotional sobriety, one day at a time (A.A., 1953: 88, 90). Recognizing that "all people, including ourselves, are to some extent emotionally ill, as well as frequently wrong" (A.A., 1953: 92), A.A. offers, through its steps and its daily meetings, a structure of tools and a supportive group environment in which the problematics of living sober may be dealt with (A.A., 1976: 554). A.A. thereby locates the recovering alcoholic in a materialistic, social, and historical world that is filled with other individuals who are also emotionally ill, if not alcoholic. In this move A.A. informs the recovering alcoholic that he is no less ill than those with whom he routinely interacts. Because the alcoholic has a set of tools and a group structure at his disposal he is, in fact, better able to deal with that world than are those who have not yet found A.A.

ALCOHOLIC STIGMA AND UNDERSTANDING

Accordingly, the stigma that A.A. might attach to itself, to its members, to alcoholism, and to being alcoholic, is reduced, if not removed, by joining symbolically the recovering alcoholic with a structure of experience that is transcendent and in harmony with the "fellowship of the spirit" that A.A. has located in a power greater than the individual (A.A., 1976: 164). That power which is in the group, in the texts of A.A., and in a God as understood and defined by each member, thus becomes the core of the "fellowship of the spirit" that A.A. says restores the alcoholic to sanity and removes the compulsion to drink.

A.A. (1975: 70) suggests that the alcoholic, when comfortable in the new identity of "recovering alcoholic," share this information with others. To do so, it is argued, increases self-respect and serves to "chip away at the cruel old stigma unfairly placed by ignorant people on victims of our malady." Such statements also "help to replace old stereotyped notions of an 'alcoholic' with more accurate perceptions" (A.A., 1975: 70).

A.A. surrounds any prospective member with an aura of understanding, sympathy, and compassion that he or she may have not found elsewhere. The problem drinker who is a "real" alcoholic will know if she is in the right place when she attends her first A.A. meeting, or so A.A. contends. The new member will find others who truly understand her, perhaps for the first time. Dr. Bob, the cofounder of A.A., described his meeting with Bill Wilson as follows:

> *Of far more importance was the fact that he was the first living human with whom I had ever talked, who knew what he was talking about in regard to alcoholism from actual experience. In other words he talked my language* [A.A., 1976: 180, italics in original].

A.A. assumes and rests upon a theory of understanding that presumes that understanding derives from shared, common experiences, even when the experiences that are understood have not been experienced together (see Denzin, 1984a: 145). That is, A.A. provides a common field of shared, interactional experience that problem drinkers immediately are able to enter into. They find themselves in the company of others who have been where they have been. They find themselves, perhaps for the first time, experiencing an interaction with others that is grounded on true or authentic emotional understanding (Denzin, 1984a: 145). What they have sought and did not find in alcohol they find in front of them in the faces and the voices of persons who call themselves alcoholics. But these others are not drinking today. They have been practicing alcoholics who have sat in the same chairs when they came to their first A.A. meeting. They find a field of common experience in which emotional understanding is embedded and they will return (See Denzin, 1984a: 145).

A theory of emotional understanding and of emotionality thus underlies the inner workings of A.A. and A.A.'s theory of alcoholism and the alcoholic. This theory, which will be articulated in following volumes, sets A.A.'s view of alcoholism and the alcoholic drastically apart from the behavioral, medical, and psychological theories of alcoholism discussed in Chapter 2.

CONCLUSIONS

A.A's theory of alcoholism and alcoholics may be summarized as follows:

(1) Alcoholism is a threefold illness involving emotional illness, physical deterioration, and physical addiction, and a moral or spiritual emptiness on the part of the person.
(2) Alcoholics have an obsessive craving for alcohol that produces an allergic reaction in their bodies.
(3) Alcoholics have lost the ability to control their drinking, or to stop drinking by themselves.
(4) Self-pride, self-delusion, and denial are central to the alcoholic's alcoholism, for the self and its emotions lie underneath the public symptoms of alcoholism.
(5) Alcoholism is a family or relational illness.
(6) Recovery from alcoholism requires abstinence. No alcoholic can ever return to controlled, social drinking.
(7) Recovery requires an admission of powerlessness over alcohol and a willingness to admit a power greater than the person into one's life.
(8) A destruction of the "alcoholic ego" (surrender) is required if recovery is to occur.
(9) Surrender will eventually be accomplished by a conversion to a "spiritual" way of life.

Science has challenged A.A.'s core ideas, including the allergy theory of alcoholism, the disease conception of alcoholism, and the craving and loss of control hypotheses (Jellinek, 1960; Beauchamp, 1980; Mello, 1972, 1980; Sobell and Sobell, 1978). It may even be argued that A.A. unscientifically reifies the concept of alcoholism, making it a causal force in the life of the drinker, when the term references only an unagreed upon set of understandings concerning problem drinking. Yet A.A.'s practical theory and method for recovery remain unchallenged as one of the most effective or major treatment modalities for alcoholism (Kissin, 1977: 41).

Central to A.A.'s effectiveness is the emotional theory of understanding that underlies the working of the A.A. group. Coupled with this theory of understanding is A.A.'s basic point that the self of the drinker lies at the center of his or her problem. Most alcoholics eventually understand this argument. Bateson's theory of alcoholism, as discussed in Chapter 2, also builds from this position, as does my own. I turn in the next chapter to the lay theory of alcoholism and problem drinking that problem drinkers develop.

4

ALCOHOLICS AND ALCOHOLISM

> When I was an undergraduate I took a course on alcoholism. That was back in the early '60's. It was just about the time Jellinek's book on the disease concept came out. My instructor, who is a leader in the field, spent the entire course (as I remember it) rejecting Jellinek. When I began having problems drinking I could never bring myself to believe that I had a disease. I knew the scientific meaning of disease and A.A.'s wasn't scientific. I thought I could control it myself [field conversation, November 20, 1982, recovering male alcoholic, one year sobriety, college professor].

In this chapter I examine the folk, or lay, theory of alcoholism. This theory is organized around the meanings the heavy, or problem, drinker gives to the terms alcoholic, alcoholism, and alcohol. (See Thune, 1977; Wallace, 1982.) This will be the third theory of alcoholism the problem drinker confronts (scientific theories and A.A.'s formulations being the other two). The lay theory of alcoholism will be the primary interpretive framework the alcoholic employs, for it allows him or her to continue drinking. In fact he or she may construct (as the drinker above did) a position against these other theoretical structures.

I will take up two main topics: the structural constraints on the lay theory of alcoholism and the essential structures of this theory. These structures will be analyzed in terms of the alcoholic's theories of (1) self, time, and causality; (2) denial and rationalization; (3) successful drinking; and (4) alcoholism.

STRUCTURAL CONSTRAINTS ON THE LAY THEORY OF ALCOHOLISM

I define a lay theory as an interpretive account of human behavior developed by the person on the street (Schutz and Luckman, 1973). This theory may draw upon common sense, scientific knowledge, personal prejudice, or the collective wisdom of a social group. It may be a "well informed theory, or a theory riddled with inaccuracies and scientifically out-dated understandings. It will be fitted to the biography and life experiences of its user. It will be a theory that weaves the self and the history of the subject into a coherent tale, or story, that may be sad or happy" (Goffman, 1961a). *A lay theory is a theory of self.* It is theory that may or may not be shared or accepted by others. The alcoholic's lay theory of alcoholism seldom is acceptable to the significant others that make up his or her world.

Previous chapters have sketched in detail the scientific, cultural, historical, and social structures that shape the conceptions of alcohol, alcoholism, and alcoholics that the lay drinker in American society is likely to confront. Because alcohol consumption is woven so deeply through every fabric of society, the drinker, if he has problems with alcohol, finds it difficult, if not impossible, to avoid alcohol's presence in his life. He lives in a culture that drinks.

It is against this background of alcohol's necessary, pervasive, yet problematic presence in his or her world that the problem drinker develops a lay theory of drinking, alcohol, and alcoholism. This theory also will draw upon images of the alcoholic or problem drinker as given in the popular culture, including its national magazines, its films, its novels, its popular music, and its television. However, those social and cultural facts will be modified to fit the facticity of each drinker's drinking experience. Lay theories will draw upon, synthesize, ignore, transform, and rewrite the cultural, religious, scientific, medical, and personal facts and images in the possession of the drinker at the time she comes to the realization that she has problems with alcohol. This stock of knowledge (see Schutz and Luckmann, 1973) will be utilized in such a way as to deny the stigma that might be associated with being a problem drinker. Self-responsibility for drinking-related problems will be denied. The self-pride of the problem drinker will be drawn upon so as to place symbolically the blame for the problems she has experienced on others. The inability of others to understand the drinker and her drinking patterns will be interpreted within a resentful, interpretive framework. That is, these others (employers, family, friends) do not understand why the drinker has to drink the way she does. At root, the problem drinker will believe that it is a moral and legal right to drink. Further, the drinker will believe that she can control, through self-will, her drinking. This complex of beliefs may have been sustained for years. They are part of the core structures of the self of the drinker. They also are woven through the basic elements of the drinker's culture and society.

THE LAY THEORY OF ALCOHOLISM, ALCOHOL, AND ALCOHOLICS

This theory has a threefold structure. First, it locates the drinker centrally within the drinking act, offering temporal and interactional accounts, disclaimers, and explanations of why he drinks as he does when he does (Scott and Lyman, 1968; Hewitt and Hall, 1973; Hall and Hewitt, 1973; Hewitt and Stokes, 1975; Sykes and Matza, 1959; Dewey, 1922, Mills, 1940; Schutz and Luckmann, 1973: 208-233; Sartre, 1956: 446-447; MacAndrew and Edgerton, 1969; Rudy, 1985; Spradley, 1970). At this level, the theory locates the drinker in relation to other drinkers and to alcoholism, which is the most problematic form his drinking may take. It also attaches the drinker to a set of drinking practices that produce desired alterations in the inner and outer streams of emotional experience. Second, the lay theory focuses attention on alcohol as a meaningful social object that brings pleasure and comfort to the drinker. He or she will be attached to a favorite alcoholic beverage and to a favorite drink, perhaps scotch and water, "7 & 7," Jack Daniels, Old Busch, Blue, dry martinis, boilermakers, or gin and tonics. He will appropriate an image of himself in relationship to the drink that he drinks, perhaps deriving personal and social status from that brand and the places in which he drinks that favorite drink. Third, the lay theory will position the drinker in a world of interactional, emotional associates (Denzin, 1984a: 3, 92-93, 281). By so doing it allows the drinker to define his alcohol use against their interpretations of him as a problem or alcoholic drinker. This threefold structure of the lay theory turns, then, just as the scientific and A.A. theories discussed earlier do, on the meanings that will be given to the three terms: "alcoholic," "alcohol," and "alcoholism."

Lay Theory as Theory

These three elements of the lay theory are organized around the just outlined interpretive structures concerning (1) self, time, and causality, (2) denial and rationalization, (3) successful drinking, and

(4) alcoholism. The lay theory is more than a quasi-theory (see below) and more than a set of hypotheses the drinker holds about himself or herself, alcohol, drinking, and alcoholism. However, it contains conceptions of cause, effect, and hypotheses concerning alcohol's effects on the drinker's experiences. In this regard, it as a theory of self in relation to alcohol.

The lay theory is a theory, if theory is understood to refer to an interpretive structure that renders a sequence of experiences meaningful and understandable. It is a pragmatic theory of ordinary behavior, fitted to the particular biographical experiences of its user. It is woven through the life story the drinker tells about herself, for as life becomes problematic so too does her use of alcohol. Accordingly, her life story and theory of heavy drinking complement one another; although often it is not clear for the drinker whether the problems she has encountered in life are due to heavy drinking or whether problems occur because she is a heavy drinker. Before turning to the four major interpretive structures that organize the lay theory, it is necessary to examine briefly the place of cause, effect, and hypotheses in this theory.

Drinking hypotheses. The alcoholic's lay theory of heavy drinking (and alcoholism) contains a set of working hypotheses (Mead, 1899: 369-371) regarding the effects of alcohol upon his or her conduct. The alcoholic has learned that he or she cannot confront the world without alcohol. He or she knows when alcohol's effects are likely to be needed, when they are likely to wear off, and where to get the next drink, should it be needed. He or she has learned how to "manage" life while under the nearly continuous influence of alcohol. The alcoholic has learned where to get a drink early in the morning and late at night. He or she has learned how and where to drink while at work, at home, in the car, in public transit, and in other public places. He or she leads a secret life with alcohol, never far from its presence. Alcohol governs the alcoholic's life, thoughts, and actions in the world.

The alcoholic's theory of how and why he drinks is fitted to the practical, local knowledge he has of himself, his associates, and the taken for granted world he inhabits (Geertz, 1983: 73-94, 167-180; Garfinkel, 1967; MacAndrew and Garfinkel, 1962; Husserl, 1962). The following account, given by a 75-year-old recovering male alcoholic, sober for 15 years, reveals these features.

> I needed a drink every 30 minutes when I worked. I kept it under the counter at the store in a cleaning bottle. When I'd go into the back room to fill the bottle I'd take a drink of the stuff. My wife never knew why I had to keep the shelves of the store so clean and why it took so much

> cleanser. I also hid the stuff in a spare tire in my car, half-pints inside the inner tube. I had it buried in the garden, and hidden behind canning shelves in the basement. I wore engineering boots to city council meetings so I could keep a half-pint inside them. I went to the bathroom a lot. I was drunk all the time and could have been arrested anytime in those 40 years for a DUI, but I never was [field conversation, August 10, 1984].

Denial and causation. The lay theory of alcoholism and heavy drinking is both a theory of denial and a phenomenological theory of cause and effect; that is, it is a theory of temporality and the drinker's place in the flow of inner subjective time (Schutz and Luckmann, 1973: 212). As a phenomenological theory of personal causation (Schutz, 1962: 22, 70-72; Schutz and Luckmann, 1973: 208-223) it incorporates "in order to" and "because" motives that account for why it is that drinkers drink the way they do when they do, and why they have the problems they do when they do. They drink in order to manage problems that arise and they drank yesterday because those problems were there and had to be dealt with then. In order to and because motives thus causally connect the future and past in the lived present of the drinker.

Quasi-Theory and Theories of Self

This theory is more than a quasi-theory (Hall and Hewitt, 1973; Hewitt and Hall, 1973) because it extends beyond "ad hoc explanations brought to problematic situations to give them order and hope" (Hewitt and Hall, 1973: 367-368). It is also more than just a set of accounts (Scott and Lyman, 1968) or disclaimers (Hewitt and Stokes, 1975) about the past or about future situations that are defined as problematic. This theory is backward and forward looking at the same time, yet most fundamentally it is grounded in the present; that is, in the now of the moment when the drinker must take another drink. It is not just a set of justifications for neutralizing the drinker's responsibility in a situation (Sykes and Matza, 1959) nor just a vocabulary of motives (Mills, 1940). Rather, it is a fully grounded interpretive system that positions the drinker against a world that would hold him accountable for his actions, today, tomorrow, or yesterday. Although certainly based on "common sense notions of human behavior and social arrangements" (Hewitt and Hall, 1973: 368) the lay theory of alcoholism incorporates all of the elements of accounts, disclaimers, techniques of neutralization, and quasi-theories of problematic situations into a workable theory of temporality and personal cause. Focused as it is around alcohol and drinking, it becomes a theory of self as drinker. As a theory of self it draws into its center every contingent life situation the drinker confronts and gives him a reason for drinking in that situation and not being the cause of what went wrong or became problematic.

In this respect it is like an elegant scientific theory of cause and effect that incorporates every deviant case that might challenge its causal efficacy. Because the self stands at the center of the theory, self as theorist is able, through the use of what Garfinkel (1967) has called *et cetera* and *ad hoc* clauses, to account for every misfortune it encounters. That is, there are no negative cases in the lay theorist's theory of his or her drinking conduct. There are, however, problematic events that cause the theorist to revise his or her theory of self in relation to those events. Consider the following, which evidences the drinker's ability to incorporate the problematic into his theory of himself as a drinker. The speaker is a 50-year-old architect, sober two years.

> I found myself in a motel with an empty whisky bottle, a copy of Elizabeth Bowen's short stories, broken glasses, and wearing the suit I had worn to a conference on the weekend. It was Wednesday morning. I couldn't figure out what I was doing there. Then I remembered a fight I'd had with my wife before I left for the conference. She said, "Don't drink!" And I said "What makes you think I will?" I was furious, that she could think that I couldn't control my drinking. Then I remembered I'd had a drink after my presentation which had gone well. Everyone was toasting me. It made sense to have a drink. Why not? I had two drinks and got mad at my wife for her thinking I couldn't control it. Then I bought drinks for everybody. I can't remember what happened after that, except leaving and taking a cab. I guess that's how I got in the motel. Once I'd figured it all out it made sense. I cleaned up, shaved, ordered a clean suit of clothes and went to the bar and had a drink with lunch. When I got home my wife was all smiles. I didn't tell her what had happened. She thought the conference was for the entire week [field conversation, July 2, 1983].

Self as drinker. The self as drinker theory structures the relationship of the drinker-theorist to temporality. This theory structures the understandings the alcoholic has about himself or herself, including such matters as sexuality, family, and work history. It speaks to deep, inner feelings concerning who the alcoholic wants to be, who he or she has been and who he or she is now. It also references "good-me," "not-me," and "bad-me" self-feelings, that is, desired self-feelings, feelings that produce dread, and feelings that produce anxiety (Sullivan, 1953: 72; Denzin, 1984a: 213).

The lay theory of the alcoholic is a theory of self, denial, and temporal causality. I shall take up each of these points in greater detail, beginning with the theory of temporality that is embedded in the lay theorist's theory of self as drinker.

THE LAY THEORY OF SELF AND TEMPORALITY

The above account of the architect who found himself in a motel room reveals the inner temporal ordering of causality as it is conceptualized by the heavy drinker. That is, the architect explains the present in terms of actions taken in the past. Those actions, in turn, justify his taking a drink once he determined why he had taken the drink that got him in the motel room in the first place. Be recalling the conversation with his wife he was able to understand why he bought the drinks for everyone after his presentation. He was still angry at her. That interpretation, in turn, justified the next drink he took. By not telling his wife of his troubles *he* was able to act "as if" he, in fact, had not taken a drink at the conference.

Temporal Consciousness

In part because alcohol alters the temporal structure of his or her consciousness, the heavy drinker is always located in a temporal world that is either sped up or spread out over that long duration Bergson (1974) called the present. Yet it is not the present that the drinker lives in; he or she lives in the past or the future, never completely in the now of the present. Alcohol spreads out the inner flow of time so that the past and the future can crowd out the present. The following excerpts from a letter Dashiell Hammett wrote Lillian Hellman in 1938, after 14 months of sobriety, reveal these temporal features of the drinker's consciousness, once alcohol has begun its work:

> Darling,
>
> So after I phoned you I took a shot of scotch, the first I've had since when was it? and it didn't seem to do me any good, but I suppose it hardly ever does anybody any good except those who sell it to get enough money to buy detective stories or tickets to Elliott... and that damned barking bird is at work outside and if I don't look out I'll become a stream of consciousness writer and be discovered by Whit Burnett....I hope you can stop laughing long enough to read the rest of this letter; it gets
> better as it goes on.

That's what I'd like to think,
and like to have you
think, but I know
as well as you
do that just
about now
what lit-
tle im-
agin-
ati-
on
I
'
v
e
g
o
t
i
s
u
s
e
d
u
p
a
n
d
s
o
.
.
.

Love,
[Johnson, 1983: 150-151]

The physical text of Hammett's letter displays the effort to spread out time, to draw out the writer's passage through time as long and as dramatically as possible. More important, Hammett's thoughts are located in the past, as these thoughts of his having used up his imagination push the boundaries of the present further away from him. He is in the past as he writes in the present and it is the past that he laments. Yet the present in the form of the barking bird outside crowds in. It is, however, a self of the past that Hammett is attempting to recapture with his prose.

Temporal Causality

A confusion over temporal causality is produced, for while he or she is or was drinking the drinker loses track of time, thinking things occurred when they did not, or did not occur when they did. Berryman (1973: 17-18) offers an example:

> He heard himself looking down at the middle of the floor saying "sober for months" after Howarden, and he shuddered.
>
> It wasn't so.
>
> Not only was it not so but he had been forced to *learn* that it was not so, and now he had "forgotten" again. He was sincerely lost, relapsed back over ground gained long ago, months ago. He had given the same account of his first slip after Howarden when he came into Northeast in the spring, and happened to mention it to his wife that evening. "But Alan," she said, "that isn't so, dear. You had your first drink at the New Year's Eve party at the Browns."

Because the drinker is always present in his or her inner stream of thought, he or she is confused easily over temporal details, as Berryman was in his conversation with his wife concerning when he took his first drink after treatment. This becomes a source of confusion, producing resentment toward the other who traps the drinker in a temporal error. It produces contradictions for the self as well.

Temporal Existence

The heavy drinker lives an inauthentic temporal existence (Heidegger, 1962), for by locating herself either in the past or in the future she is unable to live in the now of the present. This inauthentic structuring of time alters the drinker's conception of causality and cause and effect. All events that occur in the world that surrounds her are filtered through a past or future temporal orientation. Hence they are given causal effects they cannot have in the actual world of the lived present. But because the drinker's temporality is teleological, the future does enter into the present and cause things to happen in the present. The following account reveals this teleological feature of the drinker's temporal thinking. The speaker is a 45-year-old male engineer, sober 2 years.

> I had stopped going to meetings and had started drinking off and on. I was going to Toronto to some meetings. I knew I was going to drink in Toronto so I bought a bottle of Jack Daniels to take with me so I would have a drink when I got there. My plane was delayed two hours so while I waited at home I decided to have a drink since I was going to have a drink in Toronto. This made sense since I was going to drink

> in Toronto anyway. In an hour I had finished the bottle. I still had time before my plane so I went out and bought another bottle. To make a long story short, I drank that bottle too, missed my plane and lost $500 in my basement. I found the money a year later stuck in a book [field conversation, October 1, 1983].

If knowing you are going to have a drink in Toronto can cause you to drink four hours before you get to Toronto, then having someone tell you they will discuss a problem with you in a day or two when you are sober also can cause the drinker to drink now. Our references to Lowry's *Under the Volcano* present the Consul as outraged because Yvonne assumed he *would be sober* at a later time.

By absorbing externally produced events, perhaps the statements or actions of other individuals, into his inner stream of consciousness, the drinker places his own stamp of temporal causality upon them. They become his thoughts, actions, or statements and take on a temporal causality that is uniquely his. That is, the drinker fits them into the flow of other events with which he or she has to deal. Causally their meaning becomes temporal for they are inserted into the inner flow of other events with which the thinker must contend. Lowry (1947: 193, 196-197) offers a complicated example. The Consul has just received a postal card mailed to him by Yvonne a year earlier stating *"Darling, why did I leave? Why did you let me? Expect to arrive in U.S. tomorrow, California two days later. Hope to find a word from you there waiting. Love Y"* (1947: 193). Upon receiving the card, the Consul and Yvonne are invited to a friend's for drinks.

A letter written a year earlier, received today, carries meaning that it could not have had, had it been received a year ago. For if that had occurred, and if the Consul had written back, Yvonne would have learned that he had gone through with their divorce, and that he had not asked her to return. Yet she did return, and he loves her today. So today, if her letter had arrived that morning he would have told her that. But he could not tell her that without a drink and of course it was because he was drinking so heavily that she had left a year ago. All of the drinks that had transpired since she wrote the letter and he received it were thereby compressed into the present by the Consul, for, just as a year earlier, he needed a drink now. Similarly, his having gotten over her leaving and her return now made the year seem as if it had not passed. In fact last year's letter had been written yesterday; or so it seems the Consul was able to reason. The logic of this reasoning is dialectical, circular, and teleological. It inserts effect before cause, allows effects to produce causes, and causes to become effects. It is interactional, temporal, and based on the premise that for the drinker his or her thoughts are always able to transcend, if not nullify the passage of time. The drinker can make anything happen if he or she has the next drink, or so it seems. Power fantasies are realized when he or she drinks (McClelland et al., 1972).

Temporal Rhythm

The drinker's inner stream of experience assumes a temporal and melodic rhythm that is sustained by alcohol's effects upon his or her consciousness. Alcohol keeps the long spread of the present alive in the drinker's mind. The pitched high that alcohol gives is what the drinker seeks, over and over again; and he or she desires to maintain that state of mental experience at all costs. Once again Lowry offers an example:

> Oozing alcohol from every pore, the Consul stood at the open door of the Salón Ofélia. How sensible to have a mescal. . . . He was now fully awake, fully sober again, and well able to cope with anything tht might come his way [Lowry, 1947: 284].

But because alcohol's effects wear off, and because he or she dwells in a world of others, the drinker finds that other events intrude into his or her stream of consciousness, altering the temporal rhythm of his or her thoughts. The drinker is forced to accommodate these intrusive thoughts into his or her inner stream of experience.

Like an angry tryant, the drinker seizes these intrusive events and forces them into his or her inner world of thought. Snatching a request from the other who has forced his or her way into his stream of consciousness, the drinker dispenses with the other's presence as quickly as possible. Dealing with the other, thinking angrily about him or her, getting emotional, the drinker acts, impulsively, quickly, so as to be done with the other. Alex, a 41-year-old male, 2 years sober, recalls an exchange with his 3-year-old daughter on Christmas Eve:

> We'd given her this damned new bicycle which was red and came in a box. The wife had made me go out and buy it that afternoon. I got it home, tore the paper wrapping it, stuffed it under the Christmas tree and went to have a drink. The kid saw the package and wanted to open it. I said "No! Not now!" After supper she tore into it and said, "But Daddy, it's not put together! Won't you put it together for me?" I said, "Not now, I'm busy." The wife said, "Come on, honey, its Christmas." "O.K.," I said, "Christ, its my night, too." I grasped the damned thing, set my beer down, told the kid to get the wrench, got the wheels on the frame, turned it upside down so I could tighten the bolts, and fell

> asleep under the damned thing. I woke up the next morning under the damned bike, feeling like a heel and mad as hell at the kid and the wife. We laugh about it today [field interview, April 2, 1983].

Acting quickly so as to move past the intrusion of an external event, the drinker places the event (in the above case a request) in his or her immediate past. But of course he or she has not acted toward these events, except in thought or impulsively through actions that leave the project unfinished. Hence, although the drinker thinks that an event has been dealt with because it was thought about, he or she has not. That the drinker fails tightens the circle of anger that attaches him or her to the other who has brought the request in the first place. Of course, in order to deal with this anger he or she must drink again.

The Temporal Self

The temporal self references those self-feelings that come at the alcoholic through the altered temporal consciousness alcohol produces. It is a self that floods the alcoholic's awareness, melodically and rhythmically, as a pulsating point of reference in his or her consciousness. It is the problematic that centers the drinker's consciousness. As alcohol's effects wear off, the drinker finds that she must return to herself for the self crowds its presence into her stream of consciousness. Lowry's Consul (1947: 223-289) exclaims the following:

> That bloody nightmare he was forced to carry around with him everywhere upon his back, that went by the name of Geoffrey Firmin . . . deliver me from this dreadful tyranny of self. (I have sunk low. Let me sink lower still, that I may know the truth. Teach me to love again, to love life. . . . Let me truly suffer. Give me back my purity, the knowledge of my Mysteries, that I have betrayed.—Let me be truly lonely that I may honestly pray. . . . Destroy the world! he cried in his heart.)

Confronting himself in this state of mind, the Consul, like all heavy drinkers, drinks again, for what he seeks is the escape from self that alcohol gives him.

When forced to be responsible for actions that he has taken only in thought, the drinker rebels against those who attempt to hold him accountable for his actions. He withdraws, claiming misunderstandings on their part. The drinker is unable to bring into the outer world of experience the feelings, thoughts, and emotions he feels toward himself and toward them. Like Lowry's Consul he cannot speak the emotions he feels. He drinks again in order to deal with these emotional feelings that he can neither express nor feel when he is criticized by others.

The Real and the Imaginary

The alcoholic's world of temporal causality is, then, a fantasized, interior, "fictional" world of cause and effect. It is, though, a world that is real. The thoughts that are thought are felt, and felt as real feelings. These feelings and the thoughts about them lead him or her to drink. The line or the division between real and imaginary, the fantasized and the actual, is dissolved in the alcoholic's inner and outer streams of experience. Time, in all its inner and outer forms—past, present, future, when a thought was thought, a feeling felt, an action taken, or not taken—is all that connects the real and the imaginary in the alcoholic's world; time that is and self and alcohol.

Alcohol prohibits the expression of the inner self and the inner feelings that the alcoholic feels and thinks. Hence her inner world of being is cut off from the world of others. She is, as Lowry describes the Consul, truly lonely, even when in the presence of others. The alcoholic seeks to sink lower in order to find the ultimate meaning of herself to herself.

Alex, the alcoholic quoted previously, phrases this dilemma as follows:

> I want to be alone, a loner. I want to live with ordinary people, but I don't want to be ordinary. But I can't live and communicate with ordinary people when I drink and when I don't drink I can't stand them either.

Summarizing the above comments on the lay theory of temporality, the following observations may be made:

(1) The inner temporal world of the heavy drinker is located within the long *dureé* of the present, yet the drinker dwells in the past or the future.
(2) The drinker drinks in order to keep the long spread of time alive in his or her consciousness.
(3) A confusion over temporal causality and the temporal ordering and flow of events is experienced continually; producing conflict, anger, and ressentiment toward others.
(4) The heavy drinker exists in inauthentic temporality.
(5) The heavy drinker imposes his or her own temporal ordering on the events and thoughts that intrude into his or her inner world of experience.
(6) His or her theory of causality is a theory of temporality that is both fictional and real. The logic of that theory of causality is dialectical, circular, and teleological.

(7) Sustained drinking maintains the structure of this inner world of dialectical temporality.

I turn now to the lay theory of denial.

THE LAY THEORY OF DENIAL

As a pragmatic interpretive structure that renders meaningful and understandable the subject's heavy drinking conduct, the lay theory of denial rests upon the conceptions of temporality and personal, phenomenological causes just outlined. More than a quasi-theory of problematic situations, it weaves the subject's theory of self as drinker into a total "worldview" that hinges on three pivotal processes: self, alcohol, and drinking.

The lay theory of denial is a theory of personal power, for the drinker feels she is in control of her world. She feels that alcohol and drinking are the keys to that control. The drinker derives power from alcohol and drinking. To take alcohol and drinking away would render her powerless. She understands power to be the control of self and other in the social situation and the lack of power to be the inability to control herself or others. Control of self and other involves interaction, the manipulation of knowledge, secrecy, and the control of information; most centrally information about how much she has had to drink. The drinker must deny, to herself and to others, the amounts she drinks, and how dependent she is on alcohol.

The power that alcohol gives to the drinker's imagination has been discussed elaborately by McClelland and associates (1972). A male alcoholic, age 29, at his second A.A. meeting, speaks of this power:

> I've been afraid to write my dissertation. I sit down with the materials, the paper and the typewriter and I have an anxiety attack. I get up, pour a glass of scotch, drink it and the fear goes away. I get courage and power to write. But I can't stop at one drink and I never get anything written [fieldnotes, June 10, 1984].

The alcoholic writer may become dependent on alcohol, finding, he or she believes, the power to create in alcohol. Athol Fugard, the South African novelist and playwrite, sober 17 months at the time of a *New York Times* interview (June 10, 1984: 19) states in regard to alcohol and writing that the alcoholic writer becomes dependent upon alcohol and upon the myth that creativity and writing come from alcohol. Such authors indulge in and endorse the romantic myth that alcohol produces creative works of art. Fugard cites the cases of Dylan Thomas, Brendan Behan, and himself to make his point.

The alcoholic's theory of power in alcohol is, Fugard suggests, a theory of self-deception. By claiming that alcohol fuels creativity, the drinker perpetuates the relationship constructed between himself or herself, alcohol, drinking, and the act of writing. The drinker reaches for power in the world through written words, yet is dependent on alcohol for that power. Hence, power is based, Fugard suggests, on a myth, a romantic notion that the power to think creatively can be given through alcohol. In this respect cause is confused for effect, the writer thinking that the cause of creativity is alcohol, when, in fact, alcohol is both the cause and the effect of the chain of thought when he or she drinks and attempts to write.

The alcoholic's power rests on an elaborate system of self-denial, knowledge manipulation, deception, duplicitous actions, secrecy, and evasion. The following statement from a female alcoholic, age 32, sober five months, underscores the centrality of secrecy in the drinker's world.

> I only drank alone, in the dark. Never in public, never with my husband, or with his family or mine. Nobody knew I drank until I came into A.A. and they said they were glad I was doing something because they thought something was odd. I got caught by my husband one morning. It was 3:00 a.m., I was alone in the living room in my chair, with my bottle of scotch, my cigarettes, the light out, the music on the stereo. He came home one day early from a fishing trip and caught me drunk in my chair. He'd never seen me like that. Then I had to tell him. It's hard for me to look at that chair today. I remember all the nights alone, when I got drunk in it, light out, being sad, angry, resentful. Full of feeling and afraid to show it [fieldnotes, April 30, 1984].

Drinking alone, in the dark, never in public, takes to the extreme the drinker's fear of being caught.

"Passing"

A system of explanation is constructed about his or her conduct that will stand the test of the everyday structures of the world the drinker inhabits. He or she must be able to "pass" as a normal human being who is not under the heavy influence of alcohol (Goffman, 1963b; Stone, 1976; Garfinkel, 1967). "Passing" as normal, he or she "disavows" any deviance he or she might produce (Davis, 1961). By so doing, or by attempting to do so, the drinker maintains a "secret deviance" (Becker, 1973). Knowing that he or she is a heavy drinker, but pretending not to be, he or she maintains his or her standing among normals, or so he or she thinks. All the while the drinker feels as though he or she is an "outsider" in a world he or she may hate, despise, resent, or regard as inferior (Becker, 1973).

Another female alcoholic, age 48, sober five years, phrased her attempts at passing in the following words:

> I always felt that only if I didn't open my mouth nobody could tell. I only drank wine, alone in my kitchen, never even in front of my husband. At parties I'd just hold my glass and smile. But then some fool would say something ignorant that I was an expert on and I'd feel that I had to hold forth. And I would, and then I'd make a fool out of myself and my husband would have to take me home. I could never keep my mouth shut [field interview, December 17, 1983].

A female alcoholic, age 33, sober one month since her last drink, who repeatedly attained 11 months of sobriety, but never one full year, described her relationship to normals while she drank:

> Oh I was good at hiding it. I kept a constant buzz at work. I'd take a short drink before 8:00 in the morning. Kept a bottle in my desk at work, would pour vodka into my coffee cup. Nobody knew. They never knew me sober until I came into A.A. and then they wanted to know what had happened to me [fieldnotes, May 15, 1983].

The Other

The lay theory of denial hinges on self and on the relation the drinker has with others. As a system of denial it rationalizes continued drinking, neutralizes any responsibility the drinker might be held accountable for, and justifies any action that must be taken in order to obtain the next drink (Scott and Lyman, 1968). By denying self-responsibility for his actions, the drinker blames the other who holds him accountable and questions his drinking. In this respect the theory of denial becomes a theory of the other who holds the drinker accountable for his actions. The drinker altercastes (Weinstein and Deuteshberger, 1962) the other into the identity of a person who makes him drink. This subtle shift in causality is accomplished through those acts of the drinker that promote guilt and counter responsibility in the other's eyes. An alcoholic, age 65, sober 12 years, describes how he manipulated his wife into believing she caused his drinking:

> I had her believing she was crazy. She hid my bottles, poured them out. I was s'posed to do the hiding, not her. She got a bad case of the "nerves" and she went to a psychiatrist. He told her my drinking was

> her fault. She should leave me alone. That is, I needed it. But she wouldn't let up on me. Then she started to going to Al-Anon, over a year before I got in A.A., and she got off my case. I went down hill fast after that [field conversation, September 10, 1982].

A 45-year-old male alcoholic, sober two years, described his relationship to his wife as follows:

> She bought the bourbon by the case. I told her I didn't like to go into liquor stores. They made me nervous. She thought that if she got it for me and made me happy, we wouldn't have fights. It didn't work though, cause I'd drink and then get mad at her for buying the wrong brand, or whatever [fieldnotes, July 11, 1983].

By manipulating the other into a position wherein she enables his drinking, the drinker absolves himself of responsibility for his drinking conduct.

If the drinker lacks a significant emotional other, or if she rejects those that she has, responsibility for her drinking is shifted to an "imaginary" other, often the other side of her divided self. A male alcoholic, age 42, in A.A. for 12 years, with 10 months of continuous sobriety stated this situation as follows:

> When I drink another side of me takes over. The drinking side. Before I drink my sober self tells me not to drink, and I don't. If I want to drink all I have to do is take a drink and then the alcohol and my other self talk to me and tell me to have another drink. Too many times I've done this. My drinking self can't stand what the sober self accomplishes and it wants to tear it down. With one drink I can start a chain of events that will destroy everything I've accomplished while being sober [fieldnotes, June 11, 1982].

This is called talking yourself into a drink. If the lines between the subject's sober and drinking self are not drawn firmly, then an emotional ambivalence will characterize the inner dialogues that precede a drink. All of the reasons for not drinking will be set aside in favor of the one reason the drinking self gives the subject for taking a drink. Calling alcohol a friend, the drinking self will talk the sober self into picking up that drink. And once the first drink has been taken the drinker will not be able to stop with one drink. The drinker sets in motion a sequence of events that will make him or her accountable once again for the state of consciousness and actions taken. Drinking himself or herself drunk, or into sobriety, the alcoholic will turn against the drinking self and hate or despise that self for having taken the first drink. The alcoholic will disclaim responsibility for drinking, blaming it on a side of himself or herself that he or she does not understand. In H.S. Sullivan's terms (1953: 161-162), he may relegate the drinking side of his self to the "not me" and the "bad me," arguing that a side of him that is not the "good me" lead him to drink. Guilt, remorse, and self-anger may dominate the self-feelings the subject feels when he allows the "bad me" to talk himself into taking a drink. He will say that it was not the "real" self that drank. Further, if the subject took actions while he drank that he cannot remember, he will claim that it was the alcohol that was acting and talking.

An alcoholic male, an academic psychologist, age 47, speaking in a detoxification center one night before he was to start treatment stated:

> My wife would bring these conversations back to me in the morning. She'd report vile things I'd said, violent actions I threatened, crude sexual gestures, promises I'd made. I could remember none of it. I'd say she was making it all up just to get back at me. I hated her for it. Who does she think she is? I'd never never say things like that. I guess it's what they call a blackout. I just don't say things like that [fieldnotes, June 11, 1984].

Blaming Alcohol

The alcohol the subject requires is blamed for the actions that are taken when he or she drinks. The viciousness of this circle of drinking, taking actions that one cannot remember and denying responsibility for them, escapes the drinker's attention. His or her system of denial denies their occurrence. The drinker's self-pride is embedded so deeply in drinking and in the myth that his or her life is under control that he or she cannot see how alcohol destroys what it is intended to produce and sustain.

The drinker's self-pride is fused with the drinking act. Hence, in order to maintain her self-esteem she must continue to drink. Alcohol is conceptualized as a positive social object that brings beneficial effects to the drinker's self-pride and to his or her relationships with others. Indeed, the drinker feels that he or she cannot deal with others except through alcohol. The act of drinking secures a socially desirable self; a self that is valued and cherished—if not misunderstood—by others.

A female alcoholic, age 36, sober 8 years, explained why she drank the most expensive scotch:

> I was high-class. I wore the best clothes, went to the best hairdresser, had the best college education, came from high-status parents. My father was the head of a hospital. I had to drink the most expensive scotch in the world. And I did, a fifth a day for 5 years. Then it became a quart, and then I knew something was going wrong. Why did it take so much scotch to make me feel good [fieldnotes, October 7, 1983]?

A male alcoholic, sober four years, age 39, stated this relationship between self-pride and alcohol as follows:

> I'm a man, a strong man. Strong men drink boilermakers, shots of V.O., and glasses of Old Mill. That's what I did. When the old lady had me locked up over night in the city jail I couldn't believe it. She told the Chief of Police to leave me there the full limit [72 hours]. I hated her for it. How could she do that to me? I could control the stuff and she knew it. She was just trying to get back at me cause of the woman from Detroit [fieldnotes, November 13, 1986].

Self-Uniqueness

Beneath this position of pride in self is the drinker's belief that he or she is unique and hence must drink the way he or she does.

> Anybody with the problems I had would have drank the way I did. Two divorces, retarded kid, bankrupt, mother dying of cancer, I drank to blot it all out. Had to, no choice. At least the booze let me forget [fieldnotes, November 19, 1982, 58-year-old male alcoholic].

The alcoholic's belief in self-uniqueness involves the following assumptions. First, she takes seriously the assertion that every social situation is imminently personal and unique (Sartre, 1956; Garfinkel, 1967: 281-283). Second, she takes to the extreme the view that every human individual is unique, and hence unlike any other individual (Schutz and Luckmann, 1973). Third, she believes that her uniqueness is more unique than that of any other individual. Fourth, like the embezzler and white-collar criminal who believes that his or her problems are unshareable (Cressey, 1947; Benson, 1985), the alcoholic assumes that her problems can only be solved through individual means. She mobilizes self-pride and risk-taking behind this assertion. Fifth, the alcoholic resorts to actions that violate the trust others have placed in her. Her alcoholic drinking becomes a means of solving insurmountable, unshareable problems. Sixth, the alcoholic neutralizes the guilt she feels about her actions (including her drinking) by claiming that it hurts no one else. She may also make an appeal to higher authorities in justification of her drinking (see Sykes and Matza, 1959). Seventh, she feels that she is not guilty of any "true" violation of trust because she is doing only what she has to do in order to survive. Eighth, the unique lifestyle that she leads, the unique set of problems that she has inherited or that have been forced upon her, and the special problems that arise in the daily world of interaction, justify continued drinking at the alcoholic level. Recovering alcoholics call this "terminal uniqueness," and suggest that problems drinkers may die from this version of their illness.

The drinker's self is attached to the world through a circle of drinking conduct. That circle defines for him the essential meaning of who he is to himself. The drinker's essence lies in the drinking act. To stop drinking, or to contemplate stopping drinking, is unimaginable. Who would he be without alcohol? Alcohol fills a void, an emptiness that other people—including the alcoholic—cannot fill.

An alcoholic, who died from internal bleeding produced by varicose veins, spoke of why he drank:

> My counselor asked me, "Why don't you stop?" I said, "What else is there? It doesn't mean anything. Life, what is it anyway? Drink, take it all the way, push it, fight it, keep fighting it. Without booze there's nothing. It's all empty, dark. Who said it? Fitzgerald, 'the fear of early morning, alone, awake, terror of darkness.' That's why I drank, to beat the hell. When I die I want 'em to drink a bottle of whiskey and dance around the fire on my grave and say, 'He gave it HELL!'" [field conversation, August 29, 1980].

The drinker's theory of denial, to summarize, has the following features:

(1) It is a theory of power in use, for alcohol is regarded as the key source of personal power in the drinker's life.
(2) As a theory of self as drinker, the system of denial focuses on self, alcohol, and drinking.
(3) Dependence on alcohol is denied and hidden from others.
(4) Secret drinking is at the heart of the theory of denial employed by the heavy drinker.
(5) Control over alcohol is basic to the drinker's daily existence and he believes he can control alcohol and its effects upon him.
(6) The drinker's denial system blames others and the "not me" or the "bad me" components of the self for his drinking.
(7) Self-pride justifies the continuation of drinking, as does the belief that the drinker is unique and has unique problems that only alcohol can handle.
(8) The drinker's self is attached to the world through a circuit of drinking. He finds the core meaning of his existence in drinking and in alcohol.
(9) The alcoholic's system of denial is sustained by the belief that he will not fail the next time he drinks.

This last point, the belief that he will not fail the next time he drinks, is the core assumption that underwrites the alcoholics ongoing drinking project. The alcoholic's denial system sustains this belief, for it allows him to justify each time he drinks and encounters trouble. I turn now to an elaboration of this element of the subject's theory of drinking. At some point in his drinking career he did drink successfully and alcohol did do all these things for him. The alcoholic's denial system is based on a past "reality" that he believes to be true. He also believes that alcohol can work for him once again, as it did before.

THE LAY THEORY OF SUCCESSFUL DRINKING

At some point in her drinking career—perhaps for a time period that spans years, if not decades—the subject regarded herself as a successful drinker. By this she means drinking gave her the good feelings, the euphoria, the creativity, the release from pressures and anxiety, the comradery, the fellowship, the love, and the warmth of fellow humans that she sought and valued. As a successful drinker she had good times with alcohol and with others who drank with her. It was possible to control her intake of alcohol. She could control her behavior while drinking, and drink in a manner that was regarded as normal, if not unique. Even during periods of "out of control" drinking she did not suffer negative consequences that she could attribute to alcohol.

This picture of the past is held onto by every problem drinker. It is for the alcoholic a factually accurate picture. Because it is "factually" accurate, as it is remembered, it becomes the cornerstone of the system of denial the drinker constructs when her experiences with alcohol begin to go bad. That is, she believes that it is always possible to get back to the time when she drank successfully. Every negative experience is dispelled as accidental, as being caused by others. Her "bad faith" (Sartre, 1956: 70) flees the facticity of each problematic drinking situation, permitting the drinker to believe what she knows is not true. The alcoholic knows she is a problem drinker, but believes that she is not. Any problematic that might occur when she drinks is disarmed in advance. At the same time she clings to and seeks out the smallest pieces of experiential evidence that would prove that she is in fact drinking successfully.

Consider the following statements. The first is by a 52-year-old male alcoholic, an owner of a construction firm, sober 12 years:

> I remember how that gin would taste: warm, right out of the bottle I kept behind the seat in the pickup truck. I'd take a long swallow about 4:30 in the afternoon, before me and the boys would stop off at the bar for a few beers. It would be warm, bitter, sweet, hot, it tasted sharp

> and clean. It would go all the way down to my toes and then come back up through my blood stream to my brain. I'd start to tingle, feel warm, then shiver and feel cold, then my head would clear. Those damned anxieties and fears would all go away. But it would come right back up and I'd vomit the gin. I'd have to do it twice more before it would stay down and then I'd start to be warm and feel good all over. I kept this up for three years. Everyday. The wife said I was crazy [field interview, May 13, 1982].

The negative experience of vomiting is disallowed in advance. It was a necessary step that had to be taken before the gin could bring the desired effects. The drinker goes on to report:

> During this time in my life I made more money than I ever have, before or since. I had 25 men working for me. We built three banks. I drove a new Chrysler every year. We built a new home. I owned three condos and a vacation home down south. How could I be an alcoholic? I told myself it was the pressure, all those men working for me.

The problematic confronted by this drinker, the vomiting when he took the first drink, was discounted because of the above successes. These successes, however, were compounded by the following experiences:

> It was after I started drinking in the morning, and getting sick when the wife could hear me, that she told me I had to do something. I told her to go to hell. We fought for weeks. I'd come home, grab a beer out of the fridge, after the gin earlier and the 6-pack I drank on the way home, go into take a bath and pass out. She knew something was wrong. Then I'd come to the supper table, yell at everybody, drive them all off, get 'em crying and all that, and then I'd either leave, or go into the bedroom with a bottle and shut the door. Finally it got so bad the wife told me to leave. I said good. I moved into the Moose, then I could drink whenever I wanted to and nobody would yell at me. That lasted a year, before I went to A.A. for help. I still didn't believe I was an alcoholic and at the old halfway house they kicked me out and told me to go drink some more. So I did, another year. Finally I gave up, went back, got help. Stayed there 6 months. Now I'm back with the wife and kids. I still remember how sweet that gin tasted [field interview, May 13, 1982].

This drinker's story of his history with problem and alcoholic drinking displays the features of the lay theory of successful drinking outlined above. Beer and gin were his favorite drinks. The taste and feel of the gin when it entered his consciousness were memories of drinking onto which he held. His financial successes during the period of the onset of his problem drinking nullified the problems he and his wife knew he was experiencing. Alcohol appeared to handle successfully the problems of anxiety he confronted in his work. His pride and self-will were attached to the drinking act. He was willing to give up his home and his family in order to continue his drinking. The problems he was experiencing while drinking were not of his making. His bad faith succeeded in convincing him that he was still a successful drinker. That is, even when the drinker has problems with drinking he still insists that he is a successful drinker.

The following statement is from a 48-year-old academic, sober 10 months. He had entered treatment 13 months earlier and drank 3 months after he was back at work. He drank off and on for 3 months. He states the following:

> I could never connect the problems I was having in my life and in my work with drinking. Somehow they were always disconnected. Drinking was just something I did. These problems just kept coming up. I would drink when I was down and I would drink when I was up. When I was up I felt strong and drank then too. I would remember all of my accomplishments and connect those to my drinking. Then I would drink more. Everything that I did that was good I always connected to my drinking; never the bad things, and there were more of those! I drank, too, out of fear of things that hadn't happened yet—a loss in my family, a sickness, whatever [field conversation, June 13, 1984].

This drinker separates problems from drinking. He regards himself as a successful drinker because his problems were never joined with his drinking. Connecting drinking to his successes and the good moments in his life, he sustains the image of himself as a successful drinker.

The following drinker, also an academic, is less sanguine. Sober seven days in A.A., after a four-month period of being dry and then slipping for two months before coming to A.A. for the first time. He states:

> Alcohol is supposed to make you happy. It cures depressions. Takes away anxiety, kills pain. Makes me laugh. Helps me sleep. But its killing me, slowly, slowly; its taking a long time, but its killing me. Why do I keep drinking this poison? It must be insanity, or irrationality. But I can't sleep. I put the headphones on from the stereo to blot out the dreams. And I dream and the dreams hurt. I get up and take a drink and kill the pain. But then I have to come off the sauce and I can't sleep then either. Its a circle and I can't seem to break out of it [field conversation, June 10, 1984].

The double-edged effects of alcohol, as a producer of both euphoria and depression, are well captured in these remarks. Drawn back to alcohol because of its killing, numbing, sometimes pleasurable effects, the drinker nonetheless feels that he is killing himself.

The same individual describes himself in greater detail, offering the following biographical information about himself and his family.

> My father was and is an alcoholic. He would close the family grocery at 6:00 and not come home until 1:30 a.m., after the tavern closed in the little Minnesota town we lived in. As a kid growing up I never saw him. Later when I was a teenager he bought a carnival. He wanted it to be a family business. Me and my four brothers worked it in the summers. It was embarrassing. He would yell at us in the kiddie rides, drunk. I left home to go to college and thought I'd escaped. I went off to become the successful drinker. I taught my friends how to drink. One night a friend asked me: 'How many drinks does it take before you become an alcoholic?' That was years ago. That line haunts me to this day. How many drinks does it take? [field conversation, June 19, 1984].

When does the drinker stop being a successful, heavy social drinker and become an alcoholic? This is the question that is being asked.

Another side to alcohol and drinking is given in the mass media, especially through its beer commercials. A male alcoholic, age 31, 2 years after treatment, during which time he had 2 slips, or returns to drinking, describes himself:

> Sometimes I don't know who I am. I watch the T.V. and see the commercials. I think I'm a product of Madison Avenue. When I think about drinking I hear, "Go For It!" "The Weekends are for Bud!" "Join the Pepsi Generation!" Who Am I? I pick up that stuff. It used to work for me. I started when I was 15, then I found grass and speed, then LSD and then coke. I've had an altered state of consciousness for so long I don't know who I am. Then I was unconscious for two years before treatment. I can't even find my own thoughts inside all the commercials and that shit! [field conversation, June 10, 1984].

This drinker nearly lost his job as a middle-level executive. He nearly lost his marriage. He was two thousand dollars in debt to drug dealers when he entered treatment, which he was forced into. Yet when he closes his eyes and thinks drinking, he sees and hears the commercials from Madison Avenue. These commecials, which do not depict the negative consequences of drinking, elaborate the inner fantasy life of the drinker because they picture only the positive effects and consequences of drinking.

This drinker knows that the picture of a successful drinker given in the mass media is not him, still he dreams of "Going For It!" The pictures in the commercials and the sounds in his mind evoke success. The heavy social drinker, the problematic drinker, and the alcoholic can all find pictures of themselves which normalize their drinking and make drinking an attractive, desirable social act. The mass media fuel that false image of self. Often the bad faith of the drinker can talk him or her into thinking he or she is like the drinker pictured in the commercials.

On other occasions the drinker will cling to a memory, or a picture of himself from the distant past, and attempts to drink himself into that picture. The speaker is 43-years-old, sober nearly 3 years.

> I had a bottle of Pouilly Fosse, 1962, in the Princess of China, a restaurant in Chinatown in San Francisco in 1968. It was a beautiful tasting wine. The meal was outstanding and the view across the bay, after dinner, with the sunset was gorgeous. That was a good night for me. Everything was the way it was supposed to be. For years I searched for that bottle of wine and looked for that taste, that moment, those feelings of that evening. I never found that bottle of wine and I never got back to that feeling. It used to make me sad as hell and I'd drink even more. Something had gone wrong and I didn't know what [field conversation, April 10, 1984].

This inability to get back into a state of consciousness that was once experienced haunts the problem drinker. His or her denial system, as outlined above, sustains this self-image image of as a successful drinker.

The essential elements of the lay theory of successful drinking are as follows:

(1) It is based on earlier historical moments in the drinker's past that are defined as having occurred.
(2) Unpleasant features of that history that might have been problematic, in which alcohol or drinking were involved, are neutralized and discounted through the drinker's bad faith.
(3) The drinker views herself in the present in terms of these past images of self.
(4) The successes the drinker achieved in the past, whether financial, family, work, or personal, are seen as being part of the picture she has of herself as a successful drinker. She connects drinking and successful drinking with successes in the other areas of her life.
(5) Even if the drinker comes from a family of unsuccessful drinkers, she regards herself as being a successful drinker, that is, not alcoholic.

(6) At some point in her career as a successful drinker, the drinker knows that she no longer drinks as her friends or drinking associates do.
(7) Beneath the image of herself that she holds onto and puts forth as being a successful drinker is the awareness that she probably is not what she claims to be. The drinker knows, in some part of her consciousness of self, that she is a problem drinker, if not an alcoholic.

It is this last awareness that produces the lay theory of alcoholism, or of heavy, problem drinking that the above pages have outlined. The lay theories of temporality, causality, denial, and normalized or successful drinking are all subsumed under what I have termed the lay theory of alcoholism, or of heavy, problem drinking.

THE LAY THEORY OF ALCOHOLISM

This theory, which is an interpretive structure that permits the drinker to go on drinking long after he and his emotional associates feel he should, revolves around the following 12 points. These points are deeply embedded in the personal history of the drinker.

(1) He may be a heavy drinker, but not an alcoholic.
(2) He deserves to drink and has to drink because he is unique and special. Even when he has to drink it is because he deserves it.
(3) There are problems in his life with which alcohol helps him deal. Without alcohol he could not deal with those problems and be a unique person.
(4) When drinking she escapes life's problems.
(5) When she has problems drinking it is due to matters over which she had no control. When she has problems it is the problems, not the alcohol, that create the problems.
(6) She is a social drinker who drinks heavily and doesn't drink any more than others do. Therefore she cannot be an alcoholic.
(7) Those people who say he has problems with drinking do not understand him.
(8) Therefore, if they make him angry, it is natural to drink more and to not interact with them.
(9) Life is still manageable and everything is under control, even if he does drink a little too much on occasion. After all he has never had a DUI.
(10) The reasons to quit are not strong enough, although quitting is possible if she wanted to.
(11) Therefore, no interference or help from others is necessary. All that is necessary is to be left alone so that she can drink and enjoy alcohol in solitude, or in the company of others who understand and who will allow her to take pleasure from the next drink.

(12) When drinking she becomes the kind of person she wants to be. Alcohol is her best friend.

CONCLUSIONS

The lay theory of alcoholism rests, as indicated above, on a threefold structure. First, it is a theory of causality that is both rational and logical, as well as being dialectical and contradictory. It is based on facticities, or lived factual experiences that are constructed and reconstructed in the drinker's mind. The drinker twists and constructs reality to fit his ongoing picture of himself as a drinker who needs alcohol. More important, he is a misunderstood drinker.

Second, the lay theory of alcoholism rests on a theory of denial that draws, third, on the drinker's theory of normalized, successful drinking. These three interpretive structures feed upon one another. They are woven or stitched into the picture of self the drinker desperately holds on to. Inscribed in his or her consciousness and in the divisions that separate the self is a deeply etched triadic picture that joins the self of the drinker with alcohol and the drinking act. His or her life is held together through and because of alcohol. To take alcohol away from him or her would be an act of destruction. It would be an act of such monumental consequences that the drinker dares not think of himself or herself as a nondrinker. To think that it is possible to exist without alcohol is unthinkable.

It is not surprising, therefore, that the drinker will go to any length to protect his supply, hide his drinking, rationalize his troubles, and exclude from his world those who say he has a drinking problem. Nor is it surprising for the drinker who has stopped for a period of time to be drawn back to drinking and to alcohol. After all, he has constructed an elaborate interpretive structure that allowed drinking long past the time when he should have stopped. In order for the drinker to start drinking again, all that is necessary is to resurrect a tiny part of that interpretive structure and he can tell himself once again that it is okay to drink because he can handle it now. Behavior modification treatment programs for problem as well as for alcoholic drinking are well suited to the alcoholic who does not wish to stop drinking. Such programs offer interpretive reasons for continuing a drinking career.

In this chapter I have developed in considerable detail the phenomenological and interpretive structures that underlie the problem drinker's theory of alcoholism. Analysis has revealed that for the problem drinker continued, heavy drinking is a necessity. The reasons for drinking are legion, the causes for drinking phenomenological and personal. The problem drinker constructs a personal theory of drinking behavior in the midst of a social, scientific, and political dialogue that surrounds alcoholism in American society today. This theory draws from this larger universe of discourse what is necessary for the drinker's survival. Knowing that alcoholics exist in the larger society and knowing that she may be one, the drinker goes to great lengths to avoid the label, as she continues to drink. In the next chapter I offer a summary of the foregoing in terms of "The Six Theses of Alcoholism." In Chapter 6, I show how this conceptual and interpretive structure that the problem drinker has built begins to collapse. I will show how the drinker must finally confront the fact that her self lies at the core of her relationship to the world. The self, caught in the webs of bad faith that she has woven, ultimately proves to be her undoing; that is, if she is to recover.

5

THE SIX THESES OF ALCOHOLISM

> *Thesis:* "A position or that which is set down or advanced for argument." (Chambers 20th Century Dictionary, 1983: 1342)

I have now examined the three major theoretical approaches to alcoholism and alcoholics that a practicing problem drinker will confront. The theories of science, A.A., and the lay individual have been discussed in detail. In this chapter I return to the Six Theses of Alcoholism that were briefly sketched in Chapter 1. These theses are drawn from the above theories. They are based also on my empirical observations of individuals who have an "alcoholic self." The theses summarize the experiences of such individuals. They are derived from the presentations of self such persons make in the social worlds of alcoholism that center around A.A. meetings.

They are stated as theses. They are not hypotheses or testable propositions as such. They reflect points of interpretation in the structures of experience that constitute *the alcoholic circle,* including problematic or alcoholic drinking, denial, surrender, and the processes that underlie recovery.

The six theses of recovery (and alcoholism) are (1) the thesis of the temporality of self; (2) the thesis of the relational structures of self; (3) the thesis of the emotionality of self; (4) the thesis of bad faith; (5) the thesis of self-control; and (6) the thesis of self-surrender. I will discuss each thesis in order. But first I must examine briefly the basic premise that organizes the theses.

THE ALCOHOLIC SELF

The theses are organized around a single premise, contained in the term "alcoholic self." Divided against himself or herself, the alcoholic is trapped within an inner structure of negative emotional experiences that turns on extreme self-centeredness and self-narcissism. This narcissism, as Tiebout (1954) suggests, is grounded in three factors: (1) feelings of omnipotence, (2) an inability to accept high levels of frustration, and (3) a tendency to "do everything in a hurry" (Tiebout, 1954: 612). Freud's term, "His Majesty the Baby" (Tiebout, 1954: 612), has been applied to the alcoholic self who wants to rule the world in its own way. Although there is questionable utility in the three personality characteristics Tiebout ascribes to the alcoholic, his general point concerning self-centeredness and feelings of omnipotence seem useful and correct.

The narcissistic, alcoholic self uses alcohol as a "mirror" to the world. This mirror produces a distorted image of the alcoholic, for it fuels grandiose feelings of omnipotence. It also fuels an inwardness of thinking that leads the alcoholic to focus upon past failures. A resentment toward self and others is produced. This resentment is focused on gaps and failures in achievement. In particular, the alcoholic has internalized a conflicting set of inner, self-ideals. These ideals are derived, in part, from an original "mothering" or "fathering" other and in part from his or her own version of those ideals as applied to himself or herself (Lacan, 1977: 2-5). The clash between these two structures of self (ideal-self derived from the mother and/or father, and self-ideal formulated by self) creates a fundamental instability of self for the alcoholic. He or she uses alcohol as a means of joining those two self-structures.

The alcoholic's unstable inner self runs to madness, fantastic self-ideals, imaginary fears, neurosis, isolation, and narcissism. It is held together through fragmented body self-images that incorporate self-dissatisfaction with a disdain, or dislike, for the physical body that houses the alcoholic's self. The alcoholic's self-other relations (Kohut, 1984) produce experiences that solidify this fundamental alienation from self. Because alcohol is his mirror to the world and the mirror to himself, the alcoholic dwells in the reflected self-images alcohol produces for him.

These inner structures of self come to life in the language, thought, and memories of the alcoholic self. Because alcohol modifies the cognitive and emotional thought processes of the subject, it is necessary to examine briefly the disorders of consciousness that are experienced by the alcoholic. These disorders are connected directly to the individual's relations with himself or herself, emotionality, time, and others. They also speak to the phenomenon of relapse, loss of control, craving, and denial.

Language, Thought, and Memory in the Alcoholic Self

Considerable evidence suggests that alcoholics in the prodomal, critical, and chronic phases of alcoholism suffer from, or display, the following language and thinking disorders: (1) short- and long-term memory loss; (2) a substantial dissociation of experience during drinking; (3) a clouding of consciousness, a disorientation of thinking, and an inability to understand language; (4) an inability to produce written or spoken language of a coherent form, evidenced in slow speech, poor articulation, improper sentence structure, an omission of small grammatical words and word endings; (5) a confusion over similar and dissimiliar terms, including the appropriate use of metaphor and metonymy, and a general inability to follow associative and syntactical rules or understandings; and (6) compensatory confabulation (Ryan and Butters, 1983: 487-520; Mello, 1972: 262-263; Wallace, 1984: 80; Keller and McCormick, 1968: 122-123; Urbina, 1984: 56; Oscar-Berman, 1984: 191; Jakobson, 1956: 90).

These disturbances, or irregularities, in thought and memory also describe the alcoholic in the first year of recovery. They are produced by the effects of alcohol and other drugs on the various hemispheres and regions of the brain, including the frontal system, and the right and left hemispheres (Ryan and Butters, 1983: 525-526). The continuity hypothesis, which suggests a continuum of impairment that extends from heavy drinkers to alcoholics with Krosakoff's disease has been proposed; that is, as the alcoholic progresses in his or her alcoholism the above effects become more and more pronounced (Ryan and Butters, 1983: 525-526).

Alcoholic Aphasia and Amnesia

These findings may be interpreted within the literature on alcoholic aphasia and amnesia. Alcoholics have been identified as suffering from Wernicke's disease (Keller and McCormick, 1968: 215). This is also termed *receptive aphasia* (Wallace, 1984: 80), and it is characterized by points two and three above (that is, dissociation of experience and a difficulty grasping and understanding language). Alcoholics also suffer a second form of aphasia termed *Brocca's aphasia* or *expressive aphasia* (Wallace, 1984: 80), which is displayed in points four, five, and six above.

Wernicke's disease often precedes Korsakoff's psychosis (or disease), which is also termed *amnestic-confabulatory psychosis* (Keller and McCormick, 168: 122) or *alcohol amnestic syndrome* (Urbina, 1984: 56). Although the "blackout" is the milder form of alcoholic amnesia, the Korsakoff syndrome evidences an inability to form new long-term memories (anterograde amnesia) and a loss of memory of past events that were once remembered (retrograde amnesia). The *organic amnestic syndrome* refers to short- and-long-term memory loss associated with organic pathology, often produced by substance abuse, including excessive alcohol use (Oscar-Merman, 1984: 191). This form of amnesia encompasses each of the six disorders outlined above. Victor (1965) argues that recovery from this syndrome "requires the formation of new memories and their integration with past experiences" (Keller and McCormick, 1968: 123). The alcoholic in the acute phase of the syndrome produces elaborate, often imaginary, conversations to cover for the fact that she has suffered a loss of memory. Problems memorizing new materials or following conversations are evidenced, as is a general inability to employ the "forward memory span" (Keller and McCormick, 1968: 122). In short, the alcoholic is able to think about and remember only the most recent of events. She has trouble incorporating new information into her memory and into conceptions of herself.

Figures from the Past

Suffering from these forms of aphasia and amnesia, the alcoholic appears to latch onto a few pieces of information about herself, to commitments she has made, and to significant others from the past. These figures from the past constitute a constant point of reference in the otherwise clouded alcoholic stream of consciousness. She knows, in short, her name, birthdate, social security number, address, spouse's name, place of employment, who her parents were, and where she is supposed to be next, although she may even forget or confuse these elementary pieces of information. She may not remember that she is an alcoholic and may drink again because of this. The alcoholic will also forget what happened the last time she drank, including the pain that was felt during withdrawal, and that she lost control over alcohol. She will experience the physical and phenomenological craving for alcohol within a temporal vacuum that does not associate drinking with past failures.

The threads that hold this discontinuous stream of thought together are emotional. Anger and resentment toward the past is held onto. A general fear of the future is experienced. A disorientation in the present is felt, as is a confused state of self-understanding concerning who the alcoholic is and why he is in the situation he now finds himself in.

The Circles of Alcoholic Thought

The alcoholic exists within a circular, conceptual, linguistic, and temporal space that confounds the effects of receptive and expressive aphasia with anterograde, retrograde, and alcoholic amnesia. The self is located in the center of this confusing linguistic circle. Bits and pieces of the past, the present, and future attach themselves to one another within this circle in ways that do not make sense. The alcoholic is like a half-completed jigsaw puzzle. Disconnected, unrecognizable pieces of the puzzle, like the fractured pieces of the self, lie all around in a disorganized pile. He or she doesn't know where to start, or how to start to put the pieces back together into some recognizable shape or form.

The alcoholically reflective self mediates these thought patterns. It attempts to make sense out of them, but finds that its every effort to be coherent, logical, rational, and orderly fails. Its thought and talk alternate between metaphor and metonymy. It races back and forth in time from distant experiences to events that occurred a moment ago. Holophrastic, repetitive speech displaces part for whole, confuses whole for part, and associates discontinuous thoughts with one another, as if they fit together in a rational, orderly thought sequence.

The ability to reason, to think coherently, logically, and with any kind of temporal order has vanished. The alcoholic's language continues to turn and twist metaphor and metonymy into patterns of speech that appear to reflect deep, inner, primary processes of self and consciousness. These primary speech patterns of self ordinarily are inhibited in common discourse. But they are the primary discursive structures of thought that order the alcoholic's self-dialogues. Partially released by alcohol, partially ingrained in his or her consciousness, they become familiar patterns of thought for the alcoholic. The twisted, poetic, metaphorical, metonymic patterns of speech thus serve to place him or her outside the realms of ordinary speech and interaction.

Consider the following account given by an intoxicated alcoholic:

> I'm crazy, like a horse who wants to jump over a house. I'm out of the saddle, flying high over houses, I look down and see the person I

> sleep with and work with lying in bed. I want to laugh at her and try to explain all of this to her but I can't. I'm afraid to go downstairs and talk to her. She's waiting for me. I want to get in the saddle and ride again, I've got all this fear inside my head. If I could just slow down it would be better.
>
> But I can't slow down. I feel like my house doesn't belong to me anymore. Nowhere is mine anymore. I want to get away and go riding [field conversation, as reported September 20, 1985, 39-year-old alcoholic, lawyer].

This jumbled sequence of thought and speech moves from statements that equate house with horse, saddle with being in control, omnipotence with looking down and seeing the woman he lives with in bed, and craziness with being like a horse. His house becomes a horse (metonymy). He is like a horse (metaphor). He mixes these tropes in his speech, as he attempts to place himself within the stream of consciousness he is experiencing.

Ten days later, in a treatment center for alcoholism, this speaker raises the topic of relapse for discussion at an A.A. meeting. He states:

> I've been thinking about relapse. I think I stood relapsed since I got out of treatment last time. Maybe for four or five months. I was drinking when I came in here. I don't remember getting a drink, and I don't remember going out and starting to drink. All I remember is that I was drunk and I couldn't stop. They told me the first time to watch for these things but I didn't understand what they meant. How did it happen? I want to know.

This statement could be interpreted within the framework of "denial." That is, the drinker denies his alcoholism and wanted to drink, so he did. It can also be interpreted within the discussion just presented. That is, 10 days earlier this thinker was trapped within an aphasic, amnesic structure of thinking that was alcoholically produced. Drunk at that time, he could not remember taking a drink. Now, 10 days hence, as he is becoming sober, he cannot remember how he started drinking after he left his first treatment center. Suffering from a form of organic, amnestic syndrome, coupled with his earlier entrapment in expressive and receptive aphasia, he is unable to remember taking the first drink. Memory loss, coupled with denial, provide the interpretation we are seeking for the situation he found himself in.

An interpretation of the Six Theses of Alcoholism, which now follows, requires that the above discussion be kept in mind. The self, language, and thought patterns of the alcoholic structure the operation of the processes the theses are meant to describe.

THE THESIS OF THE TEMPORALITY OF SELF

The thesis of the temporality of self assumes that the alcoholic knows himself only through time and the temporal structures of experience that alcohol produces for him. As a temporal being, the alcoholic exists within authentic (inner) and inauthentic (chronological) outer time (Heidegger, 1962). The alcoholic knows himself as a being who moves through time. He knows that alcohol alters the flow of time in his inner stream of experience. By drinking, the alcoholic alters his relationship to himself, to time, and to the passage of time.

The self of the alcoholic contains in its inner core a conception of self as a drinker or a nondrinker. This master identity overrides all other conceptions the alcoholic has. The self, accordingly, is attached to the world through an interactional circuit that includes drinking or not drinking as pivotal activities that define and shape who she is to herself and to others. The self is made up of three inner structures the "good-me," the "not-me," and the "bad-me" (Sullivan, 1953: 161-162). The good me references positive feelings of self; the not me, self-feelings and actions that produce terror and horror for the drinker or the nondrinker. The bad-me refers to those self-feelings that produce anxiety and negative feelings of self. Across these three structures of self are two temporal conceptions of self: The self of the past and the self of the present. For the nondrinker the self of the past is the drinking-self of the past. The not-me and the bad-me are the central elements of this part of the past self. In the past he or she may have drunk so as to feel the "good-me" features of self. Now the not-me and the bad-me are the self ideals that drinking both brings into existence and neutralizes in terms of guilt or anxiety.

Within the temporal and interactional structures of the good-me, the not-me, and the bad-me, and the self of the past and the self of the present, is the fictional "I" of the subject (Lacan, 1968). This "I" is reflected only in the inner thoughts and feelings of the subject. It stands outside his immediate discourse with others. It is attached indirectly to his "real" interactional self through his thoughts and actions in the world. However, these actions do not, for him, reflect the deep inner meanings the alcoholic holds toward himself. These inner meanings are gathered together around the "I" of his inner self-conversations. The inner "I" of the subject is the moral self, the feeling self, the self that is the "real self" of the subject (Denzin, 1984a). For the drinking alcoholic, alcohol fuels this inner, fictional "I." Indeed, he believes that only alcohol can bring that conception of self before him.

These analytic and experiential structures of self give way in the flux of concrete experience to a consciousness of self that is always within reflective range of the subject. Haunted by who she is, could be, and has been, the active alcoholic lives within a temporal world that is circular and inward turning. Located within the circular confines of time, she is hemmed in by the past, the future, and the present. She knows herself through time. Who she is, has been, or will become ultimately hinges on actions she has taken and not taken, or will take.

A recovering alcoholic, sober 30 days, phrased this relationship between time and action in the following words:

> When I was drinking I always made momentous decisions and acted decisively—in my head. When it came time to act I always hesitated, waiting for the right moment to act. Then I would let alcohol make my decision for me and I wouldn't act. I was afraid to act and to move forward. Alcohol always gave me the excuse I needed [field conversation, 39-year-old male alcoholic, academic, July 9, 1984].

The thesis of the temporality of self rests, as the above discussion suggests, on three interrelated assumptions. First, alcoholism is a disease of time. Second, the alcoholic is a temporal being. Third, temporality defines an essential core structure of the alcoholic's self. I shall examine each of these assumptions in turn.

Alcoholism as a Dis-Ease of Time

Alcoholism is a disease, an uneasiness with time, temporality, and the alcoholic's being in time. It is a dis-ease of time. Malcolm Lowry (1947: 344) offers the following description of the Consul who is reading the letter Yvonne had mailed to him a year earlier:

> "Do you remember tomorrow?" he read. No, he thought; the words sunk like stones in his mind.—It was a fact that he was losing touch with his situation—. He was disassociated from himself . . . he was drunk, he was sober. . . . Do you remember tomorrow? It is our wedding anniversary.

The Consul is lost within time. He is ill at ease within time. He drinks to escape and control time. Alcohol, as noted in Chapter 4, speeds up and spreads out the passage of time. Within this spread-out horizon of time the alcoholic, as the Consul above, loses track of himself or herself. Fearful of time, fearful of the actions he or she must take in the world, the alcoholic confronts time with alcohol.

The Consul does not know if it is six in the evening or early morning. He is unable to remember tomorrow. Yet each of his states of inner experience—drunk, sober, hungover—collapses in upon him all at once. These inner experiences are temporal and alcoholically induced. The fact that they run together in his stream of consciousness evidences his loss over time and over his being within time. The alcoholic who drinks to make time stand still becomes a victim of the very inner consciousness he or she desires.

The Alcoholic as a Temporal Being

A recovering alcoholic, age 48, a carpenter, sober four years, described his relationship to time in the following words:

> When I drank I made time stop. I would look at the clock on my mantle, it would say 10:30 p.m., I'd drink a glass of whiskey and go flying inside my head. I'd be back years ago, or ahead, 10 years from now. I'd be happy, sad, angry, afraid, all at once. I'd stretch out my legs and reach for the glass and it would be empty. I'd get up to get another, look at the clock, it was 10:35 p.m. Here I was drunk, it was still early in the evening. I wouldn't be able to go asleep yet. The kids and the wife were still up, nothing was quiet like it was supposed to be and I was drunk! And it was only 10:35 [field conversation, December 7, 1982].

The alcoholic's dis-ease of time renders him or her a temporal isolate, an anomic temporal being. By attempting to escape time the alcoholic escapes himself or herself and is free to dream, but these dreams and this alcoholic time is not time with others. It is inner, private time that is unshareable and often unbearable. He or she is placed outside other people's time and thus becomes a different kind of temporal being. He or she is drawn to those others who share this disease of time.

The Consul inhabits lonely bars early in the morning. Other drinkers seek out the solace of their own company; still others seek crowded taverns during happy hours, which legitimately begin "drinking time" early in the afternoon. A recovering alcoholic, age 43, a chemist, sober two years, described his lunch patterns:

> I only had lunch at bars that served food. I of course drank my lunch. But "The Greek Bar and Grill" had a happy hour that started at 1:00. I could take a long lunch and legitimately start drinking early in the afternoon. The drinking crowd came in around 1:30, to beat the amateurs who came in around 3:30. We'd get the music rolling—"Margueritaville" by Jimmie Buffet—and the double gins and the day'd fly by. I'd hit the sun on the sidewalk about 4:30 and have the day under control. No problem with what to do about the day after that [field conversation, February 5, 1983].

Time and Self

The drink situation the alcoholic confronts (Lowry, 1947: 303) is whether or not to drink the drink that awaits. This decision is made as she attempts to hide from others the effects the drink she has just taken is having upon her. Locating the self of her inner consciousness in the experiences that alcohol brings, her self is a fiction. It is an imaginary "I," to borrow from Lacan (1968), Jakobson (1956), and Kristeva (1974), that has little if any connection to the "real" world of others. The "I" of alcoholic thought is fictional, narcissistic, heroic, dramatic, articulate, resentful, private, and angry. It is angry because it can never realize its inner "imagined" dimensions in "real" interactions with others. Its thoughts spill over beyond the boundaries of normal, orderly discourse. The words that surround this fictional "I" in the alcoholic's inner thought cannot find a form of acceptable display in the talk that would anchor this inner self in the public world of others. Her words are hollow, yet her inner thought is alive within a dialogue that is vivid, pictorial, dialectical, and unique. The unique structures of the self are known only to her.

The most literate alcoholic, then, is trapped within an inner world that knows no acceptable mode of external expression. Because time is ungraspable and because his thoughts exist only in time, in the fictional world his fictional "I" inhabits, the alcoholic experiences himself as a void in the world. He is nothingness (Sartre, 1956). Every action taken that would or could fill out the void of nothingness fails, or seems to fail. He can never succeed in bringing the "I" of his inner existence into the interactional world of others.

Normal Time Versus Alcoholic Time

It is necessary to compare alcoholic time with normal time. In suggesting that the alcoholic experiences a dis-ease or uncomfortableness with time, I imply a normative, or "normal," conception of time. Following Heidegger (1962), Schutz and Luckmann (1973), Mead (1934), and Parsons (1951), we may make the following points regarding "normal" time. First, everyday, purposive social action grounds the individual in the present, as the past and the future are taken as orienting perspectives for accomplishing goals in the near, or immediate, present. Second, "normal" time, unlike alcoholic time, is not oppressive, threatening, or anxiety producing. That is, the experiencing of "normal time" does not require the use of alcohol so as to overcome the fear of time. Third, alcoholic time is time that is lodged in the past or in the distant future. Normal time is lived in the present. Fourth, normal, healthy time is understood reflectively as being part of the person's ongoing presence in the world. Reflection on normal time and its passage does not produce flights back into the past, as alcoholic time does. Fifth, alcoholic time lodges the self and its emotions in the past. Normal time locates the self and its feelings in the present.

These differences between alcoholic and normal time suggest Heidegger's (1962) distinctions between authentic time and inauthentic time. Authentic time is lived in the present, without a fear of the past or the future. Inauthentic time is fearful of the past and the future. However, an easy application of Heidegger's distinctions to normal and alcoholic time cannot be made, for normal time also may be experienced inauthentically, as Heidegger so forcefully argued. To say that alcoholic time is defined by the use of alcohol so as to flee from time borders on the tautological. The operative distinction between these two modes of time lies at the phenomenological level. The alcoholic is simply uneasy in time. He is unable to deal with time on his hands. He cannot let go of the past and purposive actions that would commit him to a stance in the future are avoided. By drinking, time comes to a standstill.

The alcoholic is like the "workaholic" who deals with the fear of the future and the past by overinvolvement in task activities. The alcoholic uses alcohol, the workaholic work; both classes of individuals seek to avoid or escape time on their hands.

Modern societies have produced large groups of individuals who share certain features of the alcoholic's dis-ease of time. Scheler's (1961) man or woman of ressentiment is a victim of time and the negative emotions that trap them in the past of the future. The elderly who are fearful of death, women who experience traumas after childbirth and when their children leave home, racial and ethnic minorities who live in the oppressions of the past, students who are fearful of making life decisions, the recently divorced who face the future without spouses, and the unemployed worker who has no economic hold on the future all live a version of the alcoholic's dis-ease of time. These individuals are all candidates for alcoholism and drug addiction, for in these chemicals they will find a means of escaping time's fearful oppressiveness.

THE THESIS OF THE RELATIONAL STRUCTURES OF SELF

The self of the alcoholic is embedded in the communicational and emotional structures that tie and connect him or her to others. The self is a relational phenomenon or, in H. S. Sullivan's words (1953), it is an interpersonal process. That is, the self is not in the subject. The self is in the relationships the alcoholic has with others. Alcoholism (and the process of recovery), accordingly, is a relationship to the world. It is not something located in the person, nor is it a disease or illness of the person. *The thesis of the relational structures of self asserts that the self of the alcoholic and his alcoholism can be understood only in terms of the relational structures he constructs, experiences, and gives meaning to. In short, he and his alcoholism are relational, interpersonal processes* (Bateson, 1972a: 324-325).

The alcoholic, like other subjects, conducts transactions with the world through the *relational circuit of selfness* (Sartre, 1956: 102-103; Denzin, 1984a: 60). The self does not inhabit his or her consciousness (Sartre, 1956: 103), rather it is lodged in the alcoholic's interactional relations with himself or herself and the others. Most pivotally, the self is located in alcohol and in the drinking situation.

The alcoholic's world of relational interaction consists of the following structures: (1) "real" and imagined, or fictional, others; (2) "real" and imagined "emotional" relations with these others; (3) the structures of self and self-feeling that are lodged in these relations with others; and (4) strategies and patterns of drinking and not drinking that exist alongside these relational connections that join the self with others. Each of these structures requires brief discussion.

"Real" and Imagined Others

The alcoholic's world is populated by others who are both real and imaginary. Malcolm Lowry's Consul carries on elaborate and detailed conversations with his half-brother Hugh, oftentimes confusing the "real" Hugh with the Hugh of his imagination. Similarly, the Consul finds himself engaging Yvonne, his separated and then divorced wife, in inner conversations that bear no relationship to the "real" Yvonne who appears at his doorsteps on the last day of his life.

John Berryman's (1973) Dr. Severance was an imaginary other, a fictional alter ego, with whom Berryman coversed as he charted his recovery process while in treatment. Bateson (1972a: 328) suggests that the alcoholic's others "are either totally imaginary or are gross distortions of persons on whom he is dependent and whom he may love." These others will be drawn from the alcoholic's immediate and distant family, world of work-related others, childhood, the mass media, friendships, and from the depths of his or her imagination. They are emotional associates (Denzin, 1984a: 281), or persons who are implicated in some fashion in his or her emotional worlds of experience. More specifically, however, they are "alcoholic" others, for they are entrenched in the alcoholic world he or she has constructed. They may be *enablers,* or persons who support his or her drinking, though passively and actively disapproving of it. They may be drinking associates who drink with the alcoholic and encourage him or her to drink. They may be authority figures, including a physician, member of the clergy, psychiatrist, employer, God, judge, the police, or parent.

The alcoholic's other may be a part of her, for through a disassociation of self, she may conceive of herself as being two persons: the alcoholic who drinks and the alcoholic who does not drink. The fictional "I" of the inner self may be the real other she speaks to and regards as most central to her life. In short, the line between "real" and imaginary may be virtually nonexistent in the inner self-conversations of the alcoholic. As she brings these imagined others into her inner world they assume a liveliness and presence that is felt to be real.

The alcoholic is the consequence of a chance occurrence, the meeting of a certain body and "psychosomatic reality" with a certain social environment, a certain mother, father, set of siblings or peers, a family structure, and a social world (Sartre, 1981: 48-51; Denzin, 1984a: 91). He or she emerges from a particular family unit. Those others who make up that world of family interaction indelibly impress on the alcoholic a biographical structure of experiences that will never be shaken or forgotten permanently.

The alcoholic is haunted by this childhood past, by its memories, its relationships, and its feelings. Absent mothers and fathers figure prominently in these memories. The alcoholic may drink in order to regain a sense of a past that was lost or never experienced in childhood.

The triadic relational structure of child-mother-father attaches the alcoholic to his or her family past. The adult alcoholic attempts to reestablish, through the drinking act and through the alcoholic consciousness that alcohol produces, a relationship to that triadic structure that is satisfactory. He or she lives out, in and through alcoholic consciousness, all of the anger, the resentment, the fear, the lust, the desire, the frustration, the anxiety, and the love that were or were not present in childhood and adolescence. The alcoholic may drink so as to kill his or her absent family other, or to recreate the other in his or her own eyes. In either case he or she drinks so as to live through this past what was in some sense unsatisfactory, painful, and perhaps morally horrifying. Many female alcoholics, for example, report sexual abuse experiences in their childhoods (Gomberg, 1977). They began drinking, in part, so as to blot out, or forget, these experiences.

Every recovering alcoholic I observed made reference, at some point in the recovery process, to these family others who continued to shape and influence their lives. The following account is typical:

> My father was an alcoholic. My mother was schizophrenic and a drug addict. It was painful growing up. I learned to drink to kill the pain. My mother's dead. I like my stepmother. She's good for my father. She's not my mother. I would like to see my mother today [field conversation, 38-year-old female alcoholic, accountant, in A.A. for 12 years, sober 11 months before a recent slip, June 9, 1984].

Malcolm Lowry's Consul describes (1947: 197-198) the pain of his relationship with his mother and his stepmother:

> The urgent desire to hurt...had commenced with his stepmother.... It was hard to forgive.... Harder still...to...say...I *hate you*.

Emotional Relations with the Alcoholic's Other

Bateson (1972a: 326) suggests that the relationship the alcoholic has with his or her real and fictional other is schismogenic and symmetrical. By the first term he means that the relationship is split, or divided, into competing and often self-destructive factions. Schisms have been generated. By his second term Bateson proposes that these schisms exist along an axis that both encourages and discourages more drinking on the part of the alcoholic. Rather than being complementary, as when one pattern of behavior (dominance) fits another pattern (submission), the symmetrical relation of the alcoholic and his or her other builds and escalates into more and more drinking. Though it is likely that his or her relationship to the other is both complementary and symmetrical, Bateson's point concerning the escalation of self-destructive patterns within the relationship is correct. These patterns, if allowed to persist, will destroy the *alcohol-centered relationship*.

That is, the interactional patterns within the relationship produce an alienation from the other. This fuels feelings of ressentiment (Scheler, 1961; Nietzsche, 1887), which undercut the emotional foundations of the relationship (Jackson, 1962; Steinglass and Robertson, 1983: 295-300). The alcoholic comes to hate those to whom he is closest, and is unable to either express the positive feelings of love and warmth that he feels, or feel the other's love and warmth for him. A desperate loneliness pervades all emotional relations with others.

A recovering female alcoholic, age 40, a nurse, sober four years, described her feelings toward her husband in the following words:

> When I drank I lost all touch with love and my inner feelings for my husband (and my children). They tried so hard to get me to stop drinking that I only felt fear and anger toward them. I was afraid they would catch me drinking the wine in the kitchen and it would make me feel angry. I still don't know how to show my feelings toward them and its been over four years since I've had a drink! I'm still trying to get in touch with my emotions [field conversation, April 1, 1982].

The relationship the alcoholic has with the other escalates as he or she continues to drink. Often it escalates to the point of collapse. That is, the relationship is destroyed. More often the relationship stabilizes into an uneasy structure in which both parties relate to one another in hostile, antagonistic, and spurious interactional forms. The emotional fields of experience they share become hollow and empty, filled only by the anger and the remorse that alcohol produces. The emotionality that connects the alcoholic with his or her other is, to summarize, negative, spurious, and relationally destructive. The schisms that divide the relationship are increased each time a negative interaction and a negative emotional experience is produced.

Structures of Self-Feeling

Self-loathing, self-hatred, guilt, ressentiment, including envy, desire for spite, wrath, and anger (Denzin, 1984a: 285) characterize the self-feelings the alcoholic feels toward herself and toward the other who is nearest to her. Not only does she feel misunderstood by the other, but she feels anger and guilt over the fact that she is misunderstood. Moreover, the alcoholic's actions while drinking—which may have taken her into the self regions of the not-me and the bad-me—only serve to increase her self-loathing and guilt. As her alcoholic conduct leads her to violate her inner moral standards, anxiety and guilt increase. In short, half of this relationship with the other is built on negative emotionality. The alcoholic hates and loathes herself, therefore she hates and loathes the other.

This structure of interaction is self-generating, that is, it moves forward in terms of its own inner momentum. Each occasion of face-to-face interaction generates self-feelings that are, if not negative, ambiguous and ridden with anxiety. The feeling that the alcoholic will explode and turn on the other is ever present. Such feelings permeate the self-structures of the other, leading him or her to be always on edge and fearful of what might happen next. The expectations of negative interaction, in a self-fulfilling fashion, serve to increase the likelihood that such negativity will in fact be produced. In this sense the self-structures of the alcoholic and his or her other produce interactional structures that destroy the underlying premise of the relationship that brought them together, and now holds them together as hostages of one another. I turn now to the patterns of drinking that are built into the alcoholic's relationship with his or her other.

RELATIONAL PATTERNS OF DRINKING IN THE ALCOHOL-CENTERED RELATIONSHIP

At some point—probably early—in his relationship with the other, the alcoholic drank publicly and openly. Once his drinking becomes problematic, this pattern changes. He becomes a "hidden" alcoholic within the alcoholic-centered relationship he has established with his other (see Rubington, 1973).

The following concealment strategies were typical of the alcoholics I observed: (1) hiding alcohol in the laundry basket; (2) hiding half-pints in the corner of the bedroom closet; (3) pouring alcohol in empty laundry detergent containers; (4) hiding bottles of alcohol in desk drawers at work; (5) filling beer cans with vodka; (6) burying bottles of alcohol in the backyard and in snowbanks in the winter; (7) hiding glasses of alcohol behind books in bookcases; (8) filling oranges with gin; (9) carrying bottles of wine in shopping bags and large purses and drinking in the restroom; (10) drinking one or two large drinks before going to social gatherings; (11) drinking large amounts after the rest of the family had gone to bed; and (12) stopping for drinks before coming home for dinner.

The alcoholic's other may enter into this "hiding game" by pouring out her alcohol, throwing away bottles, asking her to mark the bottles or marking them herself, or fixing drinks for her. The other attempts to control the alcoholic's drinking through these actions and in so doing enables her. That is, an environment is promoted in which drinking becomes a competitive activity and a battle of wits. Each party focuses attention on the drinking act. The emotional content of the relationship is thereby reduced to the amount of alcohol the alcoholic drinks on a daily basis. In short, a chemical takes control of the interpersonal relationship.

THE THESIS OF THE EMOTIONALITY OF SELF

The thesis of the emotionality of self states that alcoholism, in addition to being a temporal dis-ease, is an emotional dis-ease, or a dis-ease of emotionality and self-feeling. The alcoholic is emotionally sick and inhabits a world of painful self-feelings and painful emotional experiences. His or her relations with others are emotionally distorted as well. That is, ressentiment, anger, fear, and the negative emotions outlined above permeate his or her emotional relations with others.

The alcoholic is uneasy in this emotionality, feeling pain and conflict in those emotional self-feelings that disclose his or her inner self to others. His or her inner self and inner feelings are masked through the manner of sociable comportment that alcohol gives. Yet basic to the alcoholic's relationship to the world are his or her self-feelings. These feelings, and the inner and the outer selves they are attached to, are negative, spurious, and fleeting. Their existence is dependent on the effects alcohol brings to the drinker's stream of experience. That is, the drinker feels himself or herself and his or her self-feelings first through alcohol and then through the reflected appraisals of others.

Accordingly, the interactive effects others have upon him or her are distorted by alcohol. The alcoholic's inner self is always at least slightly out of line with the self that is presented to and perceived by the other. Furthermore, his or her inner self-feelings are feelings that cannot be shared with the other, for they are alcoholically mediated emotions.

A recovering alcoholic, age 47, an academic, sober three years, reported the following conversation with his former wife:

> She said she never knew me except when I was drinking. She said she thought I never heard her when she said she loved me. She said I always seemed either too happy or completely depressed and all she ever wanted to do was make me happy. She couldn't understand who I was when I stopped drinking. I don't think I ever knew her either [field interview, July 10, 1983].

The self-feelings and emotionality of the drinking alcoholic have a three-fold structure: (1) a sense of emotionality in terms of an awareness that is filtered through the altered temporal consciousness that alcohol produces; (2) a sense of self feeling these feelings in terms of the emotional feeling that alcohol brings; and (3) a revealing of the inner, moral, deep, feeling alcoholic, drinking self through this experience (see Denzin, 1984a: 51; Heidegger, 1982: 137).

The Alcoholic Body

Because self-feelings are embodied states of consciousness (Denzin, 1985b) and because alcohol produces both minor and major alterations in his or her lived, physiological body, the alcoholic's sense of emotional experience is one in which bodily sensations play a major part. An undoubted authenticity is granted to emotional experiences simply because alcohol alters and affects the functioning of nearly every one of his or her vital organs. As the alcoholic drinks and feels the feelings he or she feels, and as he or she interprets those feelings, especially those that are emotionally significant, his or her central nervous system is processing this information within an alcoholically based biochemical environment. The drinking alcoholic's sense of self and emotionality is, then, quite literally alcoholic, for he or she experiences himself or herself only through the effects of alcohol.

His or her sense of self and emotionality is real in the illusively fictitious sense that alcohol makes effects real. The alcoholic is, after all, more than what alcohol does to him or her, but interactionally the other may not know this. Hence when he or she is defined as an alcoholic by the other the label is resented for the alcoholic knows that he or she is more than the label conveys. But because the drinker can only present himself or herself alcoholically, or through the structures of experience that alcohol produces for him or her, the other's assertions and labels are correct. This self-awareness serves to increase the ressentiment he or she feels toward the other.

The emotionality of self thesis, which suggests that alcoholism is an emotional dis-ease, points to the underlying emotional foundations of the everyday world the alcoholic must inhabit. That is, the taken for granted world that surrounds the alcoholic is one that is based on unproblematic emotionality (Denzin, 1984a). By making emotionality problematic through the drinking act, the alcoholic makes himself or herself a problematic member of the world of which he or she is a part. I turn now to the problem of bad faith and the alcoholic.

THE THESIS OF BAD FAITH

The Thesis of Bad Faith states that the alcoholic and his or her other attempt to escape the facticity of alcoholism by denying its existence. The alcoholic's theory of denial and his or her theory of normal, successful drinking supports the structures of bad faith that allow him or her to continue to drink. Blackouts and alcoholic amnesia produce a "learned" forgetfulness about the destructive effects his or her alcoholic drinking is producing.

The structures of bad faith that sustain the alcoholic's commitment to drinking are fourfold. They come before the drinker as *coefficients of adversity* (Sartre, 1956: 482), which are self-defined obstacles to action. In a self-fulfilling fashion the drinker prophesizes his or her own defeat in the face of these forces. He or she defines the situational forces as being insurmountable.

The four structures of bad faith are (1) the problematic of physiological addiction; (2) the problematic of social support and the strength of the enabling system to which the drinker belongs; (3) the obstacle of self, self-pride, self-defined fear, and the fear of failing; and (4) the problematic of time, typically phrased as follows: "How can I stop drinking for the rest of my life?"

These four problematics are the reasons the drinker gives to himself for not stopping drinking. He tells himself that the difficulties in stopping are more painful (as he imagines them) than are the current difficulties he encounters as a drinker. Accordingly, the alcoholic convinces himself that not only does he not need to stop drinking, but that he cannot stop drinking, even if he wanted to, which he does not. Therefore, there is no reason even to attempt to stop drinking because he cannot do so. In order to sustain this fourfold structure of bad faith he must bring, if only tacitly, the full force of his lay theory of drinking into place. The thesis of bad faith envelopes his theories of denial, of temporality, and of normal as well as problematic drinking. Each of these problematics requires a brief discussion.

The first structure of bad faith is embedded in the physiological structures of the drinker's body. She is addicted to alcohol. Her body needs alcohol on a regular basis, whether she wants a drink or not. As she interprets the signals and the feelings of her lived body, which produces trembling hands, headaches, morning vomiting, loss of appetite, and the craving for a drink, she drinks. The physiological and mental pain of not drinking is too great. She can never go long enough without a drink to overcome the pain of not drinking.

The second structure of bad faith is lodged in the social world of the alcoholic and in her circle of enablers. Her friends drink, so why can't she? The alcoholic sustains the myth that she is still a normal, social drinker. She succumbs to the social pressures of others who encourage her (or so the alcoholic believes) to drink.

The third structure of bad faith is located in the self of the drinker. He defines himself as a drinker. To not drink is to be without control over the fear that engulfs him every time he is in the presence of others. Closely connected to the third structure of bad faith is the fear of failing. Should the drinker make a commitment to stop drinking and not succeed, he would lose face in his own eyes and the eyes of his peers and family. Fearing that he cannot stop, not being sure that he wants to stop, the alcoholic brings the fear of failing in front of himself as a further justification for not stopping.

The fear of failing is embedded in the drinker's self-pride, and in his belief that he should be in control of himself (Bateson, 1972a: 312, 320). This belief, inscribed as it is in Western culture, leads the alcoholic to continue to pit his willpower and strength against alcohol. Indeed, by failing the alcoholic proves to himself that he cannot stop drinking. This becomes another reason for not stopping.

The fourth problematic is time. To think of herself as a person who will never take another drink again is impossible. The alcoholic confronts herself, then, with the insurmountable problematic of the universe of time that engulfs her lifetime. The drinker knows that she will never be able to stop drinking for the rest of her life, and that even if she can stop for a day, or a week, or a month, before she dies she will drink again. Knowing this, she conceives of stopping drinking as an impossibility. Hence, the alcoholic allows time to deter her from stopping.

These four obstacles, or problematics—the pain felt in the lived body, the social pressures of others, self-pride, fear, and the dilemma of time and temporality—are the self-defined adversaries that keep the alcoholic drinking long after he or she wants to stop. They are woven into his or her system of bad faith, always giving him or her a reason for not quitting today.

The following account, given by a drinker 35 years sober, a 68-year-old bartender, displays these four structures of bad faith that are at the heart of the drinker's self-system:

> I'd get up in the morning (it was after the War in Germany where I learned how to drink that good German wine), and puke in the throne, on my knees, my head in the bowl. I'd be shaking so that I'd have to tie a string around the first glass of beer at Shorties' Tavern around the corner. I'd pull the drink up to my mouth and get the first one down. Then I'd follow it with a double shot of Old Fitz. Then I'd go to the can and vomit, then come back and do the same thing all over. I'd keep the second round down and the shakes would start to stop. The boys from the Ford plant would cheer me on. "Have another one, Bill," they'd say. And I would. Then we'd be off to work. I'd be O.K. until 10:00 in the morning. We'd slip off for a couple of snorts and I'd make it till noon. Noon was eight beers and eight double shots. That would carry me until supper when we'd go back to Shorties and drink till closing time at 1:00 a.m. when I'd stumble home to start the whole thing over the next day. I wanted to sober up, but I could never get past the shakes. Everytime I thought about it I'd shake all over and get sick inside. How could I confront the boys and work sober. I knew I couldn't, and I'd

take another drink. Finally it go so bad the boys told me I had to quit. Even then I didn't stop [field conversation, July 27, 1982].

Alcoholic subjects stand in a bad faith relationship to themselves. Every time they take a drink they act as if they believe what they do not believe for they know they are alcoholics (see Sartre, 1956: 70). They do not want to believe that they are alcoholics; perhaps problematic drinkers, but not alcoholics. They want to believe that this time it will be different.

A music instructor, 49 years old, sober five years, described her drinking in the following words:

I kept telling myself that if I could only drink a little bit before parties, and not talk too loud, that nobody would know that I had been drinking. Except that I'd drink too much before parties because I was nervous about talking too loud. Then I'd talk too loud and people would whisper to my husband that I was drunk [field conversation, December 4, 1982].

A 46-year-old male recovering alcoholic, a biochemist of international fame, with over 2 years of continuous sobriety, described this dilemma as follows:

I had been sober for six months, going to A.A. every Monday night and I was happy. I kept going to those meetings and hearing those sayings and reading those readings and saying I was an alcoholic. Then after six months I stopped going. I was in ________, my old drinking place with some engineers from Japan. They said, "Come on, have a drink." I said, "No, I can't." Then I thought to myself. I have not had a drink for six months. Alcoholics must drink every day. I have not been drinking. Therefore I must not be an alcoholic. Therefore I can drink. So I took a drink. Three months later I called my wife from my laboratory at midnight and said, "I want to kill myself. Did she want to come get me?" She said "No." So I got in my car to drive to my friend's house 300 miles away. I had consumed a bottle and a half of Scotch in two hours. I woke up at 3:00 a.m. outside Detroit. I didn't know how I got there. I came back to A.A. and now I don't drink and now I do believe that I am an alcoholic. I have been all over the world and those meetings and slogans keep me sober today [fieldnotes, November 1, 1983].

A male alcoholic, age 43, an advertising executive, spoke of the relationship between his drinking and his nondrinking self:

When I take a drink it takes control. It's not me talking to me anymore. It's alcohol talking to me and I like what alcohol tells me. It tells me I

> can drink and control it. If I want to lie to myself and talk myself into a drink all I have to do is to take the first drink. Then alcohol tells me everything will be O.K. But it never is [field interview, November 7, 1983].

By acting as if he accepted what he does not believe about himself the alcoholic subject repudiates any argument that might be advanced against his taking another drink.

The drinking act and alcohol are two adversaries the alcoholic must place before himself so as to overcome them, thereby proving his power and control. He seeks a self and a structure of self-feelings that he believes only alcohol can give. Alcohol becomes, then, another coefficient of adversity the alcoholic subject places in front of himself. By setting the challenge of alcohol in front of himself the alcoholic sets a constraint on his behavior that challenges him to fail (Bateson, 1972a: 322). As he falls back in failure against the barrier that alcohol has set for him the alcoholic locates the adversary, not in alcohol, but in the situation that arose when he drank. The alcoholic flees into the defeated freedom that alcohol gives, claiming victory, when all who know him understand that he has failed once again to control his drinking.

Locating her adversary in others, the drinker seeks to escape the temporal and interactional constraints they place upon her by continuing to drink. Freedom lies in alcohol and in the state of consciousness alcohol produces. Her drinking situation is one that only she understands. That is, no other person can understand the problematic the alcoholic must overcome in order to prove herself to herself. Even failure will be done with a style and a grace that is uniquely hers. This is her challenge and no one else's. The drinker displaces the challenge that alcohol sets by claiming that it is others, not alcohol with which she is competing. In this way the alcoholic flees the facticity of her own drunkenness, blaming others for her failure—not herself and alcohol.

Bad faith allows the alcoholic to lie to himself. Believing what he knows is a lie, in his innermost self the alcoholic knows he is an alcoholic and cannot control either himself or alcohol. I turn next to the thesis of self-control.

THE THESIS OF SELF-CONTROL

The thesis of self-control asserts that the alcoholic believes he is in control of the people, places, and events that constitute his world. He believes as Bateson (1972a: 312) states that "he could be, or, at least, ought to be 'the captain of his soul.' " The alcoholic is in control of herself, her drinking, and her behavior. She believes that she has not acted insanely or irrationally while under the influence of alcohol. The alcoholic believes, rather, that the problematic events that have occurred while she has been drinking were the result of events produced by other individuals who were out of control or were acting irresponsibly.

The alcoholic believes, too, that he or she can overcome, through the force of willpower, self-manipulation, deception, lies, and economic means, the problematic events that have appeared in his or her world. If required to, he or she will move, change jobs, spouses, friends, and even withdraw completely from the world, so as to be able to continue drinking. In such actions the alcoholic will maintain his or her belief in self-control. He or she will give up anything and everything in order to keep on drinking.

In these beliefs the alcoholic clings to the myth of his invincibility in a world that has gone out of control. Positioning himself at the center of that world, the alcoholic looks out upon it as if he were "an actor who wants to run the whole show. . . forever trying to arrange the lights, the ballet, the scenery and the rest of the players in his own way" (A.A. 1976: 60). He is, as A.A. says, self-centered, full of self-delusion, self-seeking, self-pity, self-will run riot, and a victim of troubles "basically of his (our) own making" (A.A., 1976: 62).

Consider the following statement. The speaker is 39 years old. He has been sober one year and is self-employed in the insurance business.

> I was hospitalized three times with a swollen liver, pancreatitis, malnourishment, high blood pressure, and the D.T.s, was driving on a suspended license, had a trial date coming up. My wife had left me for the third time. I'd been to two detox centers and in treatment two times. I was losing customers hand over fist and the bills weren't paid. I sat at my desk, looked at everything and called a cab to get me a bottle. I drank that bottle and went on a two-week binge. I wrecked the car, damned near ran into my house and still kept on drinking. I thought I could control it. I thought I was having a run of bad luck. All I needed to do was get a change of scenery. That's when I went to South Carolina and tried to start all over again. Trouble was I took myself with me and I just kept on drinking because nothing would go right [field conversation, September 8, 1982].

Our drinker believed that he was in control of his world, of himself, and of his drinking. Through bad faith he continued to talk himself into the position of believing that he could drink successfully.

THE THESIS OF SELF-SURRENDER

This thesis asserts that only through surrender of self does recovery begin. This is A.A.'s first step, which states that "we admitted we were powerless over alcohol—that our lives had become unmanageable" (A.A., 1976: 59). The admission of powerlessness is intended to bring the alcoholics face-to-face with their inability to control their drinking. To state that their lives are unmanageable similarly expresses powerlessness over people, places, and things. Tiebout (1944, 1949, 1953, 1954) argues that the alcoholic's feelings of omnipotence and pure self-centeredness must be punctured and destroyed if he is to admit a power greater than himself into his life. The alcoholic will be unable to accept help for his alcoholism until he admits and surrenders to his powerlessness.

Tiebout (1944) contends that the alcoholic is intent on maintaining at all costs his or her feelings of omnipotence. At the core of the alcoholic's self-system is the myth of self-control, and that myth realizes itself in the self-serving narcissism the alcoholic cherishes. The alcoholic is defiant, and stubbornly persists in believing that he or she has the right to do things in his or her own way. The means to solve his or her problem lie within, in self-will, and in defiance.

The thesis of self-surrender assumes that this defiant structure of self-beliefs, grounded as it is in bad faith, must be demolished. But it can be demolished only by the alcoholic, not by others.

Surrender occurs when the alcoholic hits bottom, that is, when she is no longer able to control herself or the world that surrounds her. Every individual's bottom is unique. It may involve a loss of a husband, a job, income, and home. The drinker may become destitute and be living on the street before hitting bottom. She may hit bottom when the pain of fighting becomes too great. In every case, however, the individual must find what is to her a state of being in the world that is no longer tolerable.

When this state is reached, the alcoholic's theory of problem drinking, his theory of causality, temporality, and structures of bad faith begin to collapse. Indeed, these interpretive structures must collapse in upon him and he must recognize that they have collapsed. Only then will the alcoholic begin to understand that his theories of self-control and denial are myths, built on fabrications, self-deceptions, and self-destructive beliefs.

Surrender is a destructive process that requires a fundamental realignment of every interpretive structure the alcoholic has constructed. She must relinquish her self-centeredness, desire for control, and she must stop drinking. The ego, what Freud termed her "majesty the Baby," must be penetrated so that her systems of denial, false pride, and bad faith are exposed to the critical scrutiny of sober, nonalcoholic thinking.

The process of surrender is threefold, involving first an admission of powerlessness and failure, second, an acceptance of that failure, and third, a deep, inner surrendering to that fact. That is, the alcoholic must come to understand in his inner-most self that he is an alcoholic and powerless over alcohol (A.A., 1976: 30). This is regarded by A.A. as the first step in recovery.

If this last step in surrender is not accomplished, accepted, and repeated over and over again, the alcoholic is likely to become a *verbal convert* and not a *total* convert to A.A.'s point of view. (See Rudy, 1986; Lofland and Stark, 1965.) That is, the alcoholic may well profess his or her alcoholism, but not believe it, because he or she either still wishes to drink, or does not feel totally powerless over alcohol. Verbal converts may become convinced or pure alcoholics, or they may only tangentially accept alcohol as being at the center of their problems. What Rudy (1986: 86) terms pure, convinced, tangential, and converted alcoholics reflect variations on the degree to which the alcoholic has completely surrendered his or her self to alcoholism.

Whether verbal or total, partial or complete, the admission of alcoholism on the part of the drinker is a step toward recovery. Whether that admission occurs prior to coming to A.A. or occurs afterwards is immaterial as far as recovery is concerned. As long as the drinker's admission to himself of his alcoholism stops him from taking the first drink he has successfully taken the first step toward recovery.

Surrender, for A.A., as indicated in Chapter 3, involves more than "fully conceding" to the innermost self the facticity of alcoholism. It requires, as well, the commitment to allow into the alcoholic's life a power greater than himself or herself. Only by being humbled before a power greater than himself or herself, can the alcoholic hope to be relieved of the obsessive compulsion to drink. A.A. states the following:

> The alcoholic at certain times has no effective mental defense against the first drink. Except in a few rare cases, neither he nor any other human being can provide such a defense. His defense must come from a Higher Power [A.A., 1976: 39, 43].

Surrender requires a shattering of self in the face of a power greater than the individual. That power is first understood to be alcohol, that source of friendship, solace, and courage on which the alcoholic has for so long relied. But because that power has failed him or her, another power is inserted in its place: the power of A.A. and the power of a Higher Power, which some call God. The alcoholic finds that recovery, if it is to occur within the confines of A.A., will require a confrontation with spirituality and a reconceptualization of what he or she understands power and control to be in his or her life. These problematics will be taken up in Chapter 7.

CONCLUSIONS

It is now necessary to organize the Six Theses of Recovery (and alcoholism) into a summary statement. I understand alcoholism to be a mode of being in which the human subject places alcohol between himself or herself and the world. Alcoholism is a dis-ease in the world that is temporal, relational, and emotional. It is based on deception, bad faith, and the myth of self-control.

Each of the six theses references structures of experience that are part of the alcoholic circle of existence. Taken together they form a unitary point of view that locks the alcoholic into the self-destructive patterns of conduct that will destroy all that she calls hers. As the alcoholic lives out the six theses she will destroy or irrevocably influence those who come in contact with her on a daily basis. Through her alcohol leaves its destructive imprint on the world.

However, alcoholism is a two-sided phenomenon as designated by the two phrases, active alcoholic and recovering alcoholic. The six theses of alcoholism simultaneously refer to the active and the recovering sides of the phenomenon. Recovery, once surrender in its three phases has been set in motion, reverses the self-destructive consequences of the other five theses. The thesis of surrender exposes the fallacious foundations of the other five interpretive structures that constitute the active alcoholic's worldview.

These theses are not in the immediate reflective range of the alcoholic's consciousness. That is, they are taken for granted and firmly rooted in the cognitive and emotional structures that shape and dictate his or her actions in the world. Because they are so deeply entrenched in the very marrow of his or her interpretive structures, the alcoholic holds to them with a ferocious stubbornness that defies reason and rationality. But within his or her interpretive point of view these theses are perfectly rational and understandable. They are, after all, what sustain him or her in the face of failure, criticism, and pain.

The alcoholic's self, then, is attached firmly to each of the six theses. To let go of even one of these interpretive structures is to experience a loss of self that is severe and felt to be an admission of self-failure. For this reason the alcoholic will cling to these beliefs as he dies before his own eyes. However, this may not be an entirely willful act. The aphasia and amnesia that he suffers from serve to keep him locked within a clouded stream of experience that perpetuates drinking. These disorders in thought, language, and memory organize his self-understandings and support his systems of denial and bad faith.

In the next chapter I take up the problem of the alcoholically divided self. It will be necessary to show how the lay theory of alcoholism and the six theses of alcoholism (and recovery) actually operate in the world of the active alcoholic who must, finally, surrender to the facticity of his or her alcoholism and ask for help—if he or she is to get help, that is.

Part II

THE ALCOHOLIC SELF

6

THE ALCOHOLICALLY DIVIDED SELF

The alcoholically divided self (and its other) lives two modes of existence, referenced by the terms *sober* and *intoxicated.* These two modes of existence contradict one another, producing deep divisions within the inner and outer structures of the subject's self and the self of the other. Alcohol thickens these divisions, leading the subject to live an emotionally divided self. The subject, like his or her other, is in the grip of negative emotions, including ressentiment, anger, fear, self-loathing, self-pity, self-hatred, despair, anguish, remorse, guilt, and shame (see Denzin, 1984a: 283 on ressentiment and resentment). The alcoholic's self is disembodied. He or she experiences a separation between an alcoholically distorted inner stream of consciousness and a painful, often bruised, bloated, and diseased body he or she lives from within. His or her alcoholic self-pride mobilizes the negative feelings held toward the other.

The following argument organizes my analysis. *The alcoholic and his or her other are trapped within an interactional circuit of progressively differentiated alcoholic and nonalcoholic conduct (schismogenesis) that transforms their relationship into a painful field of negative, contrasting emotional experience. If unchecked, this relationship moves slowly toward self-destruction.* Like the violent family (Denzin, 1984b: 490-491), the alcoholic relationship will move through nine interactional stages: (1) denial of alcoholism and violence; (2)

pleasure derived from alcoholism and violence; (3) the building up of mutual hostility; (4) the development of misunderstandings; (5) jealousy (especially sexual); (6) increased alcoholic violence; and either (7) the eventual collapse of the system; or (8) the resolution of the situation into an unsteady, yet somewhat stable state of recurring alcoholic violence; or (9) the transformation of the relationship into a "recovering" alcoholic situation.

A three-act play titled "A Merry-Go-Round Named Denial" structures this drama of destruction (Kellerman, 1969). Its three acts are (1) the alcoholic situation; (2) violence and the Merry-Go-Round of Trouble; and (3) collapse and surrender. A fourth act, "Recovery," may be added to these three acts. It is the topic of the next chapter. I will present the destructive life story of the alcoholically divided self in terms of this play the alcoholic and his significant others enact. I will analyze each of the above facets and phases of the alcoholic's experiences in terms of its place in this temporal structure. My topic, then, is alcoholism as a relational dis-ease of self, other, temporality, and emotion.

ACT ONE:
THE ALCOHOLIC SITUATION

Four categories of persons are present in Act One: the alcoholic, his family, friends, and coworkers (Kellerman, 1969: 2). In Act One the alcoholic has passed through the stage of being a heavy social drinker into the phases of crucial or chronic alcoholism. As with our drinker in Chapters 4 and 5, the alcoholic still believes that he is in control of his own destiny. The alcoholic lives in a culture that sanctions drinking in a wide variety of contexts, yet he seems to be unable to drink like normal drinkers. He has learned that alcohol makes him feel better, yet he drinks hard and fast, often secretly (Kellerman, 1969: 3). The power to choose whether to drink or not is lost. When drinking, the alcoholic ignores rules of social conduct, often becomes emotionally uncontrollable, and continually embarrasses his significant others. He often creates a crisis that requires that they intercede on his behalf. In the process the drinker becomes increasingly more dependent on them, yet persists in believing that he is independent and in control of the situation. He adopts a reactive stance toward the problems he creates, waiting for others to react to him, while the alcoholic reacts to their reactions.

The alcoholic and his other have built up, through years of heavy drinking, an alcoholic-centered relationship. His spouse, or lover, has supported his drinking. The spouse or lover has denied the problems alcohol has created, and has attempted to control his drinking, all the time maintaining the myth that he is a heavy social drinker.

The following interaction is typical of the experiences the alcoholic and his other confront in Act One. The speaker recounts an experience before he came to A.A.

> I'd gotten mad at my family. They'd come home and found me drunk. They left and went to Burger King for dinner and left me alone. I called a cab, got a bottle of gin, and checked into a hotel under another name. Late that night I called home and said I was going to kill myself. Did she want to do anything? She asked where I was and I wouldn't tell her. I hung up, passed out, and woke up the next morning and called home and asked for a ride to work. They came and picked me up and dropped me off. They looked at me and said "What's going on?" I said, "Nothing, I just needed to get away." Then I got mad. I screamed at them. I said, "Get off my case. You're driving me crazy," and I slammed the door and left them there. That night I took them out for dinner and brought home roses. Everything was "lovey dovey" [field conversation, April 3, 1981].

In Act One the alcoholic and his other coexist in a field of contrasting emotional experiences. Emotional violence, sexual intimacy, physical abuse, gifts offered out of guilt, DUIs, suicide threats, and trips to counselors chart the emotional roller coaster the alcoholic and his other ride in Act One (see following). This act will continue until the alcoholic produces a situation that neither he nor alcohol can handle. That is, he requires the massive assistance of others, including financial aid, legal counsel, medical attention, and help from his coworkers. However, until this occurs, the alcoholic and his others remain within the uneasy interactional space they have created for one another.

Together they have produced *the alcoholic situation* that represents four interactional patterns organized around alcohol and its consumption by the alcoholic. The *open drinking context* displays the drinker with a drink in his hands. The *closed drinking context* references those situations in which the drinker attempts to hide the fact that he has been drinking. The *sober context* is a nondrinking situation in which it is evident that the alcoholic probably is sober. The *normally intoxicated but in control context* references the setting in which the alcoholic is maintaining a level of alcohol intake that others regard as normal and acceptable (see Glaser and Strauss, 1967).

Each time the alcoholic interacts with his other, the other must determine if he has been drinking, and if so, how much. Two interpretive frameworks (Goffman, 1974: 10-11; Bateson, 1972d: 187) compete for attention in the alcoholic situation. The "sober" framework produces one set of definitions regarding accountable and nonaccountable violent, emotional conduct. The "intoxicated," or "he has been drinking" framework produces another set of meanings and interpretations. These two frameworks may exist side by side in the same interactional situation. Drunk, the alcoholic confronts his sober other, attempting to move her into the "intoxicated" framework, or the alcoholic denies his intoxication and attempts to speak to the other from the "sober" framework. The clash of these two interpretive points of view leads to hostility, feelings of anger, and ressentiment. Witness the follwing account, offered by Merryman (1984: 6). The interactants are an alcoholic wife Abby and her husband Martin. Abby has just returned from a weekend escape to the family's cottage on the New England coast. Martin has picked her up from the airport. They are driving home. Afraid of what her husband will say about her drinking, Abby has taken a drink of vodka in the women's restroom at the airport.

> Abby sat silent, waiting, watching, intensely aware of Martin. . . . She could see right now from his hurt mad expression that the next words from his mouth would be sarcastic hints for self-improvement—unconnected to any tenderness or sensitivity. And then she would defend herself, and they would be at it again, and there would be no real hope.
>
> Presently, Martin's eyes flicked away from the highway and glanced over his glasses toward Abby. "You look completely burnt out," he said, "Had your nose in the sauce?"
>
> Abby twisted toward him, hands clenched in her lap, voice controlled. "It so happens I almost missed the plane and haven't had any breakfast. I feel like I've been in a Waring blender set on chop. . . ."
>
> Martin's eyes remained unswervingly on the road, his face set and grim. When he spoke again, his voice was cutting, punishing. "How much did you drink?"

Reading the Alcoholic

Fearful of the effects alcohol may have upon the alcoholic's conduct, family members, like Martin above, are, as Jackson (1962: 475-477) observes, always alert to what phase of the drinking cycle the alcoholic is in when he or she comes before them. The interaction patterns in the alcoholic-dependent relationship vary, as Steinglass and Robertson (1983: 272) suggest, by whether or not the alcoholic is in a stable or nonstable, sober or "wet" state. The stability of the alcoholic's emotionality, whether predictable or nonpredictable, intentional or nonintentional, whether it is charming or cruel, harsh and aloof, self-pitying and withdrawn, fawning and concillatory, hostile and angry, will be seen to vary by real and imputed states of intoxication. Confronted with the self-fulfilling definition that she has been drinking before she comes into their presence, the alcoholic may, as did Abby above, attempt to mask the effects of alcohol upon her conduct. Or the alcoholic may react with anger and produce the negative experiences family members wish to avoid.

The underlying premise of all interactions in the alcohol-dependent relationship questions the presence or absence of alcohol in the drinker's consciousness. This premise makes problematic the intentionality of the alcoholic's conduct, for her actions and meanings can always be interpreted from within the "she has been drinking" framework. Such a premise diminishes the alcoholic's standing in the relationship, making her dependent on others for the valued self-definitions she seeks. That is, the alcoholic knows and they know—and she knows that they know—that she could have been drinking. Doubt and anger thus cling to every interaction between the alcoholic and her other. Because alcohol has become the central social object in the alcohol-dependent relationship, it—not emotionality or the mutual exchange of selves—becomes the dominant, if not the hidden, focus of all interactions.

Violent Emotionality

The alcoholic and her other live in emotional violence, which I define as negative emotionality turned into active, embodied, hostile interactions with herself and with others. If violence is understood to reference the attempt to regain through force something that has been lost (Denzin, 1984a: 169), then the alcoholic attempts to use emotional and physical force to regain the sense of self-pride she has lost to alcohol and to the other.

The violence the alcoholic engages in may be verbal or physical, or both. It may be sporadic or frequent, and it may involve such actions as the sexual abuse of a spouse or child, the threat to use a weapon (including knives and guns), the actual hitting or beating of another, and the driving of an automobile while intoxicated and killing another. Violent alcoholic emotionality ranges from physical violence, as just indicated, to inflicted emotionality, as well as spurious, playful, real, and paradoxical violent emotional acts (Denzin, 1984a: 185-190). Violent emotionality, in all its forms, is embedded in the daily life of the alcoholic and his or her emotional associates. The interiority of alcoholic existence frightfully illuminates the emotional violence that has been observed in nonalcoholic, violent relationships (Denzin, 1984a: 190-197; 1984b: 483-513). The alcoholic relationship is an emotionally violent relationship.

The Five Forms of Alcoholic Violence

There are five forms of alcoholic violence that are woven through the four interactional-drinking situations the alcoholic and his or her other produce. As indicated above, every time the other interacts with the alcoholic he or she must determine if the alcoholic has been drinking. This master definition then structures the meanings that are applied to the alcoholic's conduct.

The first form of alcoholic violence is *emotional violence.* In emotional violence the alcoholic inflicts his or her emotionality on the other. He or she does this with emotional outbursts and in emotional scenes that get out of control. The following interaction describes alcoholic, emotional violence.

> I came home tired and beat. The house was a mess, the dogs were loose, and she was in the bedroom taking a nap. Supper wasn't even started yet. I fixed a drink, turned on the news. She came out, yelled at me for having that drink. I'd heard it a thousand times before. I couldn't take it anymore. I threw the drink in her face, grabbed her arm and yelled, "Where's my God damned supper! You never do anything around here." She hit back at me, called me no good. She ran and got my wood carving that I'd been making her for Christmas. She laughed at it, called it stupid and dumb. She threw it against the wall. That's when I lost it. I ran at her. She called the police. How can she ever trust me again? How can we start over? I don't know what's wrong with me. I ain't been the same since I got home from Nam. (Denzin, 1984b: 501)

The second form of alcoholic violence is *playful, alcoholic violence.* Here the alcoholic, usually in the open drinking context, plays at being violent, but serious violence is not intended. He playfully slaps his child on the shoulder, or smacks his wife on the cheek, for example. He takes a step away from "literal" reality and makes a play at being violent, but in a nonviolent way. Playful violence is conveyed through winks, smiles, voice intonations, shrugs, hand and shoulder movements, a toss of the head, and so on (Lynch, 1982: 29).

The third form of negative, violent emotionality is *spurious* and/or *accidental alcoholic violence.* As with playful violence, deliberate nonviolence is intended. However, the alcoholic's actions carry the meaning of real, intended violence. His hand slips as he reaches out to touch the other and he slaps her, rather than caressing her. He stumbles, falls, and crashes through a window. He passes out while driving and runs the car through the front door of his house. Though inwardly the alcoholic does not intend to be violent, his outward actions convey violence to the other. Unlike playful violence in which the alcoholic communicates through playful actions that his actions could be interpreted both as violence and nonviolence, in accidental violence, real violent consequences follow from his conduct.

Real alcoholic violence is the fourth form of negative, violent emotionality. Here the alcoholic intends to be violent, is violent, and his or her violent intentions are felt by the other. He or she may hit, hurl an insult, throw a knife, or fire a gun at the other. In real violence the alcoholic embodies a violent line of action from which he or she cannot willfully walk away. Real, alcoholic violence is felt in the bodies of both the alcoholic and his or her other who becomes a victim. It is "naked emotion," often raw and brutal.

The following account illuminates the differences between playful, accidental, and real violence.

> When my husband drank he would do crazy things that he didn't mean. But it got to the point where it didn't matter if he meant it or not. The first time he threw my daughter's teddy bear at me and missed and knocked over the vase of flowers on the dining room table and we both laughed at how absurd it was. We thought something crazy was going on. How could he be mad at me if he threw a teddy bear at me? But it got worse. The next time he knocked me down the stairs and said it was an accident. I knew he was mad at me and he was trying to hit me. He said it was accidental. I never believed him. Finally he got out of hand. He came home slightly drunk. I asked him "How much have you been drinking?" He swore at me. Slammed the kitchen door. I guess he went to the basement and got a drink. He came back up with the drink in his hands and threw it at me. He missed and it went through the front window. Then he came at me, grabbed me by the throat, and started to shake me. He was screaming all the time. He said he hated me and wanted to kill me. I got loose. Ran out of the house. Called the police. They came and arrested him. I filed for separation after that. We're divorced now [field conversation, September 1, 1983, 42-year-old female, occupational nurse].

If violent interactions are to be interpreted as being present, then the other must be able to distinguish between playful, accidental, and real alcoholic mood states. He or she must also be able to understand those moments when *real violence* of a nonalcoholic nature is intended. In this situation the alcoholic is held, without doubt, fully accountable for these actions.

More often, however, alcohol is present in the situation when the alcoholic's violent emotionality erupts. His or her actions occur within the following message frame:

> Because I have been drinking all messages here are untrue.
> I don't want to be violent.
> I want to be violent.

The alcoholic and his other are trapped within this message system. *Paradoxical alcoholic violence* of a "real" order is produced and experienced, but seemingly it is nonintended. This is the fifth form of alcoholic violence. Hence the other must choose whether or not to listen to the alcohol speaking. He or she may discount the alcohol and listen to the words that were not spoken, but would have been spoken, if the alcoholic had not been drinking. If he or she is not willing to suspend disbelief in the words that were in fact spoken, there is no recourse other than to hear what in fact was said. He or she is trapped. If the other knows the alcoholic didn't mean what was said, then how can the other discount the effects of the emotional and physical violence just inflicted upon him or her? Further, if the other feels that the alcoholic has self-control over his or her drinking, then he or she believes that the alcoholic drank in order to be violent. In which case the alcoholic is doubly accountable for his or her actions.

The confluence of playful, accidental, real, and paradoxical violence within the sober and intoxicated interactional contexts that the alcoholic and his or her other produces causes recurring emotional chaos. This situation serves to locate emotional violence, in all its forms, at the center of the alcohol-dependent relationship.

Alcoholic Identities

The alcoholic relationship solidifies into a set of reciprocally expected, alcoholic identities that center on alcohol and drinking. Children may become scapegoats for the family's problems. In reaction to the alcoholic situation, they may become rebellious, withdrawn, or delinquent. They may attempt to become pseudo-parents, taking over the mothering or fathering responsibilities of the alcoholic. They may become family stars, or heroes, and they may become overachievers. What they will become, to use the currently employed phrase, are adult children of alcoholics (Woititz, 1983).

Spouses, family members, friends, lovers, coworkers, employers, physicians, and children become *enablers* and *coalcoholic dependents* in the relationship. These others assist the alcoholic when she gets in trouble. They buy the alcoholic drinks and bring alcohol home for her. They give the alcoholic money when she needs it. They become dependent upon the alcoholic's dependency and mold identities that place them in a "helping" relationship with her. Enablers often become *victims,* for they are victimized by the alcoholic's inability to meet the ordinary demands that have been placed upon her. Victims do the alcoholic's work for her. Victims may also become *provokers.* The provoker becomes the other who feeds back into the alcoholic relationship all the bitterness, resentment, fear, anger, and hostility that is felt when the alcoholic turns against him or her and attacks the provoker for attempting to control the alcoholic's drinking (Kellerman, 1969). Resenting such control, the alcoholic flails out. The victim in turn becomes a *martyr,* bearing the cross of the alcoholic relationship upon his or her shoulders. The victim resents the alcoholic's resentment.

Resenting this attitude, the alcoholic builds a deep hatred toward the victim. He or she provokes the alcoholic's anger. The victim is blamed for everything that goes wrong in the relationship. The alcoholic may drink in order to blot out the painful loss of control experienced from the victim's hands. A recovering alcoholic reported the following angry thoughts he held toward his mother while he was drinking:

> She was domineering and tried to control me. We lived together in a little house trailer she bought. She'd say "Now, Harry, don't drink today." I'd get mad as hell, storm out, go to the bar on the corner and have me a drink. I'd look at her face in the glass and drink to it. I'd say, "Set em up. I'm getting drunk today. She can't tell me what to do!" And I would [field conversation, 36-year-old male, in treatment for the third time, June 22, 1984].

THE ALCOHOLIC SITUATION AS A STRUCTURE OF CONTRASTING EMOTIONS

Contrasting emotional experiences, as first indicated, are layered through the alcoholic relationship. First charming and loving, then cruel and hostile, the alcoholic generates a field of experience that is negative, positive, alienating, ambiguous, ambivalent, and ultimately self-destructive. The alcoholic and his or her others stand at the center of this field of shifting, contrasting emotions. The following account speaks to this feature of their shared life. The speaker is at his first A.A. meeting. He offers the labels Jekyll and Hyde for the two sides of his emotionally divided self. In his mid-forties, he is married, has two children and works for a large accounting firm. His father and grandfather were alcoholics. Before he stopped drinking, seven days earlier, he had been told to leave work because he was drunk. Not believing this, he had checked into a local hospital to have his blood alcohol level tested. The test confirmed that he was, in fact, intoxicated. He speaks the following:

> When I drink I become another person. Like a Dr. Jekyll and a Mr. Hyde (or whatever they're called). I get violent. I swear, I throw things. Last Saturday, a week ago, I threw the kitchen table at my father-in-law. I grabbed my wife (she only weighs 98 pounds) by the throat 'cause she said I was drunk when I came home. My little girls were hanging on my leg, telling me not to hurt Mommy! Christ! What's wrong with me? I'm not violent. I don't swear. I'm quiet. I always wear a smile. I'm easy going. Even when things are going bad I smile and say it'll work out. But I stop and have that first beer and the next thing you know I'm drunk and there till the bar closes. Then the wife's mad. Screaming at me when I come in the door. I feel guilty, mad. Mad at myself. Mad at her. Hell, I know I'm drunk. She don't have to tell me. Why'd she throw it up at me like that? I don't want to be like this any more than she wants me to be drunk. I get crazy, like last Saturday, last week. Then we don't talk. Now she's gone! Took the girls. Told me to get professional help. Are you people professional? I guess you must be cause you're not drinking. You must have something I don't have. Maybe I can get it. I'll be back [field conversation, September 25, 1984].

Self-pride lies behind this alcoholic's anger at his wife. He knows that he is drunk when he comes home. He knows that he has failed to control his drinking once again. His violence represents an attempt to regain a sense of self-worth, or self-pride, in the face of this humiliating situation. He resents her failure to acknowledge this fact. The structures of contrastive experience that are confronted by the alcoholic self and his other revolve around the negative emotions of self-hatred, fear, anxiety, anger, and violence, but most centrally the master emotions of *ressentiment* (Nietzsche, 1897: 35-39, 63-65, 77-78, 90, 110; Scheler, 1961: 39-44, 224-228, 283), and *self-pride* (see Denzin, 1986c).

Negative Emotionality

Restless and uneasy, the alcoholically divided self is always on the move, always seeking new experiences to fill, if only momentarily, the loneliness of self that is felt.

The emotions that divide the self alternate between momentary feelings of positive self-worth, and deep, underlying feelings of doubt, self-hatred, despair, and anguish. Alcoholic drinking, fueled by self-pride and risk-taking, is pursued in a futile attempt to overcome the deep inadequacies that are felt. The alcoholic is unable to sustain over any length of time a positive definition of self.

The following account addresses this aspect of the alcoholic self. The speaker is a 45-year-old advertising executive. He has been in A.A. for over 12 years, but has never had more than 11 months of continuous sobriety. He has been married and divorced. He drives expensive cars, wears expensive, yet casual clothes, and once owned an expensive home. He has been in over five treatment centers and has been exposed to reality therapy, EST, hypnosis, and Individualized Alcohol Behavioral Therapy. He has been addicted to valium and has smoked marijuana on a regular basis. When he starts drinking he begins with very dry Beefeater martinis, but usually ends with sweet liquors, including Southern Comfort and Irish Mist. He has been diagnosed manic-depressive, depressive, an alcohol addict, and a sociopath. He speaks of himself in the following words:

> I have two parts to me. One part wants to take credit for what I accomplish. Like the magazine. Its beautiful. Its one of the best in the country. Best photos. Best layout, best writers. [He had published a monthly magazine for six months, before he lost it during his last binge.] Its just like me. Pretty on the outside, empty, nothing on the inside. Pretty boy, call me. Nothing in here [points to his chest].
>
> You see, that's why the other part of me wants to destroy what the good part creates. I don't deserve for good things to happen to me. The sick side of me says destroy it all. If that side gets too strong I drink. I want to drink. And I do, and once I have the first drink the alcohol starts to talk to me and it says have another drink. You're rotten. Run, you don't deserve what you have. Blow it all. Run and leave. Kill yourself. You won't live to be 50 anyway. Remember your old man killed himself with this stuff when he was 45.
>
> These thoughts fill me up. I can't get away from them. I feel guilty if I do well. I'm so damned sick, even when I'm well I'm sick. Pretty Boy on the outside [looks vacantly outside through the windows]. Pretty Boy's sick. Ready to go? [field conversation, April 1, 1983].

Uniqueness and Fear

The alcoholic self cultivates a particular moral individualism that rests on the felt uniqueness of its own alienation. The alcoholic cuts herself off from the rest of society, feeling a profound alienation from all with whom she comes in contact. The alcoholic self nurtures an inner goodness, seeking to hide within a solitude that is solely hers. Rejecting objective experiences with others, the alcoholically divided self lives within the private world of insulated madness that alcohol produces. She assigns a sense of moral superiority to this inner world that is uniquely her own (see Laing, 1965: 94-95). From the unsteady vantage point of this alcoholically produced position, the alcoholic subject directs a world that threatens to come apart at any instant. All the while she lives an inner fear, knowing that the false walls she has built will crumble at any moment.

Consider the following account given by a recovering 44-year-old alcoholic, four years in A.A.

> I felt that nobody else knew how to live their life. I felt that my way was superior; that I knew something other people didn't. It was impossible for me to work or deal with others because I felt this way about them. I lived my life in my studio and in my tiny office where I worked. I stayed at home as much as I could. When I drank I felt that I knew who I was and what was right. In those feelings I gained a strength and a way of thinking that was unique to me. But then I collapsed. Everything came in on me. I went crazy. I came to A.A. and I found out that my way, that all the certainties I had held onto, that all my thoughts were empty too. I didn't know how to live either! I'm still learning [field conversation, June 17, 1984].

ALCOHOLIC RESSENTIMENT

Ressentiment (Scheler, 1961: 39-40) toward the past, toward others, toward the present and the future is felt. The repeated experiencing and reliving of this temporal and emotional attitude toward others and toward time itself characterizes the alcoholic self. The emotional attitude of ressentiment is negative, hostile, and includes the interrelated feelings of anger, wrath, envy, intense self-pride, and the desire for revenge (Denzin, 1984a: 283). Behind alcoholic ressentiment lies alcoholic pride (see below). This emotional frame of reference is fueled by alcohol that elevates the alcoholic's feelings of self-strength and power. However, the power that is felt is illusive and fleeting, always leaving in its wake the underlying ressentiment that the alcoholic drank to annihilate.

The centrality of resentment in the alcoholic relationship is revealed in the following interaction between J, and A. A, the male companion of J, has recently started attending Al-Anon meetings. He has been sponsored by a woman who has been in Al-Anon since 1968. Her name is Mary. J is speaking to C and K, two recovering alcoholics who have come to see him. J has been drinking for 2 days, after having been sober for 30 days. He found a full bottle of vodka in a closet when he was cleaning his and A's house.

> Come in, I'm drunk again. Here, come meet Mary [pointing to A who is seated at the dining room table]. She's been going to Al-Anon. Haven't you, Mary! Oh my, we're so much better now. Aren't we, Mary? Mary knows how to handle me now. Mary taught her "Tough Love." Well, YOU can take your TOUGH LOVE, A, and shove it. Oh, look at him, I hurt his little feelings. I'm so sorry, A, you see, I'm a sick man. You can't get mad at me. You have to love me [field conversation, as reported, September 16, 1984].

The satire, sarcasm, and double meanings that are evident in J's monologue, including his referencing of A with the feminine Mary, while he, J fills the feminine, housewife position in the relationship, speaks to the inability of the alcoholic to form "a true partnership with another human being" (A.A., 1953: 53). Using alcohol to reverse his position in the relationship, J attempts to dominate A through his words and his actions. As he expresses his hurt feelings through retaliatory vindictiveness he drives A further away from him. Resentful over A's attendance at Al-Anon meetings, he blocks and rebuffs any efforts by A to move forward in the relationship.

The return to drinking by J brings to the surface latent ressentiment that exists in his alcoholic relationship with A. Unable, or unwilling, to free himself of the anger, fear, wrath, and envy he feels toward A, his desire for revenge surfaces as he drinks.

Alcoholically induced and experienced emotionality lies at the heart of J's alcoholism. The euphoric and depressive physiological and neurological effects of the drug alcohol magnify the emotional divisions that exist within his self. His relations with A are similarly distorted when he drinks. Alcohol has become a sign, which when brought into the relationship, signifies J's alienation from A.

John Berryman (1973: 102-103) describes the telephone interactions Wilbur, an approximately 60-year-old recovering patient, had with his parents, whom he called two to five times daily from the treatment center:

> "They need me," he said many times. His father, drunk from morning to night was urging him to come home, and Wilbur was anxious to go—although they fought like madmen right through every call and it was perfectly clear to everybody but Wilbur that he got a *bang* out of holding his own against his frightful Dad from a safe telephone distance (Father's

ax, kept in the kitchen where *he* drank: "I'll chop you, Wilbur, late one night, I'll chop you"), reveling in the fact that he himself was not only sober at the moment but being *treated* for the disease that was killing them both. "They need me," he said stubbornly.

The fuel for stubbornly felt ressentiment is present in this account, including Wilbur's desire for revenge. The key to ressentiment is the repeated experiencing and reliving of the emotional feelings that draw the subject to another. Each occasion of interaction between Wilbur and his father becomes an occasion for the production of new feelings of anger, wrath, and perhaps hatred. These new feelings become part of the emotional repertoire that binds the father and son together. They experience the new feelings of ressentiment against the backdrop of all previous negative interactions. Drawn to one another through negativity, they both know that the self-feelings they derive from this relationship can be found nowhere else. The father and son are participants in the classic alcoholic relationship in which both partners are alcoholic. The complexity of their interaction is increased by the fact that they stand in a father-son relationship to one another. They both exist as alcoholically divided selves. The pivotal emotions that join their emotionally divided selves are lodged in the ressentiment they share and produce together.

The anger that the alcoholic feels toward his or her other turns into hatred. That hatred, when reciprocated, as in the case of Wilbur and his father, is increased. It destroys the affection that perhaps once existed between them. Thus it is with alcoholic ressentiment, for hatred and anger are layered upon one another, until the interactants in the social relationship are bound together only through negativity and mutual self-disdain.

Self-Pride

The threats of self-pride that ressentiment magnifies are evidenced in the following statement. The speaker is J, the male homosexual quoted above. He is intoxicated as he speaks. His remarks are directed, as before, to A:

> I hate you. You're cruel to me. You're a pig! You're not half the man W. is. You can't hold a candle to him. You take away my respect. You don't tell me my flowers are nice. You've been mean to me. You undercut me. You make me feel ugly. My sister loves me. My aunt loves me. I don't care if you do hate me. You make me hate myself. When I'm sober you can't do this to me. I feel good about myself. I feel proud to be a man. Why do you make me drink like this? I want to feel good

> about myself and have some pride again in what I do [field conversation, July 15, 1984].

Here the speaker blames the other for making him drunk, but he also blames his other for undercutting his self-pride. The ressentiment that flows through his talk masks a desire to regain a sense of self he feels he has lost to A, but also to alcohol. Pride in self, then, organizes and structures the alcoholic's deep-seated feelings of anger and wrath toward the other. The desire for revenge is embedded in this emotional attitude, which is best interpreted within the larger framework of ressentiment toward the other and toward self.

End of Act One

The drinking alcoholic and his or her other(s), to summarize Act One, live inside a recurring structure of negative, contrastive emotional experiences that become self-addictive. Each member of the relationship is trapped in this cycle of destructive emotionality, which becomes, for the alcoholic, nearly as addictive as the alcohol that he or she consumes. The alcoholic and his or her other live hatred, fear, anxiety, anger, and ressentiment. Never far from the next drink, or the next emotional battle with his or her significant other, each day becomes a repetition of the day before. They have stabilized their relationship at this brittle level. Act Two begins with either (1) the eruption of violence that goes beyond emotional attacks on the other; or (2) the alcoholic producing a problematic situation that traps him or her and exposes his or her alcoholism to others. Both of these sequences of action provoke a radical restructuring in the alcoholic's relationship with himself or herself and the significant other.

ACT TWO: VIOLENCE AND THE MERRY-GO-ROUND OF TROUBLE

In Act Two all the key figures in the alcoholic's self-destructive drama are in place. The alcoholic's dependence on alcohol is evident to all of his or her significant others, who have become enablers, coalcoholic dependents, victims, provokers, martyrs, scapegoats, pseudo-parents, family stars, and heroes. Each figure has learned how to adjust to the alcoholic's emotionality, to his or her crises, drunkenness, and unpredictability. Each in their way has rescued the alcoholic from the problems he or she has produced. In so doing they have enabled his or her drinking and dependency upon them and their dependency upon him or her.

The Phases of Negative Symbolic Interaction

The members of the alcoholic's family have passed through the first five states (as noted above), of negative symbolic interaction that characterize families of violence (Denzin, 1984b: 490). They have (1) denied the alcoholic's alcoholism and violence; (2) seen the alcoholic derive pleasure from drinking, and they derive pleasure from their dependence upon him or her; (3) experienced a buildup of mutual hostility and alienation between themselves and the alcoholic; (4) lived through misunderstandings concerning their respective commitments and responsibilities to one another; and (5) experienced sexual jealousy and violent emotionality because of the alcoholic's conduct (especially the spouse or lover). The alcoholic has placed himself or herself and the significant others in the classic double-bind relationship (Bateson, 1972c: 212). If the alcoholic truly loved them he or she would stop drinking. Because the alcoholic continues to drink he or she must not love them. Yet when the alcoholic drinks and seeks forgiveness, he or she brings gifts and showers them with the positive affection that is missing when he or she is emotionally violent. Trapped in this double bind, the alcoholic's other soon begins to experience a version of the alcoholically divided self that had previously been the sole possession of the alcoholic. That is, the alcoholic begins to drive the other insane.

Witness the following situation. The speaker is a 51-year-old nurse. Her husband is an active alcoholic:

> He's got me going to the psychiatrist. I'm on Valium because I can't sleep or hold my attention at work. He plays games with me. He says he'll cut down and only drink at home. So he keeps beer in the frig and a bottle under the sink. That's supposed to be all he's drinking. Ha! That's a big laugh! He took that new afternoon job, 3-5 delivering prescriptions for the hospital. He gets off the other job at noon. He says he comes home from noon till 3:00 to see me. What a joke. He's passed out on the sofa by 2:30. Says he needs a rest cause of the two jobs. Rest, my foot. He's drunk on his ass at 2:30 in the afternoon. The other day I played a joke on him. I didn't wake him up. Just let him sleep. He woke up at 4:30 and asked what time it was. I said 4:30 dear, are you supposed to be someplace? He knew what I meant. He grabbed one of those beers and left through the back door. Now I mark his bottles and he changes them around. I know he fills them back up after he drinks. Christ, I feel like a God damned kid! Like a child. I can't believe what he's got me doing. The doctor's no help. He just says take the pills and try to relax. Who can relax? I'm ready to check myself in. I don't give a damn what he does anymore. But I love him. Christ, why is he doing this? [field conversation, August 23, 1985].

Thus does the alcoholic relationship stabilize at the end of Act One.

Alcoholic Violence and the Merry-Go-Round of Trouble

Act Two begins with a sudden shift in the interactional structure the alcoholic and his or her others have constructed. The unsteady, fragile order that had been in place suddenly escalates to a new level. This is often precipitated by an act of violence that gets out of hand. The following episode is representative. The speaker is a 32-year-old, in treatment for the second time. His wife is in the process of divorcing him. He is under a court order not to see his wife or children. He describes how this occurred:

> I'd come home drunk on my ass. Ain't nothin different 'bout that. Done it a thousand times before. Don't know what got in her damned head. I threw her up 'gainst the kitchen wall. Told her to get off my fuckin' case. I didn't need her shit anymore, I said. Give me space, I said. Kids was screamin all 'round. My teenage girl was havin' a party in the front room. They was dancin' to that God damned punk music. I told 'em to turn it down. Man got to get some peace. Then the bitch (my old lady) turned on me. Said this was enough. She wasn't taking this shit anymore. She grabbed the kitchen knife and told me to get my ass out of the house and be gone for good. Said she didn't want to see me again. Fuck, I didn't want to stick around if I wasn't wanted. I'm no dummy, you know. But, Christ she'd drove me out of my house. Told me to get. That's my house, you know. She'd throwed the beer out after me. So I went, and I went mad. I broke the door when I left. I climbed in my new truck, went to town and got me a six-pack. Then I drove back home, drinkin' it and gettin' madder as I went. I drove that truck on the front steps of the house, laid back on the horn and kept her and kids up til one o'clock. She called the sheriff and they came and took me off. I had a gun on the front seat, but I'd never of used it. Just wanted to scare her. It ain't that I can't drink and it ain't that I don't get crazy when I drink. I just want her to talk to me when I get like that. 'Cept she gets scared, runs away from me. I just get madder and all hell breaks loose. I guess I'm an alcoholic. I sure can't control what the damned stuff does to me and what I think when I get to going [field conversation, April 1, 1983].

The drinker in the above account seeks to force his way violently into an understanding relationship with his wife. He does not drink so that he can be violent, as some have claimed (Gelles, 1972, 1979). Nor does he become violent because alcohol necessarily releases aggressive behavior that is pent up inside him, as others have argued (Hetherton and Wray, 1964; Carpenter and Armenti, 1972). The ressentiment he feels is exaggerated and highlighted in his stream of experience as he drinks. Furthermore, as he drinks he calls out in his wife negative, hostile feelings she has toward him when he drinks. The drinker is not pathologically violent, as others have suggested (Mark and Ervin, 1970).

This drinker, instead, craves and seeks a sense of self and a relational involvement of intimacy with his other that he has lost through his drinking. His violence, then, is not necessarily a display of an underlying pathology, nor is he using the "time-out" period of drinking (MacAndrew and Edgerton, 1969) as an excuse to be violent. He knows, his wife knows, and his culture has told him, that violence is not an appropriate line of action to be taken when intoxicated, especially toward a family intimate. If he forgot this, the sheriff jogged his memory for him.

Our drinker was trapped within a line of action that built upon itself. As his anger got out of hand, it turned to violence. The violence was fueled by his drinking, and his drinking was fueled by his violent emotionality. In a circle of violent, drinking emotionality, he acted out his feelings of despair and frustration by driving the truck up the front steps of the house.

The outcome of the above event was to bring this alcoholic into a treatment center. His display of emotional and physical violence moved his relationship with his family into stages six and seven of the violent family. That is, the increased violence shifted his alcoholism out of the private arenas of his home into the public sphere where the police, the courts, and now a treatment center have become involved. His relationship with his wife will either (1) collapse, (2) be stabilized at this somewhat stable state of recurring violence, or (3) be transformed into a "recovering" relationship wherein he and his family seek assistance for their jointly experienced alcoholism. His actions brought others into his alcoholic situation in ways that had never occurred before. He had finally produced an episode of violence that could no longer be denied. Although he saw his violence as being no different from his actions a thousand times before, his wife took a different view. This was real violence; violence for which he must be held accountable. It no longer mattered if he was drunk or sober, or whether his actions were playful or accidental. Somehow, in a previously unnoticed fashion, their relationship moved into a new phase of interaction. What they had before had suddenly slipped through their fingers.

Alcoholic Troubles

The key to Act Two, as suggested, is the sudden eruption of a new problematic that can or no longer will be handled within the interpretive, accomodative structures the alcoholic and his or her other have previously constructed. Violence of a new order is one form this problematic may assume. But other alcoholic troubles will also occur. A DUI, causing an automobile accident, killing a person while intoxicated, having a love affair that comes to the attention of the alcoholic's spouse, failing to deliver a work assignment at the appointed time, becoming intoxicated at a family dinner, abusing one's in-laws, getting fired, being hospitalized for an alcohol-related illness or injury, making obscene telephone calls during a blackout, firing a gun at a neighbor's house, or setting fire to a spouse's clothing in the front yard of one's home may be the event that produces the radical alteration in the alcoholic's interactional situation that is the key to Act Two. Whatever the event is, it will produce the following consequences.

First, it will shatter the significant other's denial system, leading the other to finally begin to understand that an alcoholic inhabits his or her life. He or she must come to understand that they are enabling the alcoholic's alcoholism. If the other does not come to this recognition, he or she will continue to come to the alcoholic's assistance when he or she confronts the round of troubles just outlined.

Second, this event must bring home to the alcoholic the point that he or she has problems with alcohol. If this does not occur, and if he or she continues to deny that alcoholism, Acts One and Two will continue. That is, the alcoholic will continue to drink, denying that a drinking problem exists, that he or she is an alcoholic, and that alcohol is causing him or her trouble (Kellerman, 1969: 7). The alcoholic will deny also that he or she has caused the family any harm. The alcoholic may even blame the family for the problems they have caused him or her (Kellerman, 1969: 7).

Third, this event will serve to discredit the alcoholic in his or her own and in the other's eyes. It will leave a memory of failure, self-disgust, embarrassment, and self-pain. He or she will fall back on alcoholic pride in an attempt to deny that the event occurred. Or, if he or she accepts the occurrence of the event, he or she will not take responsibility for it.

Fourth, the alcoholic and his or her other will vow that what happened will never happen again. The alcoholic may promise never to drink again, and the other will state that he or she will never help the alcoholic again.

If the other and the alcoholic continue to deny the alcoholic's troubles, the latter's dependency will only increase. Act Two will continue with the alcoholic having been saved once again by his or her enablers. He or she will end up back at home, in a safe place. The alcoholic will have been propped up in his or her job and restored to his or her usual place in the family. Kellerman (1969: 6) states:

> As everything has been done *for* him and not *by* him, his dependency is increased, and he remains a child in an adult suit. The results, effects and problems caused by his drinking have been removed by others. . . . The painful results of the drinking were suffered by persons other than the alcoholic. This permits him to continue drinking as a way to solve his problems. In Act One the alcoholic killed his pain and woe by getting drunk; in Act Two the trouble and painful results of drinking are removed by other people. This convinces the alcoholic he can go on behaving in this irresponsible way.

The following situation describes these reactions of the alcoholic and his other to the problematic events that structure Act Two. The speaker is an engineer. He describes how he came to burn his wife's clothing in the front yard of their home:

> We'd had another of those damned fights over my drinking. I'd come home drunk again, yelled and screamed as always. She stonewalled me. Turned her back on me. Got the kids, got the suitcases, took the car keys, walked out of the front door and drove off. I was flabbergasted. What an insult. But she hadn't taken everything. Her winter clothes were all there in the closet. I went in, took them off the hangers, real neat-like, stacked them up, got a laundry basket, carried them to the front yard, took four trips. I made a cross out of them. Then I got the gasoline can for the lawnmower, and the bag of charcoal. Put that charcoal in the shape of a cross, on the top of the clothes, then I poured gas on everything. Then I went and called her and told her please come home. I'd never drink again. She fell for it. She was back from her folks in 20 minutes. I turned the lights off when she drove up, stepped outside, waved to her and the kids, dropped a match on the clothes, and the whole front yard went up in flames. I stood at the top of it and screamed "Here I am, here's your God damned alcoholic. Do you want to crucify me?" All hell broke loose after that. I passed out drunk on top of the clothes, she had to call the fire department and take me to the hospital for burns. When I came to she told me everything. The neighbors in the street, the police and fire department, the story in the newspaper. Everything. I vowed I'd never drink again. She swore this was the last time she was coming back. Course we were both lying. I drank again, she left again, but the next time she was gone for a year and when she came back that time I'd been in A.A. for three months [field conversation July 22, 1985].

End of Act Two

The alcoholic in the above account is at the end of Act Two. He and his spouse have passed through the sixth and seventh stages of the violent, alcoholic family. All the structures of denial, violence, pain, ressentiment, and alcoholically produced troubles are out in the open for public inspection. Rescued once again, the alcoholic stands ready to enter Act Three, in which his interactional situation will either be completely destroyed, or he will collapse and surrender to his alcoholism.

ACT THREE: COLLAPSE AND SURRENDER

Act Three returns to Act One, for the alcoholic drinks again. This time, however, it is different. A past history of not being able to control drinking is by now common knowledge, as are the troubles and violence the alcoholic has just produced in Act Two. From the end of Act Two onward all of her drinking and conduct are interpreted within the "alcoholic" framework, even though she still may deny her alcoholism. The transition from Act Two to Act Three is critical. This is the most strategic moment for intervention. As Kellerman (1969: 9) notes, Act Two (and I add the beginning of Act Three) is the only act in which the destructive course of alcoholism can be changed.

Three factors are pivotal to Act Three. The first is the withdrawal of support from the alcoholic's other. The second is a collapse in the alcoholic's world of interaction, often accompanied by an act of insanity, an accident, or the onset of an alcohol-related illness. The third factor is surrender, which, as noted earlier (Chapter Five) is threefold: the admission of alcoholism, acceptance of this fact, and an inner surrender to this situation.

The following two cases summarize the above analysis of the alcoholic's situation as Act Three begins. Indeed they may be said to encapsulate all of Act Three, insofar as they both involve dramatic changes in action on the part of the alcoholic and his or her other.

The first case involves an *intervention,* which is the "process by which those close to the alcoholic—family, employer, friends, and coworkers—confront the alcoholic. The goal of the intervention is to force the alcoholic to seek treatment" (Wholey, 1984: 227).

The speaker, H, describes how he got into a treatment center.

> J [the woman he had been living with] kicked me out. I guess I was drunk, anyway I'd been drinking, even tho' I'd said I was sober. I packed everything up and went to a friend's house. I really gave him no choice. I started going crazy. I heard sounds, I couldn't sleep, I stayed up talking to my friend and his wife all night. The next day I was in no shape

> to go to work. They called my supervisor who got somebody else to cover for me. It kept getting worse. I was afraid to leave the basement where I was staying. I thought I was going crazy. Then they called some people from A.A. and two of them came over, along with a relative, my supervisor, and somebody else from work who is in A.A. There I was, up against the wall, holding my head. The room was filled with all of these people. They told me how I hadn't been able to do my work. How I was worse off than the last time. How I had to do something. "What was I going to do?" That's what they kept saying. I couldn't hear it. Didn't want to hear it. I kept saying I wanted to stop drinking but didn't know how. They asked me if I wanted to go to detox. I said no. They asked me if I wanted to get sober. I said yes. They said, "How are you going to do it?" Finally I agreed. I didn't want to, but I did [field conversation, September 20, 1985, 38-year-old researcher, in treatment for the third time in nine months].

As of this writing this individual is in his third week of treatment. He calls himself not an alcoholic, but an alcohol abuser. Whether or not he remains sober and fully surrenders to his alcoholism (see discussion below) remains problematic at this time. This case reflects the three key factors in Act Three. His significant others withdrew support. His world collapsed in upon him, and he surrendered, if only begrudgingly, to his alcoholic situation and entered a treatment center. The goal of the intervention was accomplished.

The next case is more clear-cut in terms of outcome. The speaker has been sober nearly five years. He is 41 years old, and is an electrician. He attends five A.A. meetings a week, and is the treasurer of one A.A. group. He talks of how he got to A.A.:

> The wife backed off. Damned if she didn't go to Al-Anon over at the Catholic Church. They told her to let me drink. She did. I went at it free as hell for six weeks. Got up one Friday morning. Sat at the kitchen table. Sun coming in. She'd gone into town to work. I'd called in sick. By myself, all alone. I looked at them six empty bottles of beer in front of me on the table. I'd finished the Peppermint Schnapps. I felt empty, sick, scared. What was I doing? I called A.A. and they said they had a noon meeting. I went, scared as hell. Been coming ever since.
>
> Its funny, bout the wife. She'd gone to see the priest. He'd told her that there was nothing she could do. He said men drink. It was her lot to take care of me. And she did. She'd buy the stuff for me. Hold my head when I was sick. Turn the other way when I was drunk. Even have sex with me sometimes. The boss was O.K. too. I think he knew something was wrong but he never said anything when I called in sick.

> Course I was hell to live with all this time. I was never happy, could never get high from the booze. Depressed all the time, drinking to stay even. God I'm glad that's over. Haven't had a drink today. Thank God! [field conversation, November 4, 1981].

This alcoholic and his wife lived out all three acts of the alcoholic's play. She was his enabler, his victim (as was his boss), his provoker, his source of comfort. They lived denial. When she stopped attempting to control his drinking his illness moved quickly to the point at which he was forced to confront the problematics of his drinking situation. He surrendered and reached out for help. It is now necessary to discuss briefly the phenomenon of collapse and surrender and reaching out for help.

Collapse and Surrender

The "help" the alcoholic reaches out for is of two varieties. A request for *enabling help,* characteristic of Acts One and Two, is a cry for assistance to get the alcoholic out of his or her troubles. There is not a sincere desire to stop drinking, although the alcoholic may declare verbally that he or she is an alcoholic and will never drink again. It is an inauthentic declaration of alcoholism. His or her alcoholism will be used as an excuse to continue drinking. When trouble again occurs the alcoholic will fall back on his or her disease as an excuse for what he or she has done.

A request for *sincere help,* on the other hand (which appears in Act Three), represents a call for help that is accompanied by the alcoholic's initial authentic surrendering to his or her alcoholism. The drinker openly confronts the problems produced by his or her drinking. He or she asks for help in order to stop drinking. The alcoholic expresses this plea for help with the words of a total convert to alcoholism (see Lofland, 1977: 57; Rudy, 1986). He or she cries out for help and sincerely means what is said or so the alcoholic and the significant others believe. The first two steps of surrender are passed through. The alcoholic has admitted an inability to control his or her drinking and appears to accept this failure.

It is nearly impossible to distinguish inauthentic from authentic statements of alcoholism by the words the alcoholic speaks, just as it is impossible to distinguish clearly a request for enabling help from a request for sincere help. The proof of the difference lies in the actions the drinker takes, once he or she has made the request for help.

Hitting Bottom

In order for the alcoholic to surrender he or she must "hit bottom." Two "bottoms" are distinguished by A.A.: "high bottom" and "low bottom." In A.A.'s early days its cofounder Bill Wilson stated:

> Those of us who sobered up in A.A. had been grim and utterly hopeless cases. But then we began to have some success with milder alcoholics. Younger folks appeared. Lots of people turned up who still had jobs, homes, health, and even good social standing. Of course, it was necessary for these newcomers to hit bottom emotionally. But they did not have to hit every possible bottom in order to admit that they were licked [A.A., 1967: 209].

When an alcoholic will hit bottom can never be predicted in advance. An A.A. member with 15 years in A.A. and a veteran of 12 Steps (an act that carries A.A.'s message of recovery to an alcoholic who requests help) states: "You never know when it will happen. I've taken one man to detox 14 times. He's still drinking. Someday he'll get it. You never know. It's a gift. You never give up on anybody [field conversation, October 3, 1983].

The bottom that is hit is emotional, economic, physical, personal, and social. The drinker must find the situation intolerable and confront the fact that the life he is living is not the life he imagined. He also must come to see that all the reasons he gave to himself for drinking are no longer working. His theory of successful drinking must be demolished. The structures of bad faith that stood in the way of the drinker confronting his alcoholism similarly must be destroyed.

Collapse

Collapse coincides with "hitting bottom." It takes three forms: physical, interactional, and phenomenological or psychological. Physical collapse refers to the physical deterioriation of the drinker's body, which often requires hospitalization for alcohol-related illnesses. Interactional collapse points to the withdrawal of support from significant others. As her others draw away, the drinker finds herself alone in the world. Without a theory to explain her conduct, the drinker experiences phenomenological or psychological collapse. She experiences an "insanity of self" (see the account of H above and M below) that may lead to suicidal thoughts. In such a state she may surrender and reach out for help.

Surrender

The thesis of self-surrender asserts that only through surrender does the recovery process begin. The alcoholic cries out for help and her cry may be sincere. There is no one to turn to. Nobody will buy her a drink, loan her money, drive her to a bar, pay the bills, or call her employer and say she is sick and won't be in today to work. Her enabling system has collapsed. Surrender is a threefold process: She must admit failure, accept this failure, and concede to her innermost self that she believes this fact.

Confronting the Alcoholic Label

At this point the alcoholic must, at some level, confront the fact that she is an alcoholic and no longer a problem drinker. She cannot hide behind the label, use the label, or run away from it. She must accept the facts that confront her. She cannot drink like ordinary people. Further, she must understand that no amount of will power or self-knowledge will keep her from taking that first drink. This has been proven time and time again, yet in the past she has denied this fact. The stigma that she has placed on the label *alcoholic* must now be understood to be no greater than the degradation experienced at her own hands. That is, if she is not an alcoholic, then whatever is wrong with her has created a situation that could be no worse than calling herself alcoholic. If the drinker does not understand this about herself she will continue to deny her alcoholism.

The following account, given by a 43-year-old middle-level management executive in his second week of treatment, illustrates the dilemma the alcoholic confronts:

> I don't think I'm a real alcoholic. Sure I drank too much, but it was the work, the house payments, the kids in college, the wife's bills. When I had that DUI and passed out and hit the light pole I had a heart attack. That's what my doctor said. He said you're overweight, you need to exercise, take a good rest, stop drinking for awhile. That's why I'm here. This is good for me but I don't think I'm an alcoholic [field conversation April 16, 1981].

This man changed his name while in treatment, refusing to allow the staff or the other patients to call him by his real name. He was still in a denial phase.

The following speaker has been in contact with A.A. for over 12 years, making annual calls to A.A. asking for help. He has never gone through treatment nor attended more than five A.A. meetings (by his words). He is dressed in a green hospital gown, 62 years old, over six feet tall, yet he weighs less than 135 pounds. Retired from the Air Force, now on pension and social security, he lives in a trailer with his wife who is not alcoholic. His teenage daughter left home several months ago because he sexually abused her. He speaks the following:

> Hell, I'm an alcoholic, but I don't want to stop. I got all those good "old boy" friends. They know I can't hold the stuff anymore. Just as I get sobered up they come over with a case of beer and a bottle of whisky. I woke up from a blackout and there was two six packs of beer next to me in bed. They'd brought it to me. What can I do? Hell, it'd kill me to pour it out! [field conversation, October 2, 1984].

This drinker is in a detoxification unit to dry out so that he can go home to drink again. He uses the alcoholic label to continue his drinking.

The following drinker used A.A. and treatment to deal with a problem of wife battering. Drunk one night, he beat up his wife. She filed charges. Three days prior to his court hearing he entered treatment. He completed his treatment. The court dropped the charges. He drank the next day. He has not attended an A.A. meeting since treatment.

> Sure I'm an alcoholic. I can't hold the stuff. But I like it. I like the stuff. I ain't got time to come to these here meetings though, I got to get me a job. You folks got a good thing here, though [field conversation, December 15, 1981].

The above drinkers have made insincere calls for help. They have made a verbal, inauthentic surrender to their alcoholism. They have passed through the first two phases of surrender, but not the third.

Complete, Inner Surrender

The following two alcoholics have surrendered authentically to their alcoholism and have been sober since that time. The first speaker has been sober three years, the second five years.

M is 41 years old, an academic, twice married. In this field conversation (November 28, 1982), he is speaking to two recovering alcoholics (O and R) who have been called to his house by M's wife (B), after he attempted suicide.

> M [to O and R]: I want to die. I tried to kill myself last night. See [points to his slashed wrists], but it didn't work. You know I was in A.A. before. I don't believe in God. I stopped thinking I was an alcoholic. I think Albert

Camus was correct. Suicide is the ultimate act of freedom. I tried to be free and failed.

O [to M]: I think Camus changed his mind in his later work. Have you read *The Plague?*

M [to O]: No. Doesn't matter. I'll have to think about that though. When I stopped going to A.A. things started to get worse. I was invited to a conference in Berlin. My host offered me a drink. I knew that I shouldn't take it. I debated with myself. I didn't want to hurt his feelings. I took it. Nothing happened. I drank every day after that when I was on my trip. When I got home I started buying wine and having it with dinner. Then I had to have it with lunch. Then wine wasn't strong enough and I started buying gin. See [points to half gallon of gin], that would last not quite two days. Last June I was at a conference in Paris. I fell in love. I want to marry that woman. I've told my wife about it. She doesn't know what to think. I've been writing this woman since June and I started drinking more heavily. I guess I went crazy. Last night we had company for dinner. After they left I started drinking gin. I got more and more depressed. I went into the bathroom and tried to kill myself. I still want to. See the blood on the floor [takes O and R into the bathroom and points to the blood stains on the floor].

R [to M]: M, do you think we should go to the fifth floor [the local psychiatric ward]?

M [to O and R]: Yes. I know I'm crazy right now. I also know I can't drink. I'm an alcoholic. I belong in A.A. Will you take me? Can we get rid of the gin?

O [to M]: Yes, M, come on, let's put it outside for the garbage men. Are you ready to go?

M [to O and R]: Yes, just let me kiss the kids goodbye. B, where are they?

B [to M]: They're on the table, dear [points to three stuffed teddy bears on the dining room table who are positioned in front of a small television screen, which is on, without the sound].

M [to teddy bears]: Bye kids, you be good while Daddy's gone. He's going to the hospital to get well. He's sick. He's an alcoholic.

M spent two weeks on the psychiatric ward. He attended A.A. meetings during that time and told his story at an open A.A. meeting. When he left the hospital he entered a treatment center for three weeks. He has been sober since November 28, 1982. At the time of this writing he is in Europe with the woman he fell in love with in the summer of 1981. He is again divorced. His suicide attempt was his bottom. Sometime during the day and evening of November 28, 1982, M authentically surrendered to his alcoholism.

The second alcoholic is R, age 48, who was with O when they called upon M. Sober five years, he describes his moment of surrender in the following words:

> S [his wife] and I had gone to Detroit to visit her family. I was drinking heavily. We had a fight and I went to a hotel. I took two six packs with me. I got drunk. I was in my underpants. I went out in the hallway and closed the door to the room. I passed out, blacked out. I came to in the hotel lobby, in my underpants, asking the hotel clerk for my room key. There I was, practically naked. My God! What was wrong with me? I knew then that I was an alcoholic. I'd called A.A. six months earlier. Somebody on the answering service told me about the meetings and said I should sober up. I got mad. Who the hell were they to tell me to sober up? I stayed drunk off and on for six months, trying to control it. I'd drink vodka in half pints and beer. I hid the half pints in the bedroom closet behind my clothes. Once S was looking for something and a bottle fell out and hit her on the head! Prior to this six months I'd had 3 DUI's, rolled the car once and spent three nights in the drunk tank. I knew I was an alcoholic. But I thought I could control it. After that night in Detroit I knew I couldn't control it any longer. I called A.A. when we got home. I've been going ever since. That first year I went every night to a meeting. S and my daughter go to Al-Anon three to four times a week now [field conversation March 10, 1983].

R surrendered to his alcoholism that evening in the hotel in Detroit. He hit his low bottom when he found himself in the hotel lobby in his underpants.

End of Act Three

Act Three has one of two basic endings, given in the terms *authentic* and *inauthentic surrender*. For the alcoholic who inauthentically surrenders to his or her alcoholism and returns to drinking the scenario is as follows. His or her destructive drama stabilizes into one of three variations on Acts One and Two. The first variation repositions the alcoholic and his or her other in an alcohol-centered relationship. They carry on as if nothing had happened or been accomplished as a result of his surface surrendering to his or her alcoholism. The relationship settles in the final stages of the violent, alcoholic relationship. It is an uneasy truce, in which the alcoholic continues to drink and his or her other continues to enable.

The second variation witnesses the collapse of the marriage or relationship with the other. The alcoholic and his or her other go their separate ways; the alcoholic to continue drinking, and the other perhaps to form a new relationship, often with another alcoholic. The third variation places the other in treatment for the alcoholism he or she experienced with the alcoholic, and the alcoholic continues drinking. In this case the spouse or other joins Al-Anon, or a similar self-help group for spouses, friends, and family members of alcoholics. In the case of immediate (or near immediate) authentic surrender, both the alcoholic and his or her other enter treatment. The alcoholic goes to A.A. and the spouse to Al-Anon.

The following case encompasses these three variations on Act Three. The speaker is 51 years years old, a successful salesman. He has been sober one year, although he has been in and around A.A. for 12 years.

> T [his wife] and I separated 12 years ago. We've been back together for two years. She'd been raising hell about my alcoholism back then. I'd gone to a few meetings. She'd gone to Al-Anon. I said I was an alcoholic, but I didn't believe it, and she knew I didn't believe it. Anyway, one night I came home drunk, as usual, and she had all my clothes in grocery bags by the front door. She told me to get out. So I left. I stayed away 10 years. Moved out west, found a friend, kept drinking. T stayed here, with the kids, I sent money off and on, not much though. We kind of lost touch with one another. She stopped going to Al-Anon, made friends with somebody from the A.A. side who went back out [started drinking again]. That didn't last. My new friend was a drunk, too. She's still drinking, far as I know. Anyway, 2 years ago I'd finally had it. Still loved T. Knew she wouldn't take me back if I was drunk. So I went into A.A., got sober, came back, we got set up again, I slipped once or twice, but I got a good sponsor and he made me go to meetings. I've got a year tonight [of sobriety] and I think we're going to make it. T's back in Al-Anon and we're trying [field conversation, November 2, 1982].

This case represents a happy conclusion to the alcoholic's three-act play. It must be remembered, however, that this drama took over 12 years to reach this position. Other alcoholics reach this point but do not remain there, as the following case reveals. Here the alcoholic takes back the act of surrender.

Angel

Angel was 53 years old when he killed himself on January 23, 1982, by asphyxiation. He had closed the door to his garage at approximately 8:30 p.m., started his car, and left a suicide note to his wife leaving all of his money to her and his daughter. Angel was a recovering alcoholic who had been sober six years. He was a regular attender of A.A. meetings. Six months prior to his death he left his wife and started drinking. His small business had gone bankrupt. He became more and more depressed. He made repeated attempts to make contact with his wife. Every time he contacted her he was intoxicated. He stopped attending A.A. meetings, but he kept up regular telephone conversations with friends in A.A. One month before he committed suicide he bought a gun and went to his wife's home. He asked to see her and to talk with her, but she refused to let him in the house. He pulled his gun out and threatened to shoot her. She slammed the door and called the police. A court injunction was issued against his coming onto the premises of his wife's home. He began to call her at all hours of the day and night. Each time he talked to her he was drinking.

The night that Angel killed himself he had gone to his wife's house. He said goodbye to her and tried one more time to get into the house to talk to her. She again refused to see him. Leaving her he said that "it was all over." She repeatedly tried to call him at his house but the phone was busy. She called the police. They went to Angel's house and found him dead, slumped over the steering wheel of his car.

Angel's death was reported as "death by reasons of heart failure." Although his earlier surrender to alcoholism had produced a happy conclusion to his version of the alcoholic's three act play, his return to drinking shattered all of that. The facts of Angel's case are kept alive in the A.A. community I studied.

The second basic ending to Act Three is produced by authentic surrender. In complete authentic inner surrender, the alcoholic sets in motion a process that carries the potential of changing him from an active, drinking alcoholic, to an alcoholic seeking recovery. The meanings he holds toward himself, alcohol, alcoholism, and alcoholics are slowly tranformed. Alcohol becomes a poison, a liquid that can kill him or drive him crazy. The drinking act, long the center of his life, is now defined in negative terms. Alcoholics and alcoholism slowly are given new meanings, now that he has defined himself as being an alcoholic. In his surrender the alcoholic begins to turn his back on the drinking self of the past. Perhaps unwittingly he seeks a new self, not knowing, however, what this self will feel like, or how it will comport itself in the world. His act of surrender has brought him to the edge of a new life.

Authentic surrender also alters the alcoholic's relationship with his or her other. By surrendering to alcoholism and entering treatment or A.A. (or both), the alcoholic makes a move that destabilizes the alcohol-centered relationship with the others in his or her life (see the case of R above). He or she and the other enter a new interactional space that alcohol and drinking previously filled. The alcohol-centered identities that he or she and the other had earlier shared must now be reconstructed, if not destroyed, and replaced by new identities that focus on the "recovery process." The end of Act Three for the alcoholic who authentically surrenders sets the stage for Act Four, which is "Recovery," the topic of the next chapter.

CONCLUSIONS

I have analyzed the drama of destruction the alcoholically divided self experiences. The three acts of this drama, (1) the alcoholic situation, (2) violence and the merry-go-round of trouble, and (3) collapse and surrender, were discussed in detail. The various scenarios that flow from the original alcoholic situation, with its denial and enabling structures, were sketched. I have shown how the alcoholic and his or her other live contrasting, negative emotionality on a daily basis.

I also examined the centrality of emotional and physical violence in this drama. Although it has not been my intention to offer a full-scale analysis of the relationship among alcohol, alcoholism, and violence, my observations warrant the following conclusions. First, the relationship between alcohol and violence in the alcoholic family is not spurious as some have suggested (Berk et al., 1983: 120; Gelles, 1979: 173). The alcoholic marriage does not give the alcoholic a license to hit his or her spouse, and he or she does not become drunk so that in this time-out period he or she can be violent.

Second, I concur with Steinglass and Robertson (1983: 299), who argue that "the preponderance of research evidence suggests the existence of some relationship between alcohol abuse and family violence." Third, this relationship perhaps can be best interpreted from within the framework I have offered in this chapter. That is, violence is woven through every interactional structure of the alcoholic relationship. It is emotional and physical, real and spurious, paradoxical and playful. It is also indicative of the "insanity of self" that the alcoholic experiences when he or she drinks. In her intoxication the alcoholic holds violent thoughts toward herself and her other. If the alcoholic continues far enough in her drinking she may, as in the case of Angel, kill herself, and threaten to kill her family. Drinkers such as Angel drink and become violent in an attempt to regain something that has been lost. What they have lost is self-pride and the intimacy the other can offer. Alcohol produces for these drinkers those forms of behavior American society defines as violent, criminal, insane, and alcoholic. Until the forms of insanity that alcoholism produces are better understood, the relationship between alcoholism and violence will remain misunderstood.

The alcoholically divided self and his or her other have played out the three crucial stages of alcoholism. As recovery begins they find themselves in a drinking culture that has victimized them. How to adjust to that fact is one of the major problems they must confront jointly in recovery. The following alcoholic, a female with over one year of sobriety phrases this problem as follows:

> We bought the whole thing. They told us to drink and be happy. So that's what my ex-husband and I did. Boy did we drink and try to be happy. Now he's my ex and I'm an alcoholic trying to recover. And everywhere I look there's an ad or a sign telling me to drink and have a good time. We were sold a bill of goods and we bought it! It's no wonder I don't trust them anymore. This is a fucked up society we live in! [field observation, October 14, 1985].

I turn now to the topic of recovery, offering an outline of the major steps in the recovery process. A detailed analysis of this process is reserved, however, for the second part of this study, *The Recovering Alcoholic.*

7

THE RECOVERING ALCOHOLIC SELF

> M [a female alcoholic] never got it. She'd been through treatment twice. She had three years one time, then her husband divorced her and she went back. She'd come to this Friday night meeting drunk on vodka and say she was a crazy, grateful alcoholic. And she was drunk. She loved all of us, would do anything for anybody. When she died in the hospital everybody cried. It was a cold day in February when we buried her. Her memory helps me stay sober today. They say no alcoholic dies in vain. M didn't. God bless her [male alcoholic, speaking at a meeting, 10 years sobriety, 65 years old, retired].

I turn now to the topic of recovery. My point of departure is the alcoholic who has reached the end of Act Three in the play called "A Merry-Go-Round Named Denial." Authentic and inauthentic surrender have brought the alcoholic into the social world of recovery A.A. and treatment centers provide. He or she now enters Act Four, which is "Recovery." However, this act is better conceptualized as a new three-act play for it represents a radical break or rupture in the life experiences of the alcoholic and his or her other. As such, it may be interpreted in terms of three interrelated acts, or phrases, which I term (1) sobriety, (2) becoming an A.A. member, and (3) two lives. My analysis focuses on the individual's experiences in A.A. I will not examine the process of recovery that begins in treatment centers (see future volumes). The recovery that I describe in this chapter is understood properly as a relational, interactional, and often family-based process. Because of the complexity of this process my analysis focuses primarily on the alcoholic, not on his or her other. (See future volumes for a fuller discussion of the other's place in the recovery process.)

Transformation of Self

The recovering alcoholic undergoes a radical transformation of self (see Travisano, 1981: 244). Not only does he or she become sober, but a new language of self is acquired, as are a new set of meanings concerning alcohol, alcoholism, alcoholics, and the drinking act. By becoming a part of the lived history of A.A. the individual is transformed into a "recovering alcoholic" within a society of fellow alcoholics. At the same time the individual becomes an outsider (Becker, 1973) to the larger society that continues to sanction the cultural and interactional use of alcohol on a regular basis.

If, during the active stages of her alcoholism, the alcoholic also stood outside the boundaries of society, then now, in recovery, she is doubly outside that society. That is, by no longer drinking, the alcoholic can now pass as a "normal" within society. But this is a duplicitous "normalcy," for the recovering alcoholic carries the previous label of having been an alcoholic. And, knowing this, she looks somewhat askance at the normal world that previously judged her, knowing that it does not understand alcoholism as she does. Furthermore, the alcoholic now looks differently at herself, for attempting to be "normal" was what caused her, in part, to become an active alcoholic. Hence, she desires not to be normal as others understand being normal. She desires, rather, to be a recovering alcoholic, with all the meanings A.A. gives to that identity. The alcoholic has, then, not undergone an alternation in personal identity. She has experienced what Travisano (1981: 242-244), James (1904), Burke (1954), Berger and Luckmann (1967), Thune (1977), Wallace (1982), and Strauss (1959) would term a radical transformation of personal identity that signals a conversion and commitment to a new way of life (Becker, 1960, 1964). How this deep transformation in the alcoholic's identity is accomplished is the central topic of this chapter.

The Alcoholic's Other

It must be noted that the alcoholic's other is more likely to experience an alternation, but not a transformation, in personal identity (although this may occur). That is, the other undergoes a transition in identity from being the spouse or lover of an active alcoholic, to being the spouse or lover of a recovering alcoholic. The other's changes in identity are contingent, in large part, on the actions the alcoholic takes or does not take. Although the other may become an "Al-Anon," or a member of a group of significant others of alcoholics, or join a group of "Adult Children of Alcoholic Parents," he or she (1) does not have to stop drinking, or have a desire to stop drinking in order to do so; and (2) will not have been ordered by the court to attend such meetings, or sent through treatment, as is often the case for the alcoholic. In short, the other's changes are more voluntary, less a matter of societal knowledge or concern, and the identity that is assumed is less deviant, or stigmatized, than is the label of "alcoholic" that the alcoholic assumes. The other, like the alcoholic, will find, though, a social group that fosters and supports the changes in identity that are sought. Recovery for the other is a wholly different process and it is not well understood.

Structural Constraints on the Alcoholic's Recovery

Racial, ethnic, gender, family, economic, and cultural factors intervene in the recovery process. If the alcoholic is a male, black or Hispanic, he is likely to live in a culture that encourages heavy drinking as a sign of manhood. Economic frustrations, including lack of work, coupled with peer pressures, increase the rewards that are found in heavy alcohol consumption. Indeed the black or Hispanic male may find himself in a totally alcohol-centered environment (see Kane, 1981; Cahalan, 1970). These factors work against recovery. The alcoholic who wishes to stop drinking finds little support for the new transformation in identity he wishes to pursue.

If the alcoholic is female (Gomberg, 1976), she lives in a culture that has a double standard toward alcoholism and alcohol consumption. The tolerance for drunkenness in women is low in our culture. The female alcoholic carries a double stigma. She is (1) a female who is alcoholic and (2) one who has been a secret alcoholic, having lived out her alcoholism in the private confines of the family home. Because her society has positioned her in the protective position of the home, the normal excuses for becoming an alcoholic have been removed, that is, pressures of work or peer pressure. She may carry also the stigma of sexual abuse in childhood (Vander Mey and Neff, 1986).

American society, then, has produced four basic classes of alcoholics: male, female, white, and nonwhite. Not surprisingly, the recovery probabilities are highest for white males (see Kane, 1981). However, recent trends (*Time,* 1985: 68-78) indicate changes in this situation. That is, as American society becomes less alcohol- and drug-centered, and as the social worlds of recovery expand and become more and more a part of the collective consciousness of the society, the stigmas from alcoholism are likely to decrease. At the same time the recovery rates for alcoholics from the other three classes noted above also should increase. However, the factors that structure alcohol consumption in adolescence, when drinking is learned, must also undergo change, for problem drinking first erupts in the early and mid-twenties for both males and females (Mandell and Ginzburg, 1976). I turn now to the first act of the three-act play called "Recovery."

ACT ONE: BECOMING SOBER

Becoming sober involves living a nondrinking self into existence. This involves the following interrelated process that may be repeated several times before the alcoholic establishes a stable sobriety trajectory (that is, a period of continous sobriety defined within A.A. in terms of 1, 3, 6, 9, and 12-month sequences). These phases, or processes are (1) hitting bottom; (2) reaching out for help; (3) making contact with A.A. and presenting one's self to an A.A. group; (4) announcing one's self as an alcoholic in an A.A. meeting; (5) slipping and returning to A.A.; (6) maintaining contact with A.A. and learning how not to drink on a daily basis; (7) becoming a regular member of A.A.; (8) learning A.A.'s Twelve Steps; and (9) becoming integrated into an A.A. network, getting a sponsor, and working the Steps, especially Steps Four and Five. (On A.A.'s steps see, A.A., 1953, 1976; Leach and Norris, 1977; Maxwell, 1984; Kurtz, 1979.)

Phases One and Two were analyzed in the last chapter. They will be relived in A.A. as the alcoholic learns to talk and tell his or her story. Phases Three, Four, and Five are the proper subject matter of Act One for they speak directly to how A.A. teaches the alcoholic not to drink (in practice Phases Three and Four are often combined, see below). Steps Six through Nine constitute the focus of Act Two, "Becoming an A.A. Member," and will be dealt with in the discussion of that act.

It is important to point out that the recovering alcoholic may move through all nine of these phases and still return to active alcoholism. The case quoted at the outset of this chapter establishes this fact. What occurs is a progressive funneling process that slowly solidifies the alcoholic's recovery program. It may take several movements through these phases before a solid recovery trajectory, or career, is secured.

A recovering alcoholic phrases this process in the following words:

> It is like an elevator that keeps going down to lower levels and lower floors until it hits bottom. I have stopped drinking, surrendered, come to A.A. and worked the Steps, but each time before it was at a level that still allowed me to drop lower. I started at too high a level. It took me a long time to hit the lowest level. I have finally hit what I hope is the bottom floor for me. But I don't know. I thought this before, too. There's always a new bottom for me to hit. Last time it was a DUI. But I've had those before too. It has taken me a long time, a long time, to learn this program. I just pray that I have it today [field observation, December 5, 1984; recovering alcoholic, 37-year-old graduate student].

An alcoholic may abstain from alcohol and not move through these eight phases. An alcoholic within A.A. may work only a portion of the Steps and also maintain sobriety. But for the alcoholic to be defined as working an A.A. program these nine phases will be experienced.

A recovering alcoholic with 11 years of sobriety speaks to the distinctions implicit in the above paragraph:

> You can get sober on just the First Step. You can stay sober and never go to meetings. You can get sober but you'll go crazy. You may be dry, and somewhat sober, but you won't have any peace of mind. You might as well be drinking. I know. That's what I did for the first four years of my sobriety. I went back to drinking. Life was just hell. You have to work all of the program. I do, anyway [field observation, July 15, 1984].

The First A.A. Meeting and Presenting an "Alcoholic" Self

Making contact with A.A. by attending one's first meeting is, of course, a basic step in the recovery process. This is Step Three in the recovery trajectory of the alcoholic. It must be followed up by subsequent A.A. meetings if the alcoholic is to learn the A.A. way of life. When an alcoholic attends his or her first A.A. meeting, by custom and tradition the meeting is turned into a *First Step Meeting*. (A.A.'s First Step states: "We admitted we were powerless over alcohol—that our lives had become unmanageable.") This means that each member at the meeting will speak to the processes of hitting bottom, surrendering, and coming to his or her first A.A. meeting. In these dialogues each member tells a story that will not be unlike the story the person at their first meeting will tell. This sharing of stories immediately joins the new alcoholic with a group perspective that has been constructed out of each individual's experiences with alcoholism before he or she got to A.A.

The following alcoholic is at his first A.A. meeting. He has been asked if he wants to speak by the chair of the meeting. Dressed in blue jeans, a heavy woolen shirt, hands shaking, face ashen and unshaven, eyes blurred, and tearing, he stated:

> I couldn't find the place. Walked by four times before I saw the A.A. sign on the front door. 'Fraid to come in. Guess that's why I'm here. My name's G, guess I'm an alcoholic. Can't stop by myself. God its good to be here. You make me feel good. Don't like to talk, though. I'm a loner. That's why I go to the bars. For the company. Never talk there either. Just drink and listen to people. Live by myself. Afraid of people. Been doin' this for 20 years. Keep gettin' into trouble when I drink. Don't even drive to the bar anymore. Walk. Can you people help me? Please [field observation, as reported, October 30, 1984].

Here the drinker presents an "alcoholic self" to the group. He asks for help, as he relates a portion of his story as a problem drinker. He calls himself an alcoholic and expresses an awareness that there must be help for alcoholics at A.A. This suggests that he knows that there are two kinds of alcoholics: his kind and those to whom he is speaking. This alcoholic has found his way to his first A.A. meeting. The group to which he presented his "alcoholic self" has since become his "home group" and he now attends three or more times a week. Having not yet announced a "dry date" for himself, he has become, in the eyes of the regular group members a "regular" at this group.

After G had spoken, the 14 A.A. members present at the meeting talked and told their stories involving the First Step. Each member spoke briefly, no longer than two to three minutes. The following comments are typical:

> My name's M and I'm an alcoholic. It took me 12 years to get to my first A.A. meeting. I came at just the right time. A day earlier and I wouldn't have been here. A day later and I wouldn't have come. It took me 18 months to get one year of sobriety. I'd been drinking for 20 years. Drunk the first time I drank, drunk every day after. I lost 3 wives, 14 cars, 2 houses, but kept the same job. I went to treatment and still drank. I came to A.A. meetings drunk and I drank after I left A.A. meetings. I didn't want to quit. I didn't want to give up. I finally surrendered. Today my miracle goes on. I didn't have to have a drink. So G, you're in the right place. Keep coming back. At least you didn't have to die before you got here [field observation, as reported, October 30, 1984; recovering male alcoholic, 52 years old, upper-level manager].

The next alcoholic speaks more directly to G:

> My name's L, I'm an alcoholic. Welcome to your first meeting. I'm glad to see you here. Its newcomers like you who help me stay sober. I know what kind of hell you've been through. I drank in bars, too. I was afraid to drive, too. I was in the emergency room at the hospital so many times they knew my clinic number. They told me if I drank again, I'd die. And I drank again. I had to come and keep coming. They told me to keep coming until I wanted to. They said come to a meeting every day. Some say 90 meetings in 90 days. I just go to a meeting every day. They said get a *Big Book*. Learn the Steps. Find a sponsor. Clear away the wreckage of your past. You're not a bad person, you are a sick person trying to get better. I have a disease called alcoholism and I can't drink. My medicine is A.A. and the poison is alcohol. I come here for my medicine. I get a little bit better everyday. Get involved with these people. You've got friends here you never knew you had [field observation, as reported, October 30, 1984, recovering male alcoholic, 44-years-old, chemist].

In the comments of these two speakers, G, the newcomer, was exposed to the A.A. theory of alcoholism, alcoholics, and alcohol. A process of socialization was at work. A new view of self, other, language, and meaning was being communicated. Of course the "new" self the alcoholic presents contains the term "alcoholic." In presenting this "alcoholic" self to the group the speaker announces a verbal (at least) commitment to the identity of alcoholic. Placing his name before or after the word alcoholic locates the speaker, for himself and for others, in the identity of alcoholic (see Stone, 1962, on identity placement).

Presenting Self

This simple speech act (Searle, 1970) which states "I am an alcoholic," carries manifold implications for the speaker. Not only does it mean more than the speaker intends, but it means exactly what is said: The speaker is an alcoholic. But more is given in this simple utterance. In a frightening sense it reflects an attempt on the part of the speaker to convince himself that he is, in fact, an alcoholic. The utterance is both an expression of a self-affirmation, and a request the speaker makes to himself, asking himself to, in fact, believe what he has just said.

The sincerity of this speech act also must be considered, for the speaker may utter the phrase "I am an alcoholic" and not believe it. He makes the utterance because others expect it or because one part of him believes it to be true and another part denies this label.

In these senses the speaker commits an act that connects him to a line of action that is produced by the effects of the utterance itself. In short, to himself and to others, the alcoholic publicly has defined himself as an alcoholic. This speech act signals, then, a conversion to an identity the speaker has heretofore gone to great lengths to avoid, if not deny. But having once made the statement, "I'm an alcoholic and my name if Bill," the speaker has crossed the verbal line from denial to surrender. He or she has begun the move from active alcoholism to recovery from alcoholism.

The following speakers display in their utterances these three attitudes toward the meaning of the phrase "I am an alcoholic."

The first speaker is at his first A.A. meeting. He states the following:

> My name's ________ and I'm an alcoholic. I guess. I hope, I'm afraid to say the word. I must be, I can't stop drinking. On New Year's Eve I got drunk and beat up my girlfriend because she left her apartment and locked the door. I don't want to do this anymore. I am an alcoholic [field observation, January 8, 1985].

This speaker fearfully pronounces the word "alcoholic," distancing himself from the word as he draws near to it. Commanding himself to believe what he has uttered, he offers the evidence he needs to make himself believe that he is, in fact, an alcoholic.

The next speaker describes his relationship to the word "alcoholic" in the following words:

> I've said I was an alcoholic for four years at these meetings. But deep down, inside, I didn't believe it. I still wanted to drink. I came here and said what you wanted me to say. Today I believe, as deeply as I can, that I am an alcoholic. It's a miracle that I haven't had a drink today. The reason I haven't, in part, is because I believe and know that I am an alcoholic and I can't take the first drink. You people have taught me that [field observation, October 27, 1983].

Here the speaker moves from insincerity to sincerity. He describes the transition he made from not believing in what he said and what he meant when he said he was an alcoholic, to the position of belief.

This simple speech act is the alcoholic's verbal ticket into the A.A. experience and into the A.A. meetings. What she does with it is wholly up to her. But if she chooses to follow through with this self-presentation at an A.A. meeting she must return. This new self that she has defined for herself and presented to others has been waiting for her.

The first A.A. meeting sets in motion, then, a process of socialization that will put the alcoholic on a sobriety trajectory, if that trajectory is desired. The socialization process turns on four levels of interpretation that move from the abstract to the specific. The first, and most abstract, level of interpretation is given to the object *alcohol* which is defined as "poison" for the alcoholic. The second level of meaning is given to the term *alcoholism,* which in A.A. is defined as a disease or an illness. The third level of meaning references the *alcoholic,* who is seen as suffering from an obsession to drink that is physical, mental, and spiritual. The fourth interpretive level speaks directly to the *problem drinker* who believes herself to be an alcoholic. A.A. tells the drinker that she is an alcoholic if she says so. And, if the drinker agrees, then she has come to the right place, for they will help her not to take a drink today.

Slipping and Returning to A.A.

It is nearly axiomatic that an alcoholic will drink after attending the first or second A.A. meeting. Slips, or returns to drinking, may be planned or accidental—that is, the alcoholic takes a drink with no prior plan of doing so. In order for recovery to occur within A.A. the alcoholic must, after slipping, return to A.A. He or she must grasp the idea that for A.A. not drinking is the key to recovery. The following speaker makes this point. After attending his first A.A. meeting, he was sober for three months, then he drank three beers at a party. He states the following:

> I feel so bad I want to cry. You know I didn't get drunk. But I did drink. I guess for you people that counts as a drink, right? I'll just have to start all over again. I don't know why I did it. Control I guess [field conversation, September 12, 1985, 46-year-old painter].

This alcoholic slipped and returned to A.A. He is struggling not to drink. He still keeps alcohol in his house. He still socializes with drinking friends. His A.A. attendance is erratic. His attendance at A.A. confirms, however, the A.A. adage that "If you drink after you come to A.A. it will never be the same again."

Reasons for Slips: Becker's Model

Slips are caused by the following factors: (1) the alcoholic's belief that he or she can once again control alcohol; (2) a desire to return to old drinking contexts in which sociability and fun were experienced (Bateson, 1972a: 328-329); (3) a phenomenological craving for alcohol coupled with a high stress situation in which drinking, in the past, was used as a means of reducing stress and anxiety; and (4) a failure to commit fully to the A.A. program. (See Denzin, 1986a, Chapters 4 and 5 for a more detailed discussion of slips and relapse.)

Two kinds of "slips" are defined by A.A. First, there are the slips experienced by the newcomer who is starting to "get" the program. These are regarded as normal and to be expected. The second kind of "slip" is experienced by the member who has had a period of continuous sobriety and is defined as a failure in the program. This return to drinking is often regarded as deliberate and not appropriately termed a slip. A.A.'s speak of these as planned drunks.

Slipping may be explained in terms of Becker's (1960, 1964) model of situational adjustments to problematic situations. That is, alcoholics slip when the transformation of self that has occurred in the early stages of recovery has not been complete. If it has produced only an alternation, but not a transformation, in identity (Travisano, 1981), then a return to drinking is likely. A complete transformation in identity, including a commitment to A.A., to the First Step, to A.A.'s concept of a Higher Power, and to the A.A. meeting structure, appears to secure the alcoholic's sobriety for that length of time that the commitment is sustained. If the alcoholic withdraws from A.A., drinking will be taken up again. His or her sobriety was, then, just a situational adjustment to a momentary problematic situation in life. He or she did not make the commitments and side bets into A.A. that would have anchored the recovering self in the A.A. way of life.

Situational adjustments to A.A. are likely when the alcoholic is forced to attend meetings, either because of pressures from work, home, or the courts. He or she will learn how to talk at an A.A. meeting, will call himself or herself an alcoholic, and may even put together a long list of attended meetings, with dates and places duly recorded. If, however, the commitment to A.A. is produced externally, a transient "alcoholic" identity is likely to be created. This will often occur for large "classes" of alcoholics, that is, those who go through a treatment center together. In this case situational adjustment becomes a collective phenomenon, shared within a group perspective.

The process of commitment to A.A. (see below) will work against slips. The alcoholic will have built up consistent lines of action toward not drinking that crisscross through the many life situations he or she might confront. He or she will have learned how to reject situational alternatives or contingencies that might provide an excuse for drinking. He or she will, that is, no longer regard not drinking as a temporary situational adjustment to a problem situation in life.

A.A. offers a social structure in which these commitments and side bets can be made. If the alcoholic chooses to anchor himself or herself in the A.A. way of life, sobriety can be secured. That is, he or she will become a member of a society of recovering alcoholic selves. In this case recovery becomes both a collective and an individual phenomenon. Slips—returns to drinking—will, for such an individual, be momentary and short lived. For the alcoholic who has not made these commitments slips may be permanent. He or she may never return to A.A.

A.A. phrases this position as follows:

> Why all this insistance that every A.A. must hit bottom first? The answer is that few people will sincerely try to practice the A.A. program unless they have hit bottom. For practicing A.A.'s remaining Eleven Steps means the adoption of attitudes and attitudes that almost no alcoholic who is still drinking can dream of taking. Who wishes to be rigorously honest and tolerant? Who wants to confess his faults to another and make restitution for harm done? Who cares anything about a Higher Power, let alone mediation and prayer. Who wants to sacrifice time and energy in trying to carry A.A.'s message to the next sufferer? No, the average alcoholic, self-centered in the extreme, doesn't care for this prospect—unless he has to do these things in order to stay alive himself [A.A., 1953: 24].

A.A.'s position is clear. In Becker's language, commitments and side bets into A.A. will not be made until the alcoholic hits bottom.

The next alcoholic makes this clear. After four and a half years of sobriety he returned to drinking.

> I still liked the taste of that damned stuff. I stayed on top of your A.A. bus for more than four years. I came to you folks so I could learn how to drink socially. After four years I told myself I could drink again. In three months I was crazy again, back on the mental ward. When I came back I got inside the A.A. bus. I learned how to rub shoulders with you people. I got involved [field observation, October 16, 1984].

This alcoholic has passed through stages one through five. After four and a half years he is ready to enter Act Two. He is ready to commit himself to A.A.

ACT TWO: BECOMING AN A.A. MEMBER

As indicated earlier, Act Two, "Becoming an A.A. Member," has four phases; (1) maintaining contact with A.A. and learning how to not drink on a daily basis; (2) becoming a regular member of A.A.; (3) learning the Steps; (4) becoming integrated into an A.A. network, finding a sponsor, and working Steps Four and Five. (Because Steps Four and Five reference the transition between the old and the new life the alcoholic learns to live, I will discuss them under Act Three, below.) I begin with phase one of Act Two, giving it the title "Building Sobriety." (See Leach and Norris, 1977: 483-484, and Rudy, 1986, for alternative views of "becoming an A.A. member.")

Building Sobriety

A.A. recognizes two types of sobriety: continuous and interrupted. Individuals who become A.A. members endeavor to build a continuous sobriety trajectory measured, after the first days and months of sobriety have been obtained, by years. On the other hand, sobriety is measured on a one day at a time model, which is given in A.A.'s often repeated statement "Who ever got up first this morning has the most sobriety in this room." As the member builds sobriety he or she accumulates medallions or tokens, which symbolically mark the length of time he or she has been sober. Each person is responsible for announcing a "dry date," or a birthday date. Their sobriety is measured, henceforth, from this date. On the occasion of the first year of continuous sobriety the member has a birthday party with one candle on a cake, signifying the first year of his or her new life.

Becoming a Regular

As the member builds a sobriety career within A.A. he or she begins to be recognized around the tables. They become a regular at one or more A.A. groups. They will find a "home" group, often the first group they attended. In this group they will become regular "readers" of the A.A. materials that are read at the outset of every meeting (that is, "How It Works," "The Twelve Traditions," and "The Thought for the Day," for the groups I studied). He or she also may become a temporary chair of the group, agreeing to lead its meetings for a month or more. Later an elected position within the group may be obtained. The member may become the group's General Service Representative or its treasurer, although this probably will not happen until after a year or more of sobriety. The member also may be asked to tell his or her story at an open A.A. meeting. The key to becoming a group-recognized, responsible regular is continuous sobriety.

Learning the Steps

A.A. describes the importance of its Twelve Steps for recovery:

> Many of us had long been booze-fighters. Time after time, we had stopped drinking and tried to stay stopped, only to return to drinking sooner or later. . . . But those Twelve Steps of A.A. mark our road to recovery. Now, we do not have to fight any more. And our path is open to all comers [A.A., 1976: 85].

> A.A.'s Twelve Steps are a group of principles, spiritual in nature, which, if practiced as a way of life, can expel the obsession to drink and enable the sufferer to become happily and usefully whole [A.A., 1953: 15].

The discourse between the following two A.A. speakers, both female, gives meaning to the Steps as they are applied to the member's recovery program.

The following speaker, a 37-year-old musician, has been sober 10 months. Her husband is an active alcoholic.

> I don't know, I don't know, you know, it's like, it's like, you know what it's like, like when you make a long distance telephone call and talk in the receiver to somebody and nobody answers, it's like there's no connection. My husband's like that. He'll make plans, get drunk, forget the plans, make new plans, get drunk, and never get anywhere. Now he's got me doing it. It's like, I don't know how I'm going to pay the bills. You know on New Year's Eve it was the greatest night of my life. I was with old friends, musicians, they were drinking and I wasn't. There was so much love there. It's like, do you know what I mean, it's like there was all that love there all around and I missed all of it because I was always drunk. I went home and cried. How could I have done that to myself? You know I think I might still be crazy, I just can't make any connections anywhere. Can anybody help me? [field observation, January 10, 1985].

A speaker with four years sobriety came forth in the meeting:

> Have you tried the Steps? Have you tried turning your life over? Have you done the Fourth and Fifth Steps? Do you do daily prayer and meditation? How many meetings do you go to? You know I was just like you my first year. I was all crazy. Then my sponsor told me to get to work on the Steps and stop feeling sorry for myself. It worked

> for me [field observation, January 10, 1985, 39-year-old female, middle-level executive].

Two modes of sobriety are expressed in these statements. The first speaker is sober with A.A.'s First Step, but not the other Steps. By her own words she is not sane. The second speaker suggests that this is because she hasn't used the Steps. But more is at issue. The first speaker has not committed herself fully to the A.A. program. She attends meetings so as to stay sober, but she has gone no farther into the transformations in self that A.A. prescribes.

A.A.'s Steps may be understood as guidelines for self-transformation. They suggest a clearing away of the alcoholic's past (Steps Four and Five), so that the program of recovery A.A. offers may be embraced fully. If the Twelve Steps are followed the identity of alcoholic is made a central part of the alcoholic's self.

Speaker L, in the above account of G's first A.A. meeting, addresses the major points in learning the Steps. These turn on regular meeting attendance (90 meetings in 90 days), which ensures that the alcoholic will hear, over and over again, A.A.'s Twelve Steps read and discussed. In the community I studied the alcoholic also could attend regular Step Meetings that devoted 12 weekly meetings in a row to each one of the Steps. Thus, over the course of 12 weeks the alcoholic would be exposed to an in-depth discussion of each Step. At the end of Step Twelve the group would then start over with Step One.

The following alcoholic speaks to the place of these meetings in her recovery:

> I went to the Sunday night Step Meeting for one year. Never missed a Sunday. We went over every Step four times that year. We read from the *Twelve and Twelve*. That's how I learned the Steps. Then I went to the *Big Book* Meetings on Saturdays and we read every chapter and story in the *Big Book*. By the end of my first year I felt like I had learned the basics of A.A. It took repetition, listening, and hearing other people read and discuss the Steps before I finally began to understand how they all fitted together [field interview, August 5, 1985].

In addition to regular meeting attendance, the alcoholic is encouraged to learn the disease concept of A.A., to make friends within A.A., to work the Steps and to find a sponsor. He or she also is told not to question why he or she became an alcoholic. In this way the newcomer is taught a new interpretive theory of alcoholism. He or she learns, through modeling, imitation, and repetition (Bandura, 1977) how to become a recovering alcoholic. The alcoholic learns how to take the attitudes of the generalized community of recovering alcoholics, and apply those attitudes and their interpretations to his or her conduct (Mead, 1934). The Steps within A.A. become significant symbols, in Mead's language, that call out interpretations toward self, alcoholics, and alcoholism that are consensual and geared toward maintaining sobriety. As significant symbols that signify lines of action to be taken in the recovery process, the Steps become integral parts of the alcoholic's self-system.

A recovering alcoholic with 30 years sobriety states the following:

> I'd be nothing today without the Steps. With them I regained self-respect, got my family back, got rid of the guilt and shame about my past and learned to live like a normal human again. I became a new kind of person. The Steps were my guide posts to a new life [field conversation, July 5, 1984].

Maxwell (1984: 128) quotes a recovering alcoholic who echoes the position of the above speaker:

> A.A. gave me a whole new way of life, so that I am still continuing on with the things that A.A. taught me—this philosophy I found in A.A. I still apply it daily as I go along. *I feel like I'm still growing....* I now have a positive outlook on life, and I understand myself. I can recognize my limitations, but I have respect for myself, and I'm much happier [Italics in original].

These accounts reference the kind of reflective self-awareness A.A.'s Steps create when they are followed and become a part of the alcoholic's life. I turn now to sponsorship.

Phase Four: Finding a Sponsor

As the alcoholic becomes a member of A.A., becomes sober, and begins to learn the Steps, a sponsor will be found. A.A. (1975: 27) defines a sponsor as "a sober alcoholic who can help solve only one problem: how to stay sober. And the sponsor has only one tool to use—personal experience, not scientific wisdom." A sponsor may, as in the early days of A.A., "sponsor" a man or woman into A.A. and into the recovery process. This may include taking an alcoholic to detox (or treatment), visting him or her regularly, meeting the alcoholic's family members, taking the alcoholic home, and then to an A.A. meeting. At his or her first meeting the sponsor will introduce the newcomer to other recovering alcoholics (A.A., 1975: 26).

A sponsor becomes a friend with whom the alcoholic shares problems that may not be discussed at A.A.'s meetings. A.A. culture recommends that sponsors not be of the same sex. A sponsor may be someone who knows secrets about the alcoholic's past. A sponsor is also someone who may take the member through Steps.

These features of the sponsor are summarized in the following account.

> When I got off the crazy ward after my last drunk I picked a sponsor who was someone I hated. I picked him because he was staying sober and I knew I could talk to the sonofabitch. I had done that plenty of times when we used to drink together at "Eddies." He even used to work for me. Then I worked for him. He took me through the Steps and I shared things with him that I never shared with nobody else. When he died I had to get someone else cause I had to have another living human being who knew this particular thing about me [field observation, June 2, 1981].

The sponsor may also become a focal point in the alcoholic's daily recovery. The following member speaks to this point:

> For 18 months I called my sponsor almost on a daily basis, sometimes more than once a day. He helped me with everything. He told me I would become a new human being. He told me I wouldn't know the old person I used to be. He taught me how to read the *Big Book*. He had me do a daily inventory (the 10th Step) and he made me commit to five or more meetings a week. I did and what he said would happen happened. He took me through the 4th and 5th Steps too [field conversation, July 2, 1984].

The sponsor is a socializing agent within the A.A. culture. The relationship he or she forms with the newcomer is purely voluntary and works only as long as both parties continue their commitment to it. Such relationships often last years. Witness the following statement:

> N was my friend for 26 years. We stayed in touch all this time. He stood up with me at my wedding. He was the Godfather for my kids. He was a friend, a family member, a confidant. He was everything you could ask of another human being. I would never have met this man, or found him, if it hadn't been for my alcoholism and A.A. [field conversation, August 22, 1983].

As the member acquires a sponsor, he or she may also become a sponsor to a newcomer. The newcomer, in turn, if he or she stays, may become a sponsor. Thus, a network of sponsors exists within any A.A. community, for behind every recovering alcoholic stands a sponsor. This dyadic relationship lies at the heart of the A.A.

experience (see Maxwell, 1984: 110-113). I turn now to Act Three of Recovery, "Two Lives."

ACT THREE: TWO LIVES

Act Three has four distinct phases that do, however, overlap. These are (1) taking Steps Four and Five; (2) acquiring a "spiritual" program as part of recovery; (3) learning how to live sober; and (4) coming to see that one has, in fact, led two lives: before A.A. and after A.A.

Steps Four and Five

A.A. tells the alcoholic that "self, manifested in various ways, was what had defeated us. Resentment is the 'number one' offender" (A.A., 1976: 64). From resentment stems the spiritual disease from which, according to A.A., all alcoholics suffer. In order for the alcoholic to recover, resentments must be dealt with, and this is the topic of the Fourth and Fifth Steps. The alcoholic is told to list his or her resentments, to identify the persons, places, and institutions that have produced them, and to locate how these resentments have affected his or her self-esteem, financial situation, and relations (including sexual) with others. A thorough review of the alcoholic's life is thus suggested. Once this searching, moral inventory is taken, the alcoholic is told to share this with God and another human being (Step Five). Having taken these two Steps the alcoholic is told to ask God (as this Higher Power is understood) to remove these defects of character that have produced these resentments and harmful actions toward others (Steps Six and Seven). Finally, A.A. suggests that the alcoholic make amends to those who were harmed before and during the active phases of alcoholism (Steps Eight and Nine).

In these moves A.A. separates the alcoholic from the past. It offers a new life with the resentments and misdeeds of the past laid to rest. At the same time A.A. locates the alcoholic within a new social world wherein other alcoholics are engaging in the same process. Recovery becomes a collective, group phenomenon.

A member with over five years sobriety speaks to the importance of Steps Four and Five for the alcoholic's recovery:

> They don't think there's anything wrong with them, except that they drank too much. They don't think the Fourth and Fifth Steps apply

> to them. They just think they drank a little too much. They come in, get dried out, sobered up, stay three months, make big speeches, and then they leave, never to be seen again. They may be too successful. I know three well-known businessmen, big money. They came for a while. They're all out now, drinking. They said A.A. wasn't for them. They didn't have problems like those drunks they saw at the meetings. They weren't willing to do the hard work the program asks. They didn't have anything in their pasts they had to share with anybody else. They were "successes" [field conversation, January 31, 1985].

Steps Four and Five cut to the core of the alcoholic's self-system. They suggest an illumination of the hidden corners of the alcoholic's self that he or she has kept from others. The good-me, bad-me, and not-me components of the self are thus addressed in these two steps.

A member speaks to the importance of these Steps for her recovery:

> It was like a giant weight was lifted from my shoulders. The past slowly began to drift away. I felt free for the first time in years. Everything fell into place, my father's alcoholism, my mother's death, my divorce, my alcoholism, what happened to me as a child sexually, why I'd had trouble with new relationships, how I was raising my son. I felt like a new woman with a new life in front of me. My sponsor took me through these steps. I trusted him and without him and what he taught me I wouldn't be here today [field conversation, April 4, 1983, female alcoholic, administrator, 4 years sober, 37 years old].

The importance of the sponsor for these two Steps is underscored in these remarks. At the same time this woman speaks to how the Steps allow the past to become understandable, as a new life within and outside A.A. is entered

Acquiring a Spiritual Program: Serenity

As indicated previously, A.A.'s Twelve Steps are organized by a set of spiritual principles (see Kurtz, 1979) that are intended to remove the alcoholic's obsession to drink. Embedded within these spiritual structures is a concept called "serenity," or "peace of mind," which carries two meanings for the A.A. member. The first meaning is the absence of negative emotion in the alcoholic's life, including anger, fear, jealousy, and resentment (A.A., 1967: 48). The second meaning is spiritual. It references a concept of "rebirth," and a peace of mind that comes when the alcoholic admits a Higher Power into his or her life (A.A., 1967: 104).

Only A.A.'s First, Fourth, Eighth, and Ninth Steps omit reference to a spiritual program or a Higher Power. Thus to enter into A.A.'s program of recovery is to enter into a spiritual program. This part of the program forgives the alcoholic for misdeeds of the past and offers a set of practices that will produce serenity or peace of mind.

These practices are situated in the A.A. meetings, wherein the Serenity Prayer opens every meeting and the Lord's Prayer closes every meeting. At the same time A.A. encourages individual meditation through the prayers that are associated with the Third, Seventh, and Eleventh Steps. Many members of A.A. also read *The Twenty-Four Hour a Day Book,* a publication of Hazelden (1954), and other meditation books, including *Each Day a New Beginning, The Promise of a New Day* and *Today's Gift* (Hazelden, 1982, 1983, 1985). In the following paragraph members discuss serenity and its meaning for them. They make reference to self-feelings that are associated with this state of mind.

The first speaker is a female, with 13 months of sobriety. Married, she is an account executive, and 53 years old:

> When I come in here everything slips away. The tension, the anxiety, the fear. The pent-up anger goes away. Today, this morning I was a fright. Just in a state. My head was like a nest of cobwebs; thoughts were crisscrossing every which way, nothing made sense. I was in a corner of my mind and couldn't get out. I think my boss set me off. I needed to come here. I feel better already. I have a tiny bit of peace of mind now that I can carry back with to work this afternoon. Thank you all for being here. I needed you today! Thank you [field observation, April 2, 1982].

In the next paragraph a member elaborates on the feelings that are experienced during a meeting. This member has been away from meetings (by choice) for five months. Sober 14 months, he is 21 years old. He states the following:

> I was afraid to come back. I don't know why. I just was. Now that I'm here I feel the peace and serenity of the group. It's just seeping into me. I'm relaxing. My fear is goin' away. I don't know why I stayed away so long. I didn't drink, but I don't know why. I need to be here every day. I remember now what it was like when I came every day. These good feelings stay with you after you leave. You carry them with you and that's why I always came every day. I need to get back to doing that. Thank you for being here when I finally got myself together to get back [field observation, February 5, 1985].

The next speaker refers to meetings he had with his group when he was in Mexico City.

> At noon everyday I'd say the Serenity Prayer to myself and repeat the Eleventh Step. Then I'd put myself at the tables for the noon meeting and I'd look at everybody, just as I remembered you. Then I'd select a topic and imagine what you would be talking about and saying. Then I'd say what I would say if I was at the meeting. This would calm me down and give me a moment of peace when I was in that crazy Mexico City trying to find my way around [field observation, August 26, 1982, 49-year-old male, two years sobriety, employed as a copy editor].

These three accounts are descriptions of personal, spiritual experiences. Modifying William James (1961: 299-301), they may be seen as having the following characteristics. First, they reference definable, self-feelings that are relational. The members speak of having to be in the presence of others (real and imagined) in order for these feelings to be produced. Second, these feelings cannot be sustained for long periods of time, but when they are recalled, they are remembered with a depth of feeling that brings the member back to the A.A. meetings. Third, the serenity, or peace of mind, the alcoholic feels and experiences in meetings, although transitory and fleeting, is grounded in an interactional context. The knowledge that these feelings will be felt when members go to a meeting draws them back to the A.A. structure of experience. The alcoholic comes to define a central part of sobriety as residing in serenity, or the peace of mind that comes from attending meetings.

Having once attempted to find this self-feeling in alcohol, the member now finds it in interactions with other recovering alcoholics. The A.A. meetings become the setting for the production of a state of mind that is both shared and entirely personal.

James (1961) stressed the importance of spiritual experiences for the self that found itself divided against itself. A.A. is more specific in regard to the centrality of spiritual experiences. Such experiences are basic to the attainment and maintenance of sobriety. The second and third speakers (above) refer directly to this point.

A.A. thus works within a conceptual structure that is circular. Taking the position that a spiritual experience is basic to the attainment of sobriety, A.A. argues that serenity, which comes, in part, from meetings, is necessary in order for sobriety to be maintained. Furthermore, sobriety without serenity, which for A.A. takes the form of "dry drunks" and negative emotionality, is to be avoided at all costs. Dry drunks lead to wet drunks. Hence, serenity stands at the center of the A.A. experience. It is both the "cause" and the "effect" of becoming and being sober. It is also the sought after state of mind that replaces intoxication. And, it is the state of mind that can be obtained best through participation in the social worlds of A.A.

Living Sober

The test of a member's program is given in the ability to confront a problematic situation and not drink. A.A. (1975) offers the recovering alcoholic a number of "tips" or protective measures that can be followed when the occasion to drink arises. These include (1) staying away from the first drink; (2) becoming active within A.A. and making commitments to A.A.; (3) calling the sponsor when the desire to drink returns; (4) not getting too tired, hungry, angry, or lonely; (5) reading the A.A. literature; and (6) being careful of drinking situations.

The probability of living sober is increased if the member's commitment to A.A.'s spiritual program is sustained (see above). At the same time, as the alcoholic becomes more committed to the identity of a recovering alcoholic, a redefinition of self in relationship to problems and drinking occurs. That is, problems that were previously defined as justifying a drink are now defined as occasions for personal, spiritual growth. This massive conceptual reordering of the alcoholic's thought patterns is accomplished through the working of the Steps, the use of the sponsor, and regular attendance at A.A. meetings.

The following alcoholic addresses this problematic:

> I don't have an excuse to drink today. A.A. took every one of them away from me. I used to think, what if my wife died, or my daughters were killed, or I lost my job, or my house burned down? What if? What if? I knew I'd drink if that happened. Today I know I'd come to a meeting and talk about it. I'd pray and ask God's guidance. I'd call my sponsor. I'd do anything I had to not to drink. A drink would not solve one of my problems today. I've finally learned what that cliché about problems being occasions for personal growth really means. I thought it was bullshit at first! They're right. I've got no excuse to drink. If I drink it's because I talk myself into it. Period [field conversation, February 2, 1982, 35-year-old male, carpenter, sober 5 years].

This alcoholic has made the transition between the two lives that a recovering alcoholic experiences. He indicates how problematic situations are redefined within A.A.'s interpretive theory. Thus far he has been successful for he has been sober over five years.

Two Lives

As the alcoholic learns how to deal with the past and as the A.A. program is internalized, he or she comes to think of his or her past life as something that happened long ago. At this point in recovery the alcoholic will have learned how to talk at A.A. meetings, will have worked the Fourth and Fifth Steps, and will have become an A.A. regular in one or more groups. (See Denzin, future volumes, for a more detailed discussion of this process.) The next two speakers make reference to this transition in self-hood that occurs.

Raymond Carver (1983: 196-197), the poet and novelist, makes the following observations regarding his alcoholic past:

> It's very painful to think about some of the things that happened back then.... Toward the end of my drinking I was completely out of control and in a very grave place. Blackouts, the whole business.... I was at Duffy's on two different occasions; in the place called DeWitt, in San Jose, and in a hospital in San Francisco—all in the space of twelve months. I guess that's pretty bad.

In these words Carver is describing how it was at the end of his drinking. Any alcoholic could give a similar story, although the details would vary, of course. In the following passage Carver describes his relationship to this past life.

> I can't change anything now.... That life is simply gone now, and I can't regret its passing. I have to live in the present. The life back then is gone just as surely—it's as remote to me as if it happened to somebody I read about in a nineteenth-century novel. I don't spend more than five minutes a month on the past. The past really is a foreign country, and they do do things differently there. Things happen. I really do feel I've had two different lives [Carver, 1983: 207].

Finally, Carver (1983: 196) speaks to the meaning of recovery. When asked by an interviewer, "How long since you quit drinking?" he replied:

> June 2, 1977. If you want the truth, I'm prouder of that, that I've quit drinking, than I am of anything in my life. I'm a recovered alcoholic. I'll always be an alcoholic, but I'm no longer a practicing alcoholic.

Carver's remarks reveal four basic features of the alcoholic's recovery story. First, the date of his last drink is fixed vividly in his memory. Second, the details of his last days of drinking are fresh in his memory. Third, he takes pride, as do all alcoholics who are recovering, in the fact that he has stopped drinking. Fourth, he now sees himself as living a new life. He has distanced himself from the old self of the past. He feels at home with the new, recovering self. He has made the full transition from the active alcoholic self of the past to the recovering self of the present.

The following speaker, the same speaker who opened Chapter 2, now sober 72 days, glimpses what Carver has seen:

> I feel that there are two me's. The old Frank of the past and the new Frank of today. The drunk Frank and the sober Frank. I don't never want to see that drunk sonofabitch again. I hope, I pray to God that he's gone away and died. I hope to meet the new Frank again in heaven when I see my maker. I pray to God I'll be sober the day I die. Last summer you never could have said that about me. I just wanted to curl up and die. I wanted to hook up one of them hoses we got at work to the back of the tailpipe of the old Chevy I got and drive down an old country lane with a pint, leave the motor runnin, maybe play some bluegrass music and jest die. Jest die. Kill myself, that's how low I felt. Lower than low, beneath a damned snake. Thank God I ain't afeelin' that way today. Thank God! Its me, the a, a, a, a. Its the New Frank a 'speakin' today. Thank God! [field observation, January 28, 1985, 53-year-old recovering alcoholic, printer].

Now 72 days away from his last drink, Frank still feels the pain of the old self that was an active alcoholic. Carver, over 6 years sober, spends less than "five minutes a month on the past." Frank is divided between the past and the present. These two alcoholics speak to the experiential distance that is traveled by the recovering alcoholic once recovery is securely in hand. Were they to sit together in the same meeting, Carver, if Frank were to hear him, would show him how much a part of his past the old Frank can become, if he stays sober.

Accepting the Alcoholic Identity

The difference between these two alcoholics is more than temporal, or their length of time in A.A. It is conceptual, moral, and lies deep within the self of each of them. Carver has accepted his alcoholic identity. He is committed fully to and invested in it, emotionally, personally, temporally, and interactionally. Frank still is learning and accepting his identity. They are in differing places in their moral careers as recovering alcoholics.

As the member makes the moves that bring this transition between the "two lives," he or she has come full circle in the A.A. experience. Starting as a newcomer at the first A.A. meeting, perhaps barely able to speak, he or she is now a recovering alcoholic. The emotionally divided self of the past has been dealt with. The horrors and traumas of the destructive alcoholic play called "Denial" have now become a part of the past. Yet that past is kept alive, as newcomers come into A.A. meetings and remind the regular where he or she used to be.

CONCLUSIONS

I have mapped the radical transformations of self that accompany the recovery process. I have structured my interpretations, as in the previous chapter, in terms of a three-act play. The phases of recovery—sobriety, becoming an A.A. member, and living two lives—represent dramatically different phases of experience. Each phase has a different focus. Phase three presumes the first two. The first two phases work back and forth upon one another, as becoming an A.A. member solidifies the member's sobriety, but one can hardly become sober within A.A. without desiring to become an A.A. member.

The key players, or figures in recovery are, of course, the alcoholic, his or her network of significant others, and recovering alcoholics in A.A. As the alcoholic becomes connected to A.A., a sponsor will be selected out of the universe of recovering alcoholics he or she comes to know. The dyadic, personal relationship that is built up between these two individuals becomes the cornerstone for the alcoholic's recovery. This dyadic structure stands, I have suggested, at the heart of the A.A. experience. From it flows the alcoholic's grasp and working of the Fourth and Fifth Steps. As the alcoholic moves beyond these steps the spiritual side of A.A. becomes more apparent. Serenity and peace of mind become sought after states of consciousness that replace the old obsession to drink that brought the alcoholic to A.A. in the first place. With spirituality comes a healing of the alcoholically divided self of the past.

The alcoholic's relationship with the other also structures the recovery process. The other may support or be negative about the new life the alcoholic wishes to lead. The other may complain about over-involvement in A.A. meetings and may miss the control he or she once exerted when the alcoholic was drinking actively. Resentment and anger may appear in the spaces that alcohol previously filled. The alcoholic and his or her other may find that nothing holds them together now that the drinking has stopped. Or they may find a new foundation for their relationship and grow more closely together (A.A., 1976: Chapter 9).

The alcoholic's recovery turns on a dialogue between two self-structures: the old self of the past and the new self of recovery. In order for recovery to begin working in the alcoholic's life a firm commitment to meetings and the A.A. Steps must be made. If this commitment is withheld, the alcoholic assumes a "transient" alcoholic identity, which represents only a situational adjustment to the problems his or her active alcoholism produced.

The new, committed "alcoholic" self that the alcoholic assumes becomes an interpersonal process (Sullivan, 1953) that is woven into the structures of experience A.A. offers. Transformed into a recovering alcoholic who is a storyteller, the member learns how to talk about the self of the past from the standpoint of humor and dramatic irony. By radically transforming himself or herself, the alcoholic transforms the world he or she lives in.

Limits of the Dramatic Metaphor

A note on the dramatic metaphor that has been employed in the last two chapters is in order. Elsewhere (Denzin, 1985a) I have criticized the use of this model because it too often produces a static, structural view of interaction. I have attempted to avoid this bias by treating the overlap that occurs between the several acts that make up the alcoholic's two plays.

With Goffman (1959: 254-255), my concern is with finding a framework that will aid in the understanding of how persons go about structuring and maintaining definitions of situations. The dramatic language of the stage is one way in which this process can be understood metaphorically. My problem has been to interpret how alcoholics and their others struggle to make sense out of a world that has gone out of control. Like actors on a stage, these individuals act out parts that they hope will make them appear (to themselves and others) to be normal. Attempting to act as normals they sink farther and farther into the destructive worlds of interaction that alcoholism produces. Like the characters in O' Neill's *Long Day's Journey Into Night* (1955), they experience ruptures and breaks in interactions that move them from one phase of experience to another. These ruptures and the new phases of experience they produce take the form of acts in a play. Different actors, different lines of action, different audiences, and different scripts are played out. Yet, in the main, it is the same set of individuals throughout. They have simply experienced new definitions of who they are in relation to one another. I turn now to reflections on the foregoing analysis.

Part III

TREATING THE ALCOHOLIC SELF
An Ethnography of the Treatment Process

8

THE PARADOXES OF TREATMENT
Introduction to the New Self

> We admitted we were powerless over alcohol—that our lives had become unmanageable [A.A.'s First Step].
>
> "Why do you think you're back in treatment?" He was not keen on the question, but he might as well give her the word. "One, I'm damned if I know, Louise. Two, I must have conned Gus Larson with my First Step; I don't see how" [Berryman, 1973: 13].
>
> I want to die. I've been trying to drink myself to death. I've lost my wife. She filed for divorce yesterday. All I've got are those two kids of mine. I don't see how this is going to work. It can't. Oh maybe they'll dry me out, that'll be all. I'm a failure. I haven't done a dammed thing for 10 years. Actually I'd rather enjoyed drinking myself to death. But this last month nothing has worked. I can't even get drunk anymore. Do you think it'll work? [Field conversation with 46-year-old male in a detoxification unit, 10 June 1984. This man has just checked himself into a 30-day treatment program].

The alcoholically divided self enters treatment feeling helplessness, frustration, despair, and a sense of mixed hopefulness. He is probably (although not always) intoxicated, or in the process of withdrawal from alcohol. He has surrendered to alcoholism, perhaps not fully, or completely. His interpretive system has collapsed. No longer able to drink successfully, his alcoholism has produced a crisis situation that has precipitated forced or semivoluntary entry into treatment. He must confront anew the meaning of surrender to alcoholism (see Denzin, 1986a: chap. 6). But more important, he must learn *how* to be treated for the disease called alcoholism. This will involve a serious confrontation with A.A.'s First Step. Treatment is organized so as to accomplish this act of surrender. How that is achieved is the topic of this and the next chapter.

The Berryman quote, cited above, suggests that this act of surrender to the First Step may not be complete or successful. Hence, the alcoholic finds himself or herself back in another (or the same) treatment center. The second alcoholic, Fritz, quoted in the opening passage, is undergoing treatment for the first time. He is depressed and suicidal.

In this chapter I study the first phase of surrender and recovery as these two processes intertwine within the quasi-total institutional settings (Goffman, 1961a), that substance abuse centers offer the alcoholic who seeks treatment. My empirical materials are drawn from the following sources. First, I shall draw heavily on Merryman's (1984) study of the recovery process as experienced by a female alcoholic who underwent a four-week residential treatment program. Second, I shall utilize John Berryman's account of his own treatment as given in his *Recovery* (1973). Having gone through several treatment centers for alcoholism, Berryman offers a considerably different view of the recovery process than does Merryman. Third, I draw from my own observations of the treatment process as it occurs in the three treatment centers described in Chapter 1.

The *Six Theses of Recovery* (and alcoholism) organize my interpretation of the treatment process. I assume that central to treatment is the temporal recovery of self that has been lost to alcoholism. Further, I assume that a relational and emotional restructuring of self occurs in treatment. Treatment *treats* alcoholism as a *dis-ease* of emotionality, temporality, social relationships, and self. Treatment locates the self of the alcoholic in the center of the disease called alcoholism. Treatment confronts and exposes the alcoholic's systems of bad faith and denial. Treatment attempts to puncture the drinker's beliefs in self-control. That is, treatment directly addresses the problematics of power and control in the alcoholic's life.

I will take up in order the following topics: (1) the paradoxes of treatment—that is, what does treatment treat, who is doing the treating, and is the alcoholic cured of an illness or a disease when he or she leaves treatment, and (2) the linguistic, temporal, and interactional structures of a "typical" treatment program as these structures are presented to the recovering alcoholic in a three- to four-week program.

THE PARADOXES OF TREATMENT

There are five paradoxes of treatment that involve dilemmas the alcoholic must confront. They may be stated as follows: (1) alcoholism is an incurable illness and disease; (2) alcoholism is an illness and disease that stands for something else; (3) the treatment for alcoholism requires that the patient become the therapist—temporal work on the self is the work of treatment; (4) alcoholism is an emotional illness; and (5) the alcoholic is not unique; rather she suffers from an illness and disease that leads her to believe that she is unique.

These paradoxes set problematics (Becker, 1960, 1964) in front of the alcoholic. Situational adjustments of a group and individual nature are made to them as alcoholics proceed through treatment together. These paradoxes define part of the "culture" of treatment centers. How the alcoholic adjusts to them will determine how he or she will become part of the culture of treatment. It is necessary to discuss each paradox.

The first paradox suggests that the alcoholic must learn that he has an illness that cannot be cured. It can only be placed in remission by abstinence from alcohol. Hence, he does not have an ordinary illness. He is told that alcoholism is a physical, mental, and spiritual illness.

Berryman (1973: 145) offers the following conversation between two patients:

> "What is the disease picture then?" . . . "Well." Severance gulped coffee. "Progressive, fatal, incurable . . . it seems to be *loss of control.* Unpredictability. That's all. A social drinker knows when he can stop. Also, in a general way, his life-style does not arrange itself around the chemical as ours does."

This disease picture of alcoholism is placed before all patients, upon entry into a treatment center. Each of the centers I studied placed Jellinek's (1960, 1962) progressive stages of alcoholism model in front of its clients. In the three treatment centers I observed, alcoholics are given A.A.'s *Big Book* (A.A., 1976) as well as *Twelve Steps and Twelve Traditions* (A.A., 1953). They are told to read A.A.'s discussion of alcoholism as a mental, physical, and spiritual illness.

The second paradox the alcoholic is confronted with elaborates the disease conception of alcoholism. She is told that this illness she has is located inside her and in her relationship to the world. Alcohol is but a symptom of her illness. She drinks alcoholically because she is an alcoholic. She is at the center of her illness. Alcohol merely made her alcoholic. She drank so as to be able to confront the world she lived in. Hence, because she has an incurable illness, she will never again be able to put in her body the symptom that produces yet masks her illness. She must learn that she is powerless over alcohol. Alcohol is poison to her.

Third, because she is at the center of her illness, only she can treat what she has. That is, she is both the patient and the therapist for her illness. This position is phrased as follows by an alcoholism counselor speaking to Berryman and the members of his group in treatment:

> It's been decided on high . . . that you Repeaters need special treatment . . . this is your Group. . . . Group is not just here in this room two hours a day five days a week. . . . Treatment goes on every minute you're awake. . . . Every one of you is on trial; if you don't show definite progress by the end of three weeks, you're out. . . . You've all got to seek each each other out and level with each other and take the risk of confronting each other, namely, give each other hell. . . . Get to work on your Programmes [Berryman, 1973: 42-43].

Several points are important in this journal entry by Berryman. Each bears on the fact that in treatment patients are responsible for treating themselves. First, the group counselor tells the patients that it is "your group." Second, he tells them that treatment does not just occur in group. It occurs during every waking hour. Even when the patients are not in group they are expected to be undergoing treatment. Third, the counselor places every member of the group on trial, charging them to make progress. This reinforces the patient's self-responsibility for treatment. Fourth, he creates a group that extends beyond the temporal boundaries of two hours a day, five days a week. The patients are to become a "pledged" group (Sartre, 1960/1976: 419), fused around the omnipresent threats of not making progress in treatment and leaving treatment to drink again. The patients are told to form relationships with one another that will permit aggressive, confrontative, self-evaluative interactions. Fifth, the patients are told to develop their own "programs" of recovery. Of course they will have to forge their own definitions of what a program is, before they can develop one.

This third paradox reverses all previous understandings the alcoholic has held concerning illness and treatment. If she has internalized her society's norms concerning the sick role (Parsons and Fox, 1978), then she understands that when you are sick you go to a physician for treatment. Now she finds that she has come to a treatment center to treat herself. This will take some time to learn. She may feel that nothing is happening to her while she is in treatment. Berryman (1973:44) offers an exchange between two patients that clarifies this point.

> "When did you come back in?"
>
> "Sunday night. How about you?"
>
> "How does it seem to be going?"
>
> "I didn't get anywhere for ten days. . . . But I made a breakthrough last Friday."

The patient, then, must learn how to treat herself, and she must learn that her treatment will occur in a setting where everyone else has the same mandate. To treat herself, to build a treatment program for herself, to confront others, to be confronted by others, this is what treatment is. A reciprocity of sharing and confrontation underlies the recovery process.

The recovering alcoholic must, under the third paradox of treatment, learn to transcend her own self-centeredness. She must learn how to apply a group perspective to her recovery. She is taught the language of A.A., which is a group, not an individual language of self. Hence, although she is responsible for her own treatment, that treatment occurs within and derives from a group point of view. She must enter a group in order to treat herself.

Berryman's conversation reveals another central theme of treatment, and that is temporality. When the woman states, "I didn't get anywhere for ten days," she underscores perhaps the most basic feature of treatment. That is, treatment occurs within time (Roth, 1963). But treatment's time is the patient's time. This is time no longer experienced through the altered temporal consciousness that alcohol once gave the alcoholic. Hence, treatment passes slowly, then rapidly, as "break-throughs" are experienced, then slowly again, as the patient waits for another breakthrough to occur. Because she produces her own break-throughs, the patient realizes treatment only through her own temporality and her own being in time (see Heidegger, 1927/1962). Because she has previously led an inauthentic temporal existence—locked into the past, or running always from the future, never living in the now of the present—the patient expects others to work time for her. They will not do this, as Berryman's counselor pointed out to his group. Waiting for things to happen within time, the patient then experiences treatment as a waste of time. Berryman offers an instance of this critical point. He states: "Sometimes long periods seemed to drag without one word being spoken by anybody in the entire room" (Berryman, 1973: 15).

Merryman (1984: 104) offers another instance. His subject is speaking with her psychiatrist. He has asked how things are going. She indicates that not much is happening and she feels that her counselor is not helping her. He states: "Can she make treatment happen for you?"

The fourth paradox the alcoholic encounters involves a further elaboration of her illness. She is told that her illness is emotional. She learns that she has never expressed the emotions that have led her to drink. She is told that she must get in touch with her emotions, for if she does not she will drink again. A counselor in Northern phrased this position as follows:

> You have an emotional illness. Alcoholism is an emotional illness. You have all lived in an emotional prison. You are all afraid and lonely. You can't trust anybody, including yourself. You're trapped in your past. You're afraid to feel. You don't know how to feel. You're all sick as Hell! Now get to work" [field observation, April 14, 1981].

Merryman reports this comment made by a lecturer on alcohol addiction:

> In the real world we were never taught to identify our feelings—glad, sad, mad, hurt, lonely. But even if our heads didn't know we were having an emotion, our bodies were feeling a whole lot of things [Merryman, 1984: 98-99].

Berryman (1973: 71) offers an additional example. A counselor is speaking to a patient: "You've got to get in touch with your feelings. If you *knew* how resentful you are, maybe you wouldn't drink. You've got to learn to level with your feelings—get them out in the open."

The alcoholic is told that if he drinks again, he will court both death and insanity. Indeed his treatment center will inform him of the casualties of his illness, perhaps relaying the recent death of a former patient who has returned to drinking (Berryman, 1973: 59; Merryman, 1984: 344, 347).

These statements are meant to suggest to the alcoholic that he has buried his emotions beneath his alcoholism. He is told that he has never been in touch with the "real" self that he has buried inside. He is told that he drinks because of his emotions. Further, he is informed that he has lived in his body the emotions he has lacked words to express.

A psychiatrist in Northern is speaking to a patient:

> You don't even have the right words for your emotions. You talk about feeling, but you can't feel. Your body does. Listen to your body. Listen to your emotional reactions in your back, in your stomach. When you feel pain in your body your emotions are trying to tell you something (field observation, April 20, 1981).

The patient is told that he has an inadequate language of emotion. He is told that his body feels what he should feel with his head. His emotions are given an autonomy of force that is seen as expressing a level of reality he has not been in touch with. Treatment teaches a new language of emotions and emotionality to the alcoholic. He or she will learn to use such words as leveling, conning, resentment, and dry drunk (see Glossary). He or she will learn to make a distinction between primary and secondary emotions and will learn how to talk about an emotion and how to feel an emotion.

The Theory of Self in Treatment

Prior to treatment the alcoholic has lived a theory of self that hinged on the denial of alcoholism and the alcoholic pursuit of a fictional "I" that alcohol would hopefully bring into existence (Denzin, 1986a; Tiebout, 1954). He has experienced a division in his inner emotional life, perhaps attempting to hide, or mask from others large portions of who he is and who he has become. He has presented a self to others that is not the self he feels in his inner self-conversations. Treatment attempts to shatter this theory of self. The alcoholic is presented with an entirely different theory of how a person comes to know the "real" self that lies beneath the facades of everyday life. Treatment rests on a fourfold theory of self. In Northern it was presented to the patients in terms of the *Johari Window* (also see Merryman, 1984: 71). Introduced into the human relations field by Luft in 1961, the Johari Window addresses the problem of self-awareness. It appears as follows:

JOHARI WINDOW

Known to Others	I Open	II Blind
Not Known to Others	III Hidden	IV Unknown

In Northern this window was modified as follows: Quadrant I was labeled "Free," quadrant II "Secret," quadrant III "Blind," and quadrant IV "Unconscious." In human relations training for self-awareness, quadrant I represents behaviors known to self and others. Quadrant II, the Blind cell, represents behaviors known to others, but not the self. Quadrant 3, the Hidden cell, represents behaviors known to the self, but not others. The Unknown quadrant, IV, represents behaviors known neither by self or by others. "One important goal of human relations training is to increase the size of the public area (quadrant I) and to reduce the blind and hidden areas (quadrants 2 and 3)" (Goodstein, 1984: 161).

Patients at Northern were told that they were blind and self-deluded and did not know who they were. They were told that they would have to learn how to *level* with others about how they felt. In so doing they would perhaps be able to find the self they had hidden from others. The Patient Workbook given to all patients stated: "We level when we take the risk of being known by spontaneously reporting our feelings. For example, we are leveling when we let someone know that we are hurt, or afraid or angry."

In addition to leveling, patients are told they must learn how to confront others. Confrontation was defined at Northern as "presenting a person with himself by describing how I see him." Rather than pleasing others by telling them what they want to hear about themselves, patients are told to be direct. This directive was phrased as follows at Northern:

> If we care about our fellow group members, and if we want them to be honest with us in return, we will present them with our picture of them. . . . Confrontation is most useful when spoken with concern and accompanied with examples of the confronted behavior or data. For example, "You seem hostile because of the sarcastic answers you give." "Your face is so red that you seem very angry." We are most useful as confronters when we are not so much trying to change another person as we are trying to help

> him see himself more accurately. Change, if it comes, comes later when a person chooses it and enlists the spiritual help that the Sixth and Seventh steps of the A.A. Program describes. Because of our egocentric *blindness* and self-delusion we are *all* dependent on others for that completed picture. Confrontation provides it [patient workbook, p. 4].

Leveling and confronting are reciprocal processes that refer, respectively, to self and other. Although based on the language of group therapy, these two terms relate directly to Cooley's (1902/1956) concept of the "looking-glass self" and Mead's "I" and "me" of social interaction. Treatment asks the alcoholic to seriously learn how to see himself from the point of view of others (me). And further, the patient is told to feel, not mask, those feelings of self that are derived from the reflected appraisals of others. He is also told that his inner "I" has been hidden from him. If he thinks he knows who he is he has deluded himself.

He is told that he has hidden behind the public self of heavy drinker. Indeed, by denying his alcoholism, he has presented himself to the world through the false sense of self alcohol has given him. The alcoholic is told that if he does not get in touch with the secret and buried selves of his past he will not recover. He is told that these structures of self are hidden behind the false emotions he presents to others. If the alcoholic does not penetrate this emotional facade he has placed in front of himself, he will not recover and uncover the deep, underlying reasons that lead him to drink. *The recovery of self through emotionality is the underlying premise of treatment.* Leveling and confrontation, coupled with group therapy and patient-to-patient interaction, are the mechanisms that treatment provides for this recovery of self.

This position is phrased as follows at Northern:

> Most of us tend to think we already know ourselves and are afraid of looking bad, so it is hard for us to take the risk of being revealing and genuine. But what have we really got to lose? Remember how unsuccessful our previous attempts to change have been. Since we can't change something until we really see it, and accept its existence, we shoud ask ourselves, "Do I really accept something if I keep it a secret?" Risking openness is the key. When you are tempted to withdraw into silence, remember, that we are all in the same boat, and a common feeling of everyone, when introduced to group, is *fear*.
>
> Try leveling with the feeling of fear for a start, and discover how that makes you feel. You will probably find, as others have, that when you report a feeling, you modify it. Keeping it a secret seems to increase its power. If we don't begin now to risk being genuine and self-revealing, when will we ever really do it?

The fourth paradox of treatment hinges on the fact that the alcoholic must undergo the painful exposure of these buried structures of self that she has kept hidden from herself and from others. Accordingly, not only must she undergo pain, but she must expose herself to others in ways that will cause embarrassment, anger, and fear. The protective structures of self that Goffman (1959) has identified, including the maintenance of fronts, impression management, collusion, the idealization of self-performances, the misrepresentation of self, mystification, secrecy, self-pride, and dramaturgical circumspection must all be set aside if the alcoholic is to recover the self she has lost to alcoholism. Similarly, treatment is organized so as to penetrate the feeling-rules individuals utilize so as to manage their emotionality in everyday life (Hochschild, 1983). Treatment attempts to lay bare the underlying emotional structures of the self. The valued presentations of self in treatment are predicated on a model of self that is distinctly not dramaturgical.

Treatment, then, rests on a theory of self that does not reside in the books of etiquette the patient has been taught to internalize and practice in everyday life. Rather, treatment presumes that a deep level of self exists beneath the surface levels of the self the alcoholic has hidden behind. Treatment assumes that the self, at the deep, inner, moral level of the person (Heidegger, 1982) is the real person. That person, the alcoholic is told, is afraid, immature, warped, distorted, and angry. Treatment attempts to bring this level of the person to the surface. It will give the alcoholic a set of tools (A.A.'s steps) by which the new (but old) self may be brought into sober existence.

The *fifth paradox of treatment* is the *paradox of uniqueness*. The alcoholic enters treatment under a unique set of circumstances. A multiplicity of events has produced a crisis situation in her life that has brought her into the treatment center. These events are uniquely hers. She brings to treatment a unique personal history. She drank in ways that were solely hers. The collapse of self she has experienced is, she believes, special and unique to her. She arrives in treatment deeply sunken inside herself, desperately holding onto the belief that she is unique and special. Merryman's female alcoholic expressed this belief in the following words: "Well, I'm not sure I'm an alcoholic. . . . I'm not like *any* of the people here" (Merryman, 1984: 63).

Treatment shatters the myth of self-uniqueness. A counselor at Eastern told her group:

> You're all a bunch of drunks. You're not special, you're not unique. You're all alcoholics. You all hid the booze, you lied to get it, you hurt

> your families. You cheated others. You lied to yourself. You'll die of terminal uniqueness if you don't get to work! [field observation, February 20, 1983].

The alcoholic is required to surrender to the myth of self-uniqueness, so as to be able to recover the inner self alcohol has taken away. An A.A. lecturer at Western phrased this position in the following words:

> We're not bad people trying to get better. We're sick people trying to get well. We each have something unique to offer. We are each unique individuals. But we're all alike. We're alcoholics. We can't find what is special inside us until we accept how we are all alike. Then we start to get better. Then we start to find a power greater than ourselves outside ourselves [field observation, May 2, 1983].

To summarize, the treatment the alcoholic receives is self-induced and self-produced, yet it occurs within a group context. Others will facilitate her self-discoveries, but she must do the temporal work of treatment. This work will only begin when she stops believing in her self-uniqueness. Only she can start her treatment and only she can end it. Treatment provides the context of discovery for the recovery of self.

The alcoholic finds that she must cast aside her previous understandings of what treatment for an illness involves. She will be given no pain killers or tranquilizers. If she receives any medication it will be given to her by the medical staff. She can no longer medicate herself. Any drugs she may have brought into treatment with her will be confiscated (see Merryman, 1984: 55, for a description of this "drug search" each patient undergoes upon admission into treatment).

Treatment presupposes a radical restructuring of self. This restructuring cuts to the very core of the open, blind, hidden, and unknown structures of the alcoholic's self. The alcoholic does not understand this process, or what it entails when she enters treatment crying out for help.

The work of treatment is biographical and historical. A new language of self and emotionality is given to the alcoholic as she attempts to discover, through the twin processes of leveling and confronting, the underlying reasons in her life that led her to drink. It is not enough for the alcoholic to get sober in treatment. She must uncover the reasons she has hidden from herself that could or will take her back to alcoholic drinking again. Treatment assumes, then, that once an alcoholic, always an alcoholic. Yet there are two kinds of alcoholics, active or drinking and recovering. Before I turn to the temporal and interactional structures of treatment that are presented to an alcoholic who enters a treatment center, it is necessary to examine briefly how the language and beliefs of A.A. are woven into the patient's treatment program.

THE TWELVE STEPS OF ALCOHOLICS ANONYMOUS AND TREATMENT

In each of the treatment centers that I observed, patients were immediately exposed to the Twelve Steps of A.A. This was done through attendance at A.A. meetings, through lectures on A.A. by counselors and outside A.A. speakers, and by reading the A.A. literature. In Northern, alcoholics were given a patient workbook when they were admitted into treatment. I quote from the first page of that workbook:

> WELCOME. . . .
>
> to our treatment program—with all the fears and frustrations that accompany you here. We wish you to know that we care about you. We are here to support you and to assist you in arresting your illness.
>
> We would like to introduce you to our program with the following message—from Chapter Five of "ALCOHOLICS ANONYMOUS":
>
> *"Rarely have we seen a person fail who has thoroughly followed our path. Those who do not* recover are people who cannot or will not completely give themselves to this simple program, usually men and women who are constitutionally capable of being honest with themselves."
>
> The "Steps" listed below are the foundation of our treatment program. You will find them easy to read, but far more difficult to understand and accept. With this, you will have help and as you accept, you will experience personal change and the start of recovery.

The Steps of A.A. (see Glossary; A.A., 1953, 1976) followed this statement. Patients were next informed that the chemical dependency program they were a part of was based on the philosophy of A.A. and that the disease they suffered from was a family illness. The patient handbook stated: "We use a multidisciplinary approach and treat the physical, emotional, social, mental and spiritual deterioration characteristic of this illness. . . . Here recovery is the patient's responsibility. Passive submission or compliance with treatment does not work." They were told that the entire family would have to be treated and that this was the purpose of "Family Week," which would occur in the last week of treatment.

Told that they and their family members were sick, the alcoholics at Northern were then reminded that their treatment would end in one short month. The prospects of maintaining a recovery program after treatment was next raised. Clients were urged to sign up for aftercare. This was an outpatient counseling program that would potentially involve the patient and his or her family for a minimum of one year in weekly therapy sessions.

The following points need to be taken from these directives that were issued to the patients at Northern. First, each of the paradoxes of treatment is addressed explicitly. The alcoholic is told that his illness can be arrested. He is told that his illness is a relational, or family, illness, and that it is physical, emotional, social, mental, and spiritual in nature. He is also told that his recovery is "almost entirely (his) responsibility." His illness is his personal problem. He will recover if he honestly expresses feelings toward other patients. This process inspires fear. He is told that he shares this fear with every other patient. In this statement the treatment center attempts to produce the interactional conditions that will promote the emergence of a "group" point of view. He is told that he may discover the "real you" that has been buried within his alcoholism.

By attempting to draw the family members of the alcoholic into treatment, Northern broadens the patient's understanding of his illness. At the same time it increases the cost of treatment. The alcoholic is told that extended treatment will last for at least one year. He is also encouraged to become involved in Alcoholics Anonymous. As this statement welcomes the patient to Northern, it suggests that he too can become a successful alumnus. This may well be the last thought the alcoholic has in his mind as he reads these words on his first day in treatment.

By presenting A.A.'s Twelve Steps on the first page of the patient's workbook, Northern anchors recovery in A.A. The quotation from chapter five of *Alcoholics Anonymous* (A.A., 1976: 58) suggests that Northern has the path to recovery. By coopting A.A.'s position, and weaving it into a treatment program that involves aftercare, Family Week, group counseling, leveling, and confrontation, Northern indicates how the modern treatment center depends upon A.A. for any success it might achieve in the field of alcohol rehabilitation. The alcoholic will soon learn that he must master A.A.'s first Five Steps before he "graduates" from Northern in "approximately one short month."

In short, a mutually beneficial partnership, or symbiotic relationship, exists between this treatment center and A.A. Indeed, this state of symbiosis underlies virtually any treatment program the alcoholic might enter. Although A.A. does not lend its name to any treatment center, affiliate with any treatment institution, or employ any treatment professionals, it willingly permits any treatment center that so desires to utilize its texts and program of recovery. This mutually beneficial relationship between A.A. and the modern treatment center permits A.A. to broaden its membership base, while giving treatment centers a successful program upon which they can base their appeal to the prospective alcoholic client. Because many treatment centers employ recovering alcoholics as counselors, or treatment directors, they are often led to rely upon A.A. for the production of these members.

THE LANGUAGES OF TREATMENT

Patients are presented with a complex and new vocabulary of terms that reference a language they must learn to speak and understand while they are in treatment. Not only must they come to understand the words and terms contained in A.A.'s Twelve Steps, but they must also master a language of group therapy. At Northern the following terms were presented to patients in their patient workbooks: communication, addiction, aftercare, Alcoholics Anonymous, black-out, chemical dependency, concerned person, confronting, congruence, treatment plan or program, controlling, defenses, delusion, dry drunk, troubled dysfunctional family (chemically dependent family), enabler, family disease, feeling, group therapy, halfway house, head tripping, intervention, letting go, leveling, locked in, nurturing family, primary disease, recovery program, self-growth, spirituality, treatment, tunnel vision, wholeness. (See the Glossary for a definition of these terms.) As given meaning, the words they define are intended to give the patient and her or his counselor a commonsense language that will permit the discovery of the "real" self of the alcoholic. They are terms that allow patients and staff to confront one another through a "group therapy" language. The use of these words sets the battleground for treatment, inasmuch as they will be used as weapons by patients as they "confront" and "level" with one another.

The following interaction, between two patients at Western, illustrates this point. The first speaker, A (a 45-year-old male, in treatment for three weeks), is confronting a new patient, C (also male, 35 years old), who has been on the unit for 6 days.

A to C: I don't like what you said in group this morning. You're not being honest with Ed. You know you don't like him. You know he reminds you of your father. Yet you told him you liked him and wanted to be his friend. You know you hate him. Come on, start leveling, get honest, you're still trying to please people and be everybody's friend. You enable yourself and Ed when you do this and you're trying to control his emotions to make him feel better. *How do you feel about you?* Get honest for Christ's sake! You know I'm only trying to help you, don't get mad [field observation, July 12, 1983].

If key terms on the above list of words were carefully defined, a large number of pivotal words that surrounded these terms were left undefined. No definitions were given to the following: blaming, placating, computing, distracting, disease, recognition, admittance, acceptance, principles of A.A., anger, rationalizing, denial, justifying, bullying, fear, intellectualizing, projection, grandiose, judgmental, intolerant, fixing, helping, hurt, sadness, rejection, joy, natural high, feeling person, cold emotional statement, high self-worth, using, defensive, compulsively, inner peace, serenity, calm, nurturing system.

Despite the fact that these words were not defined, their presence in the patient handbook sets an interpretive frame within which treatment occurs. They establish the context for an emotional language of self. That they are undefined indicates that "intellectual" definitions are not warranted. Patients must be able to feel their way into the meaning these terms have for them. Paradoxically, the emotional language of treatment requires an elaborate dictionary of meanings and definitions.

Two Languages of Emotionality

Two languages of emotionality exist side by side in treatment. The first is the *meta-language of emotionality*; a language about the language of emotions and treatment. This language includes such terms as *head-tripping, leveling,* and *confronting*. Second, there is the language of direct and indirect emotionality, expressed in the phrase "learn to communicate on a *feeling* level." At this feeling level, terms require no definition. At the meta-level definitions are required and are given. That is, the technical language of treatment in fact requires a definition of terms, including what a chemical dependent is, what a family disease is, and what a harmful dependency consists of. The meanings in this language must be conveyed before the language of emotionality that exists beneath and within it can be conveyed. That language will often be conveyed in words of vulgarity and profanity, with specific reference to biological functions.

Treatment, then, exists on two levels of meaning: the technical and the emotional. In order for the emotional work of treatment to be accomplished, the technical language must be communicated. It is that language that constitutes the framework inside of which emotional work occurs.

The language of direct and indirect emotionality is subdivided in treatment into two forms: the language *about* feelings and the language *of* feelings. A language of direct feeling is the language of anger, hurt, guilt, and resentment. A language about these feelings mediates the patient's thinking about the feeling and the direct expression of feeling. Merryman (1984: 100) illustrates this difference with the following dialogue. A counselor asks a patient what she is feeling:

> "I feel like I really want to sink right through the floor." A fellow patient replies: "Any sentence with a 'that' or a 'like' in it doesn't give a true feeling. Feelings are mad, glad, sad . . . "

This exchange reduces the expression of emotionality to the linguistic format the speaker uses when speaking of or about her emotions (see Wittgenstein, 1955). Words such as "like" or "that," which come before purely emotional words, are seen as diminishing the emotional feeling that is felt by the speaker. Such bracketing is regarded as undesirable. The patient is taught to select carefully the words she uses when she expresses her feelings.

The emotional languages of treatment (meta, of, and about) are given greater detail by the following list of words patients are presented with as they construct their treatment programs. These terms were given to patients at Northern as potential problem areas in their lives: aggressive, amoral, approval seeking, avoiding, blaming, compliant, controlling, denial, dependent, dishonest, egocentric self-centered, faith/hope lacking, financial (problems), goals (vague or none), grief stricken, indifferent, irresponsible, intellectualizing, judgmental, legal (problems), manipulative, marital, family, medical, mistrusting, passive, pride, rationalizing, self-concept, social skills, sexuality, spirituality, vocational, withdrawal.

Upon examining this list, patients at Northern were told by their group counselors that there had been a mistake in the list and that three terms had been left off. These three terms were *guilt, anger,* and *resentment*. These are the emotions A.A. says are most likely to take the alcoholic back to drinking (A.A., 1976: 54-56; 1953: 44-45; 1967: 11, 48, 68, 83, 92, 99, 140, 311).

More important, perhaps, than taking the alcoholic back to drinking, is the fact that these emotions appear on those pages of A.A.'s texts that contain discussions of the Fourth and Fifth Steps. These, of course, are the two central steps (in addition to the First) Northern asks the alcoholic to take before leaving treatment. At this fundamental level of intertexuality (Kristeva, 1974), A.A. is woven directly and deeply into the treatment experiences of the recovering alcoholic.

Alcoholics Anonymous: The Third Language of Treatment

I have identified two languages of treatment: the technical language of group therapy and chemical dependency, and the language of direct and indirect emotionality. The third language of treatment is the language of Alcoholics Anonymous. This language is contained in A.A.'s *Big Book*, in the Twelve Steps, and in the Twelve Traditions. It confronts patients immediately in the form of the Twelve Steps, as given on the first page of their patient workbook.

These Twelve Steps contain the following problematic terms and phrases: admitted, powerless, "lives had become unmanageable," "came to believe," "power greater than ourselves," restore, sanity, will, "lives," "care of God," "as we understood him," searching, fearless, "moral inventory," "admitted to God," "exact nature," "wrongs," "entirely ready," remove, "defects of character," "humbly," shortcomings, "persons we had harmed," "make amends," (direct amends), "injure," personal inventory, wrong, prayer, meditation, conscious contact, pray, "knowledge of his will for us," "power to carry that out," "spiritual awakening," carry this message, "practice these principles in all our affairs."

Informed that his treatment is based on the "Philosophy of Alcoholics Anonymous," the patient stares at this list of words and at these 12 steps and wonders what they mean. A sense of bewilderment and confusion is experienced. "What is a Step?" he asks. "How do I take a Step?" The following statement from a patient in Northern for five days evidences this confusion. A 32-year-old insurance salesman, he asks his group counselor:

> What in the hell is a Step? How do I take these dammed things? How long does it take? When do I know I'm done? What if I don't take them?

His counselor replied:

> If you don't take them you'll drink and die or go insane. You've got no choice. You'll work these steps the rest of your life if you're serious about this business. I do. It works. I've been sober on these steps 8 years now. The only step you can take successfully and to perfection is the First Step. If you don't drink today you've taken that step. If you take that step back and drink again you'll go insane, just like you were when you got here. And your life will become even more unmanageable than it already is. Get the picture? These steps are here to help you get well [field observation, May 22, 1981].

Treatment at Northern was organized so as to give the patients a working familiarity with each of the Twelve Steps. Lectures were held every afternoon on one of the Steps. Patients were required to form small groups of three and four and hold group discussions on what each step meant to their group. They were then required to select a group spokesperson who would present the group's point of view to the entire patient community.

The third language and the third level of meaning that treatment relies upon is, then, the language of A.A. This language permeates, as a threatening presence, every interaction that occurs between patients and their counselors. Knowing that they will take a Fifth Step before they leave treatment, patients are constantly asking one another if they have started on this Step. But before they can take their Fifth Step, they must take the First Step. This is the business of the first week in treatment (see next section).

I turn next to the temporal structures of treatment that mediate and give interactional meaning to these languages of self and emotionality the patient has been presented with.

THE TEMPORAL STRUCTURES OF TREATMENT

Unlike the tuberculosis patient (Roth, 1963), the chronically ill (Fagerhaugh and Strauss, 1977), the mental patient (Goffman, 1961a), or the dying patient (Glaser and Strauss, 1964), who have lingering, indeterminate temporal treatment trajectories, the patient in an alcoholism treatment center has a treatment of specific temporal duration, usually defined in terms of three or four weeks, or one month. This 21-, 28- or 30-day treatment program is further subdivided into three or four one-week intervals. Specific treatment goals are set for each of these smaller time units.

Surrender and Treatment

Treatment is organized around a four-step model of surrender and recovery. Merryman (1984: 108-109) offers a convenient summary of these four steps, quoting a lecturer who is discussing the four stages of recovery:

> "The first," he said, "is the admission that you are an alcoholic. In our definition here, an alcoholic is somebody whose personal, social, or business life is being damaged by alcohol, and who will not or cannot do anything about it. The second stage of recovery is compliance, passively going along with treatment, while inwardly defying and denying. The third is acceptance, the realization that alcoholism is not a failure of moral fiber, but a chronic, fatal disease. The fourth is surrender, the visceral certainty that you are powerless against alcohol and cannot control your addiction by yourself, without help."

Each of the weekly intervals in treatment is built upon this four-step view of surrender and recovery; the ultimate goal of treatment being the alcoholic's complete surrender to alcoholism. Week one is focused on the alcoholic taking A.A.'s first step and completing what is called a "Step One Self-Assessment." This is called the "Recognition of Illness" phase of treatment. Week two is organized around compliance and the denial of alcoholism. It is often termed the "Acceptance of the Illness" phase. It focuses on A.A.'s Second and Third Steps. Week three is focused around the preparation of a Fourth and Fifth Step. That is, patients are required to prepare a "fearless and searching moral inventory of themselves" and to share this inventory with another human being. At Northern, patients shared this with a group and with a pastoral counselor. Week four involves a further push into surrender by the alcoholic and is typically termed "Family Week." Here the patient is confronted by his significant others who share with him the effects of his alcoholism on them. Weeks three and four are termed the "Action" phases of treatment.

In this phase the alcoholic is expected to have discovered her "real" inner self and to have shared this self with others. With this phase, treatment is terminated. Depending on the treatment center, the alcoholic, her family, employer, or insurance company will have paid between $3000 and $6000 for this final act of surrender.

Upon entering treatment the alcoholic is presented with a weekly timetable that will structure each of her days in treatment. A typical daily treatment schedule is as follows:

Organizing the Treatment Day

6:30- 7:00:	wake-up (an alarm, or bell is rung)
7:00- 8:00:	breakfast
8:00- 8:45:	personal housekeeping and unit tasks
8:45- 9:30:	community meeting, lecture
9:30-11:30:	group therapy
11:30-12:15:	lunch
12:15- 1:00:	personal time
1:00- 2:00:	Step group
2:00- 3:00:	lecture
3:00- 5:00:	personal fitness
5:00- 6:00:	dinner
7:00- 8:00:	personal time
8:00- 9:00:	lecture (A.A.)
9:00-12:00:	personal time (all patients in rooms by midnight)

For the first week of treatment no visitors are allowed. Phone calls typically are unrestricted, although at Eastern patients were allowed no phone calls in the first week, which was called "filter." After the first week visitors can be seen on Saturdays and Sundays, usually from 1-8 p.m. Patients are allowed to leave the treatment center and go on walks, if accompanied by another patient. The schedule does not apply to Saturdays and Sundays, the alcoholic's two hardest days in treatment (see below).

The Activities of Treatment

The focused activities of treatment, as suggested by the previous list, are group therapy, A.A. lectures, group meals, personal fitness, or recreational activities, small amounts of personal time, fulfilling unit tasks, and sleeping. If in the outside world the alcoholic lived by a timetable that was largely of his own, his family's, and his employer's making, in treatment he finds that temporal choices have been taken out of his hands.

Furthermore, if he was accustomed to doing what he wanted to do when he wanted to, he finds that his choice has also been removed. The assignment of unit tasks is intended to bring every alcoholic down to a common level. Hence, he will find that he may be given any of the following "tasks" to do on a daily basis: (1) clean ashtrays and pick up in the patient lounge; (2) set up and fold chairs after group lectures; (3) clear tables after each meal; (4) be responsible for the distribution of clean sheets and pillowcases on the unit; (5) ring the morning bell that wakes everyone up; and (6) keep the patient snackroom clean. These menial, largely janitorial, chores are rotated among patients during their three or four weeks in treatment. The forced performance of these assignments is intended to produce a sense of self-responsibility in the patient.

THE RESPONSIBILITIES OF TREATMENT

When she receives this timetable she also receives a list of responsibilities she is expected to fulfill. She will be expected to (1) be up daily by 7:00 a.m.; (2) attend meals three times a day; (3) attend all lectures; (4) attend all group and program activities; (5) go to group therapy daily; (6) go to all unit meetings and concerned persons groups and to one A.A. meeting a week; (7) refrain from smoking in bed, halls, and elevators; (8) wear her name tag at all times (which only gives first name and last initial); (9) be on her unit by 10:00 p.m., and let staff know when she is off the unit; (10) only leave the unit with another person and to sign in and out every 1½ hours; (11) report to the nurse's station at specified times; (12) read her books and complete all written assignments; (13) complete assigned unit tasks; (14) not be in cars with visitors; (15) clear all packages received in the mail through the nursing station; (16) be responsible for preparing a treatment program; and (17) understand that grounds for dismissal from treatment are (a) campus romancing, (b) chemical usage, (c) gambling, (d) leaving unit grounds, and (e) acting out in ways that are harmful to the center as a whole. This last point states that grounds for dismissal are determined by staff consensus and by patient irresponsibility. At Northern all patients "voluntarily" signed a patient agreement form upon admission stating that they understood these responsibilities, and that they had been informed of grievance procedures they could follow should they feel their patient rights had been violated.

THE INTERACTIONAL SETTINGS OF TREATMENT

Treatment is spatially organized into seven main interactional settings. Patients typically are assigned a bed in a double room; rooms having the appearance of being and not being at the same time motel rooms, army barracks, and hospital rooms. This semiprivate room is the only personal space the patient has while in treatment. Often a curtain can be drawn across the patient's half of the room. Northern, Westside, and Eastern each had television lounges and a patient snackroom where food, coffee, and fruit juices were always available. These two settings become the places where patients comingle, come to gossip, talk, and exchange views on how their treatment is going. Berryman offers this example:

> At half past ten he . . . went off to the Snack Room for coffee. Eddie was jittering by the freezer. Jeree looked softly up, Jasper and Mike were arguing. Eddie had come in about four o'clock, in frightful shape, and driven everybody crazy.
>
> Group therapy occurs in small rooms, usually having the capacity for no more than 12 patients. A.A. posters, including the 12 Steps of A.A., the Serenity Prayer, or prints depicting peaceful nature settings may hang on the walls. Group and community lectures often occur in the largest setting in the treatment center, which is the cafeteria.

In addition to these settings, the treatment center may have a recreational or personal fitness unit, including a swimming pool, volleyball or basketball courts, pool tables, weight rooms, and tables for playing cards, chess, or checkers. There may also be, as there was at Northern, nature trails to take walks along, lakes to walk beside, and woods to walk through.

Spatially and architecturally, the treatment center may give the sense of being a sanitarium or a unit in a large countryside hospital (Northern), an old family mansion (Westside), or a downtown residential hotel (Eastern). This sense of being something other than anything the alcoholic has ever been in before locates treatment in a setting that is clearly outside the normal world of affairs. Indeed, "outside" time may stop for the alcoholic. Daily newspapers may not be allowed. The evening news cannot be watched. The alcoholic finds that his time has become someone else's. He has stepped outside time in order to be treated for his disease of time.

LIFE ON THE TREATMENT UNIT

As the alcoholic fits herself to the temporal rhythms of the treatment center, her days come to take on a predictable shape. Berryman (1973:

81) observes: "Life on the ward became *really* existential only from ten to noon five days a week, and in Mini-Group three days."

A patient, Jack, at Northern made the following comments about Easter Sunday on the unit:

> Christ, its Easter. I'm depressed as hell. I got up at 6:00 and did my laundry. Jim and Charlie and I had breakfast together. I tried to take a nap and had bad dreams. The floor is overrun with families and children. Nobody has anyplace to go. They just keep walking up and down the floor, going to the lounge and then turning around and walking back. It's funny, you know. We all seem normal here. It's the families that seem strange and out of place. It's comfortable and nonthreatening here for us. We all have made-up things to do—Charlie has the bell to ring in the morning. Jim has the ashtrays to clean. I have the laundry. But we're all into our heads. This "head-work" is screwing us up. It's like we're all here, but nobody's here. Everybody stands around and waits for a phone call from a relative or a visit. We all get dressed up. For what? Christ, Marilyn wants to know what she should wear—her yellow suit or her blue one? She's not having any visitors. Who does she think she's dressing up for anyway? Ann from Seattle just said, "How can you get your shit together on Easter? You wonder what it's like on Christmas around here." Christ, these weekends are killers. No god damned thing to do! At least we have group during the week. Who wants to read the *Big Book* on Easter? I'm ___ sick and tired of standing in front of group and saying, "Hello, my name's Jack and I'm an alcoholic." I'm tired of smiling when I say that. Christ, Andy's been here six times. How can he say that and believe it? [Field observation, April 19, 1981].

Both Berryman and the patient Jack speak to the existential structure of daily life on the treatment unit. Living a collective life that must confront the hollow gaps of weekends, holidays, Easter Sundays, and family visits, patients in treatment produce for one another a shared sense of "anomie, frustration and despair." Meaningless "make-do" jobs (Goffman, 1961a: 261) do not give the alcoholic who is in treatment a deep sense of purpose. A structure of experience that is collective and shared and that alternates between long moments of emptiness and brief, high-pitched feelings of shared emotionality is thereby lived by each patient. Each patient carves out a mode of existence that is individual and unique, yet derives from this shared group perspective.

Saturday nights, after lecture, are often occasions when patients break out of the collective gloom that pervades daily life on the unit. Merryman (1984: 198) speaks to this point:

> She came out of her room . . . and went into the large lounge. The furniture was pushed at random into one end of the space, as though painters would soon start work. There had been a record dance on Saturday night—a collection taken, pizza ordered in—Abby had gone, feeling like a teenager, relieved to detach herself in time and space.

The simple acts of ordering in pizza, of dancing and playing records can transform ward life into a temporal structure of shared emotionality that draws patients together, and out of—if only briefly—the mundane, yet troubling solitude they live on a daily basis.

Summary

I have discussed the central paradoxes of treatment, as well as the linguistic, interactional, and temporal structures that organize experience. I turn now to the First Step Inventory the alcoholic prepares during the first week of treatment.

WEEK ONE: FIRST STEP INVENTORY

Soon after entry into a treatment center the alcoholic is asked to fill out a "chemical assessment sheet." Often administered by an intake counselor, this assessment sheet asks the alcoholic questions such as the following:

(1) What chemicals have you used?
(2) How much and how often have you taken these chemicals?
(3) What is your drug of first choice? Second choice?
(4) How long have you used these chemicals?
(5) With whom do you use these chemicals?
(6) Describe how your behavior changes when you use these chemicals, compared to when you are straight.
(7) Have you ever hidden alcohol from yourself or from others?

The alcoholic is also asked to discuss the effects chemical use has had upon his relationships with others. He is asked:

(8) How do you get along with your family? Describe your relationship with each family member.
(9) Has your chemical use affected your family relationships?
(10) How does your family respond to your present situation?
(11) How has your chemical use affected your relationship with your friends?

(12) What do your friends say about your chemical use?
(13) Relate and explain any incidents or dangerous situations involving yourself or others due to your chemical use.

Questions concerning the alcoholic's self-concept are also raised:

(14) How do you feel about yourself?
(15) What are your goals and values?
(16) How have your goals and/or values changed due to your drug/alcohol use?

The alcoholic will be asked to repeat his answers to these questions in his third group day.

A consideration of these 16 questions reveals several points concerning how treatment conceptualizes the alcoholic and his "addiction." First, these questions make the alcoholic's relationship to the object alcohol and the social act of drinking problematic. By transforming alcohol into a chemical, questions 1-6 suggest to the alcoholic that he is a chemical dependent, not an alcoholic—that is, he is a drug dependent.

This transforms him into an addict, when he may have previously thought of himself as just an alcoholic. By placing him in the category of drug or chemical dependent, treatment widens the boundaries of deviance that now encircle the problem drinker. Treatment for chemical dependence places the alcoholic in the company of drug addicts, including heroin, cocaine, marijuana, PCP, and speed users. He will also find himself in the presence of prescription drug abusers, including persons addicted to Valium and other psychoactive mood-altering chemicals. The first six questions on the chemical assessment sheet tell the alcoholic that he has joined the world of chemical dependents, or drug addicts. Because his drug of choice was alcohol, he is as much of a chemical dependent as are drug addicts and persons dually addicted to alcohol and other drugs.

When the alcoholic is confronted with question 7, "Have you ever hidden alcohol from yourself or from others," he is forced to confront the fact that maybe he is not the first person who has attempted to protect his supply from others. If that is in fact the case, then perhaps he is not a normal drinker. He knows that normal drinkers do not hide their alcohol.

An alcoholic in his third day of treatment at Northern asked a fellow patient:

> Did you really hide the stuff from your wife? I kept mine behind the dictionary in the bookcase.

His friend replied:

> Hell, yes. I had it behind the tool box in the truck. The boys at work were always kidding me about my "secret supply." We all used it. The wife never knew tho' [field observation, April 20, 1982, Eastern].

By sharing this information about themselves, these two patients solidify a personal relationship. They also confirm their lack of uniqueness concerning the hiding of alcohol.

Questions 2 and 4 locate the alcoholic's drug use in personal history. The intent is to create a personal identity of the alcoholic as a user who has a particular history, or biographical relationship, with alcohol. By asking how much and how often the alcoholic takes these chemicals, the assessment sheet attempts to reveal to the alcoholic how much she in fact uses on a daily or weekly basis. Question 6 asks the alcoholic to estimate how her drug of choice affects her behavior when with others. This question is developed in questions 9, 10, 11 and 12. Question 13 locates chemical use with dangerous situations in the alcoholic's life.

The personal identity themes of this chemical assessment sheet are elaborated in the three questions on self-concept, goals, and values. Here the alcoholic is asked to assess the effects of her drinking on her goals, values, and views of herself.

These 16 questions transform *facticities*, or lived experiences, into facts. They become objective indicators of lived experiences with alcohol and with drinking. As such they shift treatment immediately up to the level of shared, social experience, for each patient is expected to share this "factual" information about herself with Group. Once shared, this information becomes part of the group's collective conscience (Durkheim, 1897/1951) regarding alcohol use and its abuse. A shared group identity of "chemical dependent," "alcoholic," "dual addict," or "user" is thus forged out of the answers to this simple chemical assessment sheet.

Those 16 questions deal with both specific instances of lived experience and with generalities, or abstractions concerning the patient's life goals and values. A two-edged reflective stance toward alcohol's presence and effects on the drinker's life is produced. That is, by reflecting on how much he drinks, how often, with whom, and by examining the effects his alcohol use has on his friends and his family, the alcoholic is forced to see that alcohol has permeated every sector of his life.

Second, because questions 15 and 16 speak to the generalities of goals and values, the drinker is forced to ask himself if he in fact has any goals or values left in life. The intent of the assessment sheet is to set in motion a chain of inner thought that reveals to the alcoholic how *unmanageable* his life has become and how *powerless* he in fact is over alcohol. These, of course, are the two key terms in A.A.'s First Step.

The first several days of treatment are meant, then, to make the alcoholic acutely aware of his powerlessness over alcoholic. However, prior to talking in Group, this self-awareness is kept inside the alcoholic's inner stream of consciousness. He has yet to admit and share this powerlessness with others. He is forced to do this in his First Step Group, which will be discussed in the next chapter.

THE GROUP LOCUS OF EMOTIONALITY

Durkheim (1893/1964; cited in Bellah, 1973) has observed that emotions and emotional experience find their location in a society that has a reality that comes before the person. He states that feelings and emotional attitudes are "ways of acting, thinking, and feeling that present the noteworthy property of existing outside the individual consciousness" (Durkheim, 1893/1964: 2). These social facts exist as pressures against the person; they are collective manifestations. They are not the sole property of individuals, although persons create the illusion that they have created the emotions that they feel. Many of the emotions that are felt in the modern world have become solidified into rituals. When followed, these emotional rituals produce sacred, moral selves.

With little difficulty it is possible to translate Durkheim's arguments into the experiences of alcoholics who undergo treatment for their emotional illness of self. Indeed, the five paradoxes of treatment and the three languages of treatment represent collective manifestations of society entering into the inner emotional life of the person. Told that she is not unique, the alcoholic is taught how to interpret emotional experiences within a structure that is outside her. She is directed to a group where she will find the kind of self-treatment it is organized to treat. The languages of treatment become ritual extensions of the alcoholic self. As these languages are learned a new form of selfhood is experienced. The Steps of A.A.—especially Steps Four and Five—ritually embed the self in a social performance that produces a new, sacred self. Yet, treatment contributes to the illusion that the alcoholic is creating these experiences of emotionality. This is done in the directives that charge alcoholics to level and confront one another. Hence, a myth of individuality is sustained within a collective structure of experience that in fact treats every individual the same.

A Durkheimian conception of emotion and treatment suggests that a phenomenology of this process will be lacking to the extent that it does not locate emotion, feeling, meaning, and selves in a collective structure of experience. A purely dramaturgical and interactional analysis of this process is also deficient. This is so because treatment presumes a theory of self and selfhood that lies beneath the surface levels of polite, everyday interaction. A structural and behavioral accounting of emotion (Collins, 1975; Kemper, 1978) will also not explain the emotional experiences alcoholics confront in treatment. Ritual interaction chains (Collins, 1981), theories of emotional arousal, and a picture of emotional interaction being governed by exchange processes will not shed sufficient light on the inner transformations of self that accompany the treatment experience.

A psychoanalytic framework, whether taken from Freud (1954), Lacan (1977), or Kohut (1984) also has limited utility in explaining the emotionality of treatment. Although such frameworks are certainly compatible with treatment's theory of self, they cannot address the collective, Durkheimian nature of emotional feelings that are lodged in a structure outside the individual.

It is apparent that a theory of meaning, language, and feeling in the alcoholism treatment center must be one that is simultaneously collective, interactional, and phenomenological. As the alcoholic learns to internalize and verbalize the disease conception of alcoholism, he or she comes to take on the deviant label of "alcoholic." Yet this label is neutralized by the medical and disease conception of his or her illness (Trice and Roman, 1970). Thus, in a collective fashion, alcoholics learn how to (1) identify the emotions that lie at the core of their illness while (2) they teach one another how to talk the language that makes such understandings and self-identification possible. Their emotions and the meanings they apply to themselves lie in the group interactions they are forced into, and they lie in the collective representations of alcoholism their society has located in the treatment center.

CONCLUSIONS

Prior to the 1972 federal act that decriminalized public intoxication and mandated the establishment of treatment centers for the treatment of alcoholism, the alcoholic in American society was commonly seen as suffering from a lack of willpower and self-control (Beauchamp, 1980; Denzin, 1986a: chap. 1). The institutionalization of this act ushered in a new conception of alcoholism as an emotional disease of self. A new set of collective representations was brought into place and put into practice in the substance abuse treatment center. In such places persons defined as alcoholic now learn how to identify the emotional sickness that lies at the core of their inner selves. The languages of emotion that treatment teaches are transmitted through group interaction processes. Collectively, alcoholics come to assume the situational identity of alcoholic. This new identity can be seen as a situational adjustment to a problematic that is collectively confronted (Becker et al., 1961).

At the core of this identity is a new emotional understanding of self. These new emotions that come to be attached to the self find their origin in a reality that comes before the alcoholic. They reside in the new culture of alcoholism that has emerged within American society since the early 1970s. A new social world of emotionality thus exists in our society. I have shown how that social world is transmitted in and through the treatment process. In so doing I have suggested that a Durkheimian conception of emotionality, when combined with a phenomenological interpretation of emotional experience, offers the fullest interpretation of this social process, which turns on the reconstruction of meaning, language, and feeling in everyday life. Alcoholism, which begins as an individual act embedded in the outer fringes of drinking groups, becomes through treatment a collective phenomenon—a phenomenon that is recreated and redefined within the organizational and institutional structures our society provides for the alcoholic deviant. By grasping the structures of this process we come to better see how the individual's inner emotional life derives its fundamental locus from society itself.

9

EXPERIENCING TREATMENT

> Today something happened. I talked with my wife. I didn't want to get drunk. I think my counselor has helped. I actually have hope today. I think I like these drunks and their meetings. I don't know what's happened. I actually want to live. Of course I'm sober today. I'm going to change my schedule this fall so I can come to those noon meetings [field conversation with Fritz, 23 days into treatment, same individual as quoted at the outset of Chapter 2].

Fritz, the alcoholic who speaks the above lines, evidences the kinds of transformations in self that may occur in treatment. Depressed and suicidal on his first day in a treatment center (see Chapter 2), he is now full of hope and promise 23 days later. In this chapter I examine the group and interactional experiences that structure these transformations in self. They begin and end in group interactions, all of which are organized around A.A.'s first five Steps.

ENCOUNTERING THE GROUP

The recovering alcoholic will encounter two distinctly different structures of group experience while in treatment. The first group she becomes a member of will number anywhere from 10 to 20 patients. This size will vary, however, depending on the treatment center's patient census at time of entry. This is her First Step Group. Her second group will be smaller, usually no more than 10 members. This is her Treatment (or Therapy) Group. Although she will spend no more than a week in her First Step Group, the remainder of her time in treatment will be in the company of her Treatment Group. The members of this group will, in all likelihood, be drawn from her First Step Group.

Both of these groups are short-lived, natural groups, formed out of the treatment encounters forged between patients and counselors. These groups are situationally bound to the treatment center, for the patient is unlikely to ever see any of his fellow group members after treatment ends. They are multiply bonded groups, based on the common identity of "alcoholic." Intense primary relationships, of a short-term duration, are thus formed; these relationships having the capacity (especially in the Treatment Group) of absorbing the patient as a total person. (On these dimensions, see Goffman, 1961b: 7-14.) That is, by the time the patient has taken his Fourth and Fifth Step in his Treatment Group, his fellow group members know more about him than he is likely to have ever shared with any other human being.

His First Step Group will be a non-sex, non-age stratified group. It will be constructed on the basis of who has come into treatment during the weekend, for group therapy presumes a five-day treatment week. Patients are cycled, then, if at all possible, through a five-day First Step Group and a three-week, 15-day, Treatment Group structure. If the First Step Group is non-age and non-sex stratified, the Treatment Group is likely to be formed along same-sex and approximately same-age lines. Intensive treatment replicates the age- and sex-stratified society the alcoholic has stepped out of. It is assumed that matters of sexuality, and deviance—although all alcoholically connected—are best handled within same-sex groups. (Some treatment centers do not follow this pattern, believing that alcoholics must learn how to deal with members of the opposite sex when sober.)

The importance of sexuality and age for the alcoholic's treatment experience is twofold. Perhaps for the first time in his adult life he is thrown into the company of males and females and asked to share his experiences in ways that he had never learned or experienced before. Second, he is likely to form friendships with individuals he would never have met in his everyday interactions in the outside world. In this way treatment exposes the protective shells the alcoholic has built around himself, opening him up to interactional experiences that are assumed to be therapeutic.

An Unexpected Community of Alcoholics: Forms and Varieties of Relationships

Same- and cross-sex relationships and friendships thus form in treatment. These relationships form out of the patient's experiences in First Step Group. In this group (and in treatment more generally, that is, community, group lectures, recreation time), the alcoholic discovers an "unexpected community" (Hochschild, 1973). This unexpected community is based on the shared identity of being an alcoholic in treatment. Out of this shared identity emerges intense social bonds that are complementary, reciprocal, primary, and secondary. Some of the bonds have the characteristic of the parent-child relationship the alcoholic may have experienced, either as a parent or as a child. It is not uncommon, for example, to see an alcoholic in treatment taking a young alcoholic adolescent under her wing and caring for her.

Like the sibling bonds Hochschild (1973: 63-69) discovered in an old-age retirement community, alcoholics form sibling bonds of brotherhood and sisterhood with one another. These bonds involve mutual helping, the sharing of past experiences, the giving of hints regarding how to fill out a Fourth Step Inventory, how to talk in Group, and so on. Rivalry and hostility may emerge within these sibling bonds.

Alongside parent-child and sibling bonds exists the deeper bond of "being alcoholic" together. The alcoholic bond, or the alcoholic relationship, is one based on the common wreckage alcoholism has brought to the lives of the individuals who form the bond. This bond is deep and emotional, admitting of a love, or a caring intimacy that the alcoholic may never have experienced before. The alcoholic bond crosscuts sexual, sibling, and adult-child relationships. It forges the ground of commonality out of which all other relationships in treatment are formed. This bond appears in First Step Group.

There is a fifth relational form the alcoholic may enter in treatment. This is the Leader-Follower relationship that forms between the patient and his or her group counselor. Through a process of identification and surrender (which may be altruistic), the alcoholic may merge her ego and her self in the experiences and the identity of her counselor. The group leader, in Freud's terms (1921/1960: 59), is the group ego ideal, for he or she is a successful recovering alcoholic.

The alcoholic as patient may surrender his identity to the identity of the counselor, perhaps experiencing a transference of emotion that is both emotional and sexual. An emotional bond is thus formed with the group counselor and this may incorporate the polarized feelings of love and hate, for the counselor may be perceived as an other who is making the alcoholic undergo pain. A patient at Northern, in his third week of treatment, expressed these ambivalent feelings toward his counselor as follows:

> You know, I kind of like that old man Walt. He's a lot like my father, but he's sober and he cares and he seems to love us. But the sonofabitch makes me want to hate him. Who in the Hell does he think he is coming off like the High and Mighty, making us eat ________ and all that! Christ, I could kill him. Did you see the way he looked at me yesterday? But you know I think I'm getting better [field conversation, 39-year-old male, June 1, 1982].

Because every alcoholic forms and experiences an individual relationship with and to his counselor, group psychology in treatment is transformed into individual psychology (see Freud, 1921/1960: 56). That is, in each case the original relationship of patient to counselor must be created and reenacted within the context of group interactions. This interactional phenomenon must be woven through the personal history of each alcoholic who comes to treatment. He must learn how to reenact the parent-child, authoritarian, subordinate relationship he he has previously experienced in the other areas of his life. And, he must do this within a structure of shared experience; that is, every other alcoholic confronts this same situation. Every alcoholic in treatment experiences, then, a shattering of previous emotional understandings concerning what a relationship with another human being is like.

These five relational forms the alcoholic experiences in treatment—cross-sex and same-sex friendships, adult-child relations, sibling bonds, the alcoholic bond, and the counselor-patient relationship—set the context from which a group solidarity is formed.

Group Solidarity in Treatment

Treatment groups are pledged groups, in Sartre's (1960/1976: 829) terms, fused around the common goal of being in treatment together. Group members create an idea of themselves as being in group together. In order to act as a group they must form themselves into something they cannot be as individuals—that is, a group. Their Group Counselor becomes a third party who compels them to act as if they were a group. They are brought together as individuals in a room sharing the identity of alcoholics and are then asked to act as a group. They do this by individually internalizing the perspective of the group counselor, and the languages of A.A. and treatment. Bringing these points of view to bear upon their individual conduct they are serially transformed from their individual states of isolation into a shared group consciousness. They learn that their alcoholism is a disease whose meanings and pains can be socially shared.

A triadic process that draws each alcoholic out of her seriality into a common group point of view operates within the treatment group. This process is structured as follows: (1) alcoholic, (2) group, and (3) counselor. The alcoholic's individuality is enveloped within a group structure that is coordinated and held together through the actions of the counselor. A collective group consciousness emerges that aligns each individual within a structure that is larger than she is. This structure is externalized and symbolizes the focus of the alcoholic's daily existence in treatment. That is, five days a week she goes to treatment in group.

In this fashion the group is both outside and inside each individual at the same time. As a collectivity the group is externalized as a process that stands ready to be mobilized each time the group comes together. Yet the group is only what its members bring to it; the counselor will not do the work of the group. That is the assignment of each individual. The counselor is, then, the symbol of what the members must do for themselves. But more important, he or she is the means by which they may individually do only what they can do in group.

Out of this process emerges a solidarity and sense of "we-ness." This solidarity is fused through the sharing of the destructive experiences the identity of alcoholic has brought to the patient who is now in treatment and in group. By revealing himself to the group and by sharing in the experience of other members doing the same thing, the alcoholic discovers a new view of himself that could only have been given by becoming a member of the treatment group. A primary group, in Cooley's (1902/1956) sense, appears. The alcoholic feels as if he has come "home" to a group he has never before belonged to. He begins, in Schutz's (1964) terms, as a "stranger" to treatment and ends up a "homecomer," for he has found a place for himself, no matter how transitory, in his "Treatment Group." If his recovery is to continue after treatment, he will have to repeat this process in the A.A. groups he will find in his "home" community. If he fails to do so, he will lose what treatment has given him. He will lose his identity of "recovering alcoholic," and become once again a "stranger" in his "home."

FIRST STEP GROUP

These preliminaries discussed, I turn now to First Step Group. I shall offer a brief narrative account of how First Step Group works in the alcoholic's first week in treatment.

It is 9:30 on a Monday morning. In a large room that looks out over rolling hills and a lake are 16 men and women seated on folding chairs in a circle. They are in Hill House, the group therapy building at Northern. Alice, their First Step Counselor, introduces herself: "My name is Alice and I'm an alcoholic. Welcome to First Step Group. Let's go around the room and introduce ourselves. Mary, you go first."

> "My name's Mary Jones." Alice cuts in. "No, your name is Mary and you are an alcoholic. We don't want to know your last name. Look at your name tag. We don't use last names here." Mary corrects herself. "My name's Mary and I'm an alcoholic." Mary starts to cry, turning away from the group, trembling. The group looks away. Alice turns to Mary and says: "That's O.K. We all had to say it for the first time."

Informed, if they had not learned this earlier, that they are to introduce themselves by their first names only, followed by the word "alcoholic," the members of the group proceed to follow Alice's instructions, each member introducing himself or herself as instructed. Alice continues:

> We're here for one purpose. To find out if you're alcoholics. That's why you have your First Step Inventories and your First Step Assessments. We are going to go through your answers to these questions. Each of you is going to talk. Who can tell me what the First Step says?

Speaking to the First Step

Although each of these speakers in this First Step group will take a different stance toward the First Step, their speech acts collectively to create a conversational context in which alcoholism is openly discussed. This is the importance of this first session in group. Each alcoholic in the room knows that he or she will have to speak and answer Alice's questions. First Step Group, then, produces a context in which the alcoholic discovers, through her own talk, how it is that she is an alcoholic. If she does not speak, she does not make that discovery. According to treatment she makes that discovery by applying the First Step to herself. She must come to see that she is powerless over alcohol.

She must understand that her life is unmanageable. First Step Group conversations are about powerlessness and unmanageability. The alcoholic speaker is forced to illustrate, from lived experiences, how alcohol has taken control of her life.

Transforming Experience

In First Step Group the alcoholic learns, then, that the unique features of his life are of no particular interest to those who are managing his treatment. He is just an alcoholic who has finally found his way into a treatment center.

This movement back and forth from the unique to the general, from the lived experiences of the alcoholic to the interpretive structures of A.A. and treatment, becomes the overriding theme of the alcoholic's experiences while in treatment. He must return again and again to the unique features of his life as an active alcoholic. From those experiences he must find the general patterns that make him an alcoholic.

In lecture the alcoholic is informed that he belongs to a selfish program. He is told that by helping others he helps himself. He is also told that in order to keep what he has, he has to give it away. If he does not have sobriety he can't help anyone else. Therefore, he must return to the presence of other alcoholics in order to remain sober and to continue recovery. He is told that nonalcoholics can neither understand his illness nor talk his language. Hence, his treatment can only be accomplished in the company of other alcoholics who are also recovering.

Returning to Group

First Step Group continues for a week. Each alcoholic repeats the answers she has given on her Step One Assessment. She witnesses other alcoholics doing as she does. She hears her story in the stories others tell about their attempts to control their use of alcohol. She learns that the problems she has confronted have also been confronted by others. In fact the litany of problems becomes familiar and repetitive: divorces, losses of jobs, bankruptcy, DUIs, hospitalizations for alcohol-related illnesses, estrangement from children, loneliness, being drunk at the wrong time, hiding alcohol, violating one's morals in order to drink, black-outs, trips to psychiatrists, psychologists, and ministers, and even previous trips to treatment centers.

At the end of week one the alcoholic is expected to have recognized his powerlessness over alcohol. The unmanageability of his life is also expected to have been recognized and accepted. He will be evaluated at the end of this time in terms of his progress: more than expected or less than expected. If he has made less than expected progress he will be held back for another week in Step One group.

The following reasons may be given for holding the alcoholic back: denial, refusal to talk, overinvolvement in the world of family or work, not taking the program seriously, or debating with counselors. This discretionary decision to hold the alcoholic back may provoke an early termination of treatment on the part of the patient. Consider the following account. The speaker had been through treatment 10 years earlier. He had recently entered Eastern. In detox for 7 days, he had completed one week of treatment when he was told he would have to repeat that week.

> Hell, they told me I was too cocky. They tried to tell me why I drank. They said it was 'cause my old man beat me when I was a kid. I said, "You ain't got it right. I drank 'cause I wanted to. Me and the old man got along just fine." Then they said you're not taking this seriously. You're too worried about setting your business straight and you got too many calls from your kids and your ex-wife. What could I say? Hell, everything's coming in on top of me. I ain't been sober for 18 months and now I got a chance to get it turned around. Why shouldn't I be trying to get back on my feet? [field observation, October 15, 1984].

Three days after he was told he had to repeat the first week of group and could have no contact with his family or his work, he left treatment.

Treatment requires that the alcoholic make treatment his first priority. Treatment places the alcoholic under the power and the control of the treatment center. Although this is voluntary, it is a mandated condition of continued voluntary treatment. This premise was rejected by the above-described alcoholic.

First Step Presentation and the Self-Fulfilling Prophecy

In the second half of the first week in treatment the alcoholics in Step One Group are expected to make a presentation to the group concerning what the First Step means to them. This sharing of a part of their autobiography to the group is intended to further the process of conversion and surrender to the alcoholic treatment point of view. Robert Lifton (1961) has documented the workings of this method in the indoctrination methods employed by the Chinese Communists after the

1949 Revolution in China. The Chinese methods were compulsory; those in the alcoholic treatment center are semivoluntary.

Treatment works through a process of *self-fulfilling prophecies* (Denzin, 1968: 349-358; Merton, 1957). That is, if the alcoholic patient publicly accepts her alcoholism, and develops a view of self that is in accord with the staff's view of a recovering alcoholic, then she will be seen as making progress in treatment. The alcoholic must come to see the treatment center as a legitimate source of help for her illness. She must view herself as being in need of treatment, and must learn to speak the languages of treatment. If she does so her treatment trajectory will be smooth and orderly and the prognosis for recovery will be judged by the staff as being good. Of course, the alcoholic may set in motion a series of self-defeating prophecies that will lead the staff to ask her to repeat one or more phases of treatment. The alcoholic who left treatment three days after he was told he had to repeat the first week of group in fact produced such a self-defeating situation for himself.

WEEK TWO: STEPS TWO AND THREE

If the alcoholic has successfully convinced his First Step Counselor that he has recognized his powerlessness over alcohol and the unmanageability of his life, he is moved into his Treatment, Therapy, or Peer Group. In this smaller group the primary alcoholic bonds that were beginning to form in First Step Group become stronger. By this time he is on a first-name, friendly basis with the alcoholics he will spend the remainder of his treatment time with. He will have spent a considerable amount of time with these alcoholics outside of group during the first week. He will have eaten three meals a day with them, attended daily lectures and community with them. He will have had talks with them, learned the names of their children and their wives, and he may have shared drinking stories with them. He probably knows where they live, what their occupation is, and he may have played gin rummy with them late at night after evening lectures.

Three males in their mid-40s are walking back from evening dinner. They are waiting for the elevator to take them up to the second floor of the treatment center. They have been discussing Bill, a 52-year-old alcoholic who had just been transferred to the psychiatric ward at Northern. Jim, a recently divorced auto mechanic and a Vietnam veteran, speaks:

> It's not fair, what his wife's done to him. Serving them divorce papers on him three days after he's here and trying to do something about the booze. Christ he's just coming off the stuff, making headway, really talking, trying to get better and now she throws this shit up in his face.

Walt, an advertising executive, speaks:

> I know. Maybe we should go over and see him. Call him. Do something to show him we love him and want to help. You know he stayed up till 3:00 this morning listening to me. He understands. He's a great guy. Its not fair. I agree.

Mike, a dentist, responds:

> He's got himself all fucked up over this divorce deal. He's just depressed as hell. Let's go and see him. Hell, all they can do is tell us we can't see him. Let's go [field observation, May 13, 1982].

The three men then walked to the psychiatric unit at Northern and were allowed to see their friend Bill. Three days later Bill attempted suicide. He did not return to the treatment unit during the time these three men were at Northern. He left the psychiatric unit after six days, started drinking again and was killed while attempting to pass a motorcycle on a country road. This death, which was reported on the unit, was deeply grieved and became a topic of discussion in the treatment group the three men belonged to.

Their counselor, Walt, stated:

> No alcoholic dies in vain. Bill's death helps me stay sober and it helps the three of you stay sober, too. His death tells me and you what can happen if we go back to drinking. Bill was sick. He had a disease called alcoholism. When he drank he got insane. Alcohol and alcoholism killed him. If one of you stays sober because of Bill's death he will not have died in vain [field observation, May 27, 1983].

Step Two

The second week of treatment examines the meaning of A.A.'s second and third steps. Step Two states: "Came to believe that a Power greater than ourselves could restore us to sanity." Step Three states: "Made a decision to turn our will and our lives to the care of God *as we understood him*." This examination, as indicated above, occurs within the small group confines of the Therapy Group.

At Northern, alcoholics were asked five questions concerning Step Two:

STEP TWO SELF-ASSESSMENT

(1) What do you understand Step Two to mean?
(2) What does a "power greater than ourselves" mean to you? Are you aware of this power and how?
(3) What specific manifestations do you think your insanity took?
(4) What do you consider sanity?
(5) How did you come to believe?

Five questions were also asked concerning Step Three:

(1) What is your definition of decision?
(2) What is your definition of "will"—"Life"?
(3) How do you decide to turn your will over to the care of your higher power?
(4) How do you decide to turn your life over to the care of your higher power?
(5) What is the difference between turning your will over and turning your life over?

There are clearly more than semantic issues involved in these 10 questions. That is, the alcoholic is being asked to do more than produce a list of definitions of such words as power, insanity, sanity, decision, will, life, and turning over. He is being asked to bring the meanings of these words into his life and to reflect on how they have relevance for him as an alcoholic. Each word is intended to reference an instance of lived experience in the alcoholic's life that might in fact be a reflection of power, insanity, sanity, decision, will, or life. By coupling the word with lived experience the questions become more than semantic exercises. They are meant to anchor the alcoholic in an interpretive structure that will give new meaning to the experiences he has lived prior to entering treatment.

In Week Two of treatment alcoholics receive lectures on A.A.'s Twelve Steps, with primary emphasis on the Second and Third Steps. A lecturer at Northern is speaking on these two Steps:

> Any of you can see that there might be a power greater than yourself in your life. It might be money, it might be your boss, it might be your mother, or your wife. Some of you might believe in a God, or a tree, or in

> electricity. This power is outside you. You can't control it. It is stronger than you are. Alcohol is a power greater than you are. You've admitted you're powerless over alcohol. Now you must find any other power, greater than you are, that won't kill you or drive you crazy. That's what these two steps are all about. When Step Three says a "power greater than ourselves can restore us to sanity" it means that you have been sane before in your life, but you're not when you are drinking. There is hope for you if you believe in this power. But you're got to see how you were insane when you drank. The Big Book and the Twelve and Twelve talk about alcoholism as an emotional illness. You are all emotionally sick people.
>
> When you drank you may have been violent, you may have hit your wives and children, you may have driven your cars when you were intoxicated. You may have written bad checks, hidden your brooze, lied, and cheated. You did anything to drink and when you drank you were crazy. If you can't believe in a power greater than yourself you'll go back to drinking because the alcoholic by himself or herself can't stay sober. It's your choice. What are you going to do about it? [field observation, June 22, 1983].

This lecturer is interpreting Steps Two and Three. She is presenting the alcoholic with the dilemmas of self-control and will power that are contained in the fifth and sixth theses of alcoholism. She is returning the alcoholic to a new consideration of surrender.

The alcoholic will be asked to share the meanings these two steps have for him in Group. At Northern at the end of the second week of treatment each alcoholic was asked to stand in front of the entire community of recovering alcoholics and speak on the meaning of the first three Steps. The following is the statement given by Jack.

> Step One. I know I'm powerless over alcohol. I take one drink and I can't stop. My life must be unmanageable. I have bills up to the ceiling and the family is about to leave and I've been put on notice at work. Step Two. I want to believe in God. I used to but I got away from the Church. But this isn't the God of my church. It's different. I want a God of love and caring. I know I was crazy when I drank. The last time I went out I ended up in a motel room across town under a different name. Now that's not sane!
>
> Step Three. I want somebody else to run my life. A.A. and treatment seem to be doing a pretty good job right now. I hope I can stay with it [field observation, June 24, 1982].

Jack has internalized the central terms of Steps Two and Three. He speaks the language of treatment and A.A. By nervously presenting his interpretation of these two steps to the entire patient community he has publicly committed himself to the identity of recovering alcoholic. Whether he means the feelings his words and gestures convey is another matter.

Feeling the Language that is Spoken

The crucial test for every alcoholic in treatment is the test of feeling. Are the words that are spoken felt in the inner self?" This is the question that is raised over and over. Language emerges as a problematic in the expression and understanding of feeling. As the alcoholic learns A.A.'s steps she acquires an interpretive structure that stands one level above lived experience. Words such as sanity, insanity, powerlessness, unmanageability, will, and life are abstractions. They are "glosses" (Garfinkel, 1967) for lived experience. The alcoholic is asked to attach a level of feeling to these abstractions; that is to ground these feelings in her biography.

Evaluating Week Two

At the end of the second week the alcoholic is expected to have confronted at a deeper level the meaning of surrender to alcoholism. If her or she is in compliance and or denial, more confrontation will be required. Consider the following exchange between a counselor at Westside and an alcoholic woman in her tenth day of treatment. The counselor, Nancy, speaks:

> Jean, who do you think you are kidding? You think you can go home and drink again don't you? Do you want a divorce? Do you want to lose your daughter? Who are you playing games with? You talk good, but you don't mean it. Tomorrow you will have a chance to talk again to Group. If you don't want to stay here, just say so. There are 10 people outside waiting to get in here and take your place. There are plenty of people who are working and trying to get better. You're playing games with all of us.

Jean replies:

> I don't know. I don't think I'm like the rest of you. A lot of this stuff never happened to me that you all talk about. Sure I want to drink again. Who doesn't? If you say you're never going to drink again you're lying. Last night I dreamed of a tall cold Mint Julep. I love 'em. This stuff may be all right for you people, but not me. I'm leaving [field observation, July 30, 1983].

Jean left treatment the next day.

By the end of the second week a judgment is made concerning whether or not the alcoholic has accepted alcoholism. If, in week one they had been asked to come to a recognition of their illness, in week two they must evidence a commitment to change their lives.

WEEK THREE: STEPS FOUR AND FIVE

In a sense, all of treatment points to the taking of the Fifth Step. Step Four is preparatory to Step Five. Step Four asks the alcoholic to "make a searching and fearless moral inventory of ourselves." Step Five suggests that the alcoholic "admit to God, to ourselves, and to another human being the exact nature of our wrongs." When the Fifth Step is taken the alcoholic reaches the final phase of treatment, which at Northern and Westside was Family Week.

Rumors abound in treatment concerning good and bad Fifth Steps. Stories are told of patients who were made to do the step over. Accounts are also told of how the person who the patient told his Fifth Step to fell asleep. Outlines for the steps are passed around. Patients can be observed working late at night on their Fourth and Fifth Steps. Depressions set in; patients become moody and withdrawn. A general fearfulness appears on the treatment unit as the time for a group to individually take these two steps is scheduled.

As the anxiety level increases patients are drawn closer together. A general caring attitude emerges. If confrontation was a recurring theme of the second week of treatment, mutual and reciprocal self-support is the theme of the third week. In part this is the case because each patient must rely upon the other members of the group for feedback when he takes his Fifth Step.

At Northern the Fourth and Fifth Steps were structured as follows. At the end of the second week of group each patient was told when he or she would be giving his Fourth and Fifth Step to group. At this time each patient was also told to make an appointment with one of the pastoral counselors. It would be with that person that the alcoholic would individually share the Fifth Step. In effect, then, patients took two Fourth and Fifth steps—the first with their group, the second with the pastoral counselor of their choice.

In their patient workbooks patients received a guide for the Fourth Step. They were told to make a list of their good qualities, and to list their resentments, anger, and fear. They were also told to write a brief history of their lives up to the time of treatment (see Denzin, 1986a:

chap. 7 for a discussion of these two steps). They were also told to read those sections of the *Big Book* and the *Twelve and Twelve* that deal with these steps (A.A., 1953: chaps. 4-5; 1976: 64-67).

Unraveling a Life

In these guides to the Fourth Step the alcoholic is presented with a method for unraveling the patterns that make up life. Couched in the languages of A.A. and treatment, the guides suggest that the problematic areas of the alcoholic's life are those focused around the emotions of resentment, anger, and fear. Social relationships are the focus of each guide. These relationships are grounded in the alcoholic's worlds of work, family, sexuality, and self. Family history is emphasized in each guide, as are the emotions of self, including self-pride, fear, and self-esteem.

The alcoholic is asked to be a participant observer of his own life. He is asked to uncover the hidden themes in his life that have influenced his relations with others. The underlying rationalizations, delusions, and self-deceptions that he has employed are also addressed. The alcoholic is asked to put all of this down on paper, in black and white. This act, in effect, transforms the alcoholic into the position of the detached observer who might be writing a life story. In writing and speaking to his life as an alcoholic, the "alcoholic-as-narrator" becomes, like Leon Edel's (1984) literary biographer, the author of an "oral text" that has meaning only within his or her lifetime.

This, then, is lay therapy, involving the alcoholic in the dual identities of therapist and patient. In treatment this lay therapeutic model is located within the context of the therapy group. It becomes, in this sense, lay psychotherapy, which is guided and directed by a counselor. The alcoholic counselor will, of course, draw on a wide variety of treatment theories. Depending on his or her background in the field of human relations, any of the following psychotherapy models may be drawn upon: client directed, psychoanalytic, Adlerian, Jungian, problem solving, behavioral, cognitive, humanistic-existential, Gestalt, rational emotive, transactional, aesthetic realism, direct decision therapy, interpersonal process recall, or intensive journal therapy (see Corsini, 1984: 223-225).

Finding the Cause of Alcoholism

Treatment presumes that the underlying cause of the patient's alcoholism can be discovered. The Fourth and Fifth Steps are the key to this attempt to find the cause of alcoholism. Berryman (1973: 78-81) located the cause of his alcoholism in his relationship to his mother. Merryman's alcoholic (1984: 125, 159-160, 174-175, 277) discovered four central events in her life that were defined as the causes of her alcoholism. These were (1) a rape when she was six years of age; (2) her anger at her mother for controlling her alcoholic father; (3) her hidden fear of her husband because he represented her controlling mother; and (4) the hysterectomy she had after the birth of her last child.

At Northern the causes of alcoholism were located in the hidden and unknown cells of the Johari Window. The following causal agents are representative of those found by therapists and patients at Northern: homosexuality, bisexuality, rape, child abuse, spousal violence, alcoholic parents, and failures at work and in education. These factors were seen as being hidden within the self-structures of the alcoholic. It was assumed that the exposure of these factors would, in part, help the alcoholic stop drinking. Similar factors were discovered in the biographies of patients at Westside and Eastern.

TAKING THE FIFTH STEP

In taking the Fifth Step, the alcoholic shares a view of life she has heretofore kept hidden from herself and from others. With the taking of this step the alcoholic comes full circle in her alcoholic understanding of self. No longer completely bewildered by her compulsive drinking, no longer existing in an alcoholic haze, she sees the pattern of her life. She sees the destructive powers of alcohol and she understands that she is powerless over alcohol.

The Fifth Step clarifies for the alcoholic the meanings of the previous four steps. By laying her life out in front of her she presumably reveals to herself how powerless she has been over alcohol. She sees how unmanageable her life has been. She confronts the moments of insanity her drinking has produced. She sees the need for a power greater than herself in her life. She sees how destructive and chaotic a life run on her will power and on alcohol has been. She sees also that she has been restored to a sense of sanity and sound thinking that she had not previously experienced. Finally, she discovers that the life that has gone astray is her own. That is, the Fifth Step turns the responsibility for alcoholic drinking and alcoholic existence back on the drinker. In so doing it isolates the alcoholic at the center of her illness, forcing her to address what she did as an individual while she drank alcoholically.

A counselor at Northern is speaking to a group of patients about to take their Fifth Step:

> You must learn to ask for forgiveness and you must learn how to forgive. You must give up the feelings of resentment towards the past that you feel. If you do not you will drink again. You have a choice today. Only you can do this. If you have taken your first three steps and believed them, then you are on the road to recovery. You have all the power on your side now [field observation, May 16, 1982].

At Northern Steps Four and Five were termed the "Action Steps." As the alcoholic takes these steps he is evaluated on two dimensions. The first dimension is "Self Inventory." His counselor makes a judgment concerning whether or not he has discovered "the real self" through his inventory. The second dimension asks if he has "shared" this self with his group and with his counselor. These two evaluations are communicated to the alcoholic after he has given his Fourth Step Inventory to his Therapy Group.

At Northern, Eastern, and Westside the alcoholic read this inventory to his or her group. After the alcoholic presents this inventory he or she is asked to leave the room. The group counselor then asks the members of the group to produce a list of words describing the "assets" and "liabilities" of the alcoholic who has just made a presentation. At Northern the following terms were frequently employed, and applied, with slight variation to each alcoholic who gave a Fourth Step Inventory:

Assets: sober, honest, clean, intelligent, articulate, responsible, likeable, friendly, reserved, open, sharing, caring, sensitive, willing, sincere, polite, respectful, loving, good mother (or father).

Liabilities: shame, guilt, hurt, anger, resentful, self-pity, hatred, mistrust, blaming, rationalizing, defiance, minimalizing, justifying, inadequate, lonely, anxiety, low self-worth, fear, dishonest to self, analytic, stuff feelings, intellectualizing.

These words are written on the blackboard in the Group Therapy room. The alcoholic is asked to read them out loud when he reenters the room. The counselor then interprets these words, applying them to the biography of the alcoholic. This process is filled with anxiety and tension. The alcoholic has just shared his life with the group. Now he is being evaluated in terms of that life and the presentation he has made. His group is likely to draw close to him. Members nod in approval as he comes into the room. Coffee is poured for him. Cigarettes are extended to him. A space is made for him at the table. As he sinks into his chair his counselor speaks reassuringly to him, telling him that he made a good presentation, perhaps informing him that "he knows he will be able to make *it* and handle *it* when he leaves."

As he fits the words his group has given him to his life, the alcoholic breathes a sense of relief; relieved that the step is over, relieved that his life is not that bad after all. He wonders too, how he will live the meaning of those words into his life. That is, how will he stop mistrusting, being analytic, lonely, or inadequate?

An alcoholic is speaking to a fellow patient after his Fourth and Fifth Step Inventory:

> How was I? What in the Hell am I supposed to do now? I've still got the guilt. I still feel bad about what I've done. Maybe it is self-pity and rationalizing. I don't know. Hell it's hard to show feelings. Maybe I do stuff the shit. I do feel a Hell of a lot better about myself. I saw things I'd never seen before about myself. You know I'm not all that bad. To Hell with all those big words. I feel better [field observation, Westside, April 25, 1983].

Wrestling with the meaning of words as they apply to his life, this alcoholic speaks to his personal inadequacies as his group has presented these to him. He feels pain in the face of this self that has been reflected back to him. The looking glass the group has given him (Cooley, 1902/1956) has reflected a self he is not entirely comfortable with. Yet it is the self he has presented, as it has been defined by his group.

As the alcoholic witnesses fellow members of his group going through the same process he has gone through, the pieces of his self begin to fall into place. He begins to see that he is like every other member of his group. He begins to understand how the same list of words can be applied to all alcoholics, not just him. He begins to see that the pain he feels and felt is the same kind of pain his fellow group members are experiencing. This shared pain solidifies the Therapy Group. What is experienced and what is revealed about self begins to lose significance. Each alcoholic comes to understand that his alcoholism is but an instance of the universal destructiveness of this disease he shares with all alcoholics.

WEEK FOUR: FAMILY WEEK

The last week of the alcoholic's treatment brings his or her family into the treatment process. Having learned that alcoholism is a family disease (illness), the alcoholic must now confront the members of his or her family. Three processes are involved. First, the family members present the alcoholic with instances of how his or her conduct has affected them. This is a painful process involving leveling and confrontation. Second, the alcoholic presents to his or her family the new found "self of recovery." This self is grounded in the languages of treatment and A.A. It is also based on a set of experiences in Therapy Group that have not been accessible to the alcoholic's family. Hence he or she is literally a "stranger" to the family when the "homecoming" that characterizes Family Week occurs. They may not know who this new person is, nor will they know how to speak to this person—who is, after all, their father, husband, wife, mother, son, or daughter. A clash of perspectives, the old one (the family's point of view) and the other new, the recovering alcoholic's new self of treatment, thus takes place in family week. Whether these two views will be joined is problematic, both during family week, and after, when the alcoholic returns home.

The third process that is involved during Family Week is the presentation of an interpretive theory of alcoholic family interactions. This theory is often an eclectic mix of several theoretical points of view: Al-Anon, Social Work, Psychotherapy, Role Theory, and Communications Theory. These points of view are all applied to alcoholism as a family disease. The alcoholic and his or her family are located within this interpretive theory. They are asked to look at themselves as participants in an interactional system that is sick, or has been distorted by the disease of alcoholism. Family Week thus addresses the Second and Third Theses of Alcoholism and Recovery; viewing alcoholism as a relational and emotional dis-ease of self and other. A principal aim of Family Week involves an attempt on the part of the treatment center to convince the alcoholic's family members that they are also sick. This is difficult to accomplish because they share the alcoholic's belief that he or she is sick—not them. Although as Kellerman (1969) notes, many family members may feel that they—not the alcoholic—are sick, if not insane.

I shall take these three processes up in reverse order.

Treatment's Theory of the Alcoholic Family

In a quaint sociological fashion, alcoholics and their families at Northern were presented with a "role theory" of the alcoholic family. This theory contains six roles: the chemical dependent, the chief enabler, the family hero, the scapegoat, the lost child, and the mascot. It assumes a six-person family, with four children playing out the respective roles of hero, scapegoat, lost child, and mascot. The wife is, of course, the enabler and the husband is the chemical dependent.

Inner and outer selves are portrayed, with distorted, negative emotionality located at the core of each inner self. Family members are told that they have become trapped within a communication system that hides anger and resentment. They are told that they have withdrawn from one another into interaction patterns that are full of fear, pain, guilt, shame, confusion, insecurity, loneliness, and rejection. They are also told that each of their adaptive patterns (enabling, being the family hero, the scapegoat, the lost child, and the mascot) displays unhealthy, maladaptive adjustments to the alcoholic situation. Because they have refused to confront the alcoholic husband and parent in his alcoholism, they have become victims of his disease. In short they are as sick as he is.

An idealized picture of a healthy American family is presented to the alcoholic's family members. This picture stresses the fact that families are nourishing of all their members, are full of love, sharing, a haven of rest, a sanctuary of peace, a harbor of love, a place where holidays are celebrated with feasting, birthdays acknowledged with gifts, and thoughts of days gone by kept alive with fond remembrances.

If the alcoholic's family is anything, it is not a haven of rest, a harbor of love, a place where holidays are celebrated with feasting and days gone by remembered with fondness. The alcoholic's family is a nightmare of confusion, terror, pain, guilt, anger, and ugliness. There may have been good days in the past, but that past has long since been forgotten.

As the family members are presented with these two pictures of the human family, they are given a chart depicting the progression of alcoholism within the alcoholic family (Jackson, 1962). They are taken through the phases of denial, the attempts to eliminate the problem, the process of disorganization, the searching for outside help, the increase in violence and financial problems, and the efforts to escape the situation, including divorce and separation. Each of their adaptive strategies are located within this progressive evolution of the illness.

They are then brought up against the fact that the alcoholic is in treatment, as are they. Their task now becomes one of confronting the alcoholic situation they have all produced. This can only be done, they are told, through communication. Communication must involve confrontation and leveling. The alcoholic's family must confront the Five Paradoxes of Treatment. They are at a disadvantage, however, because they have less than five days to do this. Further, they may have only one group session with the alcoholic during Family Week. In this session everything that has built up over the years and months of the alcoholic's alcoholism must be addressed. High drama is played out in this moment.

Confrontation and Self-Presentation

Because the presentation of old and new selves is involved in the confrontation that occurs between the alcoholic and his or her family, I will combine these two processes in the discussion that follows. In preparation for the confrontation that will occur, each individual is given a "Family Week Participation Worksheet." This sheet consists of three major questions:

(1) Prepare a list of behaviors and incidents that have been hurtful and uncomfortable for you. Do not be judgmental. Describe behaviors and/or incidents (what you have seen and heard). (A full page is given for this question.)
(2) List behaviors, incidents, and features you like about each family member (half page).
(3) List your goals, needs, and expectations in each relationship (half page).

In the moment of confrontation the alcoholic is presented by each family member with answers to these three questions. In turn, each family member (if there is time) is presented with the alcoholic's views of them.

This confrontation, as indicated above, is accomplished through a mix of languages: family therapy, role theory, A.A., treatment philosophy, and the special languages of each family member. Tension radiates through the bodies of each family member as they confront one another. Young children may be fearful of confronting their alcoholic mother or father with episodes of alcoholic violence or alcoholic misconduct. Husbands may be bitterly angry at their wives for forcing them to come to Family Week, as may children. Indeed, complex negotiations and coercions may have been required in order to secure the physical presence of the family members during Family Week.

Merryman (1984: 197-198) describes this process by which family members are brought into this phase of treatment. Abby is speaking to her daughter Judy:

> Abby said . . . "This is a very hard call for me to make. I have to ask you to come to Family Week". . . . "Mom, that's a whole week out of school. You

> want me to get good grades don't you? . . . "Stop pressuring me, Mom," Judy answered . . . "I can't take it. I don't want to come there and have all those people dig into me and analyze me." . . . Now Abby's voice was steely. "Okay, here's the word. I'm *telling* you to come to Family Week. They say it's important for my recovery and there are things you need to say to me. . . . I want us to be mother and daughter again."

The coercive structure of this conversation pits mother against daughter, while it places the mother in the demeaning position of having to ask her daughter for help. The help that is requested is not ordinary help. It is the help that comes from confrontation. The mother cannot make her daughter come and say the things she needs to say. Yet she falls back on the full authority of her parental identity as she tells her daughter to come. This is the presentation of a new self in a relationship that had previously not contained such motherly self-assertion. In order to avoid her mother's request her daughter relies upon the need to get good grades. In previous interactions this ploy by her daughter would have worked, for it would have permitted both interactants to stay out of one another's respective fields of experience. By drawing her daughter into this painful situation, the mother asserts a new self that has been learned in treatment. This new self provokes anger and resentment on the part of her daughter. This resentment adds to the earlier resentments the daughter has felt toward her mother. Accordingly, in order for the mother's treatment to move forward, the very emotions that have kept them apart must be experienced anew. That is, they must confront the emotionality that has driven them apart. In order to do this, new resentments must be produced. That resentment, in turn, is laden with fear and anger. Not only does her daughter resent having to come to Family Week, she also resents and is angry over the fact that she is the daughter of a mother who is an alcoholic. She is fearful of what this may mean for her.

The fearfulness that characterizes the alcoholic's other who does not want to participate in Family Week is elaborated in more detail in the following comments of the mother of a 35-year-old female alcoholic in her last week of treatment at Westside:

> I can't come. I can't get somebody to drive me up there [she lives 35 miles away], and it costs too much to be calling you all the time. Besides, I ain't got nothin' to do with this stuff. So what if your Old Man was one, I ain't goin' to be part of it. It scares me that you'd think I'd come. Don' t you love me? [field conversation as reported, October 22, 1984].

Faced with such a situation the alcoholic is left to the doing of Family Week without a family member present.

The following situation describes a family member who is anxious to take part in Family Week. Two parents of Norwegian ancestry and in their 60s want to help their son, Ricky, who is 24 years old and recently fired from his job as a high school janitor. He was drinking on the job. The father speaks:

> We want to help Ricky, he's our only son. We are here because we love him. I don't know why he didn't want us to come. His psychiatrist said he told him he hated us. He said Rick drank because he couldn't stand the fact that I never showed him any emotion. Now how could he believe that? [As he speaks these words Ricky's mother is sitting beside him, nodding her head, with a tightly drawn smile across her lips, hands crossed in her lap. Ricky's face is turned away, he is fighting to keep from crying. His hands are clenched, arms folded across his chest.] Ricky screams: "You never told me you loved me! YOU NEVER TOLD ME THAT! How am I supposed to know that? You just keep turning your back on me, sitting there in your chair, smoking your fucking pipe, reading your paper. We never did anything together. Nothing. Never! [field observation, Northern, April 20, 1984].

Here the alcoholic does not want the family member to participate in treatment. The frozen, angry emotion that is present in the situation speaks to the wall that exists between the father and son. The inability of the father and the mother to involve themselves emotionally in the situation suggests a gap between the words they speak and the feelings they communicate to their son.

Forms of Family Participation

The foregoing situations describe two variations on the relationship between the alcoholic and the family during Family Week. The alcoholic may desire his or her family to be present but members of the family do not want to participate (the case of Abby, the woman at Westside). The alcoholic's family may desire to be present, but he or she does not want them to come (the case of Ricky). The third variation is the situation where no part of the family wants to be present, including the alcoholic who is in treatment. At Northern this situation was frequent. The following interaction is indicative of this shared interpretation. The patient is 45 years old. His only family is his 80-year-old mother. He has been in four treatment centers. She has paid for his treatment each time in the past, but not this time. He blames her for his drinking. She blames him for all the money he has spent on "his alcoholism." She speaks:

> I don't know why Charles's counselor thought I should come here. We've tried this before. I don't want to be here. They told me I should come. I guess I had nothing better to do. Oh well, maybe it will work this time. I'll just be glad when I'm dead and I won't have to deal with this anymore.

Her son replies:

> I will be glad when you're dead, too. You old BITCH. You never loved me. You thought you could buy me off. You never let me go to college and be what I wanted to be. You made me stay home and take care of you. You get what you deserve. I wish you hadn't come either. I'll drink a case of Jack Daniels the day you die! I'll praise the Lord [field conversation, May 13, 1981].

Finally, there is the situation where the patient and his or her family all agree that Family Week will be mutually beneficial. They regard themselves as all being part of the same family illness. This orientation is most typically expressed by those families where the spouse and children have attended Al-Anon meetings and have come to adopt the A.A. and Al-Anon point of view regarding alcoholism as a family disease.

The following situation speaks to this variation on the family's attitude toward treatment.

An alcoholic's teenage daughter is speaking:

> I wish Mom could have come, but she just couldn't get off work and I believe her. I really want to be here to help Daddy and myself. I know I'm sick from this illness, too. I'm really proud of Daddy for coming into treatment. When I started going to Alateen and Daddy would take me it was like we were starting our family all over again. Mom would go to Al-Anon and we'd all go home together, maybe stop for cokes and pizza [field observation, as reported, Northern, May 16, 1981].

A process of socialization into the A.A. and treatment point of view has occurred in this family. The father reported his feelings after Family Week was over and he was about to be discharged from Northern:

> I think this has really been good for all of us. In Family Emily [his daughter] showed me how I had hurt her and how she had tried to cover it

up. She took care of me when I was sick 'cause Mom had to be at work at nights. I was scared as Hell going into this thing. I think it was worth it. We all feel closer. If we just keep up what we are doing now we have a chance to be happy as a family again [field conversation, Northern, 39-year-old male, manager of a franchise auto dealership, May 17, 1981].

Four interpretive stances underlie the family and the alcoholic's participation in treatment. Both parties may be willing and commited to participation. Both parties may be uncommitted to participation and have no desire to participate. The patient may desire to participate and the family does not. The family may want to participate and the patient does not want to confront them. Each of these variations produce, as would be expected, drastically different experiences for patients and their families as they take part in Family Week. Clearly, all agree that the first mode of participation carries the greatest promise for recovery, as recovery is conceptualized by treatment centers.

The Promise of Family Week

In the few brief hours the alcoholic and her family spend together, in and during confrontation, the bare, skeletal, ugly underside of their family is laid bare. In order for this to occur, the promise of something better is held in front of them. In lectures during Family Week they are told that families can recover from alcoholism if they all work together and if they continue to seek treatment, in the form of Aftercare, A.A., Al-Anon, and Alateen.

They are told that if they do not learn how to communicate openly and honestly with one another the destructive side of alcoholism will return to their family, even if the alcoholic does not start drinking again. They are also told they will have to change the behavior patterns they have adopted in the face of alcoholism. They are told that the alcoholic will be changing and that they will have to change as well. If they do not, the hollow marriage and family they had before treatment will return. No small undertaking, this challenge is the promise Family Week sets before the alcoholic and the family.

At Northern patients and their families were given checklists for hidden anger; anger and fight rules; lists of the risks involved in expressing anger; descriptions of destructive fight styles; 15 rules for fair intimate fighting; discussions of how silence is the real torture to direct toward a mate when angry; lists of characteristics describing nonassertive, assertive, and aggressive problem solving; a discussion of the rights of a person in an intimate relationship; a discussion of how to listen and how to focus; a discussion of the "if onlys"; an anatomy of a working relationship; a credo for having a relationship with another human being; a discussion of risks and risk-taking in an intimate relationship; a credo for an accepting community; an analysis of "letting go"; a poem celebrating "YOU"; and a statement regarding "goals for me."

Armed with this information family members were sent home after five days to attempt to repair and rebuild their family life. The family members faced many problems as they returned home. What to make of these "credos," how to put them into practice, when to use them, when not to use them, and how to give meaning to them without falling back into their old relationships together or living a life of cliches. Perhaps, most of all, they felt relief that Family Week was over. They would take the alcoholic's treatment as the promise they would build upon. For many it would be up to the alcoholic to put back together a life they had jointly allowed to deterioriate because of all of them had denied that they had an alcoholic in their midst.

ENDING TREATMENT

With the conclusion of Family Week comes the end of the alcoholic's treatment. His four weeks now over, he, along with his family, will go home to begin the process of recovery that treatment has set in motion. Treatment ends with two significant closing rituals: the giving of medallions for 30 days of continuous sobriety (or for having completed treatment), and the signing of *Big Books* and the exchange of names, telephone numbers, and addresses.

Medallions and Graduation

Graduation ceremonies were held at Northern and Westside every Friday afternoon from 3-5 p.m. This was a momemt of celebration for alcoholics, their families, fellow patients still in treatment, and staff. Cookies and fruit juices were served. Chaired by the senior counselor in residence, who typically made a short speech regarding the progress of recovery achieved by each alcoholic who was graduating, the ceremony opened with the saying of the "Serenity Prayer." Graduating alcoholics were then introduced to the group and asked to speak a few words, which typically involved mumbled thanks for what the treatment center had done for them.

Upon the conclusion of these brief speeches, round medallions—slightly larger than half dollars, gold plated, with the name of the treatment center inscribed on one side and the Serenity Prayer, or the phrase "today is the first day of the rest of my life, A.A." and "I am Responsible" inscribed on the other—were given out. On the bottom of the medallion was also inscribed Northern or Westside Alumnus. The alcoholic was told to hold onto this medallion and to exchange it at his "home A.A." group when 60 days of continuous sobriety had been achieved. Alcoholics were told that they should carry the medallion in their pocket and if they thought of buying a drink they should put the medallion in their mouth and wait until it melted before they bought the first drink.

The giving of the medallion signified four processes. First, it was a mark of accomplishment. The alcoholic had in fact completed treatment. Second, the taking of the medallion signified a commitment, probably not understood, that the alcoholic would now be living a life dedicated to recovery and to participation in A.A. Third, by connecting this first medallion with a second one that would be received after 60 days of sobriety, treatment reestablished its link to A.A. The medallion was a token that would give the alcoholic concrete entry into an A.A. group in his or her home community. The medallion also signified a new concept for the alcoholic: continuous sobriety. It would no longer be sufficient for him or her to drink only occasionally. Recovery presumes continuous sobriety. Fourth, the token was an advertisement for the treatment center. By inscribing its name on the medallion, the treatment center paved the way for its name and its program to be passed along by word of mouth through the A.A. "grapevine" the alcoholic would now be entering.

Signing Big Books

Upon the conclusion of the graduation ceremony alcoholics were free to leave the treatment center. Departure from treatment involved a related ceremony, which was the signing of the *Big Book*. Reminiscent of a high school graduation ritual, alcoholics wrote in one another's *Big Book*. Phrases such as the following are inscribed:

2 good
<u>2 be</u>
4 gotten
[Name, telephone number]

> Thanks for sharing, thanks for caring, the best of luck to you, a super guy. It's been great knowing you. I know that you will make it. [Name, telephone number]
>
> To a Great Gal and a Great Friend who made this stay much more pleasant. [Name, telephone number]
>
> With all the love you have and A.A. I know you'll make it. [Name, telephone number]

A mixture of concern, affection, and superlative is contained in these phrases. Each statement speaks to making it, to being forgotten, and to the fear and pain that was experienced while in treatment. These phrases lift the author and the recipient above the turmoil of treatment, with all its agony and fear, into a realm of platitude. It is as if all is well now that treatment has been accomplished, yet each author masks a reference to the fact that "not making it" is a possibility. Not making it, of course, is the tragedy each wishes to avoid. Each alcoholic author has lived his or her own version of hell and has, if for only 30 days, escaped that hell, only to have experienced hell in another version in treatment. Yet they are free of alcohol now. Their medallions signifying the promise treatment has given them. The alcoholics leave treatment fearful and hopeful—afraid that they will drink again, afraid that Family Week will not work when they get home, afraid that they will return to the life of hell they have escaped from.

CONCLUSIONS

Treament takes seriously (without noting) Bateson's (1972a: 310-311) argument that the alcoholic's pretreatment style of sobriety somehow drove him to drink. By restructuring the alcoholic's interpretive theory of self, emotionality, temporality, others, alcoholism, and alcohol, and by bringing the family into treatment, the treatment center changes the alcoholic's previous style of sobriety. It does so by changing his entire relational outlook on the world. Treatment attempts to locate the alcoholic within an interpretive system that is larger than he is. By grafting itself into A.A.'s philosophy, treatment gives the alcoholic the sense of a higher power. It gives him a sense of freedom from his past. It locates him, if only for 30 days, within a safe interpersonal environment wherein the depths of his hidden self can be explored. Treatment has also given the alcoholic a new language of self and it has exposed him to the Steps and the tools of A.A.

Hence, although the alcoholic may well return to the same setting he left in alcoholic despair and disarray, it is in fact a new situation he reenters. It is new because he is, if only for a brief period of time, a new person. He must learn how to live that new self into the old situations he inhabited as an active alcoholic.

Treatment as a Collective Accomplishment

The tendency to interpret treatment solely from the point of view of the recovering alcoholic must be avoided. That is, treatment is a collective, group phenomenon. This is evidenced by the central place the alcoholic's therapy group plays at every stage in the process she has experienced. From the identity of recovering alcoholic—which finds its locus in the interactions that occur in First Step Group—to the Fourth and Fifth Steps that are taken in the therapy group, the alcoholic's recovery is, in every instance, a collective, group accomplishment. Even Family Week turns on self-presentations that involve interactions with fellow group members.

The "paradoxes of treatment," as outlined in the previous chapter, thus define the culture of treatment. These paradoxes, fitted to A.A.'s first four steps, are collectively defined by each cohort of alcoholics who enter treatment together. The only constants in this system of cultural reproduction are the paradoxes, the treatment center (and its employees), and the disease called alcoholism.

Recovering alcoholics share in common with other classes of individuals who undergo group socialization experience (such as mental patients, medical students, prisoners, military recruits, college students) the following characteristics (see Becker et al., 1961; Goffman, 1961a).

First, they socialize one another. Second, they collectively develop adaptative strategies for handling problematic situations (the Fourth and Fifth Steps). Third, they develop their own meanings of the cultural problematics they are presented with (that is, the languages of treatment, alcoholism as a disease, and so on). Fourth, like prisoners who undergo a process of prisonization, or adaptation to an institutional point of view, alcoholics experience a medicalization of their illness that may be termed "treatmentization." They come to act like self-treating patients (Beauchamp, 1980; Szasz, 1975; Trice and Roman, 1970).

But more than a medicalization process occurs. Recovering alcoholics experience what may be termed a *reverse stigmatization of self*. They are taught to accept their alcoholism, to be proud of their recovery, and to carry the message of recovery to others. This experience with self, which involves radical self-transformations of a reverse stigmatizing nature, sets the alcoholic off from other classes of individuals who are also processed by and pass through socializing institutions. And of equal importance, while other institutional selves may find their progress in the outside world monitored by others (such as parole agents, military officers, senior physicians, and so forth), alcoholics do not experience this kind of supervision. That is, they are able to slip back into the world they left with their new identity hidden. As long as they do not become actively alcoholic, few people will care about their recovery career. In this respect, treatment has taught them how to be "normal" again.

If she has surrendered, then, to her alcoholism, if she has in fact worked A.A.'s first Five Steps, and if she takes up a life that makes A.A. centrally important, then her chances of recovery are excellent. If she does not, she runs the risk, as did Berryman, of returning at some later date—if she is still alive—to another treatment center to start the recovery process all over again. The following words often spoken at the end of the alcoholic graduation ceremony echo in her mind as she leaves treatment: "*Treatment is only three percent of the solution. A.A. is the other 97 percent. Treatment is discovery, A.A. is recovery.*" As she hears these words she is also told, as patients at one center were told, that "eight out of ten of you will drink again, and if you are lucky you may get back here to start all over again." I turn in the next chapter to the structures of experience that the alcoholic will confront in A.A. when she returns to her home community.

Part IV

A.A. AND THE SOCIAL WORLDS OF RECOVERY

10

THE A.A. GROUP

> Find a home group. Get a sponsor. Work the steps. Go to at least five meetings a week. Get involved. You'll get better [counselor, advice given patients leaving Northern after four weeks, June 1, 1984].

In this chapter I will examine the structures of interpretation the recovering alcoholic finds in Alcoholics Anonymous. With Maxwell (1984: 38-39) I assume that the alcoholic who enters A.A. finds a new social world. This world is structured around A.A.'s Twelve Steps, the Twelve Traditions, and around a fellowship in which "being an alcoholic" is the primary identity that is shared (Denzin, 1986a: chap. 7; Rudy, 1986).

A.A. offers the alcoholic an interpretive theory of alcoholism. That theory, which he will have confronted in treatment, must now be mastered, if only partially, if he is to remain sober and recover. Now that he is out of treatment the place he will go to learn about A.A. is A.A. meetings. It is there that he will find the answers to the directives he has received when he left treatment. That is, only in A.A. will he find a "home group," a sponsor, and five or more meetings a week to go to.

The alcoholic who leaves treatment confronts a void of experience. The close relationships with fellow alcoholics he has experienced in treatment are severed. The family context he reenters is a mixed blessing. It contains all the structures of the experience he previously drank to escape. Although "Family Week" may have set the conditions for hope and promise, he returns to his family, his job and his other interactional settings with apprehension and fear. Uncertain as to how he will present himself to others, he is caught between revealing his new identity of "recovering alcoholic" or hiding it. The desire to drink may return and he may not know how to deal with it.

His head filled with a new language, familiar with A.A.'s Twelve Steps, he may feel that he has no one with whom he can share his new-found sense of self. Yet A.A. is there, waiting for him, just as it was before he went into treatment. A.A. may, in fact, become a new family for him, if he chooses. But in order to find an outlet for the new self he has experienced in treatment, he must make the first step toward finding A.A. in his home community. The telephone listing for Alcoholics Anonymous is given in every telephone book in nearly all medium-sized communities of 5000 and over.

I will discuss, in order, the following problematics, as they reveal the underlying historical, structural, and interactional features of A.A. that the new member will confront. First, I will investigate the phenomenon of "alcoholic understanding" as this phenomenon is experienced in A.A. meetings. I will trace the meaning of "alcoholic understanding" back to the original A.A. meeting between Bill W. (William Wilson, 1895-1971) and Dr. Bob (Robert Holbrook Smith, M.D., 1879-1950). I will speak, in this context, to the issues of emotionality, self, interaction, and "types" of alcoholic understanding.

Second, I will offer an interpretation of the A.A. group, extending my analysis of the treatment group as given in the previous chapter to the A.A. group. Third, I will analyze the structure of A.A. meetings and the A.A. group, discussing the place of the Twelve Traditions, ritual, format, and temporality in the organization of A.A. meetings.

I will suggest that in A.A. meetings the alcoholic subject is transformed from a "suffering" alcoholic into a "recovering" alcoholic. How this transformation in subjectivity is accomplished is the central problem of this chapter. I will show how A.A. transforms the alcoholic into a "talking subject" who learns how to speak about his or her lived experiences within the language A.A. provides.

My intentions are to bring the structures of A.A. before the reader, as these structures are given to the new member. By offering a combination of historical, structural, textual, and interactional analyses of the "A.A. experience," I hope to reveal how the recovering alcoholic can in fact become a part of a structure of experience that is larger than he is. I will show how A.A. requires his presence and that of other newcomers for its continued existence. In so doing I will examine once again how the recovering alcoholic realizes his or her "universal singularity" in the company of fellow alcoholics who are also universal singulars in their recovery experiences. By drawing upon this universal singularity of each of its members, A.A. solves its own organizational problematic of membership replacement (and recruitment), while giving each of its members a context of interaction wherein recovery from alcoholism can occur. How this oneness of experience and purpose generates a structure of common experience that is mutually beneficial to all parties—A.A. and alcoholic alike—is my topic. Central to this process is the cultural and personal history A.A. rests upon—most important, the history of the first A.A. group. I briefly turn to this history as it is made available to the new member.

THE FIRST A.A. GROUP AND LIVED HISTORY

A.A. tradition states: "Two or more alcoholics meeting together for the purpose of sobriety may consider themselves as an A.A. group." Consider the following conversation between two A.A. members. M, 48 years old, has been sober for over three years. He has arrived early at the meeting site of an A.A. group for its usual Thursday night 8:00 p.m. meeting. D, a 21-year-old college student, has recently received a medallion for six months of continuous sobriety. It is 8:05 and they are the only two A.A. members present. M states:

> Do you want a meeting? You know two alcoholics can have a meeting if they want to. Remember Bill W. and Dr. Bob? That first meeting was just the two of them.

D nods his head and speaks:

> Yes, I do. I remember that story. I heard it in Chicago. I need a meeting. I've only had two this week. I'll chair, if you'll read "How It Works" and "The Thought for the Day" [field conversation, as reported, October 2, 1983].

The meeting began. A third A.A. member joined the group at 8:10 and the meeting that had started between M and D continued until 9:00, with each of the members speaking in turn.

This account instances the reenactment of A.A.'s original two-member group. M and D drew upon their knowledge of the first meeting between Bill Wilson and Dr. Robert Smith. They used that pivotal moment in A.A. history as justification for their two-person A.A. meeting. That D had heard this story in a meeting in Chicago reveals how this key moment in A.A. history is kept alive and passed on to the new member. This story is a part of A.A.'s lived history (see A.A., 1976, 1980, 1984; Kurtz, 1979).

A.A. dates its *inception* to the first meeting that occurred between Bill W. and Dr. Bob. That meeting occurred at 5:00 p.m. and ended at 11:15 p.m. on Sunday, May 12, 1935 in the home of Henrietta Seiberling and her husband in Akron, Ohio. The *founding* date of A.A. is given as June 10, 1935, the day Dr. Bob had his last drink. The first meeting between Dr. Bob and Bill W. has subsequently been redefined, within A.A. folklore, as the first A.A. group.

The importance of the foregoing is elaborated in the following statements made by A.A. members in meetings. The first speaker has just returned from a Young People's Convention in Chicago. Sober slightly more than one year, he states:

> It was great. The keynote speaker was sponsored by Bill W. He talked of the first groups in Cleveland and Akron. He told us to work the steps and follow the traditions. He talked about the fights they had in the early days in Detroit over the membership requirement of six months sobriety before you could come to a meeting. It was great! I'm really glad I went [field conversation, September 20, 1984].

This speaker conveys the importance of having heard an A.A. member sponsored by Bill Wilson. By listening to this man he is taken back into the early days of A.A. He is given the essential message of Wilson and Smith in 1935. He was a witness to an instance of lived history within A.A.

The next speaker is 76 years old. He has been in A.A. for 35 years. He knew Sam Shoemaker, the minister who worked with Wilson in 1934 when Wilson was trying to sober up men in Shoemaker's church in New York:

> Old Sam Shoemaker used to say, "Keep it simple. Listen to what is inside you, practice the spiritual principles but don't come down on this God thing too hard with newcomers" [field conversation, July 4 , 1983].

This A.A. member keeps A.A. history alive by mention of Sam Shoemaker, one of the early advisers of Wilson and a person listed by

Wilson as having been central to the early beginnings of A.A.

The third speaker is a female, sober seven years. She states, in regard to self and ego:

> His majesty the baby. That's me. I'm a spoiled brat. I want things my way and I want it now. I keep getting in my own way. The *Big Book* and the *Twelve and Twelve* talk about me—I prefer Her majesty the baby! [field conversation, November 25, 1982].

The phrase "his majesty the baby" is attributed to Freud by Tiebout (1954: 612), who used it to describe the narcissism of alcoholics. Tiebout also employed the phrase in a letter to Bill Wilson, suggesting that Wilson was trying to live out infantile grandiose demands (Kurtz, 1979: 127). Alcoholics often apply this phrase to themselves. The speaker, perhaps not knowing the source of her phrase, was, as she spoke, connecting herself to a moment in A.A. history when Tiebout was chastising Wilson for his own self-centeredness.

These three statements by A.A. members, and the earlier account of a three-person A.A. meeting, reveal how A.A.'s history, its key figures, its mythology, its folklore, and its key phrases are kept alive in meetings and in A.A.'s oral tradition. As an instance of a social movement—which began as a small group, then became institutionalized as it routinized charisma—A.A. has developed a body of customs, a social organization, a set of traditions, an established leadership, and an enduring division of labor with social rules, in "short a culture, a social organization, and a new scheme of life" (Blumer, 1946: 199). The problems of goal displacement and factionalization of membership that often follow the routinization of charisma within social movements have not been observed in A.A. (see Marx and Wood, 1975: 396-397; Maxwell, 1984; Zald and Ash, 1966; Zurcher and Snow, 1981; but also Kurtz, 1979).

The oral tradition that underlies the A.A. social structure keeps the culture alive. It is conveyed through the stories and the voices of A.A. members. The sources and the details of the stories are authenticated in the printed texts Wilson took pains to create (see A.A., 1984; Kurtz, 1979).

ALCOHOLIC UNDERSTANDING

Consider the following interaction as reported. The scene is a hotel room in Minneapolis. Three men in their early forties are seated around a table. They have known one another for seven years. J has been in A.A. for three years. M has been recently hospitalized several times because of drinking-related illnesses. He has a bottle of Jack Daniels in front of him on the table. D, a friend of J and M, is a moderate drinker. He listens as J and M speak to one another.

M to J: You're not drinking. Can I get you something?

J to M: No, I've stopped. Go to A.A. now, been three years. Been hard. 'Specially after the break-up with Mona. Christ, before that I'd get up at 2:00 in the morning and drink. Walk into the closet to go the bathroom. Get lost in the apartment. Drive the back alleys home so the police wouldn't stop me. Hid the stuff all over the place. Couldn't stop.

M to J: I guess I'd like to. Try to, can't. Don't know what's goin' on. Get drunk when I don't want to. 'Fraid to go to class anymore, start to shake and lose my train of thought. They told me I might need to go into treatment. I'm afraid to.

J to M: I wish I had. I know what you're talking about. I was afraid too. But you know, this old drunk told me, he was an elevator operator downtown. He saw me shaking one night, he said, "It doesn't have to be this way anymore." I said, "What do you mean?" He said, "It doesn't have to be this way anymore. It isn't for me anymore, and I used to shake more than you do. I go to A.A. now." You know, those words stayed with me. Couldn't get them out of my mind. For months. I'd be at Curley's drinking. His voice would come back, "it doesn't have to be this way anymore." One night I said ___ it. I called up A.A. and went to a meeting in the neighborhood. Still kept drinking, but after three months I stopped. You know, M, it doesn't have to be this way for you. Do you want to do something about it?

M to J: Yeh, I guess so. What are your meetings like? Can I go to one?

J to M: Sure, there's one at 8:00 tonight. I'll take you.

M to J: O.K., I'll go. What do you think about treatment?

J to M: I know somebody to call. We'll look into it.

M to J: You know, you're the first person I've talked to who understands what in the hell I've been going through. The doctor told me I had to get out of town for treatment if I couldn't stop by myself. Christ, I can't stop by myself. My family doesn't understand. I want to stop, but I can't. I keep going back to it, even when I don't want to.

J to M: They told me that will power had nothing to do with it. They said it was a disease, like diabetes. I go to A.A. meetings for my treatment. Maybe it'll work for you. It does for me. Let's go [field conversation, as reported, April 9, 1981].

Three days later M entered treatment, after attending two A.A. meetings with J.

This account may be interpreted in light of Robert Smith's description of his conversation with Bill Wilson on May 12, 1935: "He was the first . . . human being . . . who knew what he was talking about in regard to alcoholism from actual experience" (A.A., 1976: 180). M makes nearly the same statement in his comment to J: "You're the first person I've talked to who understands what in the hell I've been going through."

This interaction between M, J, and D instances a moment of shared "alcoholic understanding." (It is also an example of a Twelfth Step call in A.A..) M and J had an A.A. meeting. J carried the message of recovery to M. He did so in a language that was based on his lived experiences with alcoholism. However, the conversation between the two men made no mention of alcoholism or of alcoholics, except when A.A. was brought up. There was no need to speak to these terms because M knew he was an alcoholic and J knew that he was, just as M knew that J was a recovering alcoholic. J put the phrase "it doesn't have to be this way anymore" in front of M. He recounted his own experiences with the phrase, in terms of his interactions with the man on the elevator. He conveyed to M the point that it could in fact be different for him, too. How it would be different was the problematic, for the fact that M wanted it to be different was not at issue. J offers three lines of action for M: staying as he is, A.A. meetings, and treatment.

J reenacts the original A.A. meeting between Wilson and Smith. He communicates the disease theory of alcoholism. He shares with M his own failed attempts to stop by himself, and he relates moments of humiliation when he acted under the influence of alcohol. In a few words he secures M's attention and shares his experience with active alcoholism in the process. Of critical importance was the fact that J shared his experiences before he obtained M's understanding of how recovery might begin. That is, M understood that J understood him on the basis of the experiences J shared with him. Authentic emotional understanding was produced between these two men. They came to share a common field of experience and a common understanding concerning their respective locations within that field, which was active alcoholism, or uncontrolled drinking.

Emotional Understanding

Elsewhere (Denzin, 1984a: 145) I have argued the following:

> *In order for true, or authentic, emotional understanding to occur, two or more individuals must experience a common field of shared experience*

> *that they can enter into, each drawing, if necessary on his own visualizations of the other's feelings, his own productions and reproductions within himself of a common feeling, and the common participation in this publicly accessible field of experience. Experience . . . precedes emotional understanding* [italics in original].

I also argued that shared emotionality lies at the basis of authentic, deep understanding. In shared emotionality selves are joined in a common field of experience. The interaction between Wilson and Smith, and the interaction between M and J, rested on shared, authentic, alcoholic understanding. I will now unravel the meanings behind this assertion.

In shared emotional understanding a past set of experiences is shared, even if they have been unique to the two individuals in question. By drawing on that common but unique past, they are able to form a new, shareable field of experience. In so doing they appropriate the other's perspective and apply it to their own situation. A merger of shared emotional feelings is thus produced. In that emotional field the selves of the two interactants are lodged. A merger of biographies, of common pasts and a discourse in a common language that draws upon that shared past, emerges. "Feelings-in-common" about that past are felt and shared (Scheler, 1913/1970: 12-13). A sense of "fellow-feeling" (Scheler, 1913/1970: 14) occurs as each individual identifies with the feelings and the past experiences of the other. A reciprocal sense of "emotional infection" and "emotional contagion" appears. The heightened emotionality of each individual passes over to the other. Each, in a sense, becomes emotional because the other is emotional. Out of this process emerges a sense of emotional identification. Each individual identifies with and through the emotional feelings of the other. "Emotional embracement" ensues. The two individuals are drawn together into an emotional situation where relational bonding occurs. There is a merger of the two selves in the emotional situation they have produced together. A sense of warmth, fellowship, relief, togetherness, oneness, solidarity, perhaps even love and caring, appears. Embodied feelings are sensed and felt and ratify this sense of shared oneness. Tears, smiles, hugs, handshakes, and shared laughter may be experienced by both individuals (see Denzin, 1984a: 146-153, for a discussion of these forms of emotionality).

These forms of emotional intersubjectivity (feelings-in-common, fellow-feeling, emotional infection, emotional contagion, emotional embracement) are to be contrasted to "spurious emotionality." "Spurious emotionality," or "spurious emotional understanding," reflects those interactional moments when individuals mistake their own feelings and understandings for the feelings of the other. They interpret their feelings as the feelings of the other. Spurious emotionality arises in those situations where interactants refuse or are unable to enter into the other's field of experience. In such moments mistaken emotional memory may occur; that is, the subject thinks she has had an experience like the experience the other is presenting, but she is mistaken. She has not had parallel experiences.

In spurious emotionality the individual thinks she can understand and feel the pain and suffering of the other, but she cannot. As a consequence, she applies the wrong interpretive framework to the experience of the other, perhaps feeling sympathy for him when he does not want or desire sympathy. In this incorrect interpretive move the individual assumes that the feelings toward self she would apply to herself are the same feelings the other feels. She assumes that if she had had the experiences the other has had, she would feel the way he feels now, that is, prideful, hurt, guilty, angry, embarrassed. Thus, in spurious emotionality the individual views the other's experiences not from the other's point of view, but from her own. Mistaken, flawed, self-centered emotional sharing occurs. This leaves the other feeling that his experiences have in fact *not been understood.* Anger and resentment toward the "interpretive other" may be produced. The good intentions of the other are rejected. The other fails to understand how or why it is they have been misunderstood. In fact, they have not been misunderstood. They have misunderstood the experiences of the other toward whom they have spuriously (and perhaps unintentionally) directed misunderstandings and misplaced feelings.

In order for deep, authentic, shared emotional understanding to be produced and understood, a common field of shared and shareable experience must be created. This allows each individual to locate himself or herself in the experiential framework of the other. Without this condition being met, spurious emotionality or misplaced understanding is produced. Consequently, as argued previously, experience precedes emotional understanding. That is, understanding cannot be entered into a field of experience until a commonality of experience has first been shared and felt.

These conditions and forms of emotional understanding are central for the interpretation of alcoholic understanding. I turn now to the forms of alcoholic understanding.

Four Types of Alcoholic Understanding

Understanding, as the above discussion suggests, refers to "the process of interpreting, knowing and comprehending the meaning intended, felt and expressed by another" (Denzin, 1984a: 284). *Alcoholic understanding* refers to the process whereby two alcoholics interpret, know, and comprehend the meanings intended by the other in terms of previously experienced interactions with the active and recovering phases of alcoholism. Four forms of alcoholic understanding may be distinguished. The first form is the understanding that is conveyed between a recovering alcoholic and an alcoholic who is still drinking, but wishes to stop, or seeks help. The interaction between J and M in the previous account displays this form of alcoholic understanding, which may be termed *authentic alcoholic understanding.*" The second form of alcoholic understanding is that which is conveyed between two or more alcoholics who are recovering and are in, or have been in, Alcoholics Anonymous. The three statements given by alcoholics in the discussion of "lived history" display this form of alcoholic understanding, which may be termed "A.A. understanding." Each member who listened to those accounts knew who Bill W. was, had perhaps heard of Sam Shoemaker, and could relate to the phrase "his Majesty the baby."

The third form of alcoholic understanding transpires between drinkers who are active alcoholics and who may or may not have had experience with Alcoholics Anonymous. I term this *insincere alcoholic understanding*. In this mode both alcoholics justify their active alcoholism through recourse to the term *alcoholic*, or its equivalent—"lush," "drunk," "alkie."

These three modes of alcoholic understanding have all been experienced by alcoholics who regularly participate in Alcoholics Anonymous. Each member has moved from the understandings of alcoholic justification to an interaction with a recovering alcoholic who extended the understandings of alcoholic help that A.A. is based upon. Furthermore, as a recovering alcoholic, each member regularly participates in A.A. meetings where the discourse revolves around the languages and understandings of recovery.

The fourth form of alcoholic understanding is, as the foregoing might suggest, *spurious alcoholic understanding*. The alcoholic who wishes to recover, or who has recovered, has experienced this form of understanding many times in the past. His network of significant others—including his enablers—and his victims have bombarded him with the spurious understandings a nonalcoholic brings to bear upon the experiences and the relationships she has with a practicing and a recovering alcoholic. Although this other may feel sympathy and compassion for the alcoholic who is still drinking, she has not the experiences of the active alcoholic. She has not felt the pains of withdrawal. She has never hidden a supply. She has never felt the fear of a police car stopping her for drunk driving. She has not been hospitalized for alcoholic-related illnesses. She has not felt the embarrassment of seeing the word "alcoholic" on a medical record. She does not know what it means to try to stop drinking and not be able to. She has never attempted to work while under the addictive influence of alcohol or drugs.

In the absence of these and related experiences, the alcoholic's other stands as an "outsider" to the inner, lived experiences of the alcoholic's who is attempting to control and manage his alcoholism. All of the good intentions of the other produce misplaced, spurious alcoholic understandings. The following words by an alcoholic married for 45 years to the same woman address this point:

> I've lived with that woman for 45 years. For 30 of those years I was an alcoholic, drunk every day. And after those 45 years she'll never come within a hair on a gnat's ass in understanding me. She can't. She's not an alcoholic. I don't care how many of those Al-Anon meetings she goes to. She'll never understand me! Never [field observation, February 24, 1984].

This fourth form of alcoholic understanding draws the recovering alcoholic back to Alcoholics Anonymous, for in A.A. he or she finds a community of others who are understanding in ways that are not spurious. In the fields of experience that A.A. offers, the recovering alcoholic experiences, over and over again, authentic emotional understanding. And, as important, this form of understanding is experienced alongside alcoholically grounded feelings-in-common, and shared alcoholic fellow-feelings, including emotional infection, emotional contagion, and emotional embracement. In short, in the presence of recovering alcoholics the alcoholic first discovers, and then rediscovers, a sense of self that was long since lost—if ever possessed—to alcoholism.

Every alcoholic who recovers has experienced this process of having "received" the message of recovery from another alcoholic. If the alcoholic has gone through treatment this process of coming to understand alcoholic understanding will have been repeatedly experienced. As the alcoholic learns to attend A.A. meetings and becomes a regular A.A. member of the A.A. social world in his or her community, the word "understanding" will be one of the most frequently repeated terms he or she hears. Alcoholic understanding, in all its forms, and the meanings and terms that flow from that phrase, constitute the frame of reference or universe of discourse from which all other A.A. discourse flows.

I turn next to the topics of the A.A. group and the A.A. meeting. It is in the context of these two phenomena that the recovering alcoholic learns to achieve and experience the kind of self-understanding of alcoholism that was first promised when "the message" was carried to him. My intentions are to offer a view of the A.A. group that is consistent with Sartre's (1960/1976) dialectical theory of groups. It will be necessary in this discussion to define such terms as *group, fused group, pledge,* and *"Third Party."*

THE A.A. GROUP

An A.A. group is a historical structure of dyadic and triadic relationships that coheres within a shared universe of discourse. That universe of meanings (Mead, 1934) turns on the omnipresence of five unifying forces: alcohol, alcoholics, recovery (or not drinking), A.A. history, and A.A.'s conception of a "higher power." These processes give the A.A. group its reasons for being. The A.A. group is pledged, in Sartre's sense (1960/1976: 419-420) to the primary purpose of "staying sober and helping other alcoholics to achieve sobriety." As such, this purpose externalizes the group in the form of a pledge. That pledge fuses or joins the members in the pursuit of this common goal, which is both individual and collective. The group, then, mediates between the individual and active and recovering alcoholism. It provides an arena of interaction wherein recovery from alcoholism on a daily basis may be accomplished. Individual action is realized only through group action. Similarly, the group is individual action; that is, the group inserts itself into each individual. Each A.A. member embodies the A.A. group. The group extends itself through and into each group member. Conversely, the group embodies each member as a part of itself. The group, then, has a reality that is both individual and collective.

The A.A. group is opposed to seriality, or separateness. Indeed, it is a premise of such groups that the loneliness of alcoholism requires interactional and interpersonal treatment in a group context. The first A.A. group between Wilson and Smith was a "fused group." A fused group (Sartre, 1960/1976: 828) is "a newly formed group, directly opposed to seriality." Such groups are initially unstructured. The members are drawn together because of the need to not be alone. They share a common perspective and a common desire to be joined, or fused, in a common purpose. Out of fused groups emerge "pledged groups"

(Sartre, 1960/1976: 829). Pledged groups are organized around an agreed-upon distribution of rights and duties enforced by a pledge. Such groups are structured by a "Third Party" (see following discussion). The A.A. group is a pledged group organized around the Twelve Steps and the Twelve Traditions.

Institutional structures may emerge out of pledged groups, and indeed this has been the case with A.A. That is, an overall institutional structure, bound together through the "Twelve Concepts for World Service" written by Wilson, and the A.A. Service Manual (A.A., 1983-1984) organizes the workings of A.A. groups internationally.

The pledge is a historical act that connects each member to A.A.'s collective history, while it secures a biographical commitment on the part of the member. It is a pledge that works against group divisiveness, for it unifies all members against taking a stand on politics, organizations, religious sects, denominations, or institutions and causes. It becomes, as Sartre (1960/1976: 419) argues, both a mediated reciprocity and a practical device that directs members to concrete action within the group and within their individual lives. It forges group membership on the part of each individual while constituting the grounds upon which collective group membership is based.

As mediated reciprocity, the pledge seals a bond between all group members. It makes all of them equally accessible to the demands and commitments the pledge entails. A.A.'s "Slogan of Responsibility"—which reads, "I am responsible when anyone, anywhere, reaches out for help. I want the hand of A.A. always to be there. And for that I am responsible"—speaks directly to this mediated reciprocity that each member assumes when the pledge is taken. The pledge confirms a commitment to the A.A. community. It makes every member available to any other A.A. member for purposes of interaction regarding A.A.'s stated purpose.

When the member walks through the doors of an A.A. meeting, he or she also embodies the Third Tradition, which is an extension of A.A.'s basic purpose. That tradition reads, as noted previously, "The only requirement for A.A. membership is a desire to stop drinking." By entering an A.A. meeting the member announces the fact that she does not want to drink today and that is why she is present at the meeting. It is irrelevant to the A.A. members present that she may not know that this is what her actions mean, for they know what it means to them. Her presence announces a commitment, if only transitory and even inauthentic and insincere, to the identity of alcoholic and to A.A.'s pledge (see Stone, 1962, on identity and placement).

The A.A. group is unified through a duality of third parties. A third party is understood as an individual (or concept) who (or that) "unifies a group by observing or commanding it" (Sartre, 1960/1976: 830). The collective history of A.A., including the Steps and the Traditions, becomes a third party that guides and directs group conduct. This history is also realized most concretely through the lives of recovery experienced by the cofounders, Wilson and Smith. Because every A.A. group has old-timers, or their versions of Wilson and Smith, the history of how recovery may be accomplished is present in every group. But above Wilson and Smith stands the "higher power" they directed every member to find. This "higher power," or "God as we understand Him," is the most powerful missing Third Party that organizes and commands A.A. group interaction. But that missing third is present in every member. Hence, this absence is a presence (Derrida, 1973) that is realized interactionally as each member invokes his or her understanding of the "higher power." This absence, whose presence makes a *difference* (Derrida, 1973: 145), simultaneously externalizes the group while it is internalized in the lives, actions, and words of each member.

The "Third," in the form of the generalized pledge (to sobriety, A.A., and the higher power), moves at three levels within the A.A. group. First, it joins members to one another in the form of dyadic and triadic social relationships. Second, it permits each individual to have a relationship between self and the higher power, or the "Third" as the "Third" is understood. Finally, it operates at the level of the group as a momentary collectivity that exists through its "group conscience."

The pledge, then, in the form of the "Third" is inserted directly into the lives of each group member. Yet the group as a concept, embodied in the traditions, transcends the life or action of any given member. Therefore, the group resists *envelopment* (Sartre, 1960/1976) and embodiment in the cult of a single personality or charismatic leader.

At the same time, the daily or regular A.A. group works against seriality, or separateness, which would draw the individual member away from the group. For in order to maintain and sustain the pledge to sobriety and to the group, the individual must return to the group. For there, in the group, the individual can announce himself or herself as an alcoholic, and in so doing, become a part of the group once again. The daily meeting of the group reproduces for the individual and the group this experience. This solidifies the member's commitment to the pledge, to the group, and to himself or herself.

The pledge, then, mediates interactions between group members. It forms the line of action along which reciprocated group interaction flows. The A.A. group thus becomes a lever for group and individual history. Because the reality of the group lies in individual action, the group must be reconstituted as a collectivity each time its members come together. This is accomplished, as I shall show below, through the A.A. readings that structure the beginning of every A.A. meeting. The group must recreate an idea of itself each time its members assemble for a meeting. It does this by forming itself out of what it is not, and what it is not is a seriality of unrelated individuals. The group, then, externalizes itself as a "thing in itself," with separate status in the world. In so doing, it becomes an externalized-internalized force in the life of each member. At the same time it assumes its own history, and becomes a structure in its own right.

A.A. Tradition

In this dialectical duality of third parties (The "higher power," A.A. history, the pledge, the presence and absence of alcohol) the A.A. group fuses individual and joint action into a shared field of experience that becomes an "A.A. group having a meeting." This interrelationship between group and individual action and purpose is succinctly stated in A.A.'s First and Fifth Traditions, which respectively state: "Our common welfare should come first; personal recovery depends upon A.A. unity;" and "Each group has but one primary purpose--to carry its message to the alcoholic who still suffers." These two traditions are mediated by the Second Tradition, which states: "For our group purpose there is but one ultimate authority—a loving God as He may express Himself in our group conscience. Our leaders are but trusted servants; they do not govern."

The Second Tradition thus positions God, or the higher power, above and within every group. Group conscience, or the will of the group membership, is seen as embodying the ultimate authority of God. Because personal recovery depends on A.A. unity (Tradition One), each individual becomes an embodiment of the group. Each member's conception of God is thus mediated through the common welfare of the group, which in turn becomes a collective sense of God and group purpose, which is also individual purpose.

Group Conscience

Group conscience is a key to the working of the group. It is evidenced in the following interactions. The setting is as follows. A member with two years sobriety from a western city has assumed the chairmanship of one of the oldest A.A. meetings in the community. This meeting has a core of members with the longest sobriety in the community (average of 14 years). The chair makes the following motions:

> I would like to have a group conscience on changing this meeting into two groups on Wednesday. We're too big for one group. I would like to also move that we not read from the *24 Hour a Day* book because that's not A.A. I also propose that we just read "How It Works" and not the Traditions. Do I have a second?

A silence of five minutes followed in which no member (25 present) spoke. Then an old-timer of 16 years spoke:

> I helped start this meeting. As long as I come here I want everything read. That's part of how I got and how I stay sober. I vote no.

A second old-timer spoke:

> I'm with B, but I've only been here five years. But in Ohio we read everything. I don't think we should change. I like tradition.

A third old-timer spoke:

> I'm with G. I vote no. We can set here all night and have a group conscience. But I came here to have a meeting and stay sober. Let's have a meeting [field conversation, as reported, December 27, 1982].

A group conscience was taken and no one seconded the Chair's motion. His motion failed for a lack of a second. The meeting was held. Three weeks later the "Chair" made an amend to the group, speaking of his attempt to govern the group and asking for the group's forgiveness.

In this extended example, group conscience was at work. It worked through the silence of the group and through the talk of the three old-timers. In a collective sense the group—through the old-timers—asserted its collective history and took a stand on change. When the third speaker announced his primary purpose, which was to stay sober and have a meeting, he spoke to A.A.'s Fifth Tradition, and thereby joined the group conscience around a tradition that all members were committed to. In short, he announced for the group what A.A.'s primary purpose was.

THE A.A. GROUP AT WORK: THE MEETING

The "group conscience" is, as just indicated, a key to the working of the A.A. group. Infrequently invoked in an explicit fashion, the group conscience reveals how the group is simultaneously greater than its members, while being only what its members give to it.

It is now necessary to indicate how an A.A. group works. This requires an analysis of the A.A. meeting, which will involve a discussion of group names, meeting times, types of meetings, and A.A. ritual. There are two types of A.A. meetings: open and closed (see Denzin, 1986a: chap. 1). The *open meeting* is open to any individual who has an interest in alcoholism. A *closed A.A. meeting* is attended only by individuals who call themselves alcoholics and have a desire to stop drinking. In a closed meeting last names may be revealed and topics that would not be discussed in the presence of nonalcoholics may be talked about (see Maxwell, 1984: 9-10). *Speaker meetings* involve an A.A. member telling his or her story. *Lead meetings* involve a speaker talking for about 15 minutes on a topic, which is then turned over to the group.

Groups exist in and through their meetings; hence, to study an A.A. meeting is to study the A.A. group. However, groups exist over and above the meetings that they hold, for group members have interactions that occur outside the boundaries of meetings. (See Goffman, 1961: 9-11, for a distinction between groups and encounters or gatherings. In this context an A.A. meeting is a multifocused encounter, organized in terms of the sequential speaking of each member.) Groups are registered in the Annual A.A. Directory of Groups. This recording of the group's existence lists its name, and the names and telephone numbers of two A.A. members who may be contacted concerning the meetings of the group. The two A.A. members whose names are listed are typically the Group's Service Representative (GSR) and its secretary-treasurer, or alternative GSR. These two representatives of the group are nominated and elected through the group conscience. They typically represent members who have displayed a commitment to the group and its meetings. (See A.A., 1983-1984: 34-37, for a discussion of the functions of the GSR.)

Group names may take any form, drawing, for example, on A.A. slogans such as the "Day at a Time Group," the "Serenity Group," or the "Goodwill Open Discussion Group." On the other hand, the group may take its name from the address where it meets, calling itself, for example, "The Oak Street Group," the "Downtown Group," or the "Campus Group." The group may use the name of the day that it meets as its name, for example, "The Tuesday Night Group." Local A.A. knowledge within a community may connect the name of a group with its meeting place, for example, the "Tuesday Night Group at the Treatment Center." Special interest groups (women, gay, nonsmokers, Latino) may take their name from this special interest (such as the Tuesday Night Women's Group).

By assuming a special name the group identifies itself and its membership and locates itself within the universe of A.A. meetings that exist within the local A.A. community. Each group is, then, an autonomous structure within the A.A. social structure. Each group is financially independent and financially self-supporting, depending for its existence on the contributions its members make at its meetings. A contribution of one dollar or less is an expectation within the A.A. meeting structure. In order to secure this contribution a basket is passed during each meeting. These contributions go to pay the group's rent—which is often to a church—to buy the group's literature, and to pay for the purchase of coffee the group serves at every meeting. The presence of coffee and a coffee pot, along with a multitude of ashtrays for cigarette smokers, a table with chairs, A.A. slogans, and an address of a church, tell any A.A. member that he or she has found the site of an A.A. meeting. These are the universal symbols of an A.A. meeting.

Annually, semiannually, or quarterly, each group makes payments to the New York offices of A.A., to its district office, and to the local intergroup that it may belong to. A suggested ratio of 60%-30%-10% operates. After the group has paid all of its local expenses, if group conscience agrees, 30% of its funds are sent to New York, 10% are sent to its district, and 60% to its intergroup.

Although groups may have meetings at any time of the day or night, the universal starting time of all evening A.A. meetings is 8:00 p.m. The expected duration of an A.A. meeting is one hour, although meetings may extend beyond one hour. In some cities of the United States meetings may last two hours as a normal expectation. The size of an A.A. meeting may range from two members to over 50, although meetings of over 50 typically break up into smaller groups of 10 or fewer members. Members typically sit so that they are in face-to-face contact with one another, although in large meetings this may not be possible.

Within A.A. the terms *meeting* and *group* are used nearly interchangeably. Thus, members speak of "The Monday Night Group," or "The Monday Night Meeting," and in such usage convey the same information—that is, there was a meeting of the Monday Night Group. However, the above-mentioned differences between a group and its meetings must be kept in mind. Moreover, when a group dies it is because it stops having meetings. A group stops having meetings because members stop coming. Hence, the three key elements in a group's life are members, meetings, and the group name. No one of these terms can stand alone.

The Structures of an A.A. Meeting

I turn now to the actual structure of an A.A. meeting. The following is the format used for closed meetings by a group named the "Church Street Group." This group has daily noon meetings (12:00-1:00). The average size of its meetings is 15 members. This group has been in existence for two years, although its members are drawn from an earlier group that had existed for four years. Although the membership at any meeting changes, a core of five members is regularly present. Hence, the group draws from the entire A.A. community for any one of its daily meetings. The format the group uses borrows from the Al-Anon Program for its closing. The original outline for the meeting was brought to this community by a member who had acquired it in Ohio in 1979. It had previously been used as the format for another group and its meetings.

It contains the following elements: (1) salutation by chairperson, announcing himself or herself as an alcoholic and welcoming all members to the meeting; (2) a moment of silence followed by the "Serenity Prayer"; (3) a reading of A.A.'s "preamble" (see Glossary); (4) a reading of "How It Works" from A.A.'s *Big Book*, which contains A.A.'s Twelve Steps; (5) a reading of the Twelve Traditions of A.A.; (6) a reading of the "Thought for the Day" (Hazelden Foundation, 1956); (7) a short greeting to all new members; (8) a call for anniversaries and A.A. birthdays; (9) a call for announcements concerning group and A.A. business; (10) a call for a topic; (11) discussion, during which time each member of the group speaks, if he or she desires to; (12) closing remarks, including a call for seconds, asking if members wish to speak again; and (13) closing with the Lord's Prayer.

As can be seen there are 13 moments in the A.A. meeting, which range from the chairperson's introduction to reading of the Twelve Traditions and the "Thought for the Day," which is taken from a Hazelden publication, and which contains a reading for each day of the year. New members are asked to introduce themselves by their first name only, if they choose. If a member has a birthday of one year or more, a medallion will be given and often a birthday cake, with the number of candles representing years of sobriety, will be presented and eaten by the group after the meeing. Sobriety days of 30- and 90-day intervals are also marked by the giving of medallions, as are six months, nine months, and then one year.

If a newcomer to A.A. is present at the meeting, and if it is that person's first A.A. meeting, the group will by tradition discuss the First Step (see Denzin, 1986a: chap. 7). This will involve each member briefly telling the story of how he or she got to A.A. in the first place. These brief life stories (Thune, 1977: 79-88) recreate a shared past that the new member can enter into.

If the First Step is not the topic of discussion, the Chair may suggest the thought for the day. Or a member may come forth with a topic, such as depression, loneliness, resentment, anger, fear, the desire to drink, overconfidence, family, work, anonymity, gratitude, or the holidays and staying sober. Once a topic is selected, the Chair may say: "O.K., let's talk about resentment. Who would like to start?" The Chair then either calls on someone or a person volunteers to begin speaking. Each member at the meeting speaks in turn, usually for one to three minutes, depending on the size of the meeting and the member.

The following is an account of a closed meeting in which the topic of discussion was the Twelfth Step. The Chair of the meeting was Cl. I offer the interaction of that meeting as an instance of an A.A. group in action.

Members

Cl	Chair; 36-year-old male graduate student, 9½ years sobriety; divorced, one child.
N	42-year-old male professor, 1½ years sobriety; married.
Ws	72-year-old male, retired, 8 years sobriety; married.
Dk	61 years old, architect, 1 year sobriety; married.
Dn	27-year-old college senior, 3 years sobriety; single.
Je	37 years old, electronics technician, 2 years sobriety; married.
Khy	graduate student of education, 1½ years sobriety; divorced, one child.
Dr	33 years old, secretary, 2 months sobriety, in program 12 years; single.
Sh	45 years old, grocery-store clerk, 3 months sobriety, in program 5 months; married, four children.
Jn	48 years old, sales clerk, 6 months sobriety; married, children.
Jl	37 years old, gift shop clerk, 7½ years sobriety; divorced, two children.
Tn	41 years old, master craftsman, 2 years sobriety, in program 5 years; married, two children.

Dv 33 years old, supervisor, 6 months sobriety, slip last week; married.

Topic: Twelve Stepping

Cl: Does anyone have any problems or topics for discussion?

Tn: I do. Twelve Stepping. I have a problem. I got a neighbor who is fighting this thing. I've talked to him several times. Yesterday I went over and I gave it to him straight. I said he couldn't fight this by himself. He needed help. Either a treatment center, a psychiatrist, a minister and religion, or A.A. I got overinvolved. I know in my guts that I let my emotional self get too far involved. I'd like to hear your thoughts on this.

Ws: I'm Ws. I'm an alcoholic. I wasn't going to speak today. Eight years ago today they took me to the fifth floor. Not the second, not the third, but straight to the fifth. The floor for the crazies. I was Twelve Stepped while I was there. You had a successful Twelve Step, Tn. You came back sober. You carried the message.

Dk: I'm Dk. I'm an alcoholic. I wasn't going to say anything today. I'm glad to be here. It's a good environment. I think you should be complimented, Tn. You're carrying out the program. You're practicing all the steps. I hope I can do that someday.

Khy: I'm Khy. I'm an alcoholic. I don't know what got me sober. It was many different things. It had to be a sum that was greater than its parts. It was 10% this part, 20% this part. It was things I did and didn't do. I know that it finally worked and it worked when I was ready. I don't know how it worked. I don't think it is any specific thing we do.

Cl: I'm Cl. I'm an alcoholic. Two-and-a-half months ago my father killed himself. The day of the night before he killed himself I felt that something was wrong. I was at the club (city) and I called the man who got me into A.A. I said, do you need a meeting tonight? He said that he did. He came over and he told me, "I don't know if I should tell you this but 10 years ago I took your father to some A.A. meetings." That made me feel good because I knew there was nothing I could do for my Dad.

Dv: I'm Dv. I'm an alcoholic. I don't know. I'm working with someone right now. He's sober, sober, then drunk, drunk, then sober, then drunk. I don't know what works. I know I was successfully Twelve Stepped. I hope to be able to do that someday. Thank you, I'm glad to be here today.

Je: I'm Je, I'm an alcoholic. I don't know either. I remember how it was— sober, sober, drunk, drunk, I'd tear everything all up and then just want to hide hoping that if I did nothing it would all go away. But then I'd get drunk again, and it would start all over. It was hell. There are a couple of old-timers with over 30 years. I learn from them. They just sit back and wait. But they'd go out at 3:00 in the morning to help somebody. I got too emotional. I want them to be helped now. To cut out this nonsense. I see one fellow. He came for a while. Now he and the wife go to church. I see him in the grocery store. He looks like hell. He's shaking, he turns his head the other way. He's probably afraid I'll say something to him. I never do 'cause I don't want to scare him off. Maybe he'll get it someday. Thank you, I'm glad to be here and to be sober today.

N: I'm N. I'm an alcoholic. I'm glad to be here today. I don't know. It's a mystery. There's a fellow in treatment right now. I Twelve Stepped him a year ago. I did it all wrong. You're s'posed to separate the wife and the husband. That's what the *Big Book* says. Hell, she was all over him. Interrupting, talking all the time. How he had such a problem. How he was an alcoholic. They'd call me. She'd get on the extension phone and they'd both talk. She wouldn't give him a chance. She's an alcoholic, too. I did it all wrong and today he's in treatment and thanked me for the Twelve Step call a year ago. I don't know. It's a mystery [laughter throughout group].

Dv: I'm Dv. I'm an alcoholic. I don't know. Last weekend I Twelve Stepped my mother. I had a bottle of Usher's Green Label this far from my mouth [holds hand in the shape of a cupped fist next to his mouth]. I finally went to a meeting, took a piece of every bit of literature they had, took them home and put them on the kitchen table and left. It'll just keep up until something happens. My mom's only happy when she's into her wine. Maybe my dad will go to Al-Anon. Thank you. I'm glad to be here and to be sober. I'm glad I didn't have to be Twelve Stepped today.

Jl: I'm Jl. I'm an alcoholic. I don't know. I'm not very good. I called A.A. the first time and went the next night. Nobody even came and got me. Then I complained for the next two years. Before I go on Twelve Step calls I read "How It Works" in the *Big Book*. I'm usually 45 minutes late! Where I work, the gal's boyfriend is a drunk. He's afraid to look at me. They know I'm a recovered alcoholic. The guys thinks I'll turn him in to the authorities, whoever they are! I know my best effort in life got me into A.A. I'm glad to be here and to be sober.

Jn: I'm Jn. I'm an alcoholic. My only advice to Tn is to be patient. It takes time. It may take several days for everything you said to sink in. Thank you.

Dt: I'm Dt. I'm an alcoholic. I'm just glad to be sober and be here today. Thank you, Cl.

Sh: I'm Sh. I'm an alcoholic. I'm like N. When I was Twelve Stepped the whole family was there. My son (I have three kids) sat so close to me. I don't think he had ever sat that close, since he was a little boy and could sit on my lap. I went for two months for my family. Then I slipped for five weeks and then I came back for myself. I'm glad to be here and to be sober today. I hope I can help somebody someday like I was helped.

Cl to Group: Are there any other comments? If not, we'll close [Group stands, holds hands, and says the Lord's Prayer in unison].

The meeting was over at 1:05. All members had spoken. It was a normal, ordinary A.A. meeting of the noon group.

The Prose of the Group

From this record of a group meeting I wish to extract the following points. First, it will be noted that each member speaks "on topic," addressing in every instance A.A.'s Twelfth Step. However, only a specific part of the Twelfth Step was discussed—carrying the message. Second, the discourse that is produced reflects back upon itself. Member after member turns to the original topic announced by Tn, and then adds their own experience of either being Twelve Stepped, or having done a Twelfth Step. Third, as each member personalizes the topic, a part of their biography is shared with the other group members, that is, reading the *Big Book*. Fourth, the "mystery" of sobriety and of A.A. is spoken to. No member claims to know how he or she got sober. Fifth, alcoholics who are still drinking are brought into the meeting. The presence of these absent others serves to remind each member of how it was when they were still drinking. Sixth, humor emerges as problems in speaking to alcoholics who are still drinking are discussed. Seventh, each member evidences gratitude for being sober, and conveys a sense of thanks to the others for being present at the meeting. Eighth, a successful Twelve Step is defined for the group. If you carry the message and return sober you have been successful. This point is critical, for when the A.A. member enters the "alcoholic situation" of a person who asks for help, alcohol is often present. If the member is uncertain of his or her sobriety, the desire to drink may return and the member may in fact drink on the Twelve Step call, in which case the group may lose a member to active alcoholism, when the intent of the Twelve Step call was to help another alcoholic.

These eight points must be positioned within what I call the "prose of the A.A. group." This prose is an individual and collective production that speaks the language of ordinary people woven through the understandings of A.A. and recovery. It is proselike in structure, coming forth in full sentences, and in logical and illogical sequences. Each utterance is framed within the shared interpretive structures of Alcoholics Anonymous. In each member's talk, thoughtful, meaningful, biographically specific information is produced and shared. Taken for granted (Garfinkel, 1967) meanings are glossed over (Twelve Stepping, crazies, message, treatment, alcoholic), as each member speaks to the topic at hand. A reaching back into the member's biography is evidenced as talk is produced.

These are not the utterances of the workplace, the home, the telephone, the letter, the hospital emergency room, the psychiatrist's office, or group therapy (see Grimshaw, 1981: 222-226; Schenkein, 1978;

for reviews of these other forms of talk, and Goffman, 1981). These utterances are embedded in the sequential talk of A.A. members doing an A.A. meeting. The sequentiality, the biographical detail, the hovering presence of alcohol as an organizing "Third Party," and the shared constraints of A.A. tradition and ritual serve to produce a structure of "understanding" discourse that is perhaps unique to A.A. meetings. The "talk" and the "prose" of A.A. is sober talk. It is poetic, poignant, nuanced by the dialects, twangs, accents, and speaking idiosyncracies of each member. It is a prose that is at once personal and collective; as each member speaks for herself, she speaks to the group as a collectivity. But because no member speaks for A.A., the talk that is shared is "self-talk"(Goffman, 1981). By offering her prose to the group, each member thus contributes to a group discourse that is greater than the sum of its spoken parts. The totality of these parts gives a poetic and narrative unity to the group's meeting. As such, a historical continuity in the group's life is produced. This continuity derives from the contributions of each member.

A.A. Talk

A social semantics (Grimshaw, 1981: 222) of A.A. talk, involving both conversational analysis (Cicourel, 1981; Schegloff et al., 1977; Schenkein, 1978) and discourse analysis (Labov and Fanshel, 1977) suggests that this form of talk occurs within both restricted and elaborated linguistic codes (Bernstein, 1971), in which the unit of meaning is the speech event (Hymes, 1974: 52-53), not the reciprocated speech act (Searle, 1970) of ordinary conversation. As each A.A. member obtains his or her turn in the speaking event that is the meeting, an emotional footing (Denzin, 1984a: 265; Goffman, 1981: 124) is established. This footing aligns the speaker with the topic at hand (in the previous account, the Twelfth Step) and permits a projection of self in terms of the speaker's own experiences with the topic. Code switching into an emotional vocabulary that is personal is immediately evident in each speaker's talk. As the speaker draws upon personal history in the elaboration of his or her talk, the et cetera clause (Cicourel, 1974; Garfinkel, 1967) is employed. That is, each speaker is permitted to elaborate on the topic at hand, to introduce new topics, to adumbrate a topic, and to bring seemingly unrelated topics under the rubric of the main topic (e.g., Cl's mention of his father's death).

The rule-governed structure of A.A. meeting talk does not admit of easy analysis within the format of conversational analysis (Schegloff et al., 1977). That is, speech does not occur within easily analyzable adjacency pairs, nor are there problematics concerning how conversations are begun, carried on, and ended. Rather, when a speaker's turn is given, he or she will always begin with the "My name is ___ and I'm an alcoholic" introduction to the group. Once launched into his or her turn, each speaker then proceeds to relate a story or semi-story regarding the topic at hand, or to simply acknowledge the topic and then give thanks to the group for being present. The ending of each speaker's talking turn is typically signalled by thanks being given to the chair and an utterance concerning gratitude for being sober today. Hence this talk, although having rule-governed openings and closings, is filled out by middles that are wholly at the speaker's discretion. Nothing in the preceding talk of another member need by keyed upon, elaborated, or spoken to, although it often is.

Member talk, then, is primarily dialogic. That is, it entails a dialogue with self and with the A.A. group. This dialogue, which can become a monologue when the speaker only speaks to himself or herself, is dialectical and emergent. It is governed by the string of associations the topic at hand triggers in the biographical memory (pre- and post-A.A.) of the speaker. If the member has related a story or an account before, he or she will make an apology for repeating the story. A justification for the repetition will, however, be given—that there are members present who have not heard it before.

The dialogic structure of the member's talk does not involve a reciprocated conversation with another member; rather, the member speaks to the group, as in a monologue. However, a monologue is not produced, for the collectivity is addressed. Hence, what is given is a one-way dialogue that dialectically turns back on itself. Self-referential in structure, the member's talk thus incorporates the attitude of the group as the member speaks to the topic at hand.

Face-Work and Emotion

Face-work and impression management (Goffman, 1967) are not integral to the member's talk. As with the talk of treatment, which stressed emotionality and the "exposure of self" in interaction, A.A. talk similarly places a value on, and incorporates into its discourse, talk that in ordinary conversation would be defined as displaying a "loss of face." Crying, the revelation of deviance while under the influence of alcohol, discussions of bouts of insanity, mentions of crippling fears or depressions, and talk of failures in marriages and social relationships are all sanctioned and accepted within the talk of A.A. meetings. Positive face-work and the maintenance of face, or self, through the usual means of interactional social control (Grimshaw, 1981: 225) are not problematics in an A.A. meeting, as they apparently are in other areas of everyday social life (Goffman, 1974). Indeed, shows of emotionality and the apparent loss of face are valued and treated with compassion and care within the A.A. meeting.

These features are most evident when a member reveals a "slip" to the group, for at one level a "slip" could be regarded as a loss of face. But within A.A., members are praised for speaking of their "slips," for to do so indicates that the member reaffirms his or her desire to be a member of A.A. Consider the following account. The speaker is 37 years old. He had been sober for three months and then drank for four days. As he speaks, his hands shake, his face is unshaven and alcohol can still be smelled on his breath. He is crying as he talks:

> I'm back here because this is where I need to be. Always before I would wait until I was healthy again. I didn't want anyone to know that I had been drinking. My false pride would keep me away, even after I drank. I let things pile up in my head. Resentments, fears, anxieties, little things and big things. Then I decided that a drink would be all right. I started with one, then I got a bottle and then another bottle, and then another. I was afraid to stop. I couldn't bear the D.T.s and the dreams. But I made it through last night. I want to get better (breaks down crying again). I don't know what's wrong with me. I need help, God I need help [field conversation, November 30, 1985].

Each member who spoke after this individual thanked him for coming back. A box of tissues was passed to him as he cried. Members offered him rides to other meetings. His show of emotion was not taken, then, as a sign of the loss of face.

The following account speaks to another instance when face is not lost when a member shows emotion. The speaker is a valued member of the group. He has been sober over 10 years. He too cries as he begins speaking:

> I don't know what to do. Decided I had to bring it to you people. My 15-year-old daughter told me and mom that she's pregnant. Told us last night. I ordered her to her room and didn't speak to her 'til this morning. I could kill her and him. Christ, I don't know what to do. Never expected this to happen. I sure as hell ain't goin to drink 'bout it. That's for damned sure. But what in the fuck are we s'posed to do? [field conversation, December 2, 1985]

Here the member breaks down over a family crisis. Each of the 16 A.A. members at the group thanked him for sharing his problem and each offered advice, based on personal experience. Two female members of the group, who were social workers, shared their telephone numbers with him and offered family planning assistance.

These self-accounts speak to the above argument that within A.A., as in treatment, shows of emotion are valued and not taken as losses of face. An additional point may be made. The speakers in these accounts are male. The masculine show of emotion in American male culture is a proscribed, not a prescribed social act (see Hochschild, 1983). To be emotional is to be weak and feminine. A.A. inverts this cultural proscription.

This brief analysis of A.A. talk suggests, with Hymes (1974), that the speech event, not the sequential speech act, is the primary unit of analysis. A detailed ethnography of A.A. communication would reveal how each member builds a biography out of the speech events he or she produces within a sequence or network of A.A. meetings. That is, the member produces a personal oral history of recovery that is told each time he or she takes a turn at speaking at an A.A. meeting.

Only when the member tells his or her story to an open meeting will all the details of this personal history be drawn together into a single narrative account. Up until that time—which may never occur—primarily all that other A.A. members will learn of the speaker will be what he or she chooses to disclose when a turn to talk comes at an A.A. meeting. The rules that govern these self-disclosures by the speaker may be unconscious, or deeply buried within the member's biography.

The A.A. group exists, then, in and through a shared oral tradition that is structured by the rituals of Alcoholics Anonymous. This oral tradition is, as just indicated, personal and collective, but always given meaning within the overall interpretive system of Alcoholics Anonymous. In order for the oral tradition to exist, groups must have meetings. In order for groups to have meetings, they must have members. But there can not be members without groups for members to belong to. Hence, a dialectic of the personal and the group is woven through every structure of A.A. The meeting, then, is the interactional site for A.A. in action.

It is in the meeting, as the above transcripts reveal, that the alcoholic subject is transformed into an A.A. member who is recovering from alcoholism. By announcing himself or herself as an alcoholic, each member makes his or her history of recovery available for others to draw upon. By sharing this history of recovery, each member becomes part of a group that is recovering together. This can only be accomplished in and through the talk of each member. Talk, then, is the means to recovery. That talk, proselike in structure, autobiographical in nature, anchors the personal history of each member in the collective and shared history of the A.A. group. In this way the member's personal life becomes a part of the shared, group consciousness. The A.A. group becomes a public structure of private lives. I turn now to A.A. ritual, beginning with a brief discussion of ritual and group life.

Ritual and Oral History

Rituals are conventionalized joint activities, given to ceremony, endowed with special emotion and often sacred meaning (see Denzin, 1984d: 246-247). Performed around a clearly defined set of social objects, or lines of action, rituals, when performed, confer upon their participants a special sense of the sacred. The settings in which rituals are performed are given special, interactional meaning, and may be termed *ritual settings.* Ritual performances legitimize the selves of the ritual performers, and give a sense of solidarity and community to the group members who witness or participate in their performance. Permitting of few variations, rituals are subject to the pressures of interactional normalization. When performed, the ritual dramatically recreates for the group its central and basic worldview. Within the "frame" of ritual, group members act ritualistically, thereby connecting themselves to their collective past. In the same motion, they make a purchase on the future, for the ritual act secures a movement into the future that will be guided by the ritual in question.

Durkheim (1912) and Goffman (1971) have suggested that rituals are positive and negative. Malinowski (1913/1962), Radcliffe-Brown (1922), and Warner (1962) have suggested that rituals may be performed for purely magical, mystical, or religious reasons. That is, when performed, rituals are believed to give group members some control over the future or over the uncontrollable. At this level rituals provide a symbolic bridge between the person and the group, for by entering into the ritual the person is joined to the group through the ritual acts that are performed. Emotionally and symbolically, rituals, as Shils (1976) has argued, embody the central, core values of the group.

Interactionally, rituals symbolize the problematics of the group. At the heart of any organized group exists a set of rituals that, when communicated to the newcomer, serve to draw him or her into the inner fabric of the group. Rituals, then, stand at the intersection of individuals, societies, and groups (see Denzin, 1984e: 246-247).

A.A. ritual, enacted through the meeting, yet permanently recorded in the texts and readings of A.A., may be analyzed in terms of these dimensions. I shall take up the key A.A. rituals in turn, beginning with the readings that structure an A.A. meeting.

The reading of the A.A. "Preamble," "How It Works," the Twelve Traditions, and the "Thought for the Day," brings into every A.A. meeting the collective history of Alcoholics Anonymous. Although many groups do not read "The Thought for the Day" or "The Traditions" or all of "How It Works," the A.A. Preamble is always read. These A.A. readings are endowed with solemn ceremony. Members listen quietly as they are read. Each reading references a problematic in the A.A. program and a problematic in the member's own program. When the meeting is called to order by the Chair the ritual self of being an A.A. member at the meeting is brought into existence. From this moment until the last words of the Lord's Prayer, the members are within the "frame" of an A.A. meeting. This becomes a sacred moment in their day, as attending Mass might be for another individual. The A.A. readings permit few variations. They are read in order, exactly as they were read at the last meeting. Wherever an A.A. member goes these readings will be presented in the same sequence, with the same words. In this sense A.A. ritual admits of no variations.

These readings embody the A.A. worldview. By listening to them being read the member becomes a part of A.A.'s oral history. Furthermore, by hearing these readings read out loud the member obtains some measure of protection against taking a drink today. In this way the A.A. rituals serve as mechanisms for ensuring sobriety in a world that is regarded as uncontrollable and unmanageable. Because they focus explicitly on the problematics of A.A.—sobriety and its maintenance—these ritual readings keep A.A.'s primary purpose constantly in front of the member.

These rituals are positive, joining rituals. They bring members into one another's presence, providing a bridge between the loneliness of alcoholism and the community of A.A. recovery. By allowing the newcomer to read, A.A. invites that member to move more deeply into the inner structures of the fellowship. In this way newcomers are incorporated into group life.

The "talking" rituals of the A.A. meeting are meant to ensure that each member has a chance to speak. Interruptions are infrequent. Each member is allowed to speak as long as he or she desires, and usually on any topic. The talk is structured by turn taking, and ritualistically each member knows that when it is his or her turn to speak, the floor will be granted. One's place in the speech event that is an A.A. meeting is determined in one of three ways, depending on the chair's choice of rules. From the Chair, a left-to-right or right-to-left order of seating arrangement can be employed. That is, the chair speaks, then turns to the person immediately to either his or her left or right, and asks that person if he or she would like to speak. After that person speaks, the person immediately next to them speaks, and so on, until everyone around the table has spoken. Each member knows, then, when they will be called upon to speak. It is during this time of waiting to talk that each member organizes the "speech" that will be made.

If the counterclockwise or clockwise method of speaker designation is not employed, the other mode of speaker selection—common in the community I studied—is to turn the meeting over to the group and have members select who will speak next. This method of member designation involves the Chair asking a person to begin the meeting, and then asking that member to call on someone when they are done. In turn, the member who is called upon is asked to call on someone. In this manner the meeting runs itself without a Chair. The meeting concludes (as do all meetings), when all members have spoken and the Lord's Prayer is said in unison.

The talk that the member produces will contain references to the A.A. rituals, including the Steps and the Traditions. It may also contain humor and profanity. As the member speaks, he or she is accorded the full ritual status of "A.A. membership." In this sense, no member's talk is any more important than the talk of any other member. There is no ritual hierarchy between A.A. speakers, only a distinction between the person who is at his or her first meeting, and all other members. That is, A.A. ritualistically accords the newcomer the status of being the most important person in the room. This is because they are at the first meeting. This status, however, will soon wear off if the member becomes a regular in the group.

The "anniversary rituals" of A.A. were already discussed. The giving of medallions for continuous sobriety signals status passage moments within A.A.'s social structure. Length of sobriety thus becomes a ritual marker of commitment to A.A. and to the A.A. way of life. As sobriety lengthens the member grows into becoming an "old-timer" or "regular" in the A.A. group.

The "closing ritual" of the A.A. meetings centers around the saying of the Lord's Prayer. This is done by the group members standing, holding hands, and saying this prayer in unison. When the prayer is completed members often add "Keep coming back." This phrase, coupled with the A.A. handshake, which is the universal greeting when members enter one another's presence at an A.A. meeting, signals the continuity of A.A. fellowship.

A.A.'s rituals, then, are kept alive through the oral tradition of the A.A. meeting. The meeting place of the group, which is also given sacred, ritual, meaning, comes to symbolize the meaning of the group to its members. These meetings and their places join members simultaneously to the meeting, to the group, and to the fellowship of A.A. more broadly conceived. They do not embody all that A.A. is, but without them, what else A.A. *is* would not be possible. These rituals, then, transform the member into a "talking subject" who is learning and has learned how to speak to his or her experiences of recovery within the ritual structure A.A. provides.

CONCLUSIONS

Beginning with the original A.A. meeting between Wilson and Smith, I have presented the historical, textual, and interactional structures that A.A. rests upon. The several levels of A.A., which range from its historical texts to the network of meetings that exist in a single community, and extend to the international community of A.A. and to the New York offices, find their immediate meaning in the biography of the individual A.A. member who comes to find himself or herself as a recovering alcoholic within the A.A. meeting. Each A.A. meeting, like the members who make it up, is an universal singular, epitomizing in its structures, its talk, and its rituals all A.A. meetings that have occurred in the past or will occur in the future. The single-mindedness of purpose that underlies all of the structures of A.A. permits this historical continuity that joins the past with the present. A.A., at all its levels and in all its forms—personal, group, in texts, in oral histories, in its bureaucratic structures, in its rules, as a social movement, its rituals, and its traditions—is a unique social structure. Although none of the units or forms that make up the A.A. structure are themselves unique, the overall structure is.

The key to this uniqueness is alcoholic understanding and the shared experiences that A.A. draws upon. These experiences permit A.A. members to form social groups among strangers, yet to do so within a historical structure of understanding that makes no alcoholic a stranger to a recovering alcoholic. How this is accomplished has been the topic of this chapter.

The A.A. group stands in stark contrast to the primary groups studied by Cooley (1902/1956) and Schutz (1964: 106-119). The A.A.

group is a group of strangers who create a fellowship of interaction that is based on shared, common experiences that the broader culture and alcoholism have produced for each individual. Yet this community of strangers is often interpreted by the member as being family:

> I lost everything. Family, home, wives, kids, job, everything. Even my parents turned against me. I fought like hell to get it all back and it didn't work. They went off to be who they were and left me to find myself. I think they hated me. Lot of self-pity on my part. I finally found you people. Now you're my family. Wherever I go, you're there. Wherever I go. But I got me a "home group" back in L.A. and that's where my new permanent family is. Gives me everything I ever wanted and ever looked for. I feel like I'm needed again [field observation, as reported September 2, 1982; 47-year-old male, salesman, over three years sobriety].

This family that is found within A.A. envelopes the member within a noncompetitive collective structure that is larger than the member (Bateson, 1972a). Largely male based, this A.A. culture, and the "families" that it spawns, permits the creation of shared pasts, feelings of solidarity, and the sharing of common futures (Couch et al., 1986). These processes are, of course, at the center of all long-standing social groups, including families. In this sense A.A. universalizes the desire for "groupness" that lies within our culture (see Bellah et al., 1985).

In the next chapter I turn to "slips" and relapses. How the alcoholic produces and manages these events determines, in large measure, the shape and form recovery will take.

11

SLIPS AND RELAPSES

> Why did I slip? I guess it's because I never surrendered fully to myself and accepted that I was an alcoholic. Oh, I knew I was an alcoholic, but I thought I could control alcohol. Finally somebody said to me, "Why can't you stay sober?" and it hit me, "Why can't I stay sober?" And then I decided, "Why not?" [field conversation, September 13, 1984, male, 55 years old, account executive].

> Slips, there's no such thing as a slip. All my drunks were planned. I just wanted to drink, period! [field conversation, December 4, 1985, 35-year-old male, carpenter].

Slips, relapses, or the return to controlled and uncontrolled drinking are commonplace occurrences for alcoholics. Baekeland (1977: 388) observes that even if the alcoholic has received treatment for alcoholism "he is notoriously prone to relapse." Relapse is mostly likely to occur within the first year of treatment, often within six months (Baekeland, 1977: 388-389; Pattison et al., 1968: 611). It can be estimated that 7 of 10 alcoholics who are treated for alcoholism will in fact relapse (see Baekeland, 1977; Baekeland and Lundwall, 1977; Blane, 1977; Pattison et al., 1977; Pendery et al., 1982; Rubington, 1977). Whether they return to normal, controlled drinking is problematic (Pendery et al., 1982). Of the alcoholics who come to A.A. it has been estimated that 37% relapse within the first year (Leach and Norris, 1977: 489; Maxwell, 1984: 3-4).

In this chapter I examine the phenomenon of relapse, drawing my primary materials from the A.A. community I studied (1980-1985), which numbered over 300 regular members. Within that group there were over 20 members who regularly slipped and returned to A.A. meetings. It is these members that I study in this chapter. I also observed over 100 other members who slipped, or relapsed, almost immediately after leaving treatment. These individuals did not become part of the A.A. community I studied, hence their accounts provide only a background to the more intensive analysis I will offer.

In *The Alcoholic Self* (Denzin, 1986a: chap. 7) I offered a brief outline of a "situational theory" of slips and relapses. In this chapter I develop and further elaborate that interpretive structure. It is grounded (Glaser and Strauss, 1967a) in the case materials just referenced. It is my contention that recovery cannot be understood until relapse is placed within proper perspective. Relapse stands on the opposite side of recovery; indeed, it may negate a recovering career. However, relapse may be a necessary part of any alcoholic's recovery (Royce, 1981: 268-270). Hence, to study relapse is to study a basic facet, perhaps the central facet, of recovery.

My argument will proceed as follows. First, I will briefly review prior studies and theories of relapse, including those offered by social scientists and A.A. In this context I will introduce A.A.'s distinction between being dry, "dry drunks," "white knuckle sobriety," and "sobriety." A typology of slips will be offered. Second, I will present my situational interpretation of slips and relapses. I will discuss selected slips that were reported by the relapsing alcoholics in my study, distinguishing types of alcoholic identities and the slips associated with those identities. Third, and closely related to slips, are alcoholic drinking dreams. I shall examine these dreams as they relate to the alcoholic's attempts to remain sober. Fourth, I will conclude with a fully stated, grounded interpretation of slips and relapses.

PRIOR STUDIES AND THEORIES OF RELAPSE

Studies and theories of relapse fall into two basic categories: A.A.'s surveys and theories of slips (see A.A., 1967, 1975, 1976; Leach and Norris, 1977; Maxwell, 1984) and social science studies of relapse following treatment. I shall take up these categories in reverse order.

Social Science Findings

Within the sociological and psychological literature on relapse two major lines of research stand out. The first are the studies of Sobell and Sobell (1978), Sobell et al. (1980), and Pattison et al. (1977). These investigations, building on the findings of Davies (1962), argue that (1) alcoholism is a multidimensional, not a unidimensional, phenomenon, and (2) social drinking of a controlled nature is possible, even desirable for some alcoholics. Perhaps reflective of the fact that treatment, of any variety, has only modest success in producing continuous sobriety for any type of alcoholic, this literature attempts to build a multidimensional theory of alcoholism that integrates drinking for some alcoholics into its understanding of recovery. This literature does not offer a theory of relapse. It attempts to incorporate or redefine relapse within a broadened conception of normal, controlled social drinking. (See Pendery et al., 1982 and Denzin, 1986a: chap. 2 for a criticism of this literature and the approach it proposes.)

Rubington's Theory

The second major line of research and theorizing within the area of relapse can be found in the work of Earl Rubington (1977) on abstinence after participation in halfway houses.

Rubington (1977: 363), reviewing research on abstinence after participation in halfway houses, reports that on the average only 20% of exresidents are sober six months after discharge. Rubington lays the foundations for a theory of rehabilitation (recovery) as it occurs within halfway houses. He suggests the following explanation. (1) Membership in a halfway house creates strains and tensions concerning an adherence to group norms that requires sobriety. (2) The alcoholic accordingly must learn how to manage this strain and tension while submitting to the authority structures of the halfway house. (3) Two social communities, staff and residents, thus coexist within the same cultural setting. The main interest of staff is in maintaining their authority, whereas the main interest of residents is in reducing that authority. (4) Three social situations thus exist: those in which residents are in the company of one another, those that place residents in the company of staff only, and those that combine residents and staff. (5) Four social types emerge in the halfway house: mixers, who mediate between staff and residents, company men who take the staff point of view, regular guys who side with residents, and loners who give no sign of aligning with either staff or other residents. Four exresident social roles or types also emerge: alcoholism professionals who graduate from being residents in halfway houses to working in the field of rehabilitation, reformed drunks who lack membership in a group, abstainers who rejoin conventional society, and drunks who were intoxicated when they entered treatment and return to a drinking life after the halfway house. Rubington (1977: 374) predicts that mixers are likely to end up as alcoholism professionals, whereas company men will become reformed drunks, "regular guys" drunks, and loners abstainers.

Rubington's theory suggests that relapses are greatest for regular guys. This is so for several reasons. First there are always more regular guys in any halfway house. Second, regulars establish friendship with other regulars. Third, when relapses occur, they take two forms: paired and sequential. Paired-relapse occurs when two residents leave together and get drunk. In sequential relapse, one person relapses and then another "feels compelled to follow his example" (Rubington, 1977: 377).

Staff, Rubington (1977: 378) says, may seek to intervene and stop these relapse chains. They may counsel residents to take preventive action. However, Rubington argues that regular guys, by virtue of how they have adapted to the halfway house culture, are reluctant to talk about their desires to return to drinking; indeed, they may have little practice in doing so. They may also feel that it is out of character to speak of such matters. Thus, a wall is built upon between regular guys and staff, resignation sets in, and the alcoholic gives in to the inevitable, which is to drink.

Rubington's formulations have three important implications. First, they suggest that recovery and relapse are group phenomena that are embedded in social contexts. These contexts may produce relapse when recovery is intended. Second, they may be applied to treatment centers. Although the short-term nature of treatment works against a well-developed structure of social identities that Rubington finds in halfway houses, mixers, company men, regular guys, and loners also emerge within treatment facilities. Similarly, the division between staff and residents that Rubington finds in halfway houses also appears in treatment centers. However, the intensive nature of the treatment experience works against a strong countercultural point of view that seems to be evident in halfway houses. To the extent that patients in treatment form friendships with fellow patients, and if these friendships extend after treatment, then the paired and sequential patterns of relapse that Rubington observes also seem to hold (see following discussion).

The third implication of Rubington's formulations applies to A.A. That is, within A.A., mixers, regular guys, loners, and company men also emerge. Company men, also called "*Big Book* Thumpers," take the official, organizational view of Alcoholics Anonymous. Loners attend meetings, but form few friendships or A.A. attachments. Regular guys form friendships within the A.A. fellowship. Mixers attach themselves to long-term A.A. members and attempt to bridge the gap between newcomers, themselves, and old-timers. Across these four social identities must be arrayed newcomers (or pigeons), old-timers, regulars, and "slippers," or persons who regularly attend A.A. and relapse. Consistent with Rubington's predictions, newcomers who were regular guys in treatment and who maintain friendships with other regular guys (who are also newcomers) tend to slip, or relapse more than loners, company men, and mixers. They tend to relapse in the paired and sequential fashion outlined by Rubington.

Rubington's work indicates how the institutions that are created to produce abstinence may in fact lay the conditions for relapse. I turn now to those studies and theories that deal with relapse within Alcoholics Anonymous.

Relapse in A.A.: Leach and Norris

Leach and Norris (1977) and Maxwell (1984) review the results of the 1968, 1971, and 1981 A.A. "sobriety surveys." Several critical findings emerge from these and other data. First, as previously indicated, 37% of A.A. members relapse within the first year. This is of course an important finding. It suggests that the socialization experiences that occur in treatment lack the power to keep the alcoholic sober for any length of time. Because 7 of 10 alcoholics who undergo treatment appear to return to drinking—whereas 7 to 10 alcoholics who go to A.A. regularly stay sober—the interactions that occur within A.A. appear to hold the key to sustained sobriety. Second, those members who relapse tend to (1) attend fewer A.A. meetings, as well as other A.A. functions; (2) be referred by sources other than self (such as family, employer, physician, courts, attorneys); and (3) keep returning to A.A. out of a desire for fellowship and long-term sobriety. Third, the longer a member is in A.A. and does not relapse, the greater the likelihood that he will remain sober for two years or more. Fourth, in order for the sobriety career to build and extend beyond three years, the member will maintain regular A.A. meeting attendance (three or more meetings a week) at least up to and beyond five years of sobriety. Fifth, after five years this attendance pattern at meetings will decline, but not stop. In short, sustained sobriety within A.A. requires lengthy and continuous involvement in the A.A. social structure. In the absence of that participation and involvement slips and relapses will occur, and they are most likely to occur within the first year of sobriety.

The Leach and Norris and Rudy Models

Leach and Norris (1977: 483-484) offer a nine-step model for becoming an abstinent A.A. member. These steps are (1) learning of the existence of A.A.; (2) perceiving A.A. as relevant to one's needs; (3) being referred to A.A.; (4) making personal contact with A.A.; (5) attending a closed A.A. meeting; (6) participating in other A.A. activities and internalizing the A.A. norms; (7) taking the last drink; (8) making a Twelve Step call; and (9) speaking at an A.A. meeting. Noting that not every abstinent member passes through these nine stages, and that "hitting bottom" should be added as a stage, Leach and Norris suggest that members who relapse after passing through these stages must go through the stages again, at least in some fashion.

Rudy (1986) has proposed a modification of the Leach and Norris work, inserting "hitting bottom" as the first stage in his six-stage model. His other five stages are (1) going to the first meeting; (2) making a commitment to A.A.; (3) accepting one's problem; (4) telling one's story, (5) and doing Twelve Step work. Rudy then distinguishes four types of alcoholic careers: (1) pure alcoholics, (2) convinced alcoholics, (3) converted alcoholics, and (4) tangential alcoholics. Pure alcoholics regard themselves as alcoholics before coming to A.A. Convinced alcoholics become convinced of their alcoholism after A.A. participation. Converted alcoholics come to A.A. believing they have a drinking problem and become converted to the A.A. point of view. Tangential alcoholics have alcoholic self-conceptions, but do not regard alcohol as being a major problem in their lives.

The Leach and Norris and Rudy models (see also Trice, 1966, 1957; Trice and Roman, 1970) have the benefits of specifying a stepwise, temporal projection of how one becomes an A.A. member and learns how to be abstinent. However, Rudy's model is primarily concerned with A.A. affiliation and not with becoming abstinent. The Leach and Norris model glosses over the problematic of "hitting bottom" and too quickly passes over the process by which the alcoholic comes to the self-understanding concerning the desire to no longer drink. Neither model addresses the range of problematic situations that can lead an alcoholic back to drinking. Nor do these models fully locate "becoming abstinent" and slipping within group or interactional contexts, as Rubington's framework does. Consistent with Leach and Norris and Rudy, it can be argued that relapsing alcoholics are those A.A. members who have not yet hit bottom and made self-commitments to having their last drink.

Conversion

Rudy's model does have the benefits, however, of speaking to the conversion process that occurs within Alcoholics Anonymous. Following Travisano (1981), Stark and Bainbridge (1980), Lofland and Stark (1965), Rudy (1986), Greil and Rudy (1984), and Snow and Phillips (1980), conversion to A.A. may be conceptualized as a process signalling a radical transformation in personal identity. Such a process leads the alcoholic to come to see the world from the point of view of new A.A. significant others. As an identity transforming organization, A.A. produces a massive restructuring of the alcoholic's identity and meaning systems. Critical to the process of conversion that transpires for the alcoholic are the formation of affective bonds and the production of intensive interactions within the A.A. social structure. Ideologically and emotionally, A.A. encapsulates—to use Greil and Rudy's and Lofland's terms—the new alcoholic member. (See Chapter 6 for a further elaboration of these points.) I turn now to A.A.'s theory of relapse.

A.A.'S THEORY OF RELAPSE

Drinking in A.A., of course, is regarded as a taboo self-act, one to be avoided at all costs. Yet, because the A.A. group is organized around the principle of carrying the message of sobriety to the alcoholic who still suffers, the member who drinks and returns to A.A. is typically welcomed back. In a Durkheimian sense (1897/1951; 1893/1964; 1912/1961; Erikson, 1966) drinking when in A.A. defines the outer boundaries of acceptable group conduct. The interaction at the A.A. meeting described in the previous chapter, where a member who had just drank returned to a meeting, instances the typical A.A. reaction to slips.

Within A.A. (1967: 11, 52, 68, 99, 154, 184, 197, 213-214, 251-291; 1975: 4-5, 63-74) the following reasons are given for slips: (1) the drinker has not yet hit bottom; (2) he or she is not working the spiritual program;

(3) they went into "slippery" (that is, drinking) places; (4) they have not changed their friends and playmates; (5) the drinker has tried to take control over his or her life; (6) the member has not surrendered to alcoholism; (7) the member has not been attending enough meetings; (8) he or she has not been working the program, including reading the *Big Book*, doing the Steps, and getting rid of negative thinking and resentments.

A.A. sums up this position, or theory of slips, by reinterpreting a slip as a "slip in thinking." It is argued that the member has slipped away from the A.A. program, and did not fully let go of the old ways of thinking. Hence, he or she did not want the program badly enough to go to any length to get it.

The following elder member of the A.A. group I studied summarizes the A.A. position on slips.

> Slips are in thinking. Slips are what my wife wears. Slips are when you slip on a banana peel. You don't slip in A.A.. Hell no! You go out and get drunk. That's what I did. I stopped going to meetings. I got back in the driver's seat and took control of my life. I held on to imaginary resentments, went back to my old drinking places, forgot my higher power, stopped calling my sponsor and forgot just how bad it was the last time before I stopped drinking. I had to hit a new bottom before I could accept in my gut the fact that I'm an alcoholic and will be one until the day I die [field conversation, April 1, 1985].

A.A.'s interpretive theory of slips conceptualizes the return to drinking as an attempt on the part of the alcoholic to once again take control over his or her life. Drinking thus becomes a symbol of being in control (A.A., 1967: 213; see Bateson, 1972a and Denzin, 1986a: chap. 2).

The Disease of Alcoholism

A.A.'s disease, or illness, conception of alcoholism (A.A., 1975: 63) leads to a threefold view of slips. First, it is assumed that drinking is the normal state of affairs for an alcoholic; being sober is abnormal. Second, when an alcoholic slips in the early stages of his recovery a slip is expected, for he has yet to learn how to be sober. His disease is still talking him into drinking. Third, once an alcoholic has recovered and maintained one year or more of sobriety, a slip is no longer explained solely in terms of the illness. Rather, it is interpreted as being a willful self-act. These are often called "planned" drunks, in contrast to the perhaps unplanned slip of the newcomer. Thus, alcoholics who drink after a long period of sobriety are seen as using their illness as an excuse for drinking. On the other hand, newcomers are seen as drinking because their illness causes them to drink. *This interpretive strategy locates alcoholism as the cause of slips at one point in the recovery career, while inverting its causal position in the later stages of recovery.* The following member speaks to this point:

> The fucker doesn't want to get sober. He's using alcoholism as an excuse. He just wants pussy. He don't want to give up control. He wants everything he had before without making any changes. He ain't got no excuse to be drunk 'cept himself. Christ, he was sober two years before he went out. You figure it out [field conversation, May 2, 1983; speaker has been sober for seven years].

Being Dry versus Being Sober

An additional feature of A.A.'s theory of slips must be noted. This is the distinction between being dry, being sober, and being in a "dry drunk" (see A.A., 1967). Being dry references an individual who has gone without drinking for a period of time but has not worked the A.A. program. All A.A. members can reference times in their lives when they went without drinking. They may have taken a pledge not to drink, or they went on "the wagon." After entering A.A. these periods of being dry are contrasted to "being sober." Being sober means working an A.A. program that produces sobriety and serenity, or peace of mind (Denzin, 1986a: chap. 7). "Being sober" is then contrasted to a "dry drunk." In a dry drunk the member displays all of the characteristics of a person who is staying dry, but has negative emotional feelings about herself and others. A dry drunk is seen as being a prelude to drinking.

No Excuses

Once the member has internalized the A.A. program and surrendered to alcoholism, there are no longer any excuses for drinking. If the member drinks again it is because he or she has retreated into denial in a search for an excuse to drink. In the A.A. groups that I studied the following "Thought for the Day" (Hazelden Foundation, 1956) was often quoted:

> I hope that nothing can happen to me now that would justify my taking a drink. No death of a dear one. No great calamity in any area of my life should justify me in drinking.

By stripping away the excuses that could be given for drinking, A.A. attempts to locate the member within a social structure in which excuses for drinking become causes for staying sober. This presupposes a radical change in the member's relationship to the world. He or she has been schooled in the belief that drinking is a way to solve life's problems (see Bateson, 1972a; Madsen, 1974; McAndrew and Edgerton, 1969).

Should the member drink after joining A.A., he or she is encouraged to share that experience with the A.A. group. The December 7 (Hazelden, 1956) "Thought for the Day" addresses this point:

> When people come back to A.A. after having a slip, the temptation is strong to say nothing about it. No other A.A. member should force them to declare themselves. It is entirely up to them. If they are well-grounded in A.A., they will realize that it is up to them to speak up at the next meeting and tell about their slip.

A member with seven years of sobriety when he had a slip discusses what he did:

> I don't know how it happened. I found myself at the end of a bar with a shot and a beer. I drank it and was overwhelmed with guilt. We was going to Pittsburgh for a family vacation the next day. I waited 'till we got there and then I went to an A.A. group and told about it. I had to get it off my chest. I didn't want to tell the people in my home group. Pride, I guess. But later I did [field conversation, June 25, 1982].

Time and Slips

A.A. folklore divides the first year of sobriety into three-month segments and associates problems with slips at the end of the first month, three months, and then six and nine months. A self-fulfilling prophecy is created (see Merton, 1957; Thomas and Thomas, 1928). Members begin to speak of problems concerning the desire to drink at each of these temporal intervals. The following member is coming up on nine months. She states:

> I want to drink. I wanted to drink at three months and six months, but this is the worst yet. I dream of drinking. I see Manhattans in front of me. I want to escape everything. Just run and hide in a bottle. This is harder than three months. Is this what you call white knuckle sobriety? I feel like I'm hanging on with my finger nails [field conversation, July 2, 1984, 35-year-old nurse].

White knuckle sobriety is using all of one's strength not to drink. Members speak of this, as this individual does, in problematic situations when they want to drink, but do not. By creating temporal expectations for drinking at specific sobriety intervals A.A. sets in motion self-fulfilling prophecies that may in fact lead members back to drinking. In this organizational sense A.A. may work against its primary purpose.

Types, Causes, and Meanings of Slips

The following understandings concerning slips must be stated. First, slips, or relapses, only make sense in terms of the length of time the individual has been sober. That is, a relapse can only occur after the alcoholic has made an effort to be sober for a period of time. Being dry three days and then drinking is not a relapse from sobriety but a return to drinking. A.A.'s distinction between dry and sober is critical for understanding this distinction. Second, slips within and outside A.A. constitute two different phenomena. Those that occur after the member joins A.A. are interpreted as "slips from A.A." by the member and other A.A. members. Slips that occur outside A.A. are not so interpreted. Thus, a slip by an A.A. member carries implications for a recovery group, whereas solitary slips outside the program do not.

Third, the length and frequency of the slip must be considered. Some are short term, as when an A.A. member has one or two drinks and then returns to A.A. Others are long term and start a chain of controlled and uncontrolled drinking. Still others are intermittent, spaced at regular and irregular intervals. Fourth, the consequence of the slip for the drinker must be considered. It may lead to alcoholic troubles (DUIs), or no troubles at all. It may serve to bring the member back to treatment and A.A., or the member may never again enter a recovery career. Fifth, the perceived causes of the slip must be considered. If an alcoholic in a halfway program slips because a friend slips, the cause is located in the actions of another. If an alcoholic drinks because his wife dies, this is a problematic situation of another order, even though the cause is still located in another person or an event. The range and types of problematic situations that are seen as causing slips must be interpreted before the slip can be understood. The planned or unplanned nature of the slip in relationship to the problematic situation must also be considered.

Sixth, slips must be understood in terms of group and interactional processes. That is, relapse is not just an individual act. It occurs within social settings. It involves the real and imagined presence of others. It becomes an emotional (and at times instrumental) social act in which the alcoholic attempts to return to a mode of self-understanding that alcohol was seen as once producing. To the degree that it occurs in the company of other alcoholics who are slipping, it is a group and interactional production. Even if the slip is solitary—that is, the alcoholic drinks by herself—it occurs against the frame of reference that A.A. and treatment have offered. The drinker sees herself as going against the normative and cultural structures that treatment and A.A. have given her. In this sense the slip is a social act that is enveloped in the social perspectives of others, even if they are not present as the drinker drinks. A recovering alcoholic, sober four years, describes this process.

> I looked into the bottom of the glass and saw W's face there. I looked in the mirror on the wall and saw the A.A. group behind me. I turned away and they were in front of me. I thought I was out of my mind. I'd only had one drink and here I was feeling guilty and seeing A.A.s everywhere [field conversation, November 2, 1984].

To summarize, slips are multidimensional phenomena, involving more than an alcoholic taking a drink. They are social in nature, having their origins in the organizational, institutional, group, family, and interactional experiences of the alcoholic. The following types of slips may thus be identified: (1) the slip of the A.A. newcomer; (2) the slip of the A.A. member who has established lengthy sobriety; (3) the paired and sequential slips that occur after treatment in treatment centers and in halfway houses; (4) solitary slips that occur outside A.A.; (5) solitary slips that occur within A.A.; (6) short-term slips; (7) intermittent slips; (8) long-term slips; (9) slips that lead the member back to A.A.; (10) slips that divert and bring a halt to a recovery career; (11) planned slips, or drunks; and (12) unplanned slips.

It will not be uncommon for individual A.A. members to have experienced some or all of these forms of the slip. Consequently, any A.A. group will be made up of members who have experienced each of these types. The presence of these forms of "slipping experience" within the A.A. group serves to highlight the adage that any member could slip at any time for any number of reasons and for any length of time, and perhaps not get back. These considerations in mind, I now turn to the situational interpretation of slips.

A SITUATIONAL INTERPRETATION OF RELAPSE AND SLIPS

In *The Alcoholic Self* (1986a: chap. 7) I suggested the following reasons for an alcoholic's return to drinking: (1) the belief that he can once again control alcohol; (2) a desire to return to old drinking contexts where sociability was experienced; (3) a phenomenological craving for alcohol coupled with a high stress situation in which, in the past, drinking was used as a means of reducing anxiety and stress; and (4) a failure to fully commit to the A.A. program.

I next proposed that Becker's (1960, 1964) model of situational adjustments to problematic situations could be applied to the phenomenon of relapse. Stated succinctly, I argued that alcoholics slip when the transformations of self that have occurred in the early stages of recovery have not been complete. If recovery has produced an alternation, but not a transformation, in identity (Travisano, 1981), then when problematic situations arise the likelihood of the alcoholic drinking is high. This is so because the member has not committed himself to the identity of being a nondrinking, recovering alcoholic. In McCall and Simmons (1978) and Stryker's (1980) terms, the salience of the identity of recovering alcoholic is low, or not near the top of the hierarchy of identities the member holds about himself. The member has adopted a transitory identity of being a problem drinker who has overcome the problems that made him a problem drinker in the first place. Large classes of alcoholics who undergo treatment together are likely to develop this transient or uncommitted alcoholic identity. Hence, upon release from treatment, when they confront problematic situations their likelihood of drinking is high.

Problematic Situations

Three classes, or types, of problematic situations set the contexts for the return to drinking. These are (1) problems in the areas of work, money, and financial security; (2) problems in social relationships, including friendships and work relationships; (3) problems in the areas of intimate relationships, including family, lovers, parents, and children (see Adler, 1927).

Cross-cutting these problematic situations are the problematics of self, emotionality, and temporality. The Six Theses of Alcoholism (and Recovery) focus on these three processes (Denzin, 1986a: chaps. 1 and 5). Alcoholism is a dis-ease, or an uncomfortableness with self, time, and emotional feeling. The alcoholic used alcohol as a means of dealing with self-feeling, fear, anxiety, and time. He or she dwelled on the negative emotional experiences lived in the past. Fearful of the future, the alcoholic lived in the present with the aid of alcohol.

Self, emotionality, and temporality thus intersect with the three basic problematic situations the alcoholic confronts in recovery. The alcoholic may be unemployed, working marginally or financially insecure, or he may be overworked, and placed under high stress at work. Alcohol may then be used as a means of escaping the fears and anxieties that flow from these work- and money-related problems. Unemployed, he feels the crush of uncommitted time and drinks to escape time. Overworked, he feels the pressure of the future and drinks to reduce the fears of failure. In both instances, his self-definitions draw him to alcohol as a means of dealing with his emotions, the time he can't control, and the pressures he feels. The member who remains within a sociability network that still drinks may be drawn to alcohol (and friendship) out of a desire to still belong to a social group. He persists in lodging valued portions of self in alcohol-centered social settings. The individual who resides within an intimate social relationship that is still drinking centered feels the same pressures. If the relationship is in a state of emotional confusion, drinking may be turned to.

In each of these three contexts (work, friendships, and family), the alcoholic derives valued senses of self and emotional feeling. Still divided against herself, still caught in the self-centered narcissism that she experienced as an active alcoholic, the member falls and slips when these contexts and the problems they are seen as containing emerge in her life. She may create "imaginary" problems out of or in these situations and then justify drinking. A.A. (1976: 37) calls this finding some "insanely trivial excuse for taking the first drink." She will be more likely to drink if she has not become embedded in the A.A. social structure. If she attends only a few meetings a month and goes to no outside A.A. functions or gatherings, then she will drink when the situational opportunity to do so arises. Consider the followig account.

> The first time I drank was almost three months to the day after I left treatment. I was getting married that day. My wife-to-be asked if it would bother me if we had wine at the reception. I lied and said no. There was wine everywhere. When I was in treatment my counselor had said that he thought I could handle "it" again. I thought he meant alcohol. He meant living. Anway, I was anxious and nervous as hell that day. I could smell and taste the wine. Late that night I had glass of wine when nobody was looking. That started me off on a four-month slip. At that time I was only going to the Monday night meeting. That was the only time I thought of myself as an alcoholic. Then I quit going to that meeting. I had no A.A. contact at all [field conversation, July 16, 1981].

Holidays

The social occasion is a recurring problematic for the recovering alcoholic. Such occasions often intersect with work and family relationships, as given in the office Christmas Party, the New Year's Eve Party, Halloween, St. Patrick's Day, and so on. Such ritual gatherings are drinking occasions in American society (see Goffman, 1963a). In the past the member probably drank to excess on such days. Now that he is sober he approaches them with fear. The following individuals speak of Christmas. The first two are in treatment at Eastern. The first is a 32-year-old male.

> I get out on Saturday. On the 21st there's an office party. I'm leaving it up to the wife whether we go or not. Last year I was drunk and made a fool of myself. I just ain't sure what to do.

A second speaker states:

> I was drunk on every holiday. Nothin' different about Christmas 'cept everybody else is drunk, too. I liked these days 'cus the cops didn't notice me when I stumbled down the street drunk.

A member with four years sobriety states:

> The holidays are like every other day. I can't get too far ahead of today or I get drunk. To me Christmas is a day to celebrate sobriety, the greatest gift of all. You people give me this gift every day, if I come here. You can't buy it, you can't give it away, you can't keep it unless you give it away. You are my family and I come here on Christmas to be with you.

A member with seven years sobriety said:

> At these deals I just get a glass of soda as soon as I get there. People think I'm drinking gin or vodka and nobody says anything. Helps me to remember how I used to make an ass of myself at these things. The *Big Book* says we can go to drinking occasions if our purpose is to stay sober and not vicariously take part in other people's drinking. We have something special to bring to these things because we are sober.

These four accounts juxtapose two positions on the holidays and on drinking occasions. Newcomers to A.A. and treatment approach these gatherings with fear, apprehension, and in terms of a background of experience that defines these moments in drinking terms. The two regulars in A.A. had redefined these problematic situations within A.A.'s framework. They have learned how to pass as drinkers.

Because the holidays are notable occasions for excessive drinking, the meetings in November and December in A.A. are often given over to those topics. Large numbers of individuals come into A.A. during these months, seeking situational help for these problematic situations.

The following member confirms Baekeland's (1977: 388) observation that of those alcoholics who relapse after discharge, 50% do so in one month. This member relapsed eight days after leaving treatment, which was just before Thanksgiving. He states:

> Fuck, I didn't know what to do. The old man and old lady [father and mother] wouldn't let me stay in their place. I couldn't stay in detox, my bike wouldn't run. The garage didn't have my car [a Porsche] fixed. The job on the farm didn't turn up. My daughter who I hadn't seen since she was born was comin' to see me two weeks before Christmas, and I didn't have no money. What would you do? I went to find my old drinkin' buddies. Least they'd understand and maybe they could give me some work to do so I could get back on my feet. I only had three beers. That's O.K., ain't it? I didn't call none of you people [A.A.] cause I didn't want to bother you. Hell, it was the holidays. Nothin' you could do anyway [field conversation, November 30, 1985].

Not only does he confirm Baekeland's observation, but he supports the above interpretation. This individual attended only one A.A. meeting in the week after he was discharged from treatment. He confronted problematic situations in the areas of work and family. He returned to old interactional settings as a means of dealing with his problem. He did not use his A.A. connections as a way of dealing with his situation. When he drank, he drank with old friends and two former A.A. members who were also having problems in their lives. This was, in Rubington's sense, a paired relapse. This member has yet to attend an A.A. meeting since his relapse.

Side-Bets, Self, and Redefining the Problematic

This situational theory presumes that in order for a committed A.A. identity to be built the member must make side-bets, or interactional commitments into the A.A. social structure. Within the A.A. groups I studied specific indicators of side-bets included: (1) writing one's sobriety date on the group's A.A. sobriety calendar (see Glossary); (2) agreeing to open up and chair a group's meetings for a month; (3) fixing coffee for a group; (4) coming early to meetings and staying late; (5) offering members rides to meetings; (6) putting one's telephone number on the group telephone list; (7) talking with newcomers and getting involved with them; (8) interacting socially with other members outside A.A. meetings, for instance, breakfasts, coffee, and so on; (9) announcing one's 3-, 6-, 9-, and twelve-month birthday dates to the group;

and (10) introducing A.A. members to family members and friends. These actions and others like them serve to integrate the members into the A.A. network. They lock the member, so to speak, into a recovering identity.

But the member must not only become a regular A.A. member. He must become socially involved in A.A. outside meetings. If this is not done, the identity of alcoholic is only anchored in those situations where the alcoholic confronts other alcoholics, which will be A.A. meetings. If he attends few meetings, the opportunity for announcing and hence acting on this identity is reduced. As Stone (1981: 188, 193-194) suggests, one's identity is established in part by how others place him in a social situation. If the A.A. member announces himself as an alcoholic at an A.A. meeting and if others place him in the identity of alcoholic at meetings, then he is given the identity of alcoholic in that situation. If he avoids such situations this identity placement will not occur. However, if he carries this A.A. identification over into situations that extend beyond A.A. meetings, the likelihood of adopting a transsituational identity of recovering alcoholic is increased.

On the other hand, if the member does not become an A.A. regular, the chance of becoming embedded in A.A. is reduced and the identity of alcoholic becomes primarily situational. If the member adopts the "loner" identity he is not likely to become fully committed to the A.A. self. This increases his likelihood of drinking when problematic situations arise.

In addition to making side-bets into A.A. members must learn how to redefine themselves in relation to the problematic situations that arise in their lives. They can only learn how to do this by attending meetings. At meetings they will listen to members who engage in this process of redefining self in relationship to problems. They will see members who confront problems and do not drink, and they will also learn how to bring their problems to the tables and talk about them. The Leach and Norris (1977) materials suggest that newcomers who attend three to seven meetings a week learn to do this. Such members are apparently successful in building uninterrupted sobriety careers that extend beyond the first problematic year.

Borrowing from Stone (1981: 194), what such members accomplish is the building of a recovering self that is a "*validated program which exercises regulatory function over other responses of the same organism, including the formulation of other programs*" (italics in original). That is, the recovering alcoholic constructs a validated program of identity placement that governs her conduct in any and all situations that are confronted. Central to that identity is the self-understanding that the person will not drink. This transsituational self is learned in

A.A. meetings. It leads to a self-validating program that prohibits drinking in any situation.

The following member illustrates these points. At the time of this writing she has over four years continuous sobriety. She went through three treatment centers and is a regular attender of A.A. meetings. She is speaking after four months in A.A.

> I don't believe what I've done. Since I got sober this time I've had four deaths in the family, one wedding, and a graduation. I haven't had to have a drink. Before I would have been sloshed, drunk out of my mind, gin bottles at my feet. Its only because I've been coming here every day and talking about it that I've made it through. Seeing people with seven and eight years helps too [field conversation, February 5, 1982].

Types of Recovering Identities

Two basic alcoholic identities, transient and enduring, or uncommitted and committed, are thus distinguished. A member with a committed alcoholic identity will (1) closely attach himself or herself to a sponsor; (2) work all of A.A.'s Steps; (3) become an A.A. regular; and (4) carry A.A. over into the other pivotal areas of his or her life. Such a member will maintain regular contact with a sponsor and call a sponsor, or go to meetings (or both) when problematic situations arise. He or she will learn how to talk about these problems without drinking. The A.A. member who brought the problem of his daughter's pregnancy to the tables who was discussed in the last chapter is an instance of how this works. The member who drank eight days after treatment is an instance of how it does not work. The member with the uncommitted alcoholic identity may attach himself or herself to a sponsor but will not use the sponsor. He or she is unlikely to become a regular A.A. member, and the Steps will not be worked on a consistent basis. The member will compartmentalize his or her alcoholic identity, or neutralize that identity when in the presence of persons outside A.A.

As the alcoholic builds a committed recovering identity, he or she becomes more deeply embedded in the A.A. social structure. They may become regular guys, mixers, or company men; although some who remain outsiders and loners maintain sobriety through meeting attendance.

The "Hopelessly Alcoholic" Identity

A member may be fully committed to an alcoholic identity, go through treatment several times, attend meetings on a regular basis, yet return to drinking. He or she will sink into a long period of intoxication in which they ask for help while they continue to drink. Their lives may collapse around them, yet they continue this line of action. The following member is representative. He is intoxicated as he speaks at an A.A. meeting:

> I'm an alcoholic. I know that. I just don't know how to stop. I been through detox four times in the last week. I had four months after my last treatment center. Then the old lady set me off again. Christ, that's an excuse. I just started drinking. Now she wants a divorce and I'm about to be livin' on the street. Don't do like me. Come to your meetings and stay off the stuff 'cause when you start up it ain't easy to stop. I think a part of me wants to die and kill me. I'm just all fucked up. Just a god dammed drunk. That's all I am [field conversation, December 3, 1985].

This member is still drinking. He has no doubt in his mind that he is an alcoholic. He is on the verge of being either a revolving-door drunk or an institutional alcoholic (Pittman and Gordon, 1958; Straus, 1974; Wiseman, 1970).

The next member died from alcoholism at the age of 47. She had been through two treatment centers and at one time was sober for over one year. Well liked within the A.A. community, she called herself a "crazy, grateful alcoholic." She states:

> I keep thinking I can control it. Just a few drinks to feel good again. A little vodka and orange juice. But I can never stop. I try to get sobered up by Friday night so I can go to my home group. I've got no excuse for drinking anymore. None. I just do it. I know I'm killing myself. I know I'm an alcoholic and things go good for me when I don't drink [field conversation, January 2, 1983. This woman died eight days later].

Slips and Identities

When committed alcoholics slip, their slips are more likely to be short-term and are brought to the A.A. tables for discussion. These members become committed to building long-term sobriety careers. They mobilize their self-pride behind the length of time they have been sober. They also work to interpret the conditions that produced their slip or slips. The following individual slipped eight days after she had three months of sobriety. She is attempting to interpret her slip.

> I hadn't gone to meetings for nine days. I kept everything at work bottled up inside. I wasn't talking to my friend. She knew something was wrong but I wouldn't talk to her. I got resentful. I got angry at my boss and at my

> parents. Then I got mad at my friend 'cause she didn't understand me. I got pissed at myself for being mad at everybody. Finally I said, "Fuck it, go get drunk and show them." I only had enough money for a half-pint in my pocket. I bought it and drank it. Then I called my friend and told her what I was doing. Then I went out and got a fifth and went home and waited for her to come. She got there and I bitched and screamed and yelled and cried. She poured it out 'cause I asked her to. Then she took me to detox and I stayed the weekend [field conversation, 29-year-old female, September 2, 1985].

This member discussed her slip at an A.A. meeting the day she got out of detox. She has been discussing her slip ever since. She has just obtained three months of sobriety again. She has increased her meeting attendance. She discusses her problems at the tables. Her slip was short term and indicative of the slip of a member committed to building a recovering identity within A.A.

"The Neutralized" Alcoholic Identity

Alcoholics who build transient or less than fully committed alcoholic identities will gravitate within the A.A. social structure to other alcoholics who have similar identities. They will have continuously interrupted sobriety careers. Such members may, however, maintain interactional commitments to A.A. They will still attend meetings, talk at meetings, and they may even discuss their slips on a regular basis. These members confirm the Leach and Norris (1977) finding that regular "slippers" return to A.A. because they seek the fellowship A.A. offers. These members will neutralize their alcoholic identity, incorporating slips into their conceptions of themselves. They will not regard the slip as a deeply deviant act that places them outside the A.A. cultural order. They will legitimate the slip in terms of its failure to cause problems in their life. Their techniques of neutralization (Sykes and Matza, 1959) deny harm to themselves or others. Yet, as they neutralize their slips they speak from a "double bind" position (see Bateson, 1972e). That is, to the degree that they are committed to A.A. and want others to see them as being committed to A.A. they cannot justify their slips. But to themselves they must justify the slip. Hence, these members locate causes that account for the regularity of their slips. The following member is representative.

> First I thought it was the old lady and them horses she loves more than me. Then I thought it was the job and the fact that other people was getting more money than me. Then I thought it was 'cause my ma's an

alkie. Then I thought it was 'cause I got so dammed much free time on my hands with my job. Then I thought it was 'cause I don't get involved in A.A. and work with others. Now I think it's 'cause I never really hit bottom. You know I never lost everything. It wasn't as bad for me as it was for you other people. I just live this program one day at a time. I ain't had a drink today. But I did last Friday. Two Tequilla Sunrises with my brother and sister-in-law. No excuse. Just had 'em. That's all.

Sometimes I start to worry. First I had 11 months. Then 7 months, then 6 months, then 3 months three times. Now I ain't had 3 months in a year. Seems like it's gettin' worse. Maybe I ain't working this program the way I should [field conversation, October 17, 1985; 34-year-old male, middle management].

This individual attends three or fewer meetings a week and does not involve himself in A.A. social activities. His wife will not go to Al-Anon. He has moved through a sequence of causes for his slips and has ended with the one A.A. puts in front of every member; that is, hitting bottom.

Two Bottoms

There are two bottoms a member may hit (see Glossary, and Denzin, 1986a: chap. 6). There is the bottom that leads the member sincerely to seek help. The member in the last quote hit that bottom when he entered treatment over three years ago. Then there is the bottom that keeps the member from drinking. This may be the same bottom that brought him to A.A. the first time, or it may be the bottom that is hit when the member slips and relapses after coming to A.A. Some members call this "field research." This last member has not yet hit a bottom like the bottom that sent him into treatment. Until he does he will continue to relapse.

The following member speaks to the distinction between these two bottoms.

When I went into treatment everything had gone. Work, family, health, the whole dammed thing. My drinking was out of control. I couldn't stay stopped and once I started I couldn't control it. So I was sober three months and then I went on a four-month binge. It was O.K. at first. A drink or two and walk away from it. Then it was a bottle which would last two or three days. Then it was a bottle every day. Then I ended up in a motel and wanted to kill myself. I didn't, but I still drank. The last time I drove my family out of the house again. They were afraid to be around me. That next day I surrendered. I decided I just didn't want this life of hell anymore. It just wasn't worth it. I just couldn't take it anymore. Was I going to drink today or not? That day I surrendered and it's been over four

> years since I've had a drink. That last bottom did it for me [field conversation, November 22, 1985].

The "Situational" Alcoholic and Slips

The relationship between slips, bottoms, and alcoholic identities is further illuminated in the relapse of the "situational" alcoholic. A situational alcoholic is a member who adopts the A.A. identity for a specified period of time, in response to an alcohol-related problematic situation that has arisen in her life. Once that problem has been dealt with, the member then ceases to be a member of A.A., or she remains on A.A.'s margins and fringes. A common pattern is the following. An individual receives a DUI. She is then mandated to a DUI school where instructions on drinking and driving are given. Facing the loss of a driver's license, the member then seeks outpatient counseling from an alcoholism counselor, who refers the individual to A.A. She then makes contact with A.A., secures a sponsor, and becomes a regular attender of meetings. This pattern of involvement holds until the person's court date comes up. Then she asks A.A. members for letters of reference concerning her attempts to work the A.A. program. These materials are supplied. The individual has the court hearing. The judge revokes her license for one year, commends her for her recovery program, and suspends jail or prison time, although the individual is assigned a probation officer. The individual reports her success to the A.A. group and is never seen again. If the individual persists in having alcohol-related problems she may keep in touch with A.A. A member who conforms to this pattern is speaking to an A.A. member:

> The judge said fine things about me and A.A.. There were eight of us in court at the same time. He took everybody's license. He sent six people to prison for a year. He commended me for what I had done. I just want to thank A.A. for everything. Without A.A. I would have gone off for a year [field conversation, as reported, October 28, 1985; male, academic occupation. After three months of sobriety, he slips until his court date and has not been to an A.A. meeting since his court date].

This individual continues to maintain infrequent contact with A.A. members. He has returned to drinking and has indicated that he may need to go into treatment to deal with his problems.

From "Situational" to "Committed" Alcoholic

The following member came to A.A. because of a DUI. He went through the same sequence of experiences as did the last situational alcoholic. However, he made the transition from being a situational alcoholic to a committed alcoholic. He speaks:

> I came here because of the DUI and because the drinking had just gotten out of control. I just kept coming and I found something I've always wanted and tried to find in the bars. I guess it's fellowship and a feeling that you're liked and needed. Anyway, I keep coming back. I never want to go back to where I was before [field conversation, as reported, November 9, 1985, three days after the member's one-year birthday in A.A.].

This alcoholic was sober from his first meeting onward. He attended three or more meetings a week and became involved in chairing meetings and in outside A.A. affairs. Drawn to A.A. because of alcohol-related problems, he resolved those problems but became a converted, or committed, A.A. member in the process (see Rudy, 1985). The situational alcoholic has not made that transition. His relapses are thus slips away from Alcoholics Anonymous.

Slips of Old-Timers

Reviewing the previous argument, alcoholics slip when they have not fully committed themselves to the A.A. framework, and even then some may slip. A complete transformation in identity, including a commitment to the A.A. concept of a higher power, appears to secure the alcoholic's sobriety for that length of time that the commitment is sustained. If the alcoholic withdraws from A.A., drinking will be taken up again. Sobriety was just a situational adjustment to problematic situations in the alcoholic's life. Now that those problems are removed the alcoholic takes up drinking again. The return to drinking is increased if the time since the member's last drink is lengthy. The following alcoholic demonstrates these points. He had 22 years of sobriety when he slipped.

> I was Mr. A.A. in town. I worked with the courts, the hospitals, the treatment centers, with anyone who needed help in the alcoholism field. I went to meetings, sponsored scores of people. Then I retired two years ago. I got to thinking I was immune from the stuff. Stopped going to meetings, forgot the higher power, took control over my life. But I was still Mr. A.A. in my mind. Then I let go of that. Said to myself that I'd had enough with drunks. On December 15 I decided I could drink. I bought a half-pint and drank it. Then I bought a half-pint the next day and drank it. I started bringing it home in my briefcase. After my wife went to bed I'd

> have the half-pint. This went on for a month until one night she came out of the bathroom and caught me. I think I wanted to be caught. She said, "What are you doing?" I felt like my pants were down around my knees, like a little kid with his hand in the cookie jar, 'cept it was a bottle of booze in my hand. She got mad and afraid. Asked me what I was going to do. I said, "I guess I better call my sponsor and go to a meeting and tell them what I've done." I called my sponsor and that's what he told me to do [field observation, June 28, 1982, 73-year-old alcoholic].

This man sponsored his sponsor into A.A. He returned to meetings for two weeks and discussed his slip. He now attends meetings on a regular basis. At the time of this writing he has slightly over three years sobriety.

As this member told his story around the A.A. tables alarm, shock, and gratitude were expressed. He was welcomed back and thanked for telling his story. Soon members who had not discussed their slips began to talk of slips that had been hidden from the group. This man's story has become a point of reference in the A.A. community I studied, for it solidifies the belief that no member is immune from a slip. He defined the outer boundary of sobriety in the A.A. community. He provided a point of reference for other members. His case served to highlight the importance of meetings and the continual activation of the alcoholic self in the meetings.

Interpretation

I have examined the following categories of slips that were contained in the typology of slips offered previously: (1) slips of newcomers; (2) slips of regulars; (3) slips of old-timers; (4) short-term slips; (5) regular and intermittent slips; (6) slips that halt a recovery program; (7) slips that bring a member back to A.A.; (8) slips that occur outside A.A. (those are not brought to the tables); (9) paired relapses; (10) slips of a solitary nature that occur within A.A.; (11) planned slips; and (12) unplanned slips (the man who told his story in Pittsburgh).

An examination of these cases reveals that the 12 categories of slips merge into one another. That is, a member who is building an A.A. identity may have a planned, short-term slip that is immediately brought back to A.A. A member who stays outside A.A. may have an unplanned slip that is joined with the slip of another member and the slip may be short term, or take on the contours of a long-term relapse. Similarly, a member who adopts the "hopelessly" alcoholic identity will experience a sequence of drinking episodes that are punctuated by only brief periods of recovery. In this case, the member relapses into recovery, perhaps out of exhaustion. In addition, the slip of an old-timer may be long term or brief, but eventually it is likely to bring the member back to the tables. The following account speaks to this point.

> I had 17 years with you people. Then one day I decided I would take one drink and I did. It took me 10 years to get back to you people. I'm sure glad to be back. I got 10 days. Someday I'll tell you my story. Thank you for letting me talk [field conversation, October 1, 1985].

A typology of slips, then, only offers an initial point of departure into a phenomenological interpretation of the relapsing process. As a process, slips are always embedded within the situations and the biography of the individual. Any member, as indicated, may experience each form of the slip. Because A.A. groups are made up of members who have experienced each form, knowledge of them is thus passed on through the A.A. social structure. Members learn how to plan slips, how to ask for help when one occurs, how to talk about them at meetings, and how to plan against one when the desire to drink returns. In this manner slips become group phenomena, located as they are in the talk and culture of the A.A. group. A member with over four years of sobriety phrases this understanding as follows:

> You don't have a relapse in order to be an A.A. member, but if a relapse will convince you that you are an alcoholic it can be useful. But some people never make it back. I had to relapse. When I was early on in the program I heard A [a member with 15 years in A.A., but never more than 8 months of continuous sobriety] say he hadn't had his last drink. I knew then that I was going to drink again. And I did. I learned to be careful about what I said at the tables [field conversation, October 22, 1983].

I turn now to alcoholic dreams. In the discussion of their drinking dreams A.A. members socialize one another into sobriety.

ALCOHOLIC DREAMS

Alcoholics in and out of treatment report dreams of a "drinking" nature. Although these dreams may occur months and even years after the alcoholic has stopped drinking, their vivid occurrence is often cause for alarm. Their widespread discussion around the A.A. tables suggests that they are not isolated occurrences.

Recent research on the "alcoholic withdrawal syndrome" (Gross et al., 1974: 206-208, 230-236) reveals that there is little question that the alcoholic's sleep and dream patterns change in relationship to the effects of alcoholic intake and withdrawal. Sleep patterns change as a result, in part, of the effects of "alcohol upon the brain biogenic amines" (Gross et al., 1974: 208). Although alcoholic hallucinosis is common during the withdrawal process, the symbolic content of the alcoholic's dreams during and after withdrawal have not been analyzed in detail.

Interpreting the Alcoholic's Dreams

It is possible, of course, to analyze the dreams alcoholics report in any of a number of different ways (see Boss, 1958, 1963, 1977; Foulkes, 1978; Freud, 1900/1968; Hall, 1953/1966; Hall and Nordby, 1972; Hall and Van de Castle, 1966; Jung, 1961). In the main, I shall follow each of these authors in an attempt to offer an interpretive grammar of the dreams alcoholics discuss at the A.A. tables. That is, these dreams represent repressed wishes or desires to drink. Their manifest content focuses on the drinking act and on its consequences for the alcoholic. Like Jung's "little dreams" they represent continuations of waking preoccupations. When discussed at the tables they become part of the collective consciousness (and unconscious) of the A.A. group and its members. With Boss (1958) I assume that these dreams can be taken at face value. They do not necessarily have deep, hidden meanings, as Freud might propose. In any case, alcoholics take them at face value. A content analysis of them (see next section), following Hall (1953/1966), reveals that they focus on problematic events in the dreamer's life. These include problems in the areas of family, friends, sexuality, work, the pre-alcoholic past, drinking misfortunes, and guilt produced while in the active stages of alcoholism. A grammar of these dreams (Foulkes, 1978) suggest that they become reinterpreted with A.A.'s Twelve Steps. A central component of these dreams is the fear of drinking again, for in the dream the alcoholic is seen as drinking.

The following accounts are typical. A member with seven years sobriety is chairing the Wednesday Night meeting. He opens the meeting with the following topic.

> I'd like to talk about dreams. Alcoholic dreams. I've been sober seven years. Last night I dreamed I was drinking again. I had a cold martini. I was in the old lounge where I used to drink. Soft music was playing and I was with my wife. I had one martini, then another, and then we had a fight. I woke up in a cold chill. I've been nervous and anxious all day. I even called my old counselor. She said that these were typical and not to worry [field conversation, December 18, 1982].

Following this, 15 A.A. members, with varying degrees of sobriety (1 month to 15 years) proceeded to discuss their drinking dreams. A member with 1 month sobriety stated:

> I was sitting in front of a pitcher of beer. Three glasses, all mine, in front of me. I drank them real fast, then I woke up, shaking and crying. I haven't been able to get this dream out of my head. It happened last week.

Another member, with four years sobriety, stated:

> I was in my backyard, a bottle of Jack Daniels on the picnic table. I was drinking out of it. Christ, I never did that. It was getting dark and I could hear the birds chirping. I woke up with a start. I actually felt hung over. My head was foggy. I was thirsty like I used to be in the mornings after a heavy night of drinking. My hands were even shaking. I'd been sober one year and two months at the time.

Another member, with four years sobriety, stated:

> This happened last year around Christmas time. I dreamed I was drinking gin in front of the fireplace. Everybody had gone to bed. I was burning papers in the fire and suddenly the mantel caught on fire and the kids' stuffed animals started burning. I threw my drink on the fire and woke up in a cold sweat. Actually, this was pretty realistic because one Christmas I did start a fire that burned the mantel.

A member with five months sobriety reported a dream he had while in treatment.

> I had a dream that lasted two days when I was in treatment. It came to me even when I was laying on my bed in the afternoon with my eyes closed. It was like I was peering over the edge of a long tunnel that was looking down on a family dining room table in my grandmother's kitchen. It was Sunday dinner. My mother, my brother, my father, my grandfather, my grandmother, and myself. We're all fighting. My mother is pouting and crying. My grandmother is being cheerful. My brother is laughing at my mother. My grandfather is looking out the window. My father is silent because he never came to these dinners. I'm shouting at my mother. The table is filled with food and nobody is eating.
>
> In one version of this dream my two daughters are at the table, too, and their mother is sitting beside me. I'm drinking wine. Yet in the dream I'm 14 years old. It's very frightening. All of these people are alive and looking at me, but my grandparents are dead. As I look down on this situation it's

> like I'm reliving my childhood and adulthood. I'm watching myself dream. These images won't leave me!
>
> I told my counselor about this and he told me that he had had dreams like mine. He said he hated his parents and had used the booze to escape from them. He told me that I had to forgive myself and my parents and my grandparents.

The member with 15 years sobriety talked at the end of the meeting.

> I'm an alcoholic. I'll be an alcoholic until the day I die. I'm powerless over alcohol, even in my dreams. Hell, I still have those dreams. Last year on vacation I dreamed I was back with a bottle of gin and the boys at work. These dreams are like dry drunks. They help keep me sober today. They remind me of how bad it was. They also tell me that my primary purpose is to stay sober. If I have to drink in my dreams in order to stay sober when I'm awake, that's O.K. Better there than in real life. These damned dreams also tell me that the desire to drink will return. That's what the *Big Book* says.

This elder member of the A.A. group offers a definitive interpretation of the drinking dream. He locates the dreams within A.A.'s primary purpose, indicates that he still has them, and suggests that they are valuable because they prevent the member from actually taking a drink. Such a reading accords with the arguments made by the theorists already cited. They represent continuations of preoccupations that occur in the alcoholic's waking life. To the degree that the member has internalized A.A.'s position on abstinence, the dreamer who drinks is experiencing a repressed desire to drink. The guilt that is felt aligns the dreamer with A.A.'s normative position. That the dream is reinterpreted within A.A.'s First Step suggests that members who have these dreams are still struggling, at the out-of-consciousness level, with surrender and with their powerlessness over alcohol.

The discussion of these dreams around the tables indicates how A.A. members bring their personal, private conscious experiences into the collective consciousness of the group (Durkheim, 1912/1961). That these dreams in fact constitute "slips" suggests that even as the member stays sober he or she dreams of drinking. These dreams underscore the position that alcoholics stay sober in A.A. by talking about drinking. By talking about the tabooed act they kept it at a safe distance from their daily lives. According to Boss (1977) it can be argued that these dreams are not (as Freud would argue) just symbolic and the product of dream-work acting on unconscious dream thoughts and repressed wishes. Nor are they just compensatory. Rather, the alcoholic's dreams illuminate the ways in which he views his sober existence. Their symbolic content is real.

In the dream, then, and in its discussion, members enact and reenact the troubling act that brought them to A.A. in the first place. These dramatic, often traumatic, experiences that are shared awaken the alcoholic to the fact that even his or her private, dreaming life has become a part of a larger social structure.

A GROUNDED INTERPRETATION OF SLIPS AND RELAPSES

A summary of the foregoing analysis suggests the following statements concerning the alcoholic's slip. First, it cannot be predicted in advance, although a given alcoholic may know when she plans to take her next drink. Second, a slip for an A.A. member is a slip away from A.A. Third, it is a return to a mode of self-interaction in which the member attempts to escape from, or deal with, the problems of the present by placing alcohol between herself and the problem. Fourth, planned or unplanned; short-term, intermittent, or long-term; performed by a newcomer, a regular, or an old-timer; real or dreamed; the slip is a return to the self of the past. Fifth, the slip is an attempt by the alcoholic to take control over his life, to once again become the "captain of his own ship" (Bateson, 1972a). Sixth, the slip is a risk-taking act that denies the past failures and problems the alcoholic confronted when he drank alcoholically.

Seventh, the slip of the A.A. member is a group and interactional phenomenon, for until the member came to A.A. he did not conceptualize his returns to drinking as slips. Eighth, understood thus, the slip signals a failure in socialization as A.A. organizes such practices. Ninth, the member who embraces the A.A. program on a regular basis is the least likely candidate for a slip for she has internalized the A.A. position that there are no longer any excuses for drinking.

The situational view I have presented suggests, then, that alcoholics who slip do so only to the extent that they define themselves as "situational alcoholics." Such members come to A.A. out of an attempt to solve a particular problem in their life. When that problem is solved, they relinquish the identity of alcoholic and return to previous conceptions of themselves. If, however, on the way to solving the problem that got them into A.A. they fully surrender to their alcoholism and become committed A.A. members, their likelihood of slipping is minimized. Alcoholics thus pass through phases or stages as they become sober. For some, slipping is part of becoming sober. For others, slipping becomes a part of their A.A. identity.

Turning from the individual to society, it is possible now to understand how society, through its laws and its courts, enters into the production of situational and committed A.A. members. By remanding drunken drivers to DUI schools, to treatment centers, and to A.A., the courts place individuals in positions in which, through a process of surrender and conversion, they may become recovering alcoholics and committed A.A. members. This may happen in spite of the individual's true intentions or initial desires.

A.A.'s position on these matters is clear. The individual need not have an honest desire to stop drinking in order to be an A.A. member. All that is required is a desire. Hence, they welcome such individuals as society sees fit to send to them. On the other hand, A.A.'s position on abstinence is also clear. Once an A.A. member, one is expected to learn how not to drink. To hold any other position would be to open A.A. up to alternative theories of controlled drinking and problem solving. This would create factions within A.A. and produce large classes of situational alcoholics. Such a position would also undermine A.A.'s theory of alcoholism. Furthermore, it would destroy the basic, underlying premise of A.A., which is that all alcoholics are the same. No alcoholic, once recovery has started, has an excuse to drink. This fundamental principle obliterates the influence of class, status, and power within the A.A. social structure. It reduces every alcoholic to the same level. To do otherwise would be to lay the foundations for a theory of recovery that fitted reasons to drink to different classes of individuals and to different classes or types of problems. A.A. is effective organizationally because it refuses to waiver on this basic point.

CONCLUSIONS

I have offered a situational interpretation of slips and relapses. A typology of slips was offered, based on my interpretation of the experiences of alcoholics who slipped during the period of my fieldwork (1980-1985). Alternative views and theories of relapse were reviewed. I have incorporated portions of Rubington's, Leach and Norris's, and Maxwell and Rudy's formulations into my framework. Central to my understanding of the relapse is the identity the alcoholic forms about himself or herself as an alcoholic. Variations on the committed alcoholic identity were examined, including the situational, hopelessly alcoholic, and neutralized identities. The committed recovering alcoholic identity becomes a validated program of self-indications that prohibits the alcoholic from drinking in any situation.

In my analysis of slips I distinguished being dry from dry drunks, sobriety, and white knuckle sobriety. I also examined the dreams alcoholics report around the A.A. tables, suggesting that in those dreams lies a merger of personal and collective consciousness.

Slips and relapses are at the heart of the recovery process. This phenomenological and interactional analysis has attempted to reveal how this is so. In the next chapter I take up a more detailed analysis of the recovering self, showing how A.A. in fact gets inside the self-system of the A.A. member.

12

THE RECOVERY OF SELF

> I can't seem to get it. I get one foot stuck in the shit of the past and one foot ahead of me in the future and I fall flat on my ass, drunk in the present [male alcoholic, second week of treatment, third treatment center, 35-year-old painter].
>
> Those "normies" don't understand us [recovering alcoholic, sober three months, female, 48 years old].
>
> You'll change. You'll be the last person to see it, but you'll change. I have [recovering alcoholic, 14 years sobriety, age 74, male, June 30, 1982].

The problematic that organizes my analysis centers on the relationship between A.A. and the self of the alcoholic. The question that must be answered is the following: "How does A.A. get inside the self of the individual so that he or she moves from the identity of a situational alcoholic to the identity and self-understanding of a committed, recovering alcoholic?" I assume that this transition in selfhood occurs around and outside the A.A. tables. In these contexts the member learns to talk about himself or herself within the language and framework A.A. offers. This study in A.A. and the self is an analysis of talking and storytelling.

The following topics or issues must be analyzed: (1) the old self of the alcoholic that remains after treatment, the remnants of which are brought into A.A.; (2) temporality and change; (3) humor and becoming an A.A. storyteller; (4) fear and guilt, as these emotions accompany the changes in self that are experienced; (5) laying the self of the past to rest; and (6) fully accepting the alcoholic identity and becoming integrated into the A.A. social world. As these problematics are mastered, the recovering alcoholic is learning how to talk in A.A. meetings. He or she is learning how to bring "sobriety" problems to the tables. A brief discussion of the self theories of James and Mead, as well as an excursion into gender and A.A., will be required under point one above.

Conceptualizing Recovery

Upon leaving treatment for alcoholism the alcoholic is likely to confront two structures of experience: slips and relapses and the A.A. group. (He or she will, of course, also confront work and family. These contexts must be absorbed into the alcoholic's A.A. experiences, as well as into his or her attempts at remaining sober. See next discussion.) These were the topics of the last two chapters.

As indicated in Chapter 4, the alcoholic who leaves treatment confronts a void or emptiness of experience. His friendships in treatment have been severed. His family is still in a state of disorganization. His work career must be taken up again. He must learn how to live sober, if he is going to recover from his disease of alcoholism, which treatment has told him he will have until he dies. Treatment has activated, or bought to the surface, the negative emotions of his past.

In this frame of mind it is not surprising that he drinks and relapses. He experiences his alcoholism as a dis-ease of time and self. He starts his recovery career still locked within the feelings of guilt and shame that his alcoholic past has produced. These feelings create a fearfulness and anxiety concerning the present and the future. In the past he drank to deaden these feelings of self. Now sober, he fights not to drink as he attempts to overcome these negative feelings. He does this by becoming a regular member of A.A. How this occurs is the topic of this chapter.

In Denzin (1986a: chap. 7) I outlined the three-act play that I called "Recovery." This play has three acts: (1) "Sobriety," (2) "Becoming an A.A. Member," and (3) "Two Lives." I suggested that each of these acts had stages or phases within themselves. It is necessary to review briefly each of these acts and their phases. "Sobriety" involves (1) hitting bottom; (2) reaching out for help; (3) making contact with A.A.; (4) announcing one's self as an alcoholic at an A.A meeting; (5) slipping and returning to A.A.; (6) maintaining contact with A.A. and learning how not to drink on a daily basis; (7) becoming a regular A.A. member; (8) learning A.A.'s Twelve Steps; and (9) becoming integrated into an A.A. network, getting a sponsor, and working Steps Four and Five.

Act Two incorporates phases 6, 7, and 8 as just discussed. Act Three has four distinct phases: (1) taking Steps Four and Five; (2) acquiring a "spiritual" program; (3) learning how to live sober; and (4) coming to see that one has led two lives: before A.A. and after A.A.

I suggested in that earlier analysis that the alcoholic who moves through these three acts and their phases will experience a radical transformation of self. He or she will become a committed, recovering alcoholic who builds a lengthy history of continuous sobriety within the A.A. community. Previously lived alcoholic-centered family relationships will undergo change as the alcoholic and his or her other learn the languages of recovery offered by A.A. and perhaps Al-Anon. New languages of self, new meanings of alcoholism, alcoholics, and drinking will be acquired. The alcoholic and his or her other will move through transformations and alternations of identity that will make them new kinds of individuals, to themselves and to others (see Travisano, 1981: 244; Denzin, 1986a: chap. 7) This earlier discussion provides the framework for this chapter.

The Six Theses of Recovery

As in Chapter 2, the Six Theses of Recovery structure my analysis. The alcoholic recovers the self that was lost to alcoholism by working through the central processes referenced by these theses. The Six Theses, stated here for purposes of summary only, are: (1) *The Thesis of the Temporality of Self*—the alcoholic recovers self through the temporal structures of experience that A.A., not alcohol, now offers; (2) *The Thesis of the Relational Structures of Self*—recovery occurs within a radical alternation in the relational structures of experience that A.A., not alcohol, now offers the alcoholic; (3) *The Thesis of the Emotionality of Self*—recovery involves a relinquishing of the prior emotional understandings of self the alcoholic clung to; (4) *The Thesis of Bad Faith*—recovery requires a rejection of the structures of bad faith that had previously supported the alcoholic's active alcoholism; (5) *The Thesis of Self-Control*—the alcoholic must come to believe that he or she can no longer control the people, places, or events that constitute his or her world; (6) *The Thesis of Self Surrender*—only through a continual surrendering to powerlessness over alcohol will the alcoholic maintain sobriety.

OLD AND NEW SELVES

A.A. presumes a transition between two selves: the old drinking self of the past, which holds on to "old ways of thinking" and the new, nondrinking self of the present and the future, which may or may not take on the A.A. way of thinking and acting. The alcoholic's sobriety is maintained precisely because these two selves are continually kept alive in the dialogues that occur within A.A. meetings. A temporal structure that reaches back into the past, drawing always from the vantage point of the present, thus organizes the alcoholic's recovery experiences. Because the past can always be returned to by taking the first drink, the alcoholic learns to distance herself from who she has been as an active drinker. But because who she was is kept alive in the vividness of her memories of it, and because she learns to talk about it, she comes to define herself in terms of who she no longer wants to be. A negativity structures the interaction of the two selves that coexist simultaneously in the alcoholic's mind. By knowing who she does not want to be (negatively) she is drawn to the affirmative structures of experience A.A. offers.

The Old Self

The self of the alcoholic, that structure of experience that is woven through the streams of real and unreal consciousness alcohol has produced, must be presented to the A.A. group. It is a self that has degraded itself, embarrassed itself, and lost itself within alcoholic dreams and fantasies. Divided against itself, it comes to A.A., even after treatment, in shattered pieces. It is a self that has been humbled by alcohol. This self is familiar to A.A. members, for it is a self they keep alive in the daily discourse that makes up an A.A. meeting. Consider the following statement made by a member with six years sobriety.

> When I first got here I couldn't talk. I was shaking and crying. I sat in the corner. When it came my turn to talk I mumbled something, I don't even remember what. I felt like I had just crawled out of a hole. I felt lower than a snake on the ground. I couldn't look people in the eye. I was like this for months. Finally I started to be able to talk. I started to get some self-confidence back. It used to be that I couldn't go into a room with more than two people in it without being high on drugs and alcohol. I was afraid of people. Today I feel comfortable here. I can actually talk! That's quite an accomplishment for me. It helps me to remember who I was and what I used to be like. I've come a long ways [field observation, December 4, 1984, 32-year-old female, printer].

The old and the new self of the speaker are presented in this account. The speaker reflects back on who she was, laughing as she describes her previous inability to be in a room with people without being high. Thus, an old self is presented through the voice of a new self. This reflective stance toward the past is basic to the restructuring of self that occurs within A.A. That is, recovering alcoholics, as they move forward in recovery, continually distance themselves from who they were. Yet this distancing process occurs in small increments, built upon the sobriety trajectory that accumulates one day at a time. The self that is moving forward judges the momentum of this movement in terms of where it used to be.

The following speaker is quite explicit on this point. She has been out of treatment for three months as she speaks:

> The first time I went through treatment I didn't get it. I didn't want to be there. I was there for somebody else and I wanted to be like I always was, only I wanted to be able to control my drinking. This second time something happened in about the third week. My counselor said, "You know you don't have to drink anymore. You can let go of that part of your self." I surrendered right there. I thought that in order to be who I was I had to fight alcohol and still drink. That way I could prove that I was strong and the same old self I'd always been. Since that day I've had a peace of mind you can't imagine [field conversation, 47-year-old female, field of education].

The speaker let go of her drinking self. She surrendered to her alcoholism, which is the Sixth Thesis of Recovery.

The next speaker evidences an unwillingness to let go of the drinking self.

> I love that stuff. It's my love. I love it deeply. I don't want to give it up. I love it like a man loves a woman. When I was in the Hollywood Group in L.A. I wanted those sobriety buttons. I wanted the 30-day, the three-month, and the six-month buttons. I was wearing my clean sobriety T-shirt. I was going to sew those buttons on that shirt. I was proud of my sobriety. I went out after 28 days. That's the longest I've ever had. I can't get past 28 days! [field observation, January 5, 1985].

This member sets 28 days in front of himself as a barrier that cannot be broken. This obstacle, self-imposed, yet derivative of A.A.'s sobriety markers of one, three, and six months, indicates how a member can use time and A.A. in a self-defeating fashion.

Still attached to the drinking self, the member interprets the sobriety markers he has not received as symbols of self-failure. Yet he loves alcohol like a woman and does not want to give it up.

The alcoholic's love affair with alcohol is referenced in the following statement by a counselor at Northern. She is speaking to patients four days before they are to leave treatment.

> You're all going through a grieving process. It's like losing a loved one. Except you've lost your best friend, which is alcohol. You'll have to get used to this if you want to recover. You'll cry, you'll scream for it. You'll try and do anything to get a drink when the desire returns. But you can't give in. You've got to give it up if you want to get better. You'd better all get to A.A. because they'll help you replace this loved one with something else [field conversation, April 19, 1982].

The metaphor of "loved one," standing for alcohol and the alcoholic's relationship to alcohol, personalizes alcoholism. It drives alcohol deeply into the emotional structures of the alcoholic's self. The metaphor "death of a loved one" also attaches a familiar structure of experience to the death of this relationship. That is, grieving, pain, and shows of emotion will accompany this process.

Commonsense Structures of Self

MacAndrew and Garfinkel (1962) analyzed the images of sober self, drunk self, and ideal self of 62 Caucasian male alcoholics hospitalized for treatment. The findings indicated that the alcoholics in this sample associated forcefulness, persuasiveness, and assertiveness with reasons for drinking. Drinking was seen as allowing the alcoholic to be free to pursue a valued self, which is an assertive self.

At the commonsense level, alcohol releases inhibitions, relieves loneliness, reduces fears and tensions, and creates momentary sociability with others. These motives for drinking are thus associated with self-experiences that lead alcoholics to approach an ideal self that can not be given in the sober state.

The transition in selfhood that occurs within A.A. requires that the old understandings of self that the alcoholic held to must be relinquished. A *sober self-ideal*, to use MacAndrew and Garfinkel's (1962: 254) term, must be learned. The commonsense foundations of selfhood that link self with alcohol must be broken if A.A.'s version of recovery is to be established.

A.A.'s Theory of Self

A Jamesian theory of self is embedded within A.A.'s precepts concerning being good to yourself and watching out for anger and resentment. James's self—including the "Me," or the empirical self as known by others, and the "I," or self as knower—consisted of self-feelings, actions prompted by the self, and embodied feelings felt in the body of the person (James, 1890/1950: 292). Self-feelings, which radiate through the body of the subject, define the inner meaning of lived experience as that experience is confronted by the subject. The actions, which the subject's self-feelings and self-thoughts lead him to produce and embrace, create situations in which success, failures, and pretensions interact and collide. The subject's self-esteem, James (1890/1950: 320) argued, is the ratio of success over pretensions.

These formulations are familiar to the alcoholic. By setting herself up to fail, the alcoholic lowers her self-esteem, for her pretensions will always exceed her successes. Furthermore, by failing and drinking, she diminishes the value of her empirical self, or me, in the eyes of others. At the same time, her meaning to herself—as she knows herself—after failure has been experienced is also lowered. The consequence is that the self-feelings the alcoholic experiences, including those feelings accompanying a hangover, or a drunk, are negative, hostile, and focused on anger and resentment.

Until alcohol is removed from the alcoholic's embodied consciousness, these feelings will remain and be a part of the emotional repertoire he or she brings to every empirical situation that is confronted. But more is involved. The alcoholic must learn to bring expectations of self in line with the actual accomplishments of self. By making sobriety the primary goal of the alcoholic, A.A. produces a situation in which daily success can be accomplished and hence experienced. In a self-fulfilling fashion, sobriety produces the very circumstances of self the alcoholic had previously attempted to achieve through drinking.

G. H. Mead and the A.A. Self

If A.A. fills out, in empirical detail, elements of William James's theory of self, G. H. Mead's (1934) theory of self may also be fitted to the A.A. experience. Mead's "I" and "me" are located in the A.A. group. The "sober I" learns how to be sober by taking the attitudes of sober selves who are A.A. members. The A.A. group becomes a generalized other for the member. The significant symbols of the group (the Steps) slowly come to call out in the member consensual self-understandings regarding A.A. and recovery. The symbolic meanings of the word "alcoholic" similarly come to be integrated into the member's "I"-"me" inner dialogues. A self grounded in the symbols, meanings of self, alcohol, drinking, and alcoholism thus emerges. As this new structure appears, old meanings of self, alcohol, and alcoholism are pushed aside.

These social objects assume new meanings that are given in A.A.'s languages of self.

The unstable inner "I" of the alcoholic that had previously experienced various forms of madness (Lacan, 1977) discovers a new forum for selfhood. In this inner arena of self-conversations, which flow from participation in the A.A. group, a stable inner "I" and "me" is built.

In terms of Kohut's (1971, 1977; see also Benjamin, 1981: 203) psychology of self, the member experiences two kinds of interactional relationships; idealizing ones that permit dependency, and mirroring ones that allow for autonomy. A cohesive self that merges with the selves of other A.A. members thus appears. At least the potential for that merger is present.

In order for the alcoholic to become a member of A.A. she must be able to interpret meaningfully the actions of other A.A. members. She must also be able to judge and formulate lines of action based on these interpretations. These actions, in turn, must be fitted to the ongoing actions of others in the A.A. group. The A.A. language and a process of taking the attitude of the other underlies this experience. It revolves, as argued earlier (Chapter 4), on A.A. understanding.

Stages of Becoming an A.A. Self

In becoming an A.A. member the individual can be seen as passing through three stages of selfhood. In the *preparatory stage* the individual imitates and mimics the words, actions, and feelings of other A.A. members. Deep understanding of the attitudes of others is not yet present. In the *interactional stage* the individual learns how to take the attitudes of specific A.A. members, and a process of anticipatory socialization into A.A. begins to occur. The member still, however, speaks from a self-centered point of view, and misunderstandings regarding A.A. occur. In the *participatory stage* the individual learns to take the attitudes of the A.A. group as a collectivity. The generalized A.A. attitude is learned. Socialized speech of a nonegocentric nature is produced and the member slowly begins to build up friendships that connect him or her to a network of A.A. members (see Mead, 1934; Meltzer, 1972: 9-10; Stone, 1981: 200-201).

These stages of socialization into A.A. may be depicted as follows:

(1) *Preparatory Stage*:	Imitation of others, low understandings of A.A. Few interiorizations of A.A. self-structures.
(2) *Interactional Stage*:	Attitudes of specific A.A. members (sponsors) are taken. Learning of A.A. language begins to occur.

(3) *Participatory Stage*: Attitudes of the group are taken, socialized A.A. speech is produced. Friendships within A.A. are entered into. Member begins to lead meetings, sponsor other members, and so on.

Gender and Selfhood

The three stages of socialization into A.A. relate, then, to stages in selfhood. However, the self that emerges in A.A. is not gender free. Gender, sexuality, and personal biography structure the transitions in self that occur within the A.A. social group. The morality and emotionality of A.A. interactions align males to males and females to females. An axis of value and mood (Stone, 1981), or instrumental and emotional attachment (Denzin, 1986d; Gilligan, 1982: 8-9) differentiates the interactions of the two sexes in A.A.

Two moral codes—one masculine, the other feminine (Erikson, 1950; Kohlberg, 1981)—are thus evidenced in A.A. These codes revolve around instrumentality and emotionality. The masculine code represses emotionality; the feminine code releases it. Because A.A. is a male-dominated social structure, the masculine, instrumental value dimension predominates. However, a tension is produced in this code. The heart of A.A. works through the disclosure of emotionality, which underlies A.A.'s particular form of emotional understanding (see Chapter 4). Consequently, the feminine moral code—the showing of emotion and the valuing of emotionality—undercuts the masculine code.

Two important implications follow. First, women appear to acquire the A.A. point of view more rapidly than do men. Their empathetic abilities and previous socialization experiences allow them more quickly to enter the emotional space that exists within any A.A. meeting. Second, males who reach the participatory stage of A.A. selfhood move from the masculine, repressive view of emotion to the feminine mode of mood and emotionality.

The stigma that applies to female alcoholics in American society (Gomberg, 1976) and the double standards that are applied to them often produce a suppression of emotionality on the woman's part when she first enters A.A. She acts, that is, like a man in her show of emotion. If she remains in A.A. she will move more rapidly to the participatory stage of involvement than do males. This is because, as just indicated, she has a history of emotional expression that many males in American society have not had.

A middle ground on emotion (see next section) thus appears within A.A. This involves a merger of gender-specific attitudes on emotionality. It is not that gender becomes irrelevant. Rather, a neutral emotional zone of self-disclosure appears. Either sex can enter that zone and discuss self-degrading or emotionally disruptive experiences and not be evaluated negatively by members of the opposite sex.

Such an emotional social structure thus allows for the emergence of self-structures that are grounded in emotional experiences that would otherwise be denied members of both sexes. In Kohut's (1977) terms, cohesive selves, responsive to one another but not intimidated by the authority of the other, appear in this social situation. Independent selves, differentiated from one another yet intersubjectively dependent upon each other, thus emerge within the A.A. experience. Accorded recognition by members of the opposite sex, but not dominated by them, the member learns to interact with himself or herself in ways that had not been previously possible.

Selves and Slips

The foregoing remarks suggest a way of interpreting the analysis of slips offered in the last chapter. They indicate that relapses will be most likely to occur during the preparatory and interactional stages of a member's socialization into A.A. They suggest that the situational alcoholic identity will be most likely to appear in the preparatory and early interactional stages of involvement. It might also be proposed that there will be fewer slips for those members who are able to relinquish the instrumental, masculine code of emotional expression. To the extent, however, that the moral, interactional, and emotional code of A.A. remains embedded in the white, Anglo-Saxon culture, the slips of blacks and Hispanics will be high (see Madsen, 1974: 157). That is, the self that is produced in A.A. enters an androgynous zone of emotionality that still flows from the white, Anglo-Saxon culture. This interpretation can be further examined by discussing the black experience in A.A.

Madsen (1974: 156) suggests that there is an effort to repress racial and ethnic hostility in A.A. I observed this in the A.A. community that I studied. However, over a five-year period of fieldwork I observed only two successfully recovering blacks; both were males. Perhaps 100 or more black males and females entered treatment, attended a few meetings, and then disappeared back into the black community. One of the two members who succeeded started his own version of A.A. and located it within the black community. The other member regularly attended predominantly white A.A. meetings.

Summarizing, three key factors work against the recovery of blacks and Hispanics in A.A. (see Caldwell, 1983: 91; Kane, 1981; Madsen,

1974: 157; Watts and Wright, 1983). First, A.A. is a white, Anglo-Saxon social movement; it has few if any deep roots in the minority experience. Second, the repressed racial hostility against minorities still sets a tone of interaction that is filled with suppressed tension when blacks and whites meet across the A.A. tables. Third, the emotional tone of the A.A. meeting, although tilted in the direction of emotional display, is a tone that is modulated by the white, male experience. This tone allows emotion to be expressed, but contained within an "in-control" framework. The "talking" style of whites simply differs from the "talking" style of blacks (Labov, 1971). It is more likely to occur within a restricted emotional code that does not elaborate in thick detail the history, biography, and personal experiences of the speaker (see Bernstein, 1971). A black speaker fills his or her A.A. talk with contextualized meanings that are often not understood by the white listener (see Labov, 1971).

Hence, in the basic arena of talking and storytelling the black speaker experiences an alienation from his white A.A. listeners. This is because he speaks from a different linguistic background. His talk overflows with emotionality. There are few similar spaces within white A.A. discourse for such elaborated emotional talk. The following account is typical. It is given by a black male with four years sobriety. He spoke at an "open" A.A. meeting. His audience was all white; an equal number of males and females were present.

> We was in Germany, I was in the Fifth Airborne. We was at a football game. I was dressed to the tee; I mean I was a real stud, a dude in the stands. Cool man. I had me a pint of Jack. I drank it before the first quarter was over. I pissed in my pants and passed out. Puked all over a lady in front of me. My fuckin' pants were soaked. I had puke all over my jacket. I fell down three rows and had to be taken back to the base by the MPs. Woke up hung over and started all over. I was sailin' like a bird on that Jack; higher than a cloud in the sky. Kept thinkin' of my "auntie" back home and wanted to be back in Chicago, safe and with my friends. That drunk lasted two weeks [field observation, October 23, 1982].

The speaker's story lasted one-and-a-half hours. By the time he was done, members were becoming uneasy. They cringed as he told the self-degrading portions of his story. The speaker never returned to this group.

The black emphasis on close interpersonal relationships, on an affective symbolic imagery, on verbal rhythm, and on a logic that combines opposites, does not find a comfortable place within the universe of discourse that makes up white-dominated A.A. meetings (see Caldwell, 1983: 91). Yet, A.A. works for some black alcoholics (see the case presented by Caldwell, 1983: 91). It must be noted that the community I studied has a history of a well-formed black community that is not integrated with the larger white community (see Stack, 1970).

Temporality

Within A.A., as noted earlier, progress is measured in part through length of sobriety. The medallions that are given for 30 days, 90 days, six months, and one year represent significant temporal markers in the recovery process. Transformations in self are assumed to accompany each of these temporal points.

A speaker with five years sobriety comments:

> The first year is the hardest. You deal with physical problems of the addiction. The second year is psychological, dealing with the old ways of thinking that lead to drinking. The third year is spiritual, for you finally have to confront a higher power in your life. The fourth year is the hardest because you are supposed to be better by then. I'm over five years now and the fifth year has been the hardest for me. When does it end? [field observation, October 27, 1983, 37-year-old male counselor].

Change is organized around what A.A. recognizes as the three sides to alcoholism—that is, the physical, mental or psychological, and the spiritual or moral. Hence, a transformation of self that encompasses these three dimensions is presumed to be at work during recovery (see Wholey, 1984).

As the old self of the past is relinquished, the new self of A.A. comes to speak in terms of the Steps, the program, the past, spirituality, the present, and the gifts of the program. The following speaker illustrates this point.

> I'm nothing without A.A.—nothing. Without the Steps, the higher power, my sobriety which is given on a daily basis, my sponsor, these meetings, my new friends—without all this I'd be nothing and nothing was just what I was when I got here [field observation, April 2, 1982, 48-year-old male, salesman, four years sobriety].

As A.A. gets inside the self of the recovering alcoholic, recovery is conceptualized on two levels: the abstract components of alcoholism as a physical, mental, and spiritual illness, and the specific dimensions of one's "state of mind" at the moment. Thus, although an alcoholic may be judged to have a sound and stable A.A. program, on any given day his or her "serenity" or "peace of mind" is judged to be less than acceptable to another member. The following statement by a recovering alcoholic with nearly six years of sobriety speaks to this distinction.

> I'm hangin' in there. One day at a time. I got nothin' to complain about. I got my meetings, I still go to three or four a week. I got my friends. The business is going good. My spiritual program is working. I still eat too much, but I feel good and I got peace of mind. It's O.K. today.
>
> Saw H on the street yesterday. Gave him a big wave and smile. He just lifted his hand and kept his head down. That sonofabitch. I'm not getting into his shit anymore. He pulled me down for too long. Sucked me right in. Two months ago I saw him at the Monday night meeting. I said "Hi, H" two times and he didn't say a damned thing. That's enough for me. He can have what he has. That's not what the program's all about for me. I don't care if he does have over five years. I don't care how many spiritual books he reads on a daily basis. He ain't got it. And I know I'm takin' his inventory [field conversation, January 25, 1985; recovering alcoholic, self-employed, 51 years old].

This speaker indicates how the recovering alcoholic uses the criteria of "serenity" and peace of mind to measure and judge his personal progress in the program (see discussion of serenity below; also see Denzin, 1986a: chap. 7). Hence, he moves from the abstractions of alcoholism as an illness to the specifics of lived experience that, for him, embody what the program means. These dimensions of the program become the new commonsense foundations of the recovering self.

Concomitant with the appearance of the "new self" of the recovering alcoholic emerges the ability to become a "storyteller" within the lore and language of A.A. It is to this topic that I next turn.

BECOMING A STORYTELLER

The speaker at an A.A. meeting must learn that he speaks only for himself, not for A.A. or for the A.A. group. Three processes are involved in becoming a storyteller. The first involves learning how to speak and connect one's statements to the A.A. experience. The second involves learning what a story is. The third involves learning how to tell and modify that story to any specific problem that might arise that could test one's ability to stay sober.

When the speaker makes reference to A.A. or to her own experiences, she must learn not to use the pronouns "we," "us," "they," or "our." The following exchange between two male speakers reveals this A.A. understanding. The first speaker is discussing the Third Step Prayer. With over four years sobriety, he is an established member of the group.

He begins by repeating the prayer:

> God, I offer myself to thee—to build with me and to do with me as Thou wilt. Relieve me of the bondage of self, that I may better do thy will. Take away my difficulties, that victory over them may bear witness to those I would help of Thy power, Thy love and Thy way of life. May I do Thy will always!

He then states:

> This is our prayer. We say it every night before we go to sleep.

He is interrupted at this point by a speaker who also has over four years sobriety:

> You can't say "our." You can't say "we." It's your prayer. You say it. We don't say it! Speak for yourself!

The first speaker retorts:

> Shut up. Cram it up your ___. I'm talking. You can talk when it's your turn. I know its me saying the ___ damned prayer. Do you think I'm a dummy? I'm sick and tired of your coming in here and acting so ___ damned holy! [field conversation, September 17, 1982].

This angry display of emotion between two A.A. speakers is uncommon. Yet the second speaker was making an important point. No one individual speaks for A.A.; each member speaks from individual experience. However, each member is expected to learn what the Steps are, what the Traditions are, what A.A. stands for, and what sobriety and serenity mean within A.A. More than this, the alcoholic must learn how to talk about self. He must become a storyteller, but he must become a particular kind of storyteller. He must learn how to relate events that occur within his everyday life to the language and meanings of A.A. He must learn to see that everything that happens to him could cause him to drink. When he learns this he can relate this A.A. life to his other life. Becoming an A.A. "talker" and "storyteller" thus requires that the member be able to maintain an interaction between what A.A. teaches him and what he experiences in his everyday life.

The Story

A story within A.A. is an accounting of "what it was like, what happened and what it is like now." In "How It Works" (A.A., 1976: 58) the reader is told that "our stories disclose in a general way what we used to be like, what happened, and what we are like now." This definition of a story limits the storyteller's story to her life before she became an alcoholic, to a description of what happened during her active alcoholism, and to a discussion of how she has recovered. Hence, A.A. stories are stories of recovery from alcoholism. Some are called "drunk-a-logs." They are part of each member's biography, which is shared within the A.A. community at "open" meetings.

The guide for the member's story is given in A.A.'s *Big Book*, which contains 44 life stories framed around the above-mentioned three criteria. As the member learns the *Big Book* she may find a story that is close to her own lived experiences. This story may be adapted to fit the member's life story as it is told to the A.A. group. The following story is representative. The speaker, who had 34 years of sobriety when he died at the age of 76, told the following story about himself.

> Bill Wilson could have told my story. Same circumstances. Bright prospects for a prominent career in business. Good schools, loving parents, lovely wife, nice home. Everything. Heavy social drinking in the early days. The best drinks, best bars and restaurants. The good life. But the drinking got heavier. I was taking a bottle to work in my briefcase. Nips in the morning to get started. Early lunches so I could get a fix before I started to shake too much. Then I started getting home late from work. I'd stop for a few and a few would turn into all night. I became irresponsible toward my family. My work started to show it. I wasn't making the accounts like I used to. I decided I needed to switch jobs. So I did and for a while it was better. Then I started hitting the bottle more and more. Some days I'd leave at noon. Sometimes I'd call in sick on Monday. It got so I couldn't go longer than a hour without a drink. The wife left me and took the kids. I said to hell with them, and I took an expensive apartment in the city. Tried to live the bachelor life. I went down fast after that. Started ending up in the drunk tanks. Went into a sanitorium to dry out. Got drunk the day I got out. That was in the early forties. People were talking about this A.A. thing at the sanitorium. I read that Jack Alexander article. A friend got a copy of the *Big Book* and gave it to me. I looked at it and threw it away. Kept on drinking. I finally lost my job, everything. Another place to dry out but this time when I came out I was ready to stop. I got to an A.A. meeting and saw that *Big Book*. This time I read it. It fit me to a "T." I knew I was an alcoholic. They said there was hope if I followed their simple program. I started going to meetings. Got a

> sponsor. Dried out, got sober. Got my old job back and after a year the wife and kids came back. I've been in ever since. It turned my life around. I owe everything to A.A. and to Bill Wilson, Dr. Sam Shoemaker, Dr. Bob, and all those old-timers who held in there and kept A.A. going. In the early days we used to drive 500 miles a week just to make meetings every night. There weren't many then, you know. We all hung together and helped each other. Just like you people are today [field observation, May 2, 1982].

This speaker spoke from the historical vantage point of over 30 years in A.A.; the following speaker has been in A.A. seven months.

> I read that story in the *Big Book,* "The Vicious Circle." That's me. I get sober a few days, then I drink and I can't stop. I've been here seven months and I have three months sobriety. I just couldn't stay stopped. Always something. Boss would yell at me. My mother'd be sick. The car wouldn't start. Green Bay would lose a football game. Any damned excuse to go off and get drunk. I just about lost my good job. Today the boss is happy with me and everything's goin' good. I finally got a sponsor and got me a regular set of meetings I go to. It's working for me. Last night, tho', I wanted to drink. My sister called and told me I was a quitter for stopping drinking. She's an alcoholic, too. It scares her that I've quit. She wants me to keep drinking. Three months ago I would have gone out and drank a fifth over that call. Today I don't need to [field observation, January 10, 1985; 48-year-old mechanic, single].

This man is speaking at a First Step meeting to a newcomer who is at her first meeting. Seven months earlier our speaker was a newcomer. He has learned how to tell his story and he tells it exactly as it is suggested in the *Big Book*. First step meetings (as discussed earlier) are the occasions for alcoholics to tell their stories (see also Denzin, 1986a: chap. 7). Hence, part of becoming an A.A. member involves learning how to tell one's story to newcomers and regulars at First Step meetings.

Of equal importance, however, is the ability to adjust one's story to one's daily living situation. This is what the speaker in the last statement does. By weaving the telephone call from his sister into his account, he addresses a problem of staying sober, while telling how he became sober. He has joined the problematics of living sober with the A.A. experience.

A.A. Humor

In discussing the stories and experiences of A.A. members, the reader of the *Big Book* is told that

> our struggles . . . are variously strenuous, comic, and tragic. . . . There is, however, a vast amount of fun about it all. I suppose some would be shocked at our seeming worldliness and levity. But just underneath there is deadly earnestness [A.A., 1976; 16].

Laughter, self-criticism, and humor are basic to the stories A.A. members learn to tell about themselves. The self-humor that A.A. promotes instances what Flaherty (1983: 75) terms *reality play*; the transformation of serious "reality work" into playful, humorous interaction that is amusing and nonserious. Reality play draws its humorousness from the seriousness of the social situation that is transformed, by means of paradox, contradictions, and laughter, into a situation that is joked about.

A.A. members laugh at themselves and joke about their escapades while drinking. They speak with humor to the seriousness of their lived experiences as practicing alcoholics. By laughing and joking about themselves they transcend the seriousness of the past and learn how to put that past in the past tense of their lives. A.A. interaction works, then, on the dialectics of reality work and reality play, as these processes have been discussed by Flaherty (1983).

But more than the past is joked about, for the present and the future supply the alcoholic with an ample supply of experiences that can be humorously defined. The following speaker is scheduled to make a speech at a professional convention in three months. She has been asked to prepare an abstract of her paper. She speaks:

> I'm terrified. What if I get drunk on the plane? What if there is no A.A. there (she is going to San Francisco), what if I lose my paper on the way. Christ, I've got myself all twisted around. I got so upset this morning I forgot to make coffee. Finally, I got hold of myself and said, "Now listen. This is funny. You should be glad they asked you to give a paper. Of course they have A.A. in San Francisco. Get serious, you fool!" Then I laughed at myself and thought, "This is just how you used to think. You don't have to do this today." I had a good laugh at myself" [field observation, September 2, 1982; 29-year-old chemist].

As this speaker talked, laughter filled the meeting room (see also Maxwell, 1984: 45). As she laughed at herself others laughed with her. Through humor a serious situation was transformed into one that could be laughed about. In this move the situation was made manageable. It was brought back into the interpretive framework of A.A.. Humor thus is an integral part of A.A. talk and of A.A. storytelling.

A putting down of self in relationship to ordinary language is a form of A.A. humor. The following speaker illustrates this point:

> I don't know what the word "complacency" [the topic of the meeting] means. It's too big a word for me [group laughter]. If it means getting back in the driver's seat I can understand it. If it means taking myself too damned seriously I can understand it [laughter]. If it means taking A.A. for granted I can understand it. Is that what it means? [laughter] Now I know I'm a damned fool when it comes to big fancy thinking and talking. But I know I have to come to meetings and keep telling myself I'm an alcoholic. If I forget that I guess I must get complacent and the last time I got complacent I got drunk! [field observation, January 28, 1985, 75-year-old retired salesman].

Here the speaker plays on the meaning of the word "complacency." He works back and forth between its serious meanings and self-deprecating references to his lack of knowledge regarding the meaning of the word. He elaborates the word's meanings for him, connecting his talk to his alcoholism and to getting drunk. As he spoke A.A. members laughed at his statement, "I don't know the meaning of the word." In this act of turning back on himself and showing that he did in fact know the meaning of the word, the speaker distanced himself from the seriousness of the topic, while at the same time grounding his remarks in the last time he was complacent and drank. This ability to laminate, or layer humor alongside a serious topic, through self-distancing humorous asides, characterizes a great deal of A.A. meeting talk. Indeed, this feature of A.A. talk may be said to be its most distinguishing feature. Until the speaker can inject humor into his or her A.A. talk, he or she will not have learned the full meaning of being an A.A. speaker.

Humor and Self-Degradation

Humor is central to the alcoholic's recovery of self. Alcoholics have routinely experienced variations on the degradation ceremonies Garfinkel (1956) has described. They have been placed within an interpretive scheme that brought moral indignation and denunciations from others, usually members of their families and perhaps their employers. Their total identities have been affected by these denunciations, which have produced shame for them and perhaps group solidarity for their denouncers (Garfinkel, 1956: 421). Alcoholics overcome the shame of these experiences by learning to laugh and joke about them. Indeed a member's standing in A.A. is associated, in part, by the degree of humorous distance he can effect between his past and his present humorous understanding of that past. Humor becomes a "role-distancing" (Goffman, 1961b) or "self-distancing" social act.

Consider the following statement that might be negatively met in another social setting. The speaker just broke 11 months of sobriety.

> I bought a whore last night. Blew $450 on booze, cocaine, and sex. Also broke three windows in my house and smashed a table. Found out my old lady was a dealer and had been shacking up with the biggest dealer in town. Boy, was I dumb! I had to weasel the information out of her new old man. Christ, I was groveling on my feet, begging for coke and information at the same time. They was all laughin' at me. I ain't got nowhere to go but up today. I called my parents and told them. They were shocked. Didn't know what to say. Got a head that hurts, a pride that's broken. Feel ashamed of myself. What do you do? Laugh and get your ass to A.A.. Don't drink today. Thanks [field conversation, December 12, 1985; 36-year-old auto mechanic].

The member presents his account in a forthright manner. He discloses the humilating nature of his experience, yet distances himself from it. He placed himself outside normal society, but within A.A. as he spoke. Turning back on himself he laughed. His deviance was understandable because he had been under the influence of drugs and alcohol.

In order to incorporate the deviant and the degrading into the normal, taken-for-granted structures of recovery, the A.A. group (and the member) are led to adopt the self-distancing, nonmoralizing stances that humor provides. However, at the normative level A.A. admonishes the member. "We find it better to stick to our own stories. A man may criticize or laugh at himself and it will affect others favorably" (A.A., 1976: 125). The member is advised not to laugh at another unless he first laughs at himself.

TRANSITIONS IN SELFHOOD: FEAR AND GUILT

As the alcoholic learns how to talk and tell her story in the meetings, a transition in selfhood occurs. As she moves farther and farther away from her last drink she draws nearer to the new self that is sober. Letting loose of the old self is fraught with two problematics: fear and guilt. Fear first: Even if the old self was sick and insane, it was familiar. Furthermore, there was always the drug alcohol to dull the pain of confronting a world that had become totally problematic. The following alcoholic, sober eight months, speaks to this transition in self that occurs in the early days of recovery:

> I'm afraid a lot of the time. Afraid of what people will think. Afraid of what I say. Afraid that my hair is too long, afraid that I'm not clean shaven, afraid that my clothes aren't neat and clean, afraid that I might take that drink. At least when I was drinking the fear was dulled by the booze and the drugs. Now it's just me and the world. Sometimes I'm afraid to go forward. Some days all I do is not drink and not drug. I know these fears are unreasonable. I know I have the program and a higher power and you people, but sometimes I forget. Christ, sometimes I'm afraid to get up in the morning [field observation, January 23, 1985, recovering male alcoholic, age 34, draftsman].

Fear of self, fear of other people, fear of sobriety, fear of time; these fears grip this alcoholic as he, in his words, "white knuckles sobriety." He is caught in the gap between two selves. No longer divided against himself, as he was when he was drinking, he lingers still in the fear of moving forward into the world without the aid of alcohol or drugs. Faced with such a situation the newcomer is told to "Breathe Fear Out and Breathe In Faith."

Alcoholics in recovery distinguish several types of fear: the fear of taking the first drink, the fear of living sober, the fear of confronting the past. A fear of taking the first drink is regarded as healthy. The other fears are not so interpreted, for the program offers measures for living sober without fear. The following alcoholic speaks to the forms of these fears:

> When I was drinking I was afraid of everything. I had a deep, hollow sinking feeling of fear inside myself. Like a huge hole that you could see through. I would pour alcohol into that hole and get over some of the fear, but it was always there when I woke up. It was the fear of self, as the *Big Book* says. When I am overwhelmed by that fear today I say the Serenity Prayer and it helps the fear go away.
>
> My fear of taking the first drink is good. I never want to go back to drinking and those old fears that made me afraid to go outside and see people. I used to be afraid to deal with what I had done when I was drinking. The Fourth and the Fifth helped with that though. Today I see that my past is something I can learn from. It was somebody I used to be, it's not me today [field observation, February 13, 1982, 26-year-old alcoholic and addict, three years sober and clean].

This attitude toward the past, which can evoke fear, primarily turns on feelings of guilt the alcoholic feels regarding who she was when she drank and what she did when she drank. The following speaker, a female alcoholic with over four years sobriety, clarifies A.A.'s position on fear and guilt toward the past:

> My sponsor put it to me like this. You can either plead guilty for what you did in the past, or plead insanity, like the Second Step says. When I was an active alcoholic I was insane a lot of the time. The crazy things I did were done under the influence of alcohol. If I felt guilt about those things I'd go crazy again. I prefer to think of myself as having been insane when I drank and did those things. That helps take care of the fear, the guilt, and anxiety [field observation, June 23, 1983].

The Past: Regret versus Guilt

A.A. offers, as the last member's account indicates, a method for dealing with the past. The Fourth and Fifth Steps (see Chapter 3; also Denzin, 1986a: chap. 7) are explicitly addressed to the past. Of equal importance is the attitude the member is asked to take toward the past. Three processes are involved. First, the past is to be laid to rest. Second, the member is told to feel regret about the past, but not guilt or shame. Third, closely parallel to the neutralization of guilt is the attitude that those past acts that evoke guilt were in fact produced when the alcoholic was insane. Hence, to be morally accountable and guilty for past actions that were done when the member was in the active phases of alcoholism is itself regarded as an act of insanity.

In these three moves A.A. places a wedge between the member's pre-A.A. history and the experiences of recovery. Laying the past to rest, members are told to remember past mistakes, to remember how bad it was when they drank, and to keep these thoughts fresh. To do so will help keep them from drinking again. A.A. humor defuses the moral stigma of the alcoholic's past. The attitude of regret toward the past further contributes to the member's ability to neutralize the past so as to move forward in recovery.

A.A. teaches, then, a new attitude toward time, morality, guilt, and shame. Guilt is seen as being produced when the member violates a moral code of society that has been internalized and made into a personal moral standard. In order to expunge the guilt from the member's consciousness, A.A. directs the individual to a forgiving higher power. Members are told that this power has forgiven them for what they did in the past. Hence, unless they choose to play God, they should forgive themselves (Kurtz, 1979). By releasing the alcoholic from the past, A.A. puts in motion a process that locates the member in the "now" of the present. These moves reference the Six Theses of Recovery, for they produce a reconstruction in the alcoholic's temporal, emotional, and relational ways of dealing with herself and her interactional associates.

The following members speak to these points on time, morality, guilt, and shame. The first speaker is an elder member of the A.A. group. He has over 15 years sobriety.

> I'll not go to my grave with guilt. I was crazy back then. Sure, I'm ashamed of some of the things I did. But no guilt or shame. Regret, yes. That's healthy. That's good. Hell, I knew every whorehouse in three counties. Every gambler, every prostitute, every drunk. I drank and fucked with all of them. And I went to church every Sunday and asked for forgiveness. Never believed it though. Today I do because my higher power has forgiven me [field conversation, February 19, 1983].

The next speaker has four months sobriety. Divorced, she makes reference to her marriage and family:

> The first time in A.A. I couldn't let go of the past. I felt guilt about my marriage. I was guilty about my daughters and what I had done to them. I was ashamed because I became alcoholic when they were little girls. I took full responsibility for everything. I mean *everything*! Needless to say I was drunk three weeks after I got out of treatment. Today I don't look back. I can't. I can still get all stirred up. I've forgiven myself and so has God. I feel bad about what happened. But I'm not guilty or ashamed any longer. This lady's gettin' better. She's movin' forward [field conversation, December 14, 1985].

The next member speaks to not being able to deal with the past.

> Three months out of treatment I tried to take up everything that had happened to me and that I'd done when I was drunk. Family, work, everything. I got drunk in a week. I made a decision not to deal with those things until I'd had a year's sobriety. So I waited a year. By that time I'd gotten some distance. I learned that I wasn't all bad. I slowly learned to accept my alcoholism and to accept the fact that I wouldn't have done those things if I hadn't been sick, crazy, and drunk. I learned how to forgive myself. I regret that I lost those years, but I don't look back anymore. I think I'm a stronger person today because of those things. You people have shown me how to grow and get stronger and learn from my mistakes [field conversation, May 2, 1983, 51-year-old male, carpenter].

The following woman has been out of detox and in treatment for two days. She is at her second A.A. meeting. The topic of the meeting was "One Day At A Time." She speaks softly:

I've been depressed all day. All this guilt about the past. My kids, my husband, my mother. I've let everybody down. How can I stay sober for the rest of my life with all of this stuff in my head? I get so deep into this stuff. The past and the future are right next to each other. There's no room for the present in my head. I hope I can learn how to live one day at a time [field observation, December 17, 1985].

For this woman the past and the future push the present out of her thoughts. She experiences fear of the future and guilt about the past. A.A.'s theory of the past, which she has yet to learn, hinges on the disease conception of alcoholism. It also includes a theory of a higher power who is forgiving about the past. The A.A. theory makes a basic distinction between guilt, shame, and regret that she has still to learn. As the A.A. member becomes incorporated into the A.A. framework this interpretive theory becomes a part of the new self.

ACCEPTING THE ALCOHOLIC IDENTITY

Acceptance of the alcoholic identity means that the member has moved this identity to the top of his or her hierarchy of personal identities (McCall and Simmons, 1978). This identity has become a master identity (Hughes, 1951) for the alcoholic. Within the A.A. world, and perhaps his other worlds as well, there is no doubt in his mind who he is, wherever he goes. He is an alcoholic first, and then he is the other identities his other commitments in life give him. As this conception of himself is secured, his position within A.A. becomes more firm. He becomes integrated into the A.A. experience (Maxwell, 1984). He may become a GSR of a group, or a group's treasurer. He may speak before "open meetings." His name will be on the list of names that his local A.A. answering service uses when Twelve Step calls come in. His friendship network will include a large number of A.A. members and his participation in pre-A.A. social circles may diminish. He will become a sponsor of other A.A. members. He will continue to work the Twelve Steps and he will be looked upon as a stable member of his A.A. group.

The length of time it will take for these events to begin occurring in the member's life will vary from less than one year to three years. How quickly they come to pass will depend on a number of factors, including the following: (1) the size of the A.A. community; (2) contingencies that arise within that community, such as deaths, moves, and so on; (3) the number of meetings the member attends over a regular span of time; (4) the member's commitment to a particular group; (5) the desire on the part of the member to become involved; (6) other commitments the member has that restrict A.A. participation; and (7) slips.

The Stigma of Alcoholism

Beauchamp (1980), Madsen (1974), Maxwell (1984), Trice and Roman (1970), and A.A. (1975: 70) discuss the stigma of alcoholism. The belief that an alcoholic resides on Skid Row as a result of a failure of morals and self-control lies at the core of this stigma. In order for the member to move to the fully committed A.A. identity, this stigma must be overcome. A.A. is quite explicit on this point. Newcomers are told that a measure of increased self-respect will return when they are able to tell others that they are alcoholic and recovering from alcoholism (A.A., 1975: 70). Such statements, A.A. argues, help to remove the stigma of the malady of alcoholism. Hence, to speak out as an alcoholic has organizational benefits for A.A.; it spreads the understanding that alcoholism is a disease, not a failure of self-will. It also strengthens the members' self-respect and commitment to A.A.

Self-identification as "a recovering alcoholic" is a problematic that every alcoholic must deal with. Next to staying sober, it is perhaps the most difficult situation any newcomer must confront. As the alcoholic progresses through the recovery trajectory, self-attitudes toward the "stigma" of alcoholism change and take on new meanings. Like the homosexual (Boswell, 1980; Foucault, 1982), the alcoholic must, so to speak, "come out of the closet" at some point in his or her recovery career. At first, or course, this new "deviant" identity is shared in A.A. meetings, with fellow alcoholics. Then the alcoholic may share this identity with intimates, family members, and employers. Finally, strangers or brief acquaintances may be informed, as when a person is offered a drink at a cocktail party by a host and turns down the drink because of membership in A.A.

The following member accounts speak to the problematics of this self-disclosure process. The first speaker has been to one A.A. meeting and calls himself an alcoholic.

> I went to a dinner party last weekend. It was O.K. at the beginning 'cause I just got a glass of soda. Then we sat down for dinner and there was a wine glass in front of me. I didn't know what to do. The hostess filled it up and there was a toast. I drank it. I've felt guilty ever since. What should I have done? [field conversation, January 9, 1985].

The next speaker has been sober two weeks. A 40-year-old businesswoman, she states:

> We went for cocktails after work last Friday. I didn't know what to say. Everybody looked at me like they expected me to take a drink. I said I wasn't drinking anymore. I could just see all their eyebrows go up. I felt like I wanted to sink under the table. What was I supposed to say? That after 10 years of hell I finally got myself to A.A. and one drink would take me right back where I was before? [field conversation, January 9, 1985].

The next speaker has been sober nine months. A 38-year-old civil servant, he was on a New Year's Eve date with three friends.

> We were going to make an evening of it. When it came time to order drinks I said I wanted a Coke. My date looked at me and said, "What's wrong, don't you drink?" I said, "no, not today." She said, "That's good, my father was a drunk." Then I found out she takes every kind of drug I'd ever heard of, even some I hadn't [field conversation, January 9, 1985].

The next speaker has been sober three years. He recounts a drinking situation in the following words:

> I'd gone to this Halloween party. The hostess knew I'd stopped drinking. So when I went in she announced: "Here's M, he's stopped drinking. I'm so proud of him." I could have killed her. Then everybody started talking about how they'd like to stop and didn't want to yet. I sat there in front of all that booze. Four days later I went and got drunk. I still wanted to drink. I shouldn't have gone to that party [field observation, January 9, 1985].

The following speaker has been sober 14 years. He states:

> Your anonymity is precious to me. I would never disclose your identity as an alcoholic. But mine, I don't care. Everybody within four counties knew I was a drunk. I don't care who knows I'm in A.A., maybe it helped somebody come in to find out about me. That's why I have those A.A. stickers on my car. It lets people know [field observation, January 9, 1985].

This speaker announces his recovering identity with bumper stickers. He represents the opposite end of the self-disclosure continuum. The first two speakers would never announce their identities as recovering alcoholics with an A.A. slogan on their car. These accounts display, then, the differing attitudes A.A. members have toward alcoholism, drinking in social situations, and A.A.. The first four accounts represent members working through their own recovery trajectories. They reveal the heightened self-awareness and self-stigma the new member feels when sobriety is just under way.

These self-attitudes will change as the alcoholic becomes more comfortable in A.A. meetings and in sobriety. But in the early days of recovery the stigma that the alcoholic attaches to alcoholism may in fact impede sobriety. The member is afraid to go to A.A. meetings for fear of being seen by "normals." The following member speaks to this situation.

> In my early days I parked blocks away from the meeting place. I'd walk through the alleys to get there. I'd look both ways before I went in. I was afraid of who would see me. Today I don't care who sees me go in to an A.A. meeting [field conversation, January 9, 1985].

Becoming committed to the A.A. identity and to the identity of recovering alcoholic involves, as the above remarks suggest, a sequential socialization process. Beginning in the preparatory phase as a situational alcoholic, the member moves to the interactional stage where the situational identity is slowly released as the self-stigma of alcoholism is confronted. In the participatory phase the member has internalized the recovering identity, moved beyond the stigma, and accepted the alcohoism-as-a-disease understanding of A.A. The past has been dealt with; its guilt evoking feelings neutralized through A.A.'s theory of regret. In the participatory phase the member has become a fully integrated member of the A.A. group and the larger A.A. community.

As these events come to pass, the member's commitment to A.A. thickens and deepens. She invests herself (Becker, 1960) in A.A., emotionally, personally, temporally, and interactionally. As this commitment increases, her stature as an A.A. member increases. This means, in effect, that when she talks in A.A. meetings other members make it a point to listen. It also means that when they talk they know she will be listening to them. Stature, or standing in A.A., thus turns on the member's ability to talk and listen. It is to these twin topics that I now turn.

TALKING

Talking within the A.A. frame of reference requires, as noted earlier, an ability to speak to the Steps, the Traditions, and the basic A.A. texts, including the *Big Book, The Twelve and Twelve, As Bill Sees It,* and *A.A. Comes of Age*. In those A.A. groups where the *Twenty-Hour a*

Day book is read, the thought for the day is often a topic of discourse as well. That is, a member can presume, upon meeting another member during the day, that he or she has read the thought for the day.

There are two contexts for A.A. talk: in meetings, and outside meetings, including the telephone. The normative constraints that shape these two forms of talking must briefly be addressed.

Talking in Meetings

Within meetings members seldom speak longer than two or three minutes. If they speak for a longer period of time and if they are repeating themselves, or if they are not speaking on topic, the attention of other members will drift. Within meetings members may or may not direct their talk to the talk of another. Members speak, instead, to the topic of the meeting. They may, however, make reference to the talk of another, expressing agreement or disagreement with what another member has said. A member typically only speaks for one turn within a meeting, although after all members have spoken, the Chair will typically ask, "Are there any seconds?" With this invitation a member may speak again, either on or off topic.

Talk within meetings is dictated by the topic of the meeting, which may be a Step, the presence of a newcomer, the thought for the day, an emotion, or a problematic situation a member is confronting. Each member frames a statement around the topic of the meeting, speaking from personal experience and from the standpoint of the A.A. texts.

Breaking "Frame"

Two frames, or frameworks (Bateson, 1972d; Denzin, 1980; Denzin and Keller, 1981; Goffman, 1974), structure the definitions and interactions that occur within the A.A. meeting. The primary framework states, "What is happening here is an A.A. meeting." A secondary framework says, "We are alcoholics, taking turns talking at an A.A. meeting." When members who are in treatment and in treatment groups (see Chapters 3 and 4) come to A.A. meetings as a group, a clash in interpretive framework occurs. A third frame is in operation; the frame of the treatment group. This framework endorses talking at the same time, speaking out of turn, jumping into conversations, and directing advice to another member. It is a personalizing, talking framework. It is counter to the primary and secondary frameworks that structure A.A. meetings.

When members from treatment speak within the framework of the treatment group at an A.A. meeting, regular A.A. members experience what is called "breaking frame." They feel that the A.A. meeting has been turned into a treatment group. This violates their understanding of A.A. discourse. It produces discomfort, anger, and frustration.

Patients from Eastern often came to A.A. meetings as a group. A regular meeting was created in part for them. Its founders intended it as a "newcomer" meeting that would teach patients in treatment how to use A.A. to stay sober. An established A.A. member with five years sobriety became the GSR of the group. He quit after one month. He states his reasons:

> I can't take that fucking group. The members don't know how to talk. They interrupt. They talk out of turn. They gossip, they give advice. They don't stay on the topic. They talk about everything under the sun except A.A. Christ, I need my old Tuesday night group. I can't get to enough meetings as it is. I quit. Sorry, I've got to take care of me [field conversation, October 13, 1985].

The following is an example of the form of talk he found unacceptable. The topic of the meeting is how to deal with resentments.

> *First speaker:* That's a good topic for me. But I don't want to talk about it. I'm mad at my old lady. She ain't sent me any money. Course she's pregnant, got to work, and has other things on her mind. Hell, I'm worried about her and I can't seem to listen in those damned group meetings at the center.
>
> *Second speaker*: My grandmother died. My little girl's sick. I want a drink so bad I can taste it.
>
> *Third speaker:* [Interrupting second] What's your name? Your s'posed to say you're an alcoholic before you speak. We're talking about resentment, not families.
>
> *Fourth speaker*: Let N [second speaker] finish. You ain't s'posed to interrupt. Anyway, I want to talk when he's done. I'm about to do my Fourth Step. Can anybody help me?
>
> *Fifth speaker*: I can. I just finished mine. Felt great when it was done.
>
> *Second speaker*: I haven't finished yet. Can somebody tell me how to stay sober?
>
> *Sixth speaker*: I'm an alcoholic. Pay attention and listen. Let C [a regular A.A. member and Chair of the meeting] talk.

Seventh speaker: I think we should talk about N's [second speaker] problem. I had that kind of thing happen to me three months ago and I've been drunk ever since.

Chair: My name's C. I'm an alcoholic. We are talking about resentments and staying sober today. Some of these other problems we can take up after the meeting. Who wants to go next?

With this statement the meeting fell back into A.A. order, or back into the primary and secondary frameworks of an A.A. meeting. For the first 30 minutes, however, it was in the framework of a treatment group, although specific members attempted to return it to the A.A. framework.

Breaking frame is a recurring feature of A.A. meetings that combine alcoholics in treatment and alcoholics in the community. This clash of interpretive perspectives, evident in the previous account, reveals two strategies of talking in a group. As the more powerful socializing agency, A.A. quickly teaches the new member how to talk within the A.A. primary and secondary frameworks. Once the member leaves treatment this process is quickened because he or she no longer has the treatment group to draw upon within the A.A. meeting. This critical mass of talking others dissolves once its members leave treatment.

Forms of A.A. Meeting Talk

The following format underlies a typical set of utterances by an A.A. member when talking on topic:

(1) self-introduction—"My name is ___. I'm an alcoholic";
(2) self-reference to topic of meeting, such as resentments;
(3) brief discussion of personal experience with resentments;
(4) connection of topic to an A.A. text or Step (such as the Fourth and Fifth Steps);
(5) illustration of how the topic is or has been resolved in the life of the member;
(6) brief reference to member who has introduced topic (optional); and
(7) expression of gratitude for being sober and conclusion of talk.

Each member within a meeting will be expected to follow a format something like this. When he or she does not, inappropriate talk is being produced. If the member, for example, talks about a personal problem that has no relationship to the topic at hand, or if he or she begins discussing A.A.'s relationship to religion, when spirituality is not the topic, he or she will be ignored or not listened to. While such a speaker is talking other members will get up, go to the bathroom, get coffee, light cigarettes, look askance at one another, or begin looking at A.A. literature if it is on the table.

Talking Outside Meetings

The talk that occurs within A.A. meetings is only a small portion of the talk that occurs between and among A.A. members. Although meetings and participation in meetings constitute the focal point of the A.A. experience, interactions that occur before, after, and between meetings are significant as well. In these moments personal relationships are solidified among A.A. members (see Maxwell, 1984: 10). Indeed, a large amount of the socialization into the A.A. way of life occurs outside the immediate confines of meetings.

The settings for the interactions that occur outside meetings will vary by the A.A. group. Some groups have clubhouses, others have large rooms outside meeting rooms where socializing occurs. Others select a restaurant or cafe as a meeting place where "the meeting after the meeting" occurs. Such public places become known as A.A. meeting places. A member can usually expect to find other A.A. members in such places before and after meetings.

In these settings sponsors meet with newcomers, and old-timers share common experiences. These A.A. conversations extend beyond the narrow "topic"-defined boundaries of the A.A. meeting. In this regard, they are similar to the conversations that would be produced by the members of any small group. The rules that govern such conversations apply, as well, to A.A. conversations (see Grimshaw, 1980, on conversational rules). However, the focus of the talk is nearly always A.A. related. The following interaction between two A.A. members in a local cafe having breakfast is an example. The speakers are C, a middle-level employee of a large multinational communications firm with over four years of sobriety, and R, a self-employed businessman with over five years of sobriety.

> C: What's happening with Friday night? Nobody comes anymore. Only six there last Friday. Hear they threw eight out of [a treatment center] for using. They ain't got any clients right now. Seems like they got more N.A.'s (Narcotics Anonymous) than A.A.'s right now. Where's N.A. meeting on Tuesdays? Hear [name of a hospital] is closing out that meeting. Maybe we should move Friday night [name of another meeting place], least we'd have the 7:00 o'clock N.A. meeting beforehand.

Hell, I don't know about this stuff. Somebody slashed all four tires on my car last Friday night. I got other problems. I'm a drunk and I could get drunk over somethin' like that. I got a short memory. Remember, it took me 20 years to get here.

R: I can't worry about other people's meetings. I got to make the meetings that I need. When people go out and use that helps me stay sober. Seems like there a lot more "duals" coming in these days with the young people. Hell, I'm just lucky I never got hooked on drugs. I could be just like them. Friday night used to be the biggest meeting in town. Over 100 people. Now we got five meetings on Friday night. That's good. Gives more people a chance to talk. Friday night will pick back up gain. It always does. Christ, that's a shame 'bout your tires. Who do you think did it? Something like that happened to me once before I got here. I went on a drunk that lasted a week! Hell, in those days I'd use any excuse. I'm just glad I haven't had to have a drink today. I got nothin' to complain about. Where's breakfast? [laughs] Who's complaining? [field observation, as reported, October 2, 1983].

This A.A. conversation weaves problematics within A.A. around the biographical experiences of the two speakers. The Friday night meeting provides a common source of experience for both individuals. C's concern about that meeting is turned by R into a personal statement about meetings. Connecting himself to that meeting, he makes a statement concerning his pattern of meeting attendance. Each speaker makes reference to sobriety, to going out, and to what it was like when they used to drink. They use the slashed tires on C's car as an instance for reflecting on what their conduct in the past would have been like, had that happened before they got to A.A.

This shared, friendly conversation is typical of A.A. interactions outside meetings. The common A.A. identity is shared. A.A. problematics are discussed. Issues from the personal lives of the members are discussed. A sharing of the past and the present is evidenced. Most important, the speakers share their mutual commitment to staying sober today. These conversations outside meetings solidify the underground network that exists between A.A. members.

Seeing another A.A. member in a public place reaffirms a commitment to the identity of recovering alcoholics. Passing as a "normal" in a public place, the member shares his or her A.A. identity with another A.A. member in these conversations that occur over breakfast, lunch, dinner, and coffee. These public meetings, then, provide a bridge between the two worlds of the alcoholic. By being a recovering alcoholic in a public place, the member achieves an interactional accomplishment that had previously been impossible. Passing as a normal (Goffman, 1963), the member presents a public self that alcohol had previously destroyed. Indeed, at the end of the member's drinking days public places may have been avoided. Now, with sobriety in hand, the member comes and goes from the public realm, attempting, as often as possible, to anchor these public appearances in the shared company of other A.A. members.

Telephone Talk

Talking over the telephone is the third major form of A.A. talk. Members share telephone numbers and develop their own A.A. telephone directories. Newcomers are encouraged to call their sponsor, day or night, if they think they may take a drink. Sponsors work with newcomers over the telephone. A.A. friends maintain daily or weekly contact with one another through telephone calls. Arrangements for rides to meetings are made over the telephone. Initial contact with A.A. may occur over the telephone, if a newcomer calls the A.A. answering service. In these several ways the A.A. network is activated and kept alive through the mediated exchanges the telephone offers.

A fully integrated A.A. member will be the recipient of many telephone calls. As a member, because of age or illness, becomes less able to attend meetings, the telephone may be the major form of A.A. contact he or she has. The following statement speaks to this situation. The speaker is 75 years old. Ill for several months, he has not been able to attend meetings. Famous for his sponsorship work within A.A., he discusses his relationship to those he works with over the telephone.

> I was on the phone for over five hours today. Three lovely ladies called me. One from Canada, one from Florida, and one here in town. They wanted to know how I was feeling. They just shared their experiences with me. I don't know what I'd do without that phone of mine. It keeps me alive and helps me stay off the self-pity pot.
>
> You know, this program gave me my life back. I have so many dear friends. I am just so grateful [field observation, June 20, 1984. This speaker died two weeks later].

The use of the telephone and learning how to use the telephone are two major measures of how the recovering alcoholic becomes, in a fuller sense, an A.A. member. Indeed, it may be said that next to the meeting, the telephone is the most important form of interaction members have with one another. To not use the telephone is, then, to restrict severely one's participation in the A.A. world. There are, of course, members who do not have telephones and there are A.A. "loners" who are located in settings where telephones cannot be used. In these situations A.A.'s *Grapevine* becomes an important medium of A.A. interaction, as are the few meetings that the member is able to attend. The next speaker speaks to this situation.

> I was in North Africa. Ain't no meetings there. Can't call your sponsor back home, either. I read my *Big Book* and some old *Grapevines* I took with me. Then they had a flight come up to Morocco. I got myself on it. Plane stopped three times. Picked up three A.A.'s on the way. I didn't know that 'till I got to Morocco and to the A.A. meeting place. Them three guys were there, too. That meeting cost me $500. Cheap [field observation, as reported, April 2, 1983; 41-year-old Marine sergeant, over seven years sobriety].

LISTENING

In addition to learning how to talk within the A.A. frame of reference, the member must learn how to become a listener. This requires an ability to identify with the person who is speaking and to locate the central problematic the speaker is attempting to discuss. An A.A. saying, often repeated, goes as follows: "Take the cotton out of your ears and put it in your mouth. You can't learn to speak until you learn to listen." A.A. newcomers are told to listen. They are told that they will hear their stories around the tables. They are also told that they are not unique. They are told that before they can understand their problems they have to learn what A.A. is all about. This involves a loss of ego, or a loss of self-centeredness. Told to "eat your ego" and be quiet, the newcomer may be chastised for speaking too much.

The following speaker makes this point. Sober over 14 years, he has been the director of a treatment center. He is talking to a newcomer who has talked for 15 minutes, repeating himself several times:

> Learn to keep your mouth shut. Listen, don't talk. The answers are here. You don't have them. That's why you are here. Your way didn't work. Learn to swallow your pride and listen. I had to. When I first got here I thought I had all the answers. I didn't. I'm not sure I do today. But I know I had to learn to keep quiet and listen [field observation, June 20, 1983].

If listening involves learning how to keep quiet in a meeting and not "over-talking," it also involves an ability to speak to the problems of another.

The next speaker describes her sponsor:

> She's a good listener. I call her. I'm all messed up, saying a thousand things at the same time, nothin' making sense. Just confused. I can go on like this for 10 minutes and she won't say anything. Then I'll stop and she'll say something like, "Do you think you are getting in the way of your program? Have you turned it over today?" That's all she'll say, oh, maybe a little more. Like "be good to yourself." And that's exactly what I need to hear. She knows how to listen [field observation, June 20, 1982].

BRINGING PROBLEMS TO THE TABLES

Having discussed the major "forms" of A.A. talk, I now turn to the "content" of the talk that occurs around the A.A. tables. As the member learns how to talk and listen, he or she learns to bring "sobriety problems" to the tables for discussion.

Told to "talk about it in here so you don't drink about it out there," the member learns that anything can be a sobriety problem. He or she learns this in two ways. First, by listening to the topics that are discussed at the tables the member comes to understand what the other members regard as sobriety problems in their lives. Second, by inspecting her own biography, the member can discover what events she is using, or could use, as excuses to drink again. Reminded by old-timers that "anybody can get sober, but not everybody can stay sober," the new member is admonished to bring her problems to the meetings. She is told that she must be able to go to any length to achieve and maintain her sobriety.

Sobriety Problems

The problems of living sober are, in a sense, the same problems that stand in the way of obtaining sobriety. The new member who listens at meetings will learn that any of the following topics of discussion represent "sobriety problems": anger, resentment, depression, conflicts in the workplace or at home, confusions over sexual identity, disputes with A.A. members (including sponsors), broken anonymity, dry drunks that turn into wet drunks, slips that aren't returned from, temptations to drink from friends, amends that go wrong, loneliness, feelings of guilt and shame about the past, inabilities to meet high standards set by self or others, using drugs other than alcohol, frustrations with Twelve Step Calls, problems with the "spiritual" part of A.A., false pride, lack of patience, tolerance or acceptance of others, attempts to control others, criticisms of A.A. by friends, divorces, deaths, close friends in the program "going out," living too far in the past or the future, money problems, debts, loss of a driver's license, being sent to prison, jail, or a mental hospital, envy of others with more sobriety, envy of others who can still drink, promotions at work, being fired or terminated from a job, being given more choices than one can deal with, or being sober, but having no peace of mind, or serenity. In short anything can be a sobriety problem. It is not necessary, nor is it possible, to discuss all of the "sobriety" problems that are brought to the A.A. meetings. The preceding list is representative.

There are two levels to the content of the topics that are discussed at A.A. meetings: (1) the directly personal and (2) the A.A. concept that would fit the personal. In a sense, this distinction reflects Schutz and Luckmann's (1973) distinction between first-order and second-order concepts. First-order concepts, derived from lived experience, are filtered in A.A. meetings through the second-order conceptual structure of the A.A. philosophy.

The following is a depiction of these two conceptual structures:

A Problem from Lived Experience:	*A.A.'s Conceptual Re-Interpretation:*
(1) feeling lonely, fearful, wanting to drink;	(1) self-pity, faith, gratitude, primary purpose;
(2) anger with family;	(2) powerlessness, emotional sobriety;
(3) guilt about the past;	(3) Fourth and Fifth Steps;
(4) depression;	(4) get involved in A.A.; chapter 7 *Big Book*;
(5) resentments;	(5) Fourth and Fifth Steps;
(6) failing to meet standards;	(6) Easy Does It, First Things First;
(7) slips;	(7) spiritual program, First and Third Steps;
(8) impatience with work;	(8) gratitude;
(9) confused, anxious;	(9) Turning It Over, One Day At A Time; and
(10) relationships.	(10) primary purpose, Third Step, prayer and meditation.

As a member presents a problem to the A.A. group when the call for topics is made, the chairperson will if possible reinterpret that problem within the A.A. framework. The following exchange is typical, and it indicates how the above list of two topics works.

Chair: Does anyone have a topic or problem they would like to discuss?
Speaker: I do. I don't know how to put it exactly. I guess it's work. There's this guy. I used to drink a lot with him. I know he's got a problem. I've said something to him. He doesn't want help. I think I secretly hate him. Anyway he controls what I do, he's head of my division. This morning he called me in and I got so mad I could have screamed. I've been upset ever since. I'm glad I'm here. Thank you.
Chair: Sounds like resentment to me. Anybody want to start? [field observation, November 2, 1983]

The speakers that followed discussed resentments, powerlessness, anger, emotional sobriety, turning it over at work, being grateful for a job, and First Things First. Each speaker drew upon a personal instance in his or her life where the problematics presented by the second speaker had appeared. In this way this meeting addressed the specific problems one member had on that day living sober and not drinking. This is how A.A. works in the meetings.

SELVES, TALKING, AND STORYTELLING

In Denzin (1986a: chap. 8) I suggested that the recovering alcoholic experiences four forms of self-awareness. I termed these (1) self-as-loss, (2) self-as-false-subjectivity, (3) self-as-transcendent, and (4) self-as-social-critic. Every alcoholic, I proposed, moves from experiences of feeling that life is empty and lacking in meaning (self-as-loss), to attempts to locate self in material things (false subjectivity), to feelings of transcendence, which are located in alcohol and drugs and in the A.A. experience. As a social critic the alcoholic believes that he sees things about his culture and his times that other persons are unable to see.

Self as a Double Structure of Experience

Once alcoholics reach the participatory stage of A.A. selfhood and fully commit themselves to the recovering alcoholic identity, they are able to look back on their lived experiences and find a "center" to their life that was previously not present. A doubling of self occurs (see Booth, 1961/1983: 71-76, 83, 109, 151-152, 172; Dostoevski, 1846; Lacan, 1977: 3-4). That is, the individual is able to turn back on himself, see himself as subject and object, and distance himself from who he previously was (see Mead, 1934).

This doubling occurs within the stories the alcoholic tells. She sees herself reflected in the looking-glass of her past experiences. Her new self is also reflected back to her in the faces of her fellow A.A. members (Cooley, 1902/1956: 183-185). She becomes a second self within the texts of the stories she tells (Booth, 1961/1983: 83, 109). Through a variety of narrative stances toward herself and her past she tells a multitude of stories and tales about "what it was like, what happened and what it is like now" (A.A., 1976: 58).

In this process the alcoholic relives her past. She seizes it anew, retrieves it, and recenters it within her recovery experience. As she goes through her old experiences she does so from the vantage of a new recovering self. She exorcises herself from her past in retelling stories of it. In this process she becomes a different kind of self. She objectifies her past, gets outside of it, and turns it into a social object that now takes on new meanings. She locates her past within a new structure of experience, which is given by A.A..

The Stories

It is in the alcoholic's stories that the doubling of self is most frequently displayed. The A.A. member reveals two selves when speaking. The first is the self of the storyteller. The second is the self of the recovering alcoholic who is reflecting on the past, the present, and the future. These two selves merge and double back on one another. As the member speaks, the voice of the storyteller is heard. This voice provides facts, pictures, and images about events that the other members have not witnessed. The speaker molds a picture of himself that joins him to the group. He socially constructs himself as he talks.

When the member talks he offers others a privileged access to inner thoughts and past experiences. However, as a dramatic narrator of life events, the speaker may be a reliable or unreliable storyteller. He or she may be comic, serious, satiric, ironic, truthful, overly emotional, deadpan, deceptive, direct, or indirect. But as the member talks, a narrative structure of events unfolds. When speaking the A.A. narrator controls the distance between himself, the story he tells, and his audience. He may say, as does the following speaker, the following to preface his story:

> You may not like me for what I'm about to say. You may hate me. But that's all right. This is what I have to say. I've lied. I've cheated, I've stolen things. I've been violent to people, once I broke a man's back because he wouldn't give me a hit. I don't care what you think, I'm here for me [field

observation, as reported, January 14, 1985; 28-year-old recovering alcoholic and addict, third week in treatment; salesman].

As this speaker distances himself from his A.A. audience, he challenges that audience to draw near to his story. He evokes sympathy and dislike in the same breath. In this process emotion is controlled, and attempts to present a realistic, if not glossed over, view of lived experience is given. The speaker's voice, then, as he acts out his part as a storyteller, speaks the words of a self that is recovering. Direct or indirect, objective, subjective, compassionate, or neutral, personal or impersonal, humorous, pompous, ministerial, therapeutic, philosophical, fatherly or motherly, this is the voice of recovery. And it is the voice of a speaker who is able to double back on himself, reflect himself in his talk, distance himself from his experiences, and talk about himself in a way that seemingly only requires his voice in order for the talk to be accomplished. *That is, he has become a storyteller.* He is no longer a suffering alcoholic unable to speak, nor is he a lost self. He has obtained an objective view of his own subjectivity. He has discovered that his subjectivity is interactional, reflective and *in* the stories he tells to the A.A. group.

The member has become the producer of the oral text he speaks. This is the text of his life. But this work is always unfinished, for his story will never be completely told. There are too many ways to tell it. Furthermore, the meaning of these stories he tells resides in the telling, for he creates meaning as he speaks. He must, as Booth (1961/1983: 83) suggests of all authors, literally put "his self on the table" in some form or another.

The alcoholic speaker, as he experiences the doubling of self, is firmly rooted in the oral tradition of Western culture. He is the storyteller par excellence. He has learned how to define himself through his talk. However, the language of A.A. speaks, not the alcoholic. The alcoholic is the language he speaks (Heidegger, 1976). His talk, as a spoken text, produces him (Derrida, 1978). And this is his ultimate paradox: In order to find himself he has to learn to speak a language that others before him have produced. He can only learn that language by listening to others who are also learning how to talk and think within the same set of meanings. But by learning how to speak this language he finds a new image and understanding of himself. The alcoholic finds himself, in part, in the external signs and significations of A.A.. He does this by telling his story over and over again, for he resides in these stories. He knows, too, that he will always have an audience for his stories. All he needs to do is go to the next A.A. meeting. For at the A.A. meeting he will be given his turn to talk and in that talk he can accomplish what he cannot do by himself. He can, that is, double back on himself, reflect on himself, hear himself talk, and locate himself within a structure of experience in which he is both object and subject to himself. In so doing he provides the context for others who seek the same ends for themselves.

Doris Lessing (1969) provides a fitting conclusion to this discussion for she speaks directly to the doubling of self that the alcoholic experiences.

> How very extraordinary it was . . . being the person who ran and managed and kept going. . . . It was as if more than ever one was forced back into that place in oneself where one watched; whereas all around the silent watcher were a series of defences, or subsidiary creatures, on guard, always working, engaged with—and this was the point—earlier versions of oneself.

CONCLUSIONS

I have examined the relationship between A.A. and the changing self of the recovering alcoholic. I have shown how A.A. gets inside the self of the alcoholic. In this process the alcoholic moves from being a situational alcoholic to a committed member of A.A. A socializing process organizes this experience, moving the member through three stages of A.A. selfhood. I have shown how gender and race structure this process, which involves a radical restructuring of the commonsense foundations of the individual's self. Central to the recovery of self is learning how to become a storyteller about one's life, before and after A.A. membership. The self is recovered in and through the stories the member learns to tell. Talking and listening thus become the key processes that structure the member's new senses of A.A. selfhood. "Breaking frame," or talking outside the primary and secondary interpretive frameworks of an A.A. meeting, reveals how individuals in the preparatory stages of becoming members socialize one another into and away from the A.A. point of view.

Fully committed A.A. members learn how to deal with the self and societal stigmas of being alcoholic. They accept the disease conception of alcoholism, and see themselves as members of an organization that is changing their life for the better. Learning how to let go of the past and the guilt it carries for them, A.A. members live into existence the Six Theses of Recovery. In so doing they transform themselves and the worlds they live in.

13

INTERPRETING ALCOHOLISM AND RECOVERY

The desire [to drink] will return [A.A. member].

The task of offering an interpretive framework for the understanding of alcoholism and the recovery process remains. This requires a reflection on the contents of this volume and its companion, *The Alcoholic Self*. It is not my intention to offer a *theory* of alcoholism and recovery; however, the outline of an interpretation may be set forth. This will involve a reconsideration of the Six Theses of Alcoholism, and a discussion of selfhood, desire, drinking, and alcohol in American society.

THE SIX THESES

I have repeatedly examined the two sides of alcoholism, asking in a variety of ways the same two questions: "How do ordinary men and women live into existence that dis-ease of conduct called alcoholism, and then, having been labeled alcoholics, recover from this form of experience?" The center of my work has moved outward from the self of the active and recovering alcoholic. My analysis has shown that it is impossible to separate alcoholism from group, interactional, and cultural contexts. Alcoholism and recovery are group phenomena. In its active phases, alcoholism involves families, drinking groups, and interactional associates. In the recovery phases, treatment centers and Alcoholics Anonymous play central parts in restructuring the alcoholic's self. In both phases the alcoholic develops situational adjustments to the problematics her alcoholism has produced for her. These adjustments lead to situational and committed self-definitions that identify the individual as an alcoholic.

The Six Theses of Alcoholism map the interpretive structures of self, time, emotion, and social relationship that the active alcoholic develops and lives out. Alcoholism involves a denial process that leads the alcoholic to live a mode of existence that is rooted in bad faith. Committed to the belief that each individual should be the "captain of his soul," the alcoholic denies the facts of his alcoholic existence. Willful self-pride leads her to drink when the likelihood of success is minimal and the probability of failure is high (Bateson, 1972a). Alcoholism becomes a form of self risk-taking in which the alcoholic tests her will power against the drug alcohol. Only when the problematics of her life become subjectively insurmountable is the alcoholic likely to surrender to her dis-ease of alcoholism and admit that she cannot drink like "normal" social drinkers. This act of commitment may bring her into a treatment center for alcoholism where she will learn that she suffers from what her society calls a disease. Her disease of alcoholism is emotional, her drinking but a symptom of an underlying emotional disorder. Treatment and A.A. offer the languages and situations for a restructuring of self that incorporates the alcoholism-as-disease conception into the alcoholic's view of herself.

The insanity of the alcoholically divided self has been compared to the new senses of self that A.A. and treatment offer. My lengthy study of the treatment process disclosed how old structures of self are cleared away through a "stripping" process that lays bare an empty inner self that has lost itself to alcoholism.

I have shown that once the world of recovery is entered, both in treatment and in A.A. meetings, the alcoholic finds a new structure of experience that rests on "alcoholic understanding" and a dialectical group process. A new self rises out of the languages, rituals, and interactions that A.A. groups and meetings offer. As this new self appears, and as the alcoholic learns how not to drink, the old self of the past slips away, to be replaced by a radically transformed sense of selfhood.

The recovering alcoholic discovers a new interpretive theory of self, meaning, alcohol, and alcoholics. This theory replaces the system of denial and bad faith that his or her self-system had previously clung to. This theory, which is A.A.'s, blends a pragmatic understanding of conduct with a practical, spiritual ethic that has a single purpose—staying sober today.

In telling this story I have repeatedly focused on the universal singularity of each alcoholic's recovery experience. I have assumed that each alcoholic's experience is unique, particular to his or her lived situation. Hence, there are as many stories of recovery as their are alcoholics who are recovering. However, it can be argued that there is only one recovery story, the story that is given in the Twelve Steps of A.A., and in A.A.'s *Big Book*. That is, alcoholics who recover through A.A. learn and tell the same basic recovery story, the one that is given in the basic texts of A.A. Hence, recovery becomes a story-telling process involving socialization into the language and lore of A.A. (Thune, 1977).

DRINKING, ALCOHOL, AND AMERICAN SOCIETY

The schools, laws, peer groups, families, work groups, and agencies of social control in American society teach individuals how to drink, how to use alcohol, and how to act when under the influence of alcohol (Jellinek, 1962; Lemert, 1967; MacAndrew and Edgerton, 1979). American society, like other societies, ritually integrates the beverage and drug called alcohol into its interactional and moral orders. The drinking of alcohol is a symbolic ritual and interactional act in our society. Americans connect the drinking of alcohol with the occasioned release of tension and anxiety. They drink so as to solidify lines of sociable identification with one another. They utilize certain alcoholic beverages as status markers of self-worth. They connect the drinking of alcohol with the pursuit and interactional realization of a valued social self. They learn to drink so as to celebrate the good times and they drink to drown the sorrows of failures and bad times.

Accepted normal drinking is symptomatic of our culture's attitudes toward the drinking act; that is, all drinkers, when they stay within the boundaries of acceptable "drinking comportment," are culturally symptomatic drinkers (Jellinek, 1962; MacAndrew and Edgerton, 1969). The drinking act connects the drinker's self to the culture's values regarding alcohol and social drinking. However, some "symptomatic drinkers" become occasional, symptomatic excessive drinkers. They transfer alcohol from its status as a beverage to its use as a drug. They use alcohol as a means of relieving major individual stresses that are social in nature. Within this group of occasional symptomatic excessive drinkers emerge those individuals for whom alcohol becomes a "mode of living" (Jellinek, 1962: 359). These drinkers become addictive alcoholics. They lose control over the amount they drink on any given occasion and they are unable to abstain from drinking for any continuous period of time. Their use of alcohol causes them and society problems. It is this category of drinker that I have studied in this volume and in *The Alcoholic Self.*

Alcoholics appear to emerge in those social groups, families, and cultural settings where heavy drinking is permitted and where the temporary euphoria of the alcoholic "high" is valued over its dysfunctional and negative psychological effects; indeed, these negative effects are often defined as part of the cost of the high that the drinking of alcohol produces (see Cahalan, 1970: 151-154; Jellinek, 1960). Alcoholics create and seek out social spaces that legitimate heavy, regular alcohol consumption. The "drinking spaces" alcoholics live in place a high premium on the selfhood that is achieved through the drinking act. These places are also filled with sufficiently justifiable reasons for drinking. These reasons, which become motives for drinking, may include unemployment, marital or relational disruptions, loneliness, financial pressures, anxiety, and the desire to escape from the demands of ordinary life. *The core problematic that organizes the "pre-alcoholic" drinking situation is the desire to escape from self through the use of alcohol.* The inner structure of the pre-alcoholic's self tends, as Tiebout (1949) suggested, toward self-centeredness, narcissism, loneliness, and a fearfulness of self and other.

Ressentiment and Alcohol

Particular social groups, by virtue of their structural location in American society, are more likely to adopt the previously outlined definitions regarding self and alcohol. Members of such groups are characterized by the emotional attitude Scheler (1912/1961: 39-40) termed *ressentiment*. Ressentiment is a backward-looking emotionality. It is a form of self-hatred that is located in the real and imagined actions another has taken toward the person. It is a self-poisoning emotion that colors all of the interactions the subject has with others, particularly those in authority positions. Ressentiment is characterized by two key features. First, it involves the repeated experiencing and reliving of a particular emotional reaction against someone else. Second, the quality of this emotional reaction is negative, often involving hostility, anger, wrath, and a vengeful joy in the other's misfortunes. Scheler suggests that for the man or woman of ressentiment, this cluster of emotional feelings comes to form the center of their personality. Such persons look out on the world of interaction through the negative framework that ressentiment offers. Each time the subject acts toward the other for whom ressentiment is felt, a sense of inferiority and repressed rage is experienced. Because of their structural relation to the other for whom they feel this hatred, the subject is unable to express the feelings that are felt. Hence, ressentiment becomes a repressed or buried emotional attitude. Holding in these feelings, which are then turned inward, subjects come to undermine their own senses of self-worth. They feel inferior in the eyes of the other. The desire to strike out is repressed, leading to a feeling of impotence, which is surrounded by an inner seething rage.

Scheler argues that certain social structures regularly produce the emotion of ressentiment (also see Denzin, 1984a: 226). Social democracies that espouse equality of rights for all but allow wide variations to exist between expectations and what is in fact received engender ressentiment on the part of the "young, the elderly, women, the handicapped, the stigmatized, and members of racial and ethnic minorities" (Denzin, 1984a: 226). These special populations are especially prone to alcohol abuse and to higher rates of alcoholism within American society (see Gomberg, 1982: 337-343, 351-352). Certain occupational groups also experience greater degrees of ressentiment, including the military, civil servants, academic professionals, certain clergy groups, other members of the educational establishment (including students), professional athletes, the unemployed, and those on welfare. Ressentiment is greatest when self- or group-injury is experienced as destiny and as being beyond one's control. When powerlessness is great, ressentiment increases, as does alcohol use and abuse.

The man or woman of ressentiment fuels these negative emotional feelings with alcohol; indeed, drinking may be the only socially legitimate escape persons in such situations feel is available to them. When the economic, interactional, gender, moral, political, legal, and religious structures of a society regularly produce large categories of persons who experience the emotions of ressentiment, then such structures lay the foundation for higher rates of alcoholism among the members of these special populations who come to feel that ressentiment is in fact their destiny. The dis-ease of alcoholism thus becomes a structural phenomenon, attached to the emotional experiences of large categories of persons in contemporary American life. It may be argued that the structures of society produce the emotions and forms of emotionality that turn back on the very structures that produced them (Denzin, 1984a: 227). In this sense the dis-ease of alcoholism becomes a poisoning emotional attitude that reflects an inner dis-ease of self in the central social institutions of American society. Basic to this dis-ease conception are the negative attitudes toward time and emotion that I have located at the heart of the alcoholic's alcoholism. The backward-looking, temporal nostalgia that typifies much of the postmodern period (Habermas, 1985), which combines with a negative emotional reading of current social relationships (Baudrillard, 1983b, 1983c) is thus symptomatic of a contemporary version of ressentiment. Such conditions create the basis for the violent, repressed, distorted emotionality so characteristic of alcoholism and related drug abuses.

Motives, Desire, and Drinking

For individuals of ressentiment a functional autonomy of drinking motives (Allport, 1964: 29; Cahalan, 1970: 153; Jellinek, 1960: 74; Wexberg, 1951) develops. This joins the drinking of alcohol with (a) the euphoric pleasures of drinking and (b) the inner emptiness of self the individual feels on a regular basis. The reasons and purposes for drinking extend beyond the original contexts in which the individual drank for social reasons. He or she now drinks so as to relieve the stress of self that is continually felt. Drinking becomes a functionally autonomous act. It is inscribed in the basic and primary self-images the person commits to. Because alcoholics carry this picture of themselves into every situation they enter, they always have a reason to drink or to think about drinking.

The functional autonomy of the drinking motive is layered through the basic self-structures of the individual. As the alcoholic moves from the pre-alcoholic to the prodomal and then crucial and chronic stages of alcoholism, the drinking act produces a second layer of emotions and negative experiences that are woven into the underlying negative emotions the person already holds about himself (Jellinek, 1962). The individual literally produces an "alcoholic personality" for himself.

The drinking motives of the individual are driven by the "desire" to escape and then to find self. The alcoholic's desire for self seeks realization in a mode of consciousness that is in control of itself and free from fear and anxiety. Alcoholic desire is that mode of self-consciousness that desires itself through the altered streams of experience alcohol produces. Alcoholic desire is consciousness aimed at its own fulfillment. It is self- and body centered, for it is felt throughout the drinker's body as he or she drinks. In this desire the objects of the alcoholic's consciousness are under her control, for she brings them into existence as she drinks. Her desire links her to a world of others that is primarily imaginary, distorted, and inward based. The alcoholic's drug-induced desire brings her up against relations with others, which she often demolishes through alcoholic and emotional violence. Her desire shuts her off from the very world she wishes to be a part of (Denzin, 1985c: 49).

Desire and the Self

When alcoholics tell newcomers that "the desire to drink will return," they are referencing the double aspect of alcoholic desire. That is, the desire that returns is aimed at a form of selfhood that alcohol produces. Hence, the desire to drink is a desire to return to a self of the past in which alcoholic desire dominated the drinker's consciousness.

The self that the alcoholic seeks in the drinking act is a ritual, sacred self that will join him with his fellows, who may also share his ressentiment. He desires a mode of self-experience that will ratify his wholeness to himself and to others; never mind that this is a fictional wholeness based on alcohol. By producing a fictional unity with self and other he molds a sacred, ritual image of himself that purportedly allows him to pass as "normal" in the company of other "normal" interactants, with and toward whom he may share or feel ressentiment.

However, the alcoholic's fellow interactants find a valued mode of selfhood in "normal" social drinking that is filtered through social interaction. The alcoholic, on the other hand, understands that he can only find his ritual, sacred self in the privateness of alcoholic drinking. Once he finds that self in alcohol he can then bring it to the occasions of social interactions his fellows take for granted. Literally overflowing with selfhood, the alcoholic finds that his cherished, sacred, inner ritual self is unwanted in civil, social society.

The Inner, Alcoholic Self

The inner self of the alcoholic, nourished on alcohol, has been wounded, perhaps since childhood. The sources of these wounds are interactional and interpersonal. They derive from the formative matrix of interactional experiences that brought the alcoholic into the drinking cultures of his or her society. At the center of these experiences stand unstable inner self-feelings, faulty understandings of the other, emotional loneliness, a lack of trust in the others, and an inability to enter into fully consensual "I-me" dialogues with others. An "anxiety" of relating to the other (Sullivan, 1953), a preponderance of negative emotional experiences that detach the individual from close relations with others, and a failure to achieve full recognition in the "eyes" of the other contribute to the inner instability of the pre-alcoholic's self.

Distorted, unbalanced, and uneven emotional relations with "fathering" and "mothering" others lead the pre-alcoholic to place an emotional wedge between self and figures of authority. Fearful of abuse, shame, or experiencing a lack of subjectively defined proper recognition from the other, the pre-alcoholic enters the world of interaction from the vantage point of an imaginary self that has found its own center in its self. Unable to love the other fully, the alcoholic exaggerates self-love, becoming narcissistic, self-centered, and resentful. But because the other cannot or will not furnish the recognition and love that is desired, the alcoholic's self-love is tainted with insecurity, guilt, and egocentric uncertainty.

If the alcoholic's significant others are (or were) alcoholic (as was the case for nearly every alcoholic I studied), then two self interactional patterns are set in motion. First, the pre-alcoholic learns alcoholic emotions and learns how to drink alcoholically. Second, the pre-alcoholic sets out to prove that he or she *will not* become alcoholic. A battle with alcohol, which is a battle with self, follows. In an attempt to regain a measure of status and recognition in the eyes of the significant other, the pre-alcoholic sets out to drink more than the other, and yet not become alcoholic. Perhaps genetically doomed to failure, the individual becomes an alcoholic in the process.

Alcoholic Self-Comportment

Hence, those same social agencies, social groups, and individuals who taught the alcoholic how to drink so as to bring a valued social self into existence now turn against her and brand her a problem drinker, or an alcoholic. These labels, which apply to selfhood and interactional comportment, serve to undercut the drinker's standing in her social groups. She finds herself with a self that has no place to go. She has acquired the stigmatizing label of "alcohol." As a recovering alcoholic she will work to remove this stigma of self.

The foregoing suggests that those agencies and groups that teach individuals how to drink normally also teach them how to identify problem drinkers. Alongside these agencies exists a social structure that has been created to deal with problem drinkers. Alcoholism researchers, treatment centers for alcoholism, and A.A. study and teach problem drinkers how to become recovering alcoholics.

These structures remind us that although any society apparently finds some utility in having deviants who define the outer limits of normal conduct, they also need agencies that bring these deviants back in line (Durkheim, 1912/1961). So it is with the active and recovering alcoholic. He or she traverses both edges of the sacred and the profane in American society. Once a flagrant drinker, the alcoholic who recovers in A.A. becomes abstinent. The alcoholic's career thus highlights the two moral extremes American society takes toward drinking and alcohol. Yet, by learning how not to drink, but by discovering a new sense of selfhood in A.A., the alcoholic presents a dilemma to society. That is, the resources for discovering a nonalcoholic, serene self lie in interactions with one's fellows; just as it supposedly rests in the drinking groups that make up our society. Hence, either way he looks, the alcoholic finds that the foundations of his self rest in structures that are outside the mainstream interactional worlds of modern American life.

RECAPTURING SELF

The recovering alcoholic recaptures a sense of selfhood that was lost to alcoholism. A new, sacred, ritual self is given by virtue of sobriety and participation in the storytelling rituals and traditions of A.A. It must be remembered that 7 of 10 alcoholics who undergo treatment relapse. These persons adopt the situational identity of alcoholic. Those who do commit themselves to recovery assume committed, recovering alcoholic identities. In Rudy's (1986) terms they become pure, converted, and committed alcoholics. It is these alcoholics that I now speak to. Their social experiences are sociologically important because they reveal how a new social self, which flows from the sacred, collective structures of group life, may be created.

With Mead (1934), Durkheim (1912/1961), Sullivan (1953), and Wiley (1985) the following process for recapturing self may be sketched. As previously argued (Denzin, 1986a), the recovering alcoholic experiences four modes of self-awareness: self-as-loss, self located in material things, self-as-transcendent, and self-as-social-critic. The recovering alcoholic learns a new mode of selfhood that locates self in the interactional structures of the A.A. experience (Maxwell, 1984). This structure is larger than the alcoholic. It has collective, ritual properties, given in the A.A. Steps and Traditions. These properties are also evidenced in A.A. storytelling and in the other interactions that occur around the A.A. tables.

Four levels, or structures, of experience connect the self of the individual to A.A.: the personal, the dyadic, the group, and the collective. The personal level is given in the member's daily meditations with the texts of A.A. The dyadic level is given in the sponsor relationship and in the friendships that develop in A.A. In the sponsor relationship (Denzin, 1986a) the member reenacts a relationship to authority figures from the past. In this relationship members find social recognition, self-esteem, and a sense of identification that was previously lacking in their lives. They learn how to identify with and through the emotional experiences of another who has the valued, sober, sacred self they seek.

The sponsor relationship objectifies the new self that is sought. It anchors that self in the experiences of an older, more knowledgeable member, who becomes a coaching, socializing agent for the new A.A. member (see Strauss, 1959).

Within the A.A. group the member learns how to enact and present this new, sober self. Members learn how to talk about the self of the past that is slipping away as they become sober. They learn how to allow this self to become a part of the past. The old self of the past, filled with not-me and bad-me social experiences (Sullivan, 1953), is absorbed into the archetypical past (Thune, 1977) A.A. offers. As this self becomes a part of the past, the new sober self, grounded in the rituals and languages of A.A., takes its place. This self is located in the "good-me" experiences (Sullivan, 1953) that the sponsor and the A.A. group make available to the member. It becomes a storytelling, sober self that enters into the collective structures of the A.A. community.

That is, as the member becomes and stays sober, his or her biography becomes a part of the collective A.A. consciousness. The member's recovery story is shared by others. His or her home group becomes common knowledge within the A.A. social world, for instance, Jane of the Monday Night Group. At this collective level, the new, sacred self of the member becomes part of a collective group self. It enters into the group's collective understanding of itself as a group that has regular, sober members.

A.A. symbolizes the sacredness of the member's self at each of the previously stated four levels: the individual, the dyadic, the group, and the collective. This is seen in the principle of anonymity that is the spiritual foundation of the A.A. traditions (A.A., 1953). By stripping each individual of any sense of uniqueness, and by transforming each member into an anonymous member of a collective whole that is governed by spiritual principles, A.A. creates a society of co-equal selves. Each self is sacred in its own right, but sacred only because of its membership in the collectivity as a whole. Each part of that collective whole (the personal, dyadic, group) is necessary in order for the collective level to exist. A.A. cannot be reduced to the selves of its individual members. These selves are part of and produced by something that is larger than any given individual. Hence, a collective, ritual self enters the self of each member; that ritual self in turn contributes to and becomes part of something larger than it is.

By taking individuals with ruined, distorted, disorganized selves and giving them a new, sacred, whole self, A.A. reveals how the collective creates the individual. At the same time, the individual creates the collective, for without members there would be no A.A. groups. Without groups there would be no society of preexisting sober selves. Such a society, which exists *sui generis*, is necessary for the emergence of a new sober self that learns how to take the attitudes of sober, previously drinking alcoholic selves (see Mead, 1934). Mead's principle of sociality, which involves the ability to take the attitude of the other, thus organizes the key processes through which A.A. works. As Mead noted, significant symbols, meaningful social objects, and a universe of shared discourse are all requirements for the genesis and emergence of self in the social situation. A.A. makes these essential ingredients available through its texts, Traditions, Steps, and meetings.

But to Mead must be added Durkheim's insights on the ritual sacredness of the self that emerges out of the collective structures of social groups. The self that is recaptured in A.A. is a sacred, ritual self. It is a self that flows out of and into the A.A. group. Its moral significance lies in its symbolic capacity to activate and stand for the fundamental principles of sobriety and anonymity that A.A. values. This moral self becomes, as Goffman (1967) argued, a god. But it is not an isolated god; it is an intersubjectively produced, sacred, social object. Each A.A. self thus symbolizes the totality of the A.A. experience. For in each sober self lies the residues of the A.A. past that holds this society of recovering selves together.

In this manner, a ritual yet commonsense structure of self-feelings is produced in the person of the new member. These feelings and self-understandings come into existence as the member learns to fit himself or herself into the taken-for-granted meaning structures of the A.A. cultural structure. When the member slips and relapses, he or she relapses into a previously learned mode of self and cultural understanding. That is, the member draws away from the meaning structures of A.A. and seeks an old ritual self in the standardized understandings that his drinking culture has given him.

In so doing he seeks a privatized, ritual self that turns its back on the collective, ritual self of the A.A. social structure. This self is repositioned within the competitive, dualistic divisions of the broader society in which "being captain of one's soul" is paramount. Hence, in order to find the new ritual A.A. self the member must give herself to the collective structures A.A. offers. These collective structures, as Bateson (1972a) argued, following Durkheim, are outside the person, immanent in a system greater than the person, and based on a noncompetitive, nonnegotiative, nonconflictual mode of self and social interaction. This collective whole is a Durkheimian religion. As Bateson (1972a: 333) observes and Wiley (1985) suggests, this religion sacretizes the person at every level of interaction. It joins the member to a transcendent group structure that is stronger than he or she is. It envelopes the member. It gives a sense of sacred, ritual selfness that cannot be given in the solitary drinking act, or in drinking groups, which are predicated in a competitive, individualistic model of person and interaction.

The sociological foundations of this view of persons, selves, and groups thus derives, as Durkheim observed, from the sacred, symbolic impulse that organizes all human societies. By deifying the personhood of the recovering alcoholic self, A.A. symbolizes this sacred impulse that some contend has been lost in the modern, secular world. But A.A.'s move is collective, not individualistic. Hence, the A.A. self finds its locus in a cultural structure that stands to the side, if not outside, the mainstream of modern group life.

CONCLUSION

Our society, however, has created a space for the alcoholic. This can be seen in the expanding social worlds of recovery. As a social critic the alcoholic's life stories record the effects of our society upon the "civilized individual" (Spender, 1947/1984: ix). This cultural member shows possibilities of existence that would otherwise not be present if our attitudes toward drinking and alcohol were not as they are. This individual symbolizes, through his or her experiences, the fate of all persons who wish to control their own lives and live into existence a mode of selfhood that is shareable, sociable, assertive, and pleasurable. Yet, alcoholics remain outsiders to this culture, which still does not understand them. This is the alcoholic's dilemma, and the culture's, too.

14

CONCLUSION
Self, Temporality, and Alcoholism

> The real cause of alcoholism is the complete baffling sterility of existence as sold to you [Malcolm Lowry, 1984: xxx].
>
> The moral, then, is this. Since societies, like individuals, get the kinds of drunken comportment that they allow, they deserve what they get [MacAndrew and Edgerton, 1969: 173].

The alcoholic self has been my topic. A victim of a course of action he or she helps construct, the alcoholic and his or her other live through the three-act play I have, following Kellerman (1969), called the "Merry-Go-Round Named Denial." The alcoholic who collapses and surrenders to alcoholism then enters the regions of experience called recovery. I have briefly sketched the stages of recovery the alcoholic passes through.

It is now necessary to reflect on the alcoholic experience as I have presented it. I shall discuss briefly, in turn, the following topics: (1) alcoholism, science, and American society; (2) the alcoholic self; (3) self, temporality, and existence; and (4) the alcoholic as social critic.

ALCOHOLISM, SCIENCE, AND AMERICAN SOCIETY

American society, through its mass media, cultures, schools, laws, and institutions of social control teaches individuals how to drink and use alcohol. People, as MacAndrew and Edgerton (1969: 172) suggest, learn about drunkenness from what their societies teach them. Members of a culture also learn how to identify problem drinkers. Their society also makes available to them a variety of interpretations concerning how and why it is that certain people become alcoholics and others do not. If a society is contradictory, ambivalent, or less than clear-cut on the patterns of drunken comportment that it allows (Pittman, 1967), then what individuals do when they drink will vary enormously. Furthermore, if a society teaches, as ours does, that "the state of drunkenness carries with it an 'increased freedom to be one's other self' " then the variety of selves that a society produces when it encourages its members to drink will also vary enormously (MacAndrew and Edgerton, 1969: 172). American society thus gets the kinds of alcoholic selves it deserves, for it encourages the use of alcohol in the pursuit of a self that is valued, cherished, and celebrated in everyday discourse (Madsen, 1974: 107).

Modern behaviorial science aids in this pursuit of a desired self that is produced in and through the drinking act. It does so in the following ways. First, it offers evidence on the drinking patterns of "normal" drinkers (Beauchamp, 1980). Second, it offers causal theories and explanations of problem, alcoholic drinking. Third, it offers theories and methods for turning problem, alcoholic drinkers into social drinkers. Fourth, it aids in the production of scientific texts that hold out hope for alcoholics and their families, suggesting in these texts that science may one day remove the specter of alcoholism from the American scene (see Franks, 1985). Fifth, by questioning the scientific and medical status of the term "alcoholism," modern science suggests that the "alcoholism" problem it has helped create may, in fact, not exist at all (Beauchamp, 1981). In this manner, science turns the lived problems of alcoholic drinking back on the drinker and his or her family. It suggests in the process that drinkers have become victims of a scientific or folk myth. They, in fact, do not have alcoholism. They have something else.

Driven by the causal question "Why does the 'alcoholic' drink alcoholically?" this literature often has gone in circles as it debates the reality of the phenomenon it supposedly has committed itself to eradicating. Periodically a "new" cause of alcoholism is discovered. Most recently the activities of the enzyme called P-450 and the opiate compounds in the central nervous system called TIQs have been located as the causes of alcoholism (Franks, 1985).

Such discoveries by science of course cannot be discounted. They offer new narrative texts that, as just suggested, hold out hope for the suffering problem drinker and his or her significant others. They of course do not speak to the alcoholic who has been defined, by himself or herself and others, as alcoholic. For the alcoholic has something that he or she and others believe has caused the alcoholic to act in ways that society defines as deviant, abnormal, or alcoholic. Whether that something happens to be TIQs or the enzyme called P-450 really is irrelevant.

These discoveries, then, serve to divert attention away from the lived experiences of alcoholics. Indeed it is unlikely that the phenomenon called alcoholism will disappear. It will be with us as long as our society persists in holding on to the ambivalent, contradictory attitudes toward alcohol and self-hood that it now values. We will have, that is, a phenomenon with the characteristics of alcoholism long after science has discovered and secured an undebatable, verifiable cause of it. This is so because alcoholism is a disease of living that is produced, in part, in its modern forms, by societies that do not provide alternative, nonalcoholic answers and solutions to selfhood, meaning, and everyday existence.

American Society

Our society, then, provides the arenas for the production of alcoholic selves. It produces the language for describing such selves (narcissistic, self-centered, divided against itself). It creates a need for a mass media that reports on the conduct of these selves and others like them (that is, those who are spiritually bankrupt, alienated, or schizophrenic). Our society also creates the alcohol that persons defined as alcoholic drink. It creates the laws that such persons violate when they, for example, drink and drive (Gusfield, 1981). Our society provides the treatment centers that treat these selves. A new class of bureaucratic personalities (or selves) has been created also. They go by various titles: DUI instructors, alcoholism counselors, Certified Alcoholism Professionals, and so on.

At the same time American society has created a social and moral space for the emergence of Alcoholics Anonymous (see Kurtz, 1979; Maxwell, 1984; Rudy, 1986). A.A. also produces alcoholic selves of the recovering variety. I have outlined how A.A. works in Chapters 3 and 7. It is apparent that societal attitudes toward the existence of the alcoholic self are drastically changing. In the 1980s the problem drinker cannot escape the labels of alcoholic and recovering alcoholic (see *Time,* 1985).

Alcoholism as a Dis-ease of Conduct

Given the foregoing preconceptions, I have decided to examine the alcoholism that the alcoholic in the 1980s experiences as a dis-ease of conduct. Alcoholism is an uneasiness of self that draws the subject into a vicious circle of addictive, destructive drinking. Alcoholism touches nearly every area of the alcoholic's life, as I have attempted to show in Chapters 4, 5, and 6. At the heart of alcoholism lies a fear of temporality. Locked in the past, the alcoholic fearfully confronts the present and future through the temporal consciousness alcohol creates. Alcoholism becomes a dis-ease of time. This uneasiness with time is manifested in the divided self the alcoholic experiences. Trapped within the negative emotions that alcoholism produces, the alcoholic dwells within the emotions of the past. The alcoholic approaches the present and the future with an anxious, self-fearfulness that undermines the ability to generate positive, emotional feelings toward self or others.

THE ALCOHOLIC SELF

My concern in this text, accordingly, has been to examine, in a variety of ways, the same question: "How do ordinary men and women experience that form of conduct modern society calls alcoholism?" This experience, I have suggested, is structured by an alcoholic self. This self is divided against itself (see Laing, 1965). Narcissistic and self-centered, the alcoholic self uses alcohol as a mirror, seeking in the self-reflections that alcohol offers a truer picture of itself. Yet alcohol, for the divided self, fuels a resentment toward others and an inner hatred of self. The unstable, inner self of the alcoholic runs to violent emotionality, madness, insanity, and imaginary fears. The emotional and sexual relations the alcoholic has with others are similarly distorted by alcohol's effects. The alcoholic is unable to present a "true" picture of self to the other, for he or she always sees the other through alcoholically clouded streams of consciousness. Hampered by alcoholic amnesia and alcoholic aphasia, the alcoholic lives within a distorted world of self-other relations. Symbolically and interactionally attached to dominating emotional associates from the past, the alcoholic lives out a maddening inner self-drama that is scripted by resentment and hatred. I have traced the major contours of this drama in Chapter 6.

Telling the Alcoholic's Story: The Six Theses

There are, Henry James (1920) suggests, 5 million ways to tell the same story. I have distilled the stories alcoholics tell about themselves into the Six Theses of Alcoholism as given in Chapter 5. These theses organize the alcoholic's experiences with alcoholism and recovery. They refer to an interaction process that organizes the alcoholic's relationship to alcohol, drinking, self, emotionality, meaning, temporality, action, and the other.

They do not, however, always operate at the level of conscious, interpretive strategies. Rather, they structure the alcoholic's existence at a taken for granted, habitual, often preconscious level. They may, on occasion, however, evolve into consciously developed, well thought-out interpretive systems, as is the case of the alcoholic's theory of denial.

The concepts of time, social relationships (real and imagined), emotionality (positive and negative), bad faith, denial and self-deception, and beliefs in self-control and surrender reference the inner and outer forms of experience that constitute the essential structures of alcoholism (and recovery). As such they reflect an interpretive theory of self and conduct in the world.

ALCOHOLICS AND "NORMALS"

These theses also apply to the world that is taken for granted by nonalcoholics. That is, active alcoholics take to the extreme the assumptions and principles that structure the lives of ordinary people. Ordinary individuals live bad faith, lie and deceive themselves and others, and engage in distorted human relationships. Ordinary individuals also experience negative emotions, hold onto resentments, experience time inauthentically, and believe in willpower and self-control. Such persons also develop divided selves and live out imaginary self-ideals that have little to do with the worlds of the "real."

What sets the alcoholic off from the "normal" are the lived experiences that accompany his or her self-definitions. The individual's divided self leads him or her into the world of alcoholic dreams and fantasies; that world soon takes over the alcoholic's life. As the alcoholic moves farther and farther into it, his or her distance from normals and normal everyday life increases. The alcoholic becomes an outsider to society, almost by choice (Becker, 1973).

In telling the alcoholic's story I have repeatedly focused on the universal singularity of each alcoholic's experiences. I have assumed that each alcoholic is unique, yet in his or her uniqueness lies a universal generality that describes the experiences of all persons who become alcoholic during this particular period of American history. Although there are as many stories of alcoholism as there are alcoholics, the outline of every story is the same, and each can be interpreted within the structures that the Six Theses reference.

Alcoholic Time and "Normal" Time

In Chapter 5, I compared alcoholic time with normal time. I suggested that "normal" time (1) is grounded in the present, (2) is not experienced fearfully, (3) is reflectively grasped as being part of ongoing purposive action, (4) is not lodged in the past or the future, and (5) does not give rise to feelings of self that are located in the past. Normal time informs the present in a purposively useful fashion. Alcoholic time demolishes the present.

I then suggested that modern societies have produced large classes of individuals who share certain features of the alcoholic's dis-ease of time. Following Scheler (1961), I argued that the elderly, women, members of racial and ethnic minorities, the recently divorced, students, and the unemployed all experience a resentment that is grounded in time. Alcoholism, then, is just one version of the dis-ease of time that grips the modern situation.

SELF, TEMPORALITY, AND EXISTENCE

Consider the following self-statements given by alcoholics.

> I don't know who the fuckin' hell I am. It's been eight months that I've been sober and I still don't know myself. Nothin's right. I'm messin' up everything I touch and even the things I leave alone are fucked up. I come to meetings every day and I want to leave early. I talk and nothin' works. I hear the sound of my voice and I don't know what I'm sayin'. I feel like there's no space for me. No space in my head. No space where I am. I'm in the middle of nothing.

> Last night I decided to take action. Fix the frozen drainpipe on the house I said to myself. Went outside. The fucker was frozen all to Hell. Nothin' I could do. Went back to go inside and the damned door was locked. I thought maybe I could take out a window, real gentle-like. Instead I smashed it to pieces. Went all over my living room. Got inside and there was glass all over. I didn't want to be there. So I left. But I didn't know where to go. Too dumb to go to a meeting I just drove around by myself [field observation, February 8, 1985, recovering alcoholic, 35 years old, accountant].

In this account, or story, the member speaks to a loss, or emptiness of self. Indeed as he speaks he is searching for a self to which he might anchor himself.

Compare the previous account to the following. The speaker is 43 years old. He is still intoxicated, after two days of not drinking. He is at his second A.A. meeting.

> I've got everything. A good wife. A good job. A new car. Great kids. Great groups of buddies. Sure I maybe drink too much. But what the hell, who doesn't? Some days I can go with just one drink, then I stop and stay till closing time. I feel something you people got here but I'm not sure it's for me. I think I can handle this deal by myself. Don't know. Nothing makes sense. Thanks for letting me talk [field observation, October 13, 1983].

This member talks with a self-confidence that is absent in the account of the first speaker. He has a self firmly attached to material and personal things, including a wife, a job, children, a car, and friends. He speaks as if he knows who he is. The first speaker does not know who he is.

The following speaker is reflecting back on his "using days." A dentist, 29 years old, he has been "clean and straight" for three months. He has been in A.A. for over four years. He has gone through three threatment centers.

> I would get up, depressed as hell. Roll a joint and grab a beer, lay back. Get in touch with the universe. I'd fly off, out of my apartment, into space, in tune with the world. No worries, no fears. I knew everything. I had all the answers. Turn the music on high, the Stones, mellow out. No depression. I called it getting in touch with the universe. Today that all sucks. I get high with you people [field observation, January 2, 1985].

This speaker references two modes of experiencing self: the first is produced by drugs and alcohol, the second by A.A. interaction.

The following speaker is more explicit. Sober 12 years, he is 68 years old. A retired barber, he states the following:

> A.A. will be here after I'm gone. People who are still out there drinking will take my place in this fellowship. And like me they will find a peace of mind, a serenity, and a God of their understanding that I could never get with that damned booze. They will find out who they are and they will learn that they belong here, if they want to be here. They will help others find what I have found. This has been a very good way of life for me. I am just glad I found it before it was too late [field observation, October, 13, 1983].

Our barber has found himself. He speaks of a place in a fellowship that will go on after he dies. He has experienced a self-transcendence that is unlike the negativity of the first speaker. He has transcended, as well, the material foundations of self the second speaker is still attached to.

Problematics of Self and Alcoholism

Smith (1957: 279) has described the alcoholic in the following paradoxical words:

> The [A.A.] member was never enslaved by alcohol. Alcohol simply served as an escape from personal enslavement to the false ideals of a materialistic society.

These four accounts by alcoholics speak directly to Smith's position, for each alcoholic locates himself within a materialistic culture that is somehow found empty or lacking. Each, in his way, is criticizing that culture. These statements reference three problematics of self that are displayed in the alcoholic experience. These problematics may be termed (1) self as loss, (2) self as false or illusive subjectivity, and (3) self as transcendent experience.

Self as loss references the experiences of the first speaker. He is sober but his life has no meaning for him. He can feel his inner subjectivity, but he feels an emptiness of self as he speaks. His selfhood is illusive. He is haunted by a sense of self that escapes his grasp.

Self as false subjectivity is given in the account of the second speaker. He has everything: wife, job, new car, friends, house. Yet he drinks more than he wants to and suspects that he may be an alcoholic. The meaning of self he seeks in material things has failed him.

Self as transcendent is given in the accounts of the third and fourth speakers. The third speaker seeks self-transcendence in drugs and alcohol, the fourth in the A.A. experience. The transcendent-self seeks to be part of something larger than itself that is not materialistic. It seeks an immanence in a structure of experience that is both enveloping and, in a Durkheimian sense (1912), collective, and perhaps ritualistic, spiritual, or religious (Bateson, 1972a: 319, 333). The self that is transcendent is processual, outside itself objectively, but subjectively aware of its own relationships with the world. It seeks to transcend direct empirical experience in the search for a broader and larger meaning of self and existence (James, 1961: 399-400).

The transcendence that is found in drugs and alcohol is a chemical transcendence. This is a personal, unshareable selfhood that is isolating, alienating, and individualistic. This inner state of experience is not immanent in a structure larger than itself, although such an immanence is sought. Interactional self-transcendence is given in the A.A. experience as described by the fourth speaker. He has found a noncompetitive, complementary relationship with a world that is larger than he is (Bateson, 1972a: 335).

These three problematics of self are woven through every alcoholic's experiences. They reference modes of self-experiencing that move from the individual to the group. As the alcoholic becomes embedded in A.A., a shared, group conception of self is acquired. A.A.'s move, which is truly sociological, locates transcendence of self in the group, not the person. The active alcoholic had, of course, the opposite position. He or she located individuality, subjectivity, and transcendence in alcohol, drugs, and in the self. A.A.'s self is in the group, not the person.

THE ALCOHOLIC AS SOCIAL CRITIC

There is a third mode of self as transcendent. It is given in the texts of Malcom Lowry, especially *Under the Volcano* (1984). It can be located also in the discourse of nearly any practicing alcoholic. In the quotation cited at the beginning of this chapter, Lowry locates the cause of alcoholism in "the complete, baffling sterility of existence." In the transcendent mode of *self as critic,* the active alcoholic believes that she sees a sickness in society that no one else sees. In the alcoholic's transcendent critique and dreams she believes she is above the problems of society. She displays an attempt to escape and transcend a society that is seen as crumbling and falling apart from within. She searches for an alternate set of ultimate values that will locate and anchor self in a structure of experience that is eternal, transcendent, and not purely subjective. The alcoholic attempts, however, to discover the purely transcendent in the depths of her own alcoholically produced consciousness. Like our third speaker, the alcoholic seeks *in vino veritas* (Bateson, 1972a: 311). But unlike our third alcoholic, Lowry's narrator sees his vision revealing an inner structure and meaning to life that is partially reflected only in the fragmentary pieces of personal experience (Spender, 1984: ix). That is, Lowry's alcoholic Honorary Consul finds, having transcended his own existence, that the vision of life below is empty and hollow. He finds ultimate meaning only in himself. In his moment of death this shattering view of reality is finally given. He states the following:

> And now he has reached the summit. Ah, Yvonne, sweetheart, forgive me! Strong hands lifted him. Opening his eyes, he looked down, expecting to see below him, the magnificent jungle, the height. . . like those peaks of his life conquered one after another before the greatest ascent of all had been successfully, if unconventionally, completed. But there was nothing there: no peaks, no climb. Nor was this summit a summit exactly: it had no substance, no firm base. It was crumbling too, whatever it was, collapsing, while he was falling, falling into the volcano, he must have climbed it after all. . .yet no, it wasn't the volcano, the world itself was bursting, bursting into black spouts of villages catapulted into space, with himself falling through it all, through the inconceivable pandemonium of a million tanks, through the blazing of ten million burning bodies, falling, into a forest, falling [Lowry, 1984: 327-328].

Out of his own consciousness Lowry's Consul has discovered an eternal nothingness in existence. In that discovery he has become the ultimate social critic who has illuminated and revealed the eternal meaning to life by inspecting his own personal experience.

The Alcoholic's Dis-ease

The alcoholic as critic is the modern antihero "reflecting an extreme external situation through his own extremity. His neurosis [alcoholism] becomes diagnosis, not just of himself, but of a phase of history" (Spender, 1984: ix). The alcoholic's dis-ease of conduct thus is justified because it is no longer just one individual's case history or life story. Within the context of history it becomes the "dial of the instrument that records the effects of a particular stage of civilization upon a civilized individual" (Spender, 1984: ix).

The alcoholic's transcendent vision of his or her culture and times thus becomes a symbolic statement concerning the breakdown of the modern world. This expression affects other individuals in ways that they may only dimly understand or accept (see Spender, 1984: ix). But the alcoholic as critic registers feelings and insights that in some senses apply to all members of the culture at large. The alcoholic is thereby accorded a place in the culture because his or her situation speaks to everyone. And it is not just because of the alcoholic's deviance that this place is given. He or she does more than reveal the boundaries of the acceptable or the unacceptable (Durkheim, 1895). The alcoholic signals a doubt about the inner, felt truth of the culture and its times. By living that doubt into existence, and by taking it to its extremes, the alcoholic becomes the symbolic representation of every modern individual who also doubts the meaning of modern existence. Understanding this, the alcoholic as critic justifies alcoholism in the name of a higher cause. He or she buys into the place culture has accorded him or her.

Lowry's alcoholic sought transcendent insight through the analysis of his own personal experience. The fourth speaker, by contrast, searches for an alternate set of ultimate values that will locate and anchor self in a structure of experience that is not purely subjective and introspective. He finds his values in the rituals, traditions, and interactions of Alcoholics Anonymous. Like a "postmodernist" (Spender, 1984: ix; Habermas, 1983; Jameson, 1983; Updike, 1984; Lyotard, 1984), the recovering alcoholic discovers a universality of tradition (and spirituality) that is barely revealed in the distorted structures of modern life. But this approach is not purely rational or nonpersonal, it is emotional, subjective, and historical. At the deepest level, the transcendent meanings the recovering alcoholic discovers are found in the self and in a reading of the past which is taken as evidence of the failure of previous modes of self-understanding. Out of this rereading of the self appear the "shadows" of the past (Jung, 1939) that have haunted the subject. And these are shadows that haunt every modern individual, for the alcoholic has positioned doubt at the center of modern existence. From this confrontation with the past may emerge a joining of the personal consciousness of the individual with the collective, shared consciousness of Alcoholics Anonymous. And, in this process, the individual is reinserted into his or her culture as a new subject. This subject is the topic of the next book in this series, *The Recovering Alcoholic* (Denzin, 1986a).

The alcoholic, drinking or recovering, thus brings before us new possibilities of existence. He or she shows us how far we may have to go before we are forced to change our lives and the social structures that we live in. In studying the alcoholic we study ourselves.

Glossary

A.A. member Any person who calls himself or herself an A.A. member.

A.A. meeting Two or more alcoholics meeting together for the purposes of sobriety. Types: *Closed*, attended only by individuals who have a desire to stop drinking; *Open*, attended by those who have an interest in alcoholism and A.A.; *Speaker*, where one A.A. member tells his or her story to others in an open meeting; *Discussion*, where a topic of discussion (such as resentment, anger) is discussed by each member, in turn. *First Step*: a meeting (usually closed) devoted to a discussion of A.A.'s First Step, by tradition any meeting attended by a "newcomer" or a person at their first meeting becomes a First Step Meeting. *Step Meeting*: a meeting devoted to a discussion of each of A.A.'s Twelve Steps.

A.A. motives Reference reasons for attending A.A., including attempts to resolve situational problematics that have arisen in the member's life, for instance, a DUI. Such motives may become functionally autonomous. The person continues to attend A.A. after the original problem has been solved. In the process they move from situational to committed, recovering alcoholics.

A.A. calendar Any 12-month calendar hung in an A.A. meeting place upon which group members write the date of their last drink.

A.A. preamble (Read at the beginning of every A.A. meeting): "Alcoholics Anonymous is a fellowship of men and women who share their experience, strength and hope with each other that they may solve their common problem and help others to recover from alcoholism. The only requirement for membership is a desire to stop drinking. There are no dues or fees for A.A. membership; we are self-supporting through our own contributions. A.A. is not allied with any sect, denomination, politics, organization or institution; does not wish to engage in any controversy, neither endorses nor opposes any causes. Our primary purpose is to stay sober and help other alcoholics to achieve sobriety."

A.A. ritual The Steps, Traditions, opening and closing ceremonies (such as Serenity Prayer, Lord's Prayer), and birthdays.

A.A. selfhood Becoming a self within A.A. Stages: (1) preparatory, (2) interactional, (3) participatory.

A.A. talk Meeting talk that is dialogic; the speaker engages the group in a self-dialogue.

Abstinent alcohol culture (Pittman, 1967): The cultural attitude is negative and prohibitive toward any type of ingestion of alcoholic beverage.

Addict In this study, refers to a person who calls himself or herself a member of Narcotics Anonymous.

Adult child of an alcoholic parent An adult with a parent that is an alcoholic.

Alcoholic rhythm A regular pattern of drinking, established in the critical and chronic phases of alcoholism, usually involving drinking on a four-hour cycle.

Alcoholic A person who defines himself or herself as alcoholic. Characterized by an inability to control drinking once the first drink is taken, and an inability to abstain from drinking for any continuous period of time.

Alcoholism I A self-destructive form of activity involving compulsive, addictive drinking, coupled with increased alcohol tolerance and an inability to abstain for long periods of time from drinking. Phases: pre-alcoholic, prodomal, crucial, chronic. Types: alpha, beta, gamma, delta (see Jellinek, 1960).

Alcoholism II American Medical Association definition: An illness characterized by preoccupation with alcohol and loss of control over its consumption such as to lead usually to intoxication if drinking is begun; by chronicity; by progression; and by tendency toward relapse. It is typically associated with physical disability and impaired emotional, occupational, and/or social adjustments as a direct consequence of persistent and excessive use of alcohol.

Alcoholism III Alcoholics Anonymous definition: The manifestation of an allergy, coupled with the phenomenon of craving for alcohol, producing an illness that is spiritual, mental and physical.

Alcoholic aphasia and amnesia Thought disorders associated with the crucial and chronic stages of alcoholism. Wernicke's disease and Korsakoff's psychosis are types.

Alcoholic-as-social critic A mode of self-transcendence in which the alcoholic locates himself or herself outside society, seeing in society a sickness or illness that no one else sees.

Alcoholic-centered relationship A relationship between an alcoholic and an other in which alcohol has become the center or focus of interaction. Alcohol displaces intimacy, love, or conversation as the previous focus or center of the relationship.

Alcoholic dreams Dreams reported by alcoholics involving drinking, slips, and relapses.

Alcoholic identity Coming to define one's self as alcoholic. There are 10 types: (1) *transient alcoholic*—assuming the alcoholic identity so as to overcome a problematic situation. This is a situational adjustment to the problems alcoholism produces; (2) *committed alcoholic*—investing and committing one's self in the identity of recovering alcoholic as defined by A.A. This identity is produced by a transformation of self, whereas a transient identity is produced by an alternation of identity; (3) *neutralized*; (4) *helplessly alcoholic*; (5) *situational; (6) transsituational*; (7) *newcomer*; (8) *old-timer*; (9) *regular*; and (10) *alcoholic in treatment.*

Alcoholic other An emotional-interactional associate of the alcoholic; may be spouse, friend, relative, employer, fellow drinker. This other becomes a member of an alcohol-centered relationship.

Alcoholic pride (Bateson): Also called false pride, which is mobilized behind the alcoholic's belief that alcohol can be controlled. Leads to "risk taking" in drinking.

Alcoholic problematic situation A situation that produces sobriety problems, typically flowing from work, family, and relational settings. Faced with such problematics, alcoholics develop situational adjustments and identities that may or may not lead them to drink again.

Alcoholic risk taking (Bateson): Taking a drink when the probabilities of success are minimal and the likelihood of failure is high.

Alcoholic self A self divided against itself, trapped within the negative emotions that alcoholism produces. Key emotions are ressentiment and self-pride. Characterized by denial, bad faith, and emotional and physical violence.

Alcoholic situation (1) Act One of the three-act play called "A Merry-Go-Round-Named Denial"; (2) descriptive term used to reference four interactional drinking patterns the alcoholic and his or her other become embedded in: open-drinking context, closed-drinking context, sober context, in control, normally intoxicated context.

Alcoholic understanding The process of interpreting, knowing, and comprehending the meaning intended, felt, and expressed by another alcoholic. Types: (1) authentic; (2) A.A.; (3) insincere; (4) spurious.

Alcoholic violence Attempts by the alcoholic to regain through emotional and physical violence a sense of self that has been lost to alcohol and his or her other. The five types are emotional, playful, spurious, real, and paradoxical.

Alternation of identity Changes in identity that do not require transformations or a radical restructuring of self. Evidenced in alcoholics who do not remain in A.A. and in the self-changes the alcoholic's other often experiences.

Ambivalent alcohol culture (Pittman, 1967): The cultural attitude toward alcohol usage conflict between use and nonuse.

Bad faith A lie to oneself in an attempt to escape responsibility for one's actions. A denial of one's situation and one's place in it. A fleeing from what one is—alcoholic.

Big Book A.A.'s name for *Alcoholics Anonymous: The Story of How Many Thousands of Men and Women Have Recovered from Alcoholism: The Basic Text of Alcoholics Anonymous.*

Birthday (A.A. or N.A.) Measured in years, but the first year is measured by one, three, six, and nine months sobriety, or clean intervals, which must be continuous.

Blackout Amnesia, not associated with loss of consciousness, for all or part of the events that occurred during or immediately after a drinking session (Keller and McCormick, 1968).

Bottom Confronting one's alcoholic situation, finding it intolerable, and surrendering to alcoholism. Accompanied by collapse and sincerely reaching out for help. May be high or low.

Circuit of selfness The moving field of experience that connects the person to the world.

Clean date The date of one's last use of a drug (N.A.).

Codependent An alcoholic other who has become dependent on the alcoholic's alcoholism.

Confronting Telling another how you see and feel about him or her.

Craving Overwhelming desire for alcohol. Two forms: (1) *physiological*, or *nonsymbolic*, located in the withdrawal effects felt as the body detoxifies alcohol, and (2) *psychological, symbolic*, or *phenomenological*, felt as a compelling need for alcohol in the absence of any withdrawal symptom.

Culturally symptomatic drinker An individual whose use of alcohol (1) conforms to the ritual drinking patterns of the culture, (2) does not go beyond the boundaries of acceptable drinking comportment for the culture, and (3) does not become excessive, which (4) could produce occasional or regular excessive drinking, in which case (5), alcohol becomes a drug and no longer functions as a ritual beverage.

Denial Refusing to accept one's alcoholism; closely akin to being in "bad faith."

Desire (alcoholic) That mode of self-consciousness that seeks freedom from fear and anxiety through the altered streams of experience alcohol produces. It is self- and body centered.

Dis-ease An uneasiness, or disorder in health, body, or manner of living. Alcoholism is a dis-ease of conduct in the world, involving an uneasiness with self, time, emotion, and relations with others.

Drinking motive Reasons alcoholic gives for drinking; motive becomes *functionally autonomous*, that is, freed from the original ritual situations where drinking was learned.

Drunk-a-log Story told at an "open" A.A. meeting.

Drunken comportment (McAndrew and Edgerton, 1969): Culturally and socially patterned forms of behavior that occur after an individual has been drinking. Situationally, culturally, and historically determined and defined.

Dry Not drinking, but not working the A.A. program.

Dry date The date of one's last drink.

Dry drunk When an A.A. member displays all of the characteristics of being drunk, or hung over—self-centered, emotional, self-pitying, angry, resentful—he or she is said to be in a dry drunk.

DUI Driving under the influence of alcohol.

Emotion Self-feeling.

Emotionality The process of being emotional.

Emotionality I. Normal: A balance of emotional experiences, in which extreme negativity or exaggerated exhilaration are absent. An emotional ideal alcoholics seek to attain.

Emotionality II. Alcoholic Contrasted to normal emotionality, includes extreme negativity (ressentiment) and exaggerated exhilaration produced by alcohol. Tends toward emotional violence.

Emotional account Justification of a self-feeling.

Emotional associate A person who is implicated in the subject's emotional world of experience.

Emotional practice An embedded practice that produces anticipated and unanticipated alterations in the person's inner and outer streams of emotional experience.

Emotional understanding Knowing and comprehending through emotional means—including sympathy and imagination—the intentions, feelings, and thoughts expressed by another.

Emotionally divided self A self turned against itself, disembodied, characterized by self-loathing and ressentiment.

Enabler An alcoholic other who enables, or assists, the alcoholic in his or her drinking career.

Family Week Occurs during the fourth, or last, week of treatment. The alcoholic's family and significant others come to the treatment center for group and individual counseling. The alcoholic is confronted by and confronts his or her family during this week. Leveling also occurs.

Field of experience The temporal structure of meanings, definitions, and feelings that surround and situate the person in the world.

Field research Phrase used by recovering alcoholics to describe their experiences when they return to drinking.

First-Step assessment Occurs during the first week of treatment, done in the context of the First-Step Group, involving the alcoholic's answering a series of questions concerning alcohol use and abuse prior to treatment. Intended as a measure that produces a surrendering to the First Step of A.A.

First-Step group A non-sex, non-age stratified group formed within the first week of treatment. The alcoholic does a First-Step assessment before this group.

Frame An interpretation that structures the definition of a situation. Types within A.A.: (1) primary, "This is an A.A. meeting"; (2) secondary, "We are talking at an A.A. meeting, taking turns"; (3) treatment group, counter to A.A. frames, "We give advice to each other, talk out of turn, and do not focus on a single topic of discussion."

Functional autonomy An action organized as an adjustment to a situational problematic that becomes dislodged from the original situation and takes on an autonomous life of its own.

Fused group A newly formed group opposed to seriality, or separateness. Initially unstructured, yet fused, or drawn to a common purpose. The first A.A. group (or meeting) between Wilson and Smith was a fused group that later became a pledged group, and hence the archetype of all subsequent A.A. groups.

Gamma alcoholic Jellinek's term: involves excessive drinking, acquired increased tissue tolerance to alcohol, withdrawal symptoms, craving due to physical dependence on alcohol, and an inability to stop drinking once it is begun. This type is most like A.A.'s alcoholic.

Grapevine A.A.'s international monthly magazine.

Group conscience The will of an A.A. group expressed through a vote on any matter brought before the group, such as moving the group to another meeting place, changing the format of the group, or electing a GSR.

GSR Group Service Representative for an A.A. group. Such persons are responsible to the group for collecting contributions at meetings, keeping rent paid, seeing to it that coffee and supplies are available for meetings and for chairing, or securing chairpersons for the group's meetings. GSRs may move on to represent groups within A.A. districts and become delegates to national conventions. A person is assumed to have a lengthy period of sobriety before being elected to the GSR position.

Home group The A.A. group an A.A. member calls his or hers. Often the first group ever attended, but not necessarily. The member will become a regular in this group.

"How It Works" Portion of the *Big Book*, pp. 58-60 through point (c) which is read at many A.A. meetings as it contains A.A.'s Twelve Steps.

Ideal self Self-ideal individual selects for self, but often fails to achieve.

Imaginary The inner world of symbolic, imaginary conversations the person locates himself or herself within.

Integration hypothesis (Ullman): A social group will have lower rates of alcoholism when it has clear rules concerning how alcohol is to be used, that is, when drinking is ritually integrated into the group's way of life.

Johari Window A four-celled window that addresses the problem of self-awareness, covering the self that is open, unknown, hidden, and blind to self and others. This model is presented to alcoholics in treatment.

Languages of treatment There are three: (1) meta-language of emotionality; (2) language of direct feeling and emotion; and (3) the language and terms of A.A.

Lay-theory of alcoholism A threefold interpretive structure that contains theories of time, causality, denial, and successful drinking.

Leveling Spontaneously sharing one's feelings with another during treatment.

Loss of control Any drinking of alcohol starts a chain reaction that is felt as a physical and psychological demand for alcohol. Typically experienced as (a) an inability to stop drinking after one drink, and (b) an inability to predict one's behavior once drinking begins.

"Merry-Go-Round-of-Trouble" A continuous circuit of negative symbolic interaction, involving the alcoholic and his or other in an endless round of problems and troubles, such as DUIs, unpaid bills, loss of work, divorce, violence, and so on.

N.A. Narcotics Anonymous.

Narcissism The individual acts as if he were in love with himself. The state of self-love and admiration of oneself. In A.A. the phrase "his or her majesty" is taken to refer to this form of narcissism, which alcoholics believe they suffer from.

Negative symbolic interaction An interaction process characterized by violence, contrasting, negative emotions, and destructive schismogenesis.

Newcomer A person early in A.A.'s program of recovery; usually with less than three months sobriety.

Normal social drinker A drinker who can control alcohol and not become alcoholic.

Old-timer An A.A. regular with 10 years or more continuous sobriety and A.A. membership.

Overpermissive alcohol culture (Pittman, 1967): The cultural attitude is permissive toward drinking, to behaviors that occur when drinking, and to drinking pathologies.

Paradoxes of treatment Five dilemmas the alcoholic must confront in treatment, including learning how to become a therapist for the dis-ease of alcoholism.

Permissive alcoholic culture (Pittman, 1967): Cultural attitude toward ingesting alcohol is permissive, but negative toward drunkenness and other drinking pathologies.

Pigeon An A.A. term for a newcomer an old-timer is working with.

Pledge A historical act that connects individuals to a group or joint activity. A pledge produces a mediated reciprocity between members, as with A.A.'s pledge of "Responsibility."

Pledged group A group pledged to or committed to a single purpose. The A.A. group is a pledged group. Such groups share a common perspective, and are organized around an agreed-upon distribution of rights and duties enforced by a pledge.

Program An A.A. reference to the Twelve Steps and the Twelve Traditions and the spiritual program contained in the Steps. Alcoholics in treatment must develop their own program for recovery, which is not the same as the A.A. program.

Recovering alcoholic An individual who (1) incorporates the identity of recovering alcoholic into his or her self-conception; (2) having once been an active drinking alcoholic, becomes a nondrinker, and (3) calls himself or herself a member of Alcoholics Anonymous.

Recovering self A form of selfhood involving a validated program of self-indications that exercise a regulatory function over other actions of the person, including not drinking. This transsituational self is learned in A.A. meetings and in treatment.

Relapse The return to drinking by a recovering alcoholic, also called *slip*. Types: (1) paired, (2) sequential, (3) solitary, (4) planned, (5) unplanned, (6) short term, (7) long term, (8) of old-timer, (9) of regular, (10) of newcomer.

Responsibility slogan (A.A.) "I am responsible. When anyone, anywhere, reaches out for help, I want the hand of A.A. always to be there. And for that: I am responsible."

Ressentiment The repeated experiencing and reliving of a particular emotional reaction against another. The emotion is negative, hostile, and includes a cluster of interrelated feelings—anger, wrath, envy, intense self-pride, and desire for revenge.

Ritual Conventionalized joint acts, given to ceremony, that convey special emotion and sacred meaning for performers.

Ritual self New, sacred self acquired by the recovering alcoholic. Sobriety is the key feature. It is learned through interactions at the personal, sponsor, group, and collective levels of A.A. It is a moral, sacred self that flows from and into the A.A. group.

Schismogenesis (Bateson): The genesis of divisions and conflicts within a relationship such that more of one kind of behavior by one member produces more of a counterbehavior by the other member; attempts to control the alcoholic's drinking produce more drinking.

Self That process that unifies the stream of thoughts and experiences the person has about herself around a single pole or point of reference; not a thing, but a process. It is consciousness conscious of itself, referring always to the sameness and steadiness of something always present to the person in her thoughts, as in "I am here, now, in the world, present before and to myself." Involves moral feelings for self, including all the subject calls hers at a particular moment in time, such as material possessions, self-feelings, and relations to others. Also includes the meaning the person gives to herself as a distinct object and subject at any given moment, involving the meaning of the person to herself as she turns back on herself in reflection. The self is not in consciousness, but in the world of social interaction. It haunts the subject.

Self-account A member's story of self in relation to a problematic event.

Self-as-double Doubling of self within A.A., involving telling stories about self that transform the self into a subject and an object of recovery.

Self-as-false-subjectivity Living self through material things and experiencing a loss of self as a result.

Self-as-loss Experiencing the absence of an inner sense of selfness, or positive being.

Self-as-narrator The A.A. storytelling self.

Self-as-transcendent Seeking a mode of self-understanding and awareness that is located in a structure outside the self. May be produced by drugs and alcohol or by interaction in a group.

Self-feelings Sequences of lived emotionality having self-referents, including a feeling for self, a feeling of this feeling, and a revealing of the moral self to the person through this feeling.

Self-ideal Ideal self set before person by others.

Serenity A.A. term for peace of mind, emotional sobriety, and the absence of negativity in one's life.

Serenity Prayer Said at the beginning of every A.A. meeting: "God grant me the serenity to accept the things I cannot change, courage to change the things I can, and wisdom to know the difference."

Six Theses of Alcoholism Six points of interpretation in the structures of experience that constitute the alcoholic circle. They refer, in turn, to temporality, self, relations with others, emotionality, denial, bad faith, self-control, and surrender.

Slip A return to drinking by a recovering alcoholic. May be planned or unplanned. Also called relapse. It is a slip away from the A.A. program into drinking.

Sober Not drinking and working the A.A. program.

Sobriety date The date of an A.A. member's last drink, often written on the Group's Sobriety Calendar.

Social phenomenological method That mode of inquiry that returns to the things of experience and studies them from within. Involves five phases: deconstruction of previous theories of the phenomenon, capture, reduction, construction, and contextualization.

Social world of recovery The network of social experiences wherein recovery from alcoholism occurs, including treatment centers and A.A.

Sponsor An older A.A. member who assists a newcomer in getting sober and working the Steps.

Steps A.A.'s Twelve Steps (see A.A., 1976): (1) We admitted we were powerless over alcohol—that our lives had become unmanageable; (2) Came to believe that a power greater than ourselves could restore us to sanity; (3) Made a decision to turn our will and our lives over to the care of God *as we understood Him*; (4) Made a searching and fearless moral inventory of ourselves; (5) Admitted to God, to ourselves, and to another human being the exact nature of our wrongs; (6) Were entirely ready to have God remove all these defects of character; (7) Humbly asked Him to remove our shortcomings; (8) Made a list of all persons we had harmed, and become willing to make amends to them all; (9) Made direct amends to such people wherever possible, except when to do so would injure them or others; (10) Continued to take personal inventory and when we were wrong promptly admitted it; (11) Sought through prayer and meditation to improve our conscious contact with God *as we understood Him*, praying only for knowledge of His will for us and the power to carry that out; (12) Having had a spiritual awakening as the result of these Steps, we tried to carry this message to alcoholics, and to practice these principles in all our affairs (italics in original).

Stigma (of alcoholism) Accepting the belief that alcoholism is a failure of self-will, and not a disease.

Story Self-accounting, or self-story, told by an A.A. member involving "what it was like, what happened, and what it is like now."

Surrender A threefold process: (1) admitting alcoholism, (2) accepting alcoholism, and (3) surrendering in the inner self to alcoholism.

Tables A.A.'s name for the tables around which all A.A. meetings occur.

Temporality I. Normal Time experienced reflectively, merging the past, present, and future in a nonthreatening fashion. Making time a nonproblematic in everyday experience.

Temporality II. Alcoholic Time experienced through the altered consciousness alcohol creates. Characterized by a fearfulness of time and its passage, including a tendency to dwell in the past and to feel guilt about past deeds.

Therapy (treatment) group An age- and sex-stratified group that the alcoholic moves into after the first week of treatment. The Fourth and Fifth Steps were taken with this group at Northern.

Third party An individual or a concept that unifies a group by observing or commanding it. Within A.A., the Steps, the higher power, and the traditions act as third parties, as does the collective history of A.A.

Time-out period (McAndrew and Edgerton, 1969): A universal societal phenomenon in which the everyday demands for accountability over one's actions are suspended, or set aside. Drunken comportment is typically structured within these moments, as drinking is commonly associated with time-out periods of experience.

Traditions A.A.'s Twelve traditions (see A.A., 1953). (1) Our common welfare should come first; personal recovery depends upon A.A. unity. (2) For our group purpose there is but one ultimate authority—a loving God as He may express Himself in our group conscience. Our leaders are but trusted servants; they do not govern. (3) The only requirement for A.A. membership is a desire to stop drinking. (4) Each group should be autonomous except in matters affecting other groups or A.A. as a whole. (5) Each group has but one primary purpose—to carry its message to the alcoholic who still suffers. (6) An A.A. group ought never endorse, finance, or lend the A.A. name to any related facility or outside enterprise, lest problems of money, property, and prestige divert us from our primary purpose. (7) Every A.A. group ought to be fully self-supporting, declining outside contributions. (8) Alcoholics Anonymous should remain forever nonprofessional, but our service centers may employ special workers. (9) A.A.. as such, ought never be organized; but we may create service boards or committees directly responsible to those they serve. (10) Alcoholics Anonymous has no opinion on outside issues; hence the A.A. name ought never be drawn into public controversy. (11) Our public relations policy is based on attraction rather than promotion; we need always maintain personal anonymity at the level of press, radio, and films. (12) Anonymity is the spiritual foundation of all our Traditions, ever remaining us to place principles before personalities.

Transformation of self Radical restructuring of self and its basic beliefs, evidenced in recovery from alcoholism.

Twelve and Twelve A.A.'s name for its second basic text, *The Twelve Steps and the Twelve Traditions.*

Universal singular (alcoholic) A single instance of a process that is experienced by any alcoholic who seeks to recover from the dis-ease of alcoholism.

Victim An alcoholic other who becomes victimized by the alcoholic's alcoholism.

Working the Steps A phrase used by A.A. members when they are in the process of going through the Twelve Steps or focusing on a particular Step.

References

Ablon, Joan

1976 "Family structure and behavior in alcoholism: a review of the literature," pp. 205–242 in Benjamin Kissin and Henri Begleiter (eds.) The Biology of Alcoholism, Vol. 4. Social Aspects of Alcoholism. New York: Plenum.

Adler, A.

1927 The Practices and Theory of Individual Psychology. New York: Harcourt.

Al-Anon Family Groups

1977 Lois Remembers. New York: Al-Anon Family Group Headquarters, Inc.

Alcoholics Anonymous

1953 Twelve Steps and Twelve Traditions. New York: Alcoholics Anonymous World Services, Inc.

1957 Alcoholics Anonymous Comes of Age: A Brief History of A.A. New York: Alcoholics Anonymous World Services, Inc.

1963 "The Bill W.-Carl Jung letters." Grapevine (January): 26–31.

1967 As Bill Sees It: The A.A. Way of Life. Selected Writings of A.A.'s Co-Founder. New York: Alcoholics Anonymous World Services, Inc.

1973 Came to Believe: The Spiritual Adventure of A.A. as Experienced by Individual Members. New York: Alcoholics Anonymous World Services, Inc.

1975 Living Sober: Some Methods A.A. Members Have Used for Not Drinking. New York: Alcoholics Anonymous World Series, Inc.

1976 Alcoholics Anonymous. New York: Alcoholics Anonymous World Services, Inc.

1980 Dr. Bob and the Good Oldtimers: A Biography with Recollections of Early A.A. in the Midwest. New York: Alcoholics Anonymous World Services, Inc.

1983 "Treatment centers for alcoholism." Grapevine (March): 62.

1983–1984 The A.A. Service Manual combined with Twelve Concepts for World Service by Bill W. New York: Alcoholics Anonymous World Services, Inc.

1984 "Pass It On": The Story of Bill Wilson and How the A.A. Message Reached the World. New York: Alcoholics Anonymous World Services, Inc.

1985 Eastern United States A.A. Directory. New York: Alcoholics Anonymous World Services.

Allport, G. W.

1964 Personality and Social Encounter. Boston: Beacon.

American Medical Association

1968 Manual on Alcoholism. New York: Author.

American Psychiatric Association

1980 Diagnostic and Statistics Manual of Mental Disorders (DSM-III) Washington, DC: Author.

Armor, D. J., J. M. Polich, and J. B. Stambul

1976 Alcoholism and Treatment. Report R-1739-NIAAA. Santa Monica, CA: Rand Corporation.

Bacon, M. K., H. Barry, III, and I. L. Child

1965 "A cross-cultural study of drinking. II: Relations to other features of culture." Quarterly Journal of Studies on Alcohol Supplement 3, pg. 29.

Baekeland, Frederick

1977 "Evaluation of treatment methods in chronic alcoholism," pp. 385–440 in

Benjamin Kissin and Henri Begleiter (eds.) The Biology of Alcoholism, Vol. 5. Treatment and Rehabilitation of the Chronic Alcoholic. New York: Plenum.
Baekeland, Frederick and Lawrence K. Lundwall
1977 "Engaging the alcoholic in treatment and keeping him there," pp. 161–196 in Benjamin Kissin and Henri Begleiter (eds.) The Biology of Alcoholism, Vol. 5. Treatment and Rehabilitation of the Chronic Alcoholic. New York: Plenum.
Baldwin, John W.
1984 "Comments on Denzin's 'Note on emotionality, Self and Interaction.' " American Journal of Sociology 90: 418–421.
Bales, Robert F.
1946 "Cultural differences in rates of alcoholism." Quarterly Journal of Studies on Alcohol 6: 480–499.
Bandura, Albert
1977 Social Learning Theory. Englewood Cliffs, NJ: Prentice-Hall.
Barnes, Gordon E.
1983 "Clinical and prealcoholic personality characteristics," pp. 113–196 in Benjamin Kissin and Henry Begleiter (eds.) The Biology of Alcoholism, Vol. 5 Psychosocial Factors. New York: Plenum.
Bateson, Gregory
1972a "The cybernetics of 'self': a theory of alcoholism," pp. 309–337 in Steps to an Ecology of Mind. New York: Ballantine.
1972b "The logical categories of learning and communication," pp. 279–308 in Steps to an Ecology of Mind. New York: Ballantine.
1972c "Double bind," pp. 271–278 in Steps to an Ecology of Mind. New York: Ballantine.
1972d "A theory of play and fantasy," pp. 177–193 in Steps to an Ecology of Mind. New York: Ballantine.
1972e "Toward a theory of schizophrenia," pp. 201–227 in Steps to an Ecology of Mind. New York: Ballantine.
Baudrillard, Jean
1983a "The ecstasy of communication," pp. 126–134 in Hal Foster (ed.) The Anti-Aesthetic: Essays on Postmodern Culture. Port Townsend, WA: Bay Press.
1983b In the Shadow of the Silent Majorities. New York: Semiotext.
1983c Simulations. New York: Semiotext.
Beauchamp, Dan E.
1980 Beyond Alcoholism: Alcohol and Public Health Policy. Philadelphia, Temple University Press.
Becker, Howard S.
1960 "Notes on the concept of commitment." American Journal of Sociology 66: 32–40.
1964 "Personal change in adult life," Sociometry 27: 40–53.
1967 "History, culture and subjective experience." Journal of Health and Social Behavior 8: 163–176.
1973 Outsiders. New York: Free Press.
Becker, Howard S., Blanche Geer, Everett C. Hughes, and Anselm L. Strauss
1961 Boys in White, Chicago: University of Chicago Press.
Beecher, Henry K.
1959 Measurement of Subjective Responses: Quantitative Effects of Drugs. New York: Oxford University Press.

Bellah, Robert, N. (ed.)
1973 Emile Durkheim on Morality in Society. Chicago: University of Chicago Press.

Bellah, Robert, N. et al.
1985 Habits of the Heart: Individualism and Commitment in American Life. Berkeley: University of California Press.

Benjamin, Jessica
1981 "The Oedipal riddle: authority, autonomy and the new narcissism," pp. 195–224 in J. P. Diggins and M. E. Kann (eds.) The Problem of Authority in America. Philadelphia: Temple University Press.

Benson, Michael
1985 "Denying the guilty mind: accounting for the involvement in a white collar crime." Criminology 23: 583–607.

Berger, Peter and Thomas Luckmann
1967 The Social Construction of Reality. New York: Doubleday.

Bergson, H.
1947 Creative Evolution. New York: Modern Library.

Berk, Richard A., Sarah Fenstermaker Berk, Donileen R. Loseke, and David Rauma
1983 "Mutual combat and other family violence myths," pp. 197–212 in David Finkelhor et al. (eds.) The Dark Side of Families: Current Family Violence Research. Beverly Hills, CA: Sage.

Bernstein, B.
1971 Class, Codes and Control, Vol. 1. Theoretical Studies Toward a Sociology of Language. London: Routledge & Kegan Paul.

Bertaux, Daniel
1981 "Introduction," pp. 1–22 in D. Bertaux (ed.) Biography and Society. Beverly Hills, CA: Sage.

Berryman, John
1973 Recovery: A Novel. New York: Farrar, Straus and Giroux.

Biegel, Allan and Stuart Ghertner
1977 "Toward a social model: an assessment of social factors which influence problem drinking and its treatment," pp. 197–234 in Benjamin Kissin and Henri Begleiter (eds.) The Biology of Alcoholism, Vol. 5. Treatment and Rehabilitation of the Chronic Alcoholic. New York: Plenum.

Blane, H. T.
1968 The Personality of the Alcoholic: Guises of Dependency. New York: Harper & Row.

Blane, H. T.
1977 "Psychotherapeutic approach," pp. 105–160 in Benjamin Kissin and Henri Begleiter (eds.) The Biology of Alcoholism, Vol. 5. Treatment and Rehabilitation of the Chronic Alcoholic. New York: Plenum.

Blumer, Herbert
1946 "Collective behavior," pp. 166–222 in A. M. Lee (ed.) New Outline of the Principles of Sociology. New York: Barnes & Noble.
1969 Symbolic Interactionism. Englewood Cliffs, NJ: Prentice-Hall.

Booth, Wayne C.
1983 The Rhetoric of Fiction. Chicago: University of Chicago Press. (originally published in 1961)

Boss, M.
1958 The Analysis of Dreams. New York: Philosophical Library.
1963 Psychoanalysis and Daseinsanalysis. New York: Basic Books.

1977 "I Dreamt Last Night . . . ": A New Approach to the Revelations of Dreaming and its Uses for Psychotherapy. New York: Gardner.

Boswell, John
1980 Christianity, Social Tolerance and Homosexuality: Gay People in Western Europe from the Beginning of the Christian Era to the Fourteenth Century. Chicago: University of Chicago Press.

Burke, Kenneth
1954 Permanence and Change. Los Altos, CA: Hermes.

Caddy, G. R., H. J. Addington, and D. Perkins
1978 "Individualized behavior therapy for alcoholics: a third year independent double-blind follow-up." Behavior Research and Therapy 16: 345–362.

Cahalan, Don
1970 Problem Drinkers: A National Survey. San Francisco: Jossey-Bass.

Cahalan, Don and Robin Room
1972 "Problem drinking among American men aged 21–59," American Journal of Public Health 62: 1473–1482.
1974 Problem Drinking Among American Men. New Brunswick, NJ: Rutgers Center of Alcohol Studies.

Cahalan, Don and I. H. Cisin
1976 "Drinking behavior and drinking problems in the United States," pp. 77–115 in Benjamin Kissin and Henri Begleiter (eds.) The Biology of Alcoholism, Vol. 4. Social Aspects of Alcoholism. New York: Plenum.

Caldwell, Fulton J.
1983 "Alcoholics Anonymous as a viable treatment resource for black alcoholics," pp. 85–99 in T. S. Watts and R. Wright, Jr. (eds.) Black Alcoholism: Toward a Comprehensive Understanding. Springfield, IL: Charles C. Thomas.

Cappell, H. and C. P. Herman
1972 "Alcohol and tension reduction—a review." Quarterly Journal of Studies on Alcohol 33: 33–64.

Carpenter, J. A. and N. P. Armenti
1972 "Some effects of ethanol in human sexual and aggressive behavior," pp. 509–543 in Benjamin Kissin and Henri Begleiter (eds.) The Biology of Alcoholism, Vol. 2. Physiology and Behavior. New York: Plenum.

Carver, Raymond
1983 "The Paris Review interview," pp. 187–216 in Raymond Carver (ed.) Fires, Essays, Poems, Stories. New York: Vantage Books.

Catanzaro, Ronald J.
1967 "Psychiatric aspects of alcoholism," pp. 31–44 in David J. Pittman (ed.) Alcoholism. New York: Harper & Row.

Cavan , Sheri
1966 Liquor License: An Ethnography of Bar Behavior. Chicago: Aldine.

Chafetez, Morris E. and Robert Yoerg
1977 "Public health treatment programs in alcoholism," pp. 593–614 in Benjamin Kissin and Henry Begleiter (eds.) The Biology of Alcoholism, Vol. 5. Treatment and Rehabilitation of the Chronic Alcoholic. New York: Plenum.

Charmaz, K. C.
1980 "The social construction of self-pity in the chronically ill," pp. 123–146 in Norman K. Denzin (ed.) Studies in Symbolic Interaction, Vol. 3. Greenwich, Ct: JAI.

Chomsky, N.
1967 "A review of B.F. Skinner's *Verbal Behavior,*" pp. 142–171 in L. A. Jakobovitz and M.S. Miron (eds.) Readings in the Psychology of Language. Englewood Cliffs, NJ: Prentice-Hall.

Cirourel, A. V.
1974 Cognitive Sociology. New York: Free Press.
1981 "The role of cognitive-linguistic concepts in understanding everyday social interaction," pp. 87 – 106 in R. H. Turner and J. F. Short, Jr. (eds.) Annual Review of Sociology, Vol. 7. Palo Alto, CA: Annual Reviews, Inc.

Clough, Patricia T.
1979 "Sociability and public behavior in a mid-sized city," pp. 359–376 in Norman K. Denzin (ed.) Studies in Symbolic Interaction, Vol. 2. Greenwich, CT: JAI.

Cockerham, William
1981 Sociology of Mental Disorders. Englewood Cliffs, NJ: Prentice-Hall.

Collins, R.
1975 Conflict Sociology. New York: Academic Press.
1981 Sociology Since Midcentury, New York: Academic Press.

Conger, J. J.
1951 "The effects of alcohol on conflict behavior in the albino rat." Quarterly Journal of Studies on Alcohol 12: 1–29.
1956 "Alcoholics: theory, problem and challenge. II: Reinforcement theory and the dynamics of alcoholism." Quarterly Journal of Studies on Alcohol 17: 291–324.

Cooley, C. H.
1956 The Two Major Works of C. H. Cooley. New York: Free Press. (originally published in 1902)

Corsini, R. J.
1984 "Innovative psychotherapies," pp. 223–225 in R. J. Corsini (ed.) Encyclopedia of Psychology, Vol. 2. New York: John Wiley.

Couch, Carl J., Stanley L. Saxton, and Michael A. Katovich (eds.)
1986 Studies in Symbolic Interaction: The Iowa School. Greenwich, CT: JAI.

Davies, D. L.
1962 "Normal drinking in recovered alcoholics." Quarterly Journal of Studies on Alcohol 23: 94–104.

Davis, Fred
1961 "Deviance disavowal: the management of strained interaction by the visibly handicapped." Social Problems 9: 120–132.

Denzin, Norman K.
1968 "The self-fulfilling prophecy and patient therapist interactions," pp. 349–358 in S. P. Spitzer and Norman K. Denzin (eds.) The Mental Patient: Studies in the Sociology of Deviance. New York: McGraw-Hill.
1977a "Notes on the criminogenic hypothesis: a case of the American liquor industry." American Sociological Review 42: 905–920.
1977b Childhood Socialization. San Francisco: Jossey-Bass.
1978 "Crime and the American liquor industry," pp. 87–118 in Norman K. Denzin (ed.) Studies in Symbolic Interaction, Vol. 2. Greenwich, CT: JAI.
1979 "On the interactional analysis of social organization." Symbolic Interaction 2: 59–72.
1980 "Towards a phenomenology of emotion and deviance." Zietschfrift für Soziologie 9: 251–261.

1982 "Notes on criminology and criminality," pp. 115–130 in H. E. Pepinsky (ed.) Rethinking Criminology. Beverly Hills, CA: Sage.
1983a "A note on emotionality, self and interaction." American Journal of Sociology 88: 943–953.
1983b "Interpretive interactionism," pp. 129–146 in G. Morgan (ed.) Beyond Method. Beverly Hills, CA: Sage.
1984a On Understanding Emotion. San Francisco: Jossey-Bass.
1984b "Toward a phenomenology of domestic, family violence." American Journal of Sociology 90: 483–513.
1984c "Reply to Baldwin." American Journal of Sociology 90: 422–427.
1984d "Ritual behavior," pp. 246–247 in R. J. Corsini (ed.) Encyclopedia of Psychology, Vol. 3. New York: John Wiley.
1985a "Review essay: Signifying Acts: Structure and Meaning in Everyday Life." American Journal of Sociology 91: 432–434.
1985b "Emotion as lived experience." Symbolic Interaction 8: 223–239.
1985c "On the phenomenology of sexuality, desire and violence," pp. 39–56 in S. McNall (ed.) Current Perspectives in Social Theory, Vol. 6. Greenwich, CT: JAI.
1986a The Alcoholic Self. Beverly Hills, CA: Sage.
1986b Treating Alcoholism. Beverly Hills, CA: Sage.
1986c "A phenomenology of the emotionally divided self," in Krysia Yardley and Terry Honess (eds.) Self and Identity: Psychosocial Perspectives. New York: John Wiley.
1986d "A phenomenological analysis of social referencing," in S. Feinman (ed.) Social Referencing in Infancy. New York: Academic Press.
1986a The Recovering Alcoholic. Beverly Hills, CA: Sage.

Denzin, Norman K. with Charles Keller
1981 " 'Frame Analysis' reconsidered." Contemporary Sociology 10: 52–59.

Derrida, Jacques
1972 "Structure, sign, and play in the discourse of the human sciences," pp. 247–272 in Richard Macksey and Eugenio Donato (eds.) The Structuralist Controversy: The Languages of Criticism and the Sciences of Man. Baltimore, MA: Johns Hopkins University Press.
1973 Speech and Phenomena. Evanston, IL: Northwestern University Press.
1976 Of Grammatology. Baltimore, MA: Johns Hopkins University Press.
1978 Writing and Difference. Chicago: University of Chicago Press.
1981 Positions. Chicago: University of Chicago Press.

Dewey, J.
1922 Human Nature and Conduct: An Introduction to Social Psychology. New York: Henry Holt.

Dostoevski, Fyodor
1846 "The double," in The Short Novels of Dostoevski [Constance Garnett, trans.]. New York: Dell.

Duhman, Bob
1984 "The curse of the writing class." Saturday Review (January–February): 27–30.

Durkheim, Emile
1982 The Rules of Sociological Method. New York: Free Press. (1895)
1973 "Elementary forms of religious life," in R. Bellah (ed.) Emile Durkheim on Morality and Society. Chicago: University of Chicago Press. (1912)
1964 The Division of Labor in Society. Glencoe, IL: Free Press. (1893)

1961 The Elementary Forms of Religious Life. New York: Collier. (1912)
1951 Suicide. Glencoe, IL: Free Press. (1897)

Edel, Leon
1984 Writing Lives: Principia Biographica. New York: Norton.

Erikson, Erik H.
1950 Childhood and Society. New York: W. W. Norton.

Erikson, Kai T.
1966 Wayward Puritans. New York: John Wiley.

Fagerhaugh, S. Y. and A. Strauss
1977 Politics of Pain Management: Staff-Patient Interaction. Menlo Park, CA: Addison-Wesley.

Faulkner, William
1981 "Mr. Acarius," pp. 435–448 in Joseph Blotner (ed.) *Uncollected Stories of William Faulker.* New York: Vantage.

Flaherty, M.
1983 "A formal approach to the study of amusement in social interaction," pp. 71–82 in Norman K. Denzin (ed.) Symbolic Interaction, Vol. 5. Greenwich, CT: JAI.

Foucault, M.
1970 The Order of Things: An Archaeology of the Human Sciences. New York: Random House.
1977 Discipline and Punishment. New York: Pantheon.
1980 Power/Knowledge: Selected Interviews and Other Writings 1972–1977. [C. Gordon, ed.; C. Gordon, L. Marshall, J. Mepham, K. Soper, trans.]. New York: Pantheon.
1982 "Afterword: the subject and power," in H. Dreyfus and P. Rabinow (eds.) Michael Foucault: Beyond Structuralism and Hermeneutics. Chicago: University of Chicago Press.

Foulkes, D.
1978 A Grammar of Dreams. New York: Basic Books.

Fox, R.
1957 "Treatment of alcoholism," pp. 163–172 in H. E. Himwich (ed.) Alcoholism: Basic Aspects and Treatment. Washington, DC: American Association for the Advancement of Science.

Franks, David
1984 "Role-taking, social power and imperceptiveness: the analysis of rape," pp. 123–147 in Norman K. Denzin (ed.) Studies in Symbolic Interaction, Vol. 6. Greenwich, CT: JAI.

Franks, Lucinda
1985 "A new attack on alcoholism." New York Times Magazine (October 29): 46–48, 50, 61–65, 69.

Freedman, Samuel G.
1984 "Fugard traces a dark parallel on film." New York Times Section 2: 1, 19.

Freud, S,
1938 The Basic Writings of Sigmund Freud. New York: Random House.
1954 The Standard Edition. London: Hogarth.
1960 Group Psychology and the Analysis of the Ego. New York: Bantam Books (originally published in 1921)
1965 The Interpretation of Dreams. New York: Avon Books. (originally published in 1900)
1968 The Interpretation of Dreams. In The Standard Edition of the Complete Psychological Works of Sigmund Freud, Vols. 4 and 5. London: Hogarth.

Gadamer, H. G.
1975 Truth and Method. London: Sheed and Ward.
1976 Philosophical Hermeneutics. [D. E. Linge, ed. and trans.]. Berkeley: University of California Press.

Garfinkel, H.
1956 "Conditions of successful degradation ceremonies." American Journal of Sociology 61: 420–424.
1967 Studies in Ethnomethodology. Englewood Cliffs, NJ: Prentice-Hall.

Geertz, C.
1973 The Interpretation of Cultures. New York: Basic Books.
1983 Local Knowledge: Further Essays in Interpretive Anthropology. New York: Basic Books.

Gelles, Richard J.
1972 The Violent Home: A Study of Physical Aggression Between Husbands and Wives. Beverly Hills, CA: Sage.
1979 Family Violence. Beverly Hills, CA: Sage.

Glaser, Barney and Anselm Strauss
1964 Awareness of Dying. Chicago: Aldine.
1967a "Awareness contexts and social interaction." American Sociological Review 29: 669–679.
1967b The Discovery of Grounded Theory. Chicago: Aldine.

Glasser W.
1965 Reality Therapy: A New Approach to Psychiatry. New York: Harper & Row.

Goffman, E.
1956 "Embarrassment and social organization." American Journal of Sociology 67: 264–271.
1959 The Presentation of Self in Everyday Life. New York: Doubleday.
1961a Asylums. New York: Doubleday.
1961b Encounters, Indianapolis, IN: Bobbs-Merrill.
1963a Behavior in Public Places. New York: Free Press.
1963b Stigma. Englewood Cliffs, NJ: Prentice-Hall.
1967 Interaction Ritual. New York: Doubleday.
1971 Relations in Public. New York: Basic Books.
1974 Frame Analysis. New York: Harper.
1981 Forms of Talk. Philadelphia: University of Pennsylvania Press.
1983 "The interaction order." American Sociological Review 48: 1–17.

Gomberg, Edith Lisansky
1976 "Alcoholism in women," pp. 117–166 in Benjamin Kissin and Henri Begleiter (eds.) The Biology of Alcoholism, Vol. 4. Social Aspects of Alcoholism. New York: Plenum.
1982 "Special populations," pp. 337–354 in Edith L. Gomberg et al. (eds.) Alcoholic, Science and Society Revisited. Ann Arbor, MI: The University of Michigan Press.

Gomberg, Edith, L., Helene R. White, and John A. Carpenter
1982 Alcohol, Science and Society Revisited. Ann Arbor: University of Michigan Press.

Goodstein, L.
1984 "Human relations training," p. 161 in R. Corsini (ed.) Encyclopedia of Psychology, Vol. 2. New York: John Wiley.

Goodwin, Donald
1976 Is Alcoholism Hereditary? New York: Oxford University Press.

1979 "Alcoholism and heredity: a review and hypothesis" Archives of General Psychiatry 36: 57–61.
Goodwin, Donald W. and Samuel B. Guze
1974 "Heredity and alcoholism," pp. 37–52 in Benjamin Kissin and Henri Begleiter (eds.) The Biology of Alcoholism, vol. 3. Clinical Pathology. New York: Plenum.
Goshen, Charles E.
1973 Drinks, Drugs, and Do-Gooders. New York: Free Press.
Greil, A. L. and D. R. Rudy
1984 "What have we learned from process models of conversion? An examination of ten case studies." Sociological Focus 17: 305–323.
Grimshaw, Allen D.
1981 "Talk and social control," pp. 200–234 in M. Rosenberg and R. H. Turner (eds.) Social Psychology: Sociological Perspectives. New York: Basic Books.
Gross, Milton M., Eastlyn Lewis, and John Hastey
1974 "Acute alcohol withdrawal syndrome," pp. 191–264 in Benjamin Kissin and Henri Begleiter (eds.) The Biology of Alcoholism, Vol. 3. Clinical Pathology. New York: Plenum.
Grove, William M. and Remi J. Cadoret
1983 "Genetic factors in alcoholism," pp. 31–56 in Benjamin Kissin and Henri Begleiter (eds.) The Biology of Alcoholism, vol. 7. Biological Factors. New York: Plenum.
Gusfield, Joseph R.
1981 The Culture of Public Problems: Drinking-Driving and the Symbolic Order. Chicago: University of Chicago Press.
Guze, S B., V. B. Tuasvon, M. A. Stewart, and B. Picken
1963 "The drinking history: a comparison of reports by subjects and their relatives." Quarterly Journal of Studies on Alcohol 24: 249–260.
Habermas, Jürgen
1983 "Modernity – an incomplete project," pp. 3–15 in Hal Foster (ed.) The Anti-Aesthetic: Essays on Postmodern Culture. Port Townsend, WA: Bay Press.
1985 "Neoconservative culture criticism in the United States and West Germany: an intellectual movement in two political cultures," pp. 78–94 in R. J. Bernstein (ed.) Habermas and Modernity. Cambridge, MA: MIT Press.
Hall, C. S.
1966 The Meaning of Dreams. New York: McGraw-Hill. (originally published in 1953)
Hall, C. S. and V. J. Nordby
1972 The Individual and His Dreams. New York: New American Library.
Hall, C. S. and R. L. Van de Castle
1966 The Content Analysis of Dreams. New York: Appleton-Century-Crofts.
Hall, Peter M. and John P. Hewitt
1973 "The quasi-theory of communication and the management of dissent." Social Problems 18: 17–27.
Hazelden Foundations, Inc.
1956 Twenty-Four Hours a Day. Center, MN: Author.
1982 Each Day a New Beginning. Center City, MN: Author
1983 The Promise of a New Day, Center City, MN: Author.
1985 Today's Gift. Center City, MN: Author.

Hegel, G. W. F.
1980 The Phenomenology of Mind. [J.B. Braillie, trans.]. London: Allen & Unwin.
Heidegger, Martin
1962 Being and Time. New York: Harper & Row. (originally published in 1927)
1982 The Basic Problems of Phenomenology. Bloomington, IN: Indiana University Press.
Hetherton, E. M. and N. P. Wray
1964 "Aggression, need for social support and human preferences." Journal of Abnormal Social Psychology 68: 685–689.
Hewitt, John P. and Peter M. Hall
1973 "Social problems: problematic situations and quasi-theories." American Sociological Review 38: 367–374.
Hewitt, John P. and Randall Stokes
1975 "Disclaimers." American Sociological Review 40: 1–11.
Horchschild, Arlie
1973 The Unexpected Community, Englewood Cliffs, NJ: Prentice-Hall.
1983 The Managed Heard: Commercialization of Human Feeling. Berkeley: University of California Press.
Horton, Donald
1943 "The functions of alcohol in primitive societies: a cross-cultural study." Quarterly Journal of Studies on Alcohol 4: 199–320.
Hughes, E.
1951 Men and Their Work. Glencoe, IL: Free Press.
Husserl, E.
1962 Ideas: General Introduction to Pure Phenomenology. New York: Collier Books. (originally published in 1913)
Hymes, Dell
1974 Foundations in Sociolinguistics: An Ethnographic Approach. Philadelphia: University of Pennsylvania Press.
Isbell, H.
1955 "Craving for alcohol." Quarterly Journal of Studies on Alcohol 16: 38–42.
Jackson, Joan
1962 "Alcoholism and the family," pp. 472–493 in David J. Pittman and C. R. Snyder (eds.) Society, Culture, and Drinking Patterns. New York: John Wiley.
Jakobson, Roman
1956 "Two aspects of language and two aspects of aphasic disturbances," pp. 69–96 in Roman Jakobson and Morris Halle (eds.) Fundamentals of Language. The Hague: Mouton.
1962 Selected Writings, Vol. 1. Phonological Studies. The Hague: Mouton.
James, Henry
1920 "Letter to Mrs. Humphry Ward," pp. 332–336 in Percy Lubbock (ed.) Henry James: Letters. London: Hogarth.
James, W.
1950 The Principles of Psychology in Two Volumes. New York: Henry Holt. (originally published in 1890)
1955 Pragmatism and Four Essays from the Meaning of Truth. New York: Humanities. (originally published in 1910)
1961 The Varieties of Religious Experience: A Study in Human Nature. New York: Collier. (originally published in 1904)

Jameson, Fredric
1983 "Postmodernism and consumer society," pp. 111–125 in Hal Foster (ed.) The Anti-Aesthetic: Essays on Postmodern Culture. Port Townsend, WA: Bay Press.

Jellinek, E. M.
1960 The Disease Concept of Alcoholism. New Haven, CT: Hillhouse.
1962 "Phases of alcohol addiction," pp. 356–368 in David J. Pittman and C. R. Synder (eds.) Society, Culture, and Drinking Patterns. New York: John Wiley.

Jessor, R., T. D. Graves, R. C. Hanson, and S. L. Jessor
1968 Society, Personality and Deviant Behavior: A Study of a Tri-ethnic Community. Holt, Rinehart, and Winston.

Johnson, Bruce Holley
1973 "The alcoholism movement in America: a study in cultural innovation." Doctoral dissertation, University of Illinois, Urbana-Champaign.

Johnson, Dianne
1983 Dashiell Hammett: A Life. Boston: Little, Brown.

Jung, C. G.
1939 The Integration of Personality. New York: Farrar and Rinehart.
1961 Memories, Dreams, Reflections. New York: Pantheon.

Kane, Geoffrey P.
1981 Inner-City Alcoholism: An Ecological Analysis and Cross-Cultural Study. New York: Human Sciences Press.

Keller, Mark
1976 "The disease concept of alcoholism revisited." Quarterly Journal of Studies on Alcohol 37: 1694–1717.
1978 "A nonbehaviorist's view of the behavioral problem with alcoholism," pp. 381–398 in Peter E. Nathan et al. (eds.) Alcoholism: New Directions in Behavioral Research and Treatment. New York: Plenum.

Keller, Mark and Mairi McCormick
1968 A Dictionary of Words About Alcohol. New Brunswick, NJ: Publications Division, Rutgers Center of Alcohol Studies.

Kellerman, Joseph L.
1969 Alcoholism: A Merry-Go-Round Named Denial. New York: Al-Anon Family Group Headquarters, Inc.

Kemper, T. D.
1978 A Social Interactional Theory of Emotions. New York: John Wiley.
1981 "Social constructionist and positivist approaches to the sociology of emotions." American Journal of Sociology 86: 336–362.

Kissin, Benjamin
1977 "Theory and practice in the treatment of alcoholism" pp. 1–52 in Benjamin Kissin and Henry Begleiter (eds.) The Biology of Alcoholism, Vol. 5. Treatment and Rehabilitation of the Chronic Alcoholic. New York: Plenum.

Knight, R. P.
1937 "The psychodynamics of chronic alcoholism." Journal of Nervous and Mental Diseases 86: 538–548.

Kohlberg, L.
1981 The Philosophy of Moral Development. San Francisco: Harper & Row.

Kohut, H.
1971 The Analysis of the Self. New York: International Universities Press.
1977 The Restoration of the Self. New York: International Universities Press.

1984 How Does Psychoanalysis Cure? Chicago: University of Chicago Press.
Kristeva, Julia
1974 La Révolution du Langage Poétique. Paris: Editions du Seuil.
Kuhn, Manford H. and C. Addison Hickman
1956 Individuals, Groups and Economic Behavior. New York: Dryden Press.
Kurtz, Ernest
1979 Not-God: A History of Alcoholics Anonymous. Center City, MN: Hazelden Educational Materials.
Labov, W. and D. Fanshel
1977 Therapeutic Discourse: Psychotherapy as Conversation. New York: Academic Press.
Lacan, J.
1949 "The mirror stage as formative of the function of the I as revealed in psychoanalytic experience," pp. 1–7 in Ecrits: A Selection. New York: W. W. Norton.
1957 "The agency of the letter in the unconscious or reason since Freud," pp. 146–178 in Ecrits: A Selection. New York: W. W. Norton.
1966 Ecrits. Paris: Editions de Seuil.
1968 Speech and Language in Psychoanalysis. [A. Wildon, trans.]. Baltimore, MD: Johns Hopkins University Press.
1977 Ecrits: A Selection [A. Sheridan, trans.]. New York: W.W. Norton.
1978 The Four Fundamental Concepts of Psycho-Analysis. New York: Norton.
1982 Feminine Sexuality. New York: Norton.
Lasch, C.
1979 The Culture of Narcissism: American Life in an Age of Diminished Expectations: New York: Norton.
1984 The Minimal Self: Psychic Survival in Troubled Times. New York: Norton.
Leach, Barry and John L. Norris
1977 "Factors in the development of Alcoholics Anonymous (A.A.)," pp. 441–519 in Benjamin Kissin and Henri Begleiter (eds.) The Biology of Alcoholism, Vol. 5, Treatment and Rehabilitation of the Chronic Alcoholic. New York: Plenum.
Laing, R. D.
1965 The Divided Self: An Existential Study in Sanity and Madness. Harmondsworth, England: Penguin.
Lemert, Edwin M.
1958 "The use of alcohol in three Salish Indian tribes." Quarterly Journal of Studies on Alcohol 19: 90–107.
1964 "Drinking in Hawaiian plantation society," Quarterly Journal of Studies on Alcohol 25: 689–713.
1967 Human Deviance, Social Problems and Social Control. Englewood Cliffs, NJ: Prentice-Hall.
Lessing, Doris
1969 The Four-Gated City. New York: Knopf.
Levine, Harry Gene
1978 "The discovery of addiction." Journal of Studies on Alcohol 39: 143–174.
Lewontin, R. C., Steven Rose, and Leon J. Kamin
1984 Not in Our Genes: Biology, Ideology, and Human Nature. New York: Pantheon.
Lifton, R. J.
1961 Thought Reform and the Psychology of Totalism. New York: W. W. Norton.

Lindesmith, Alfred R.
1947 Opiate Addiction. Bloomington, IN: Principia Press.
1968 Addiction and Opiates. Chicago: Aldine.
1975 "A reply to McAuliffe and Gordon's 'Test of Lindesmith's Theory of Addiction.' " American Journal of Sociology 81, 1: 147–153.
Lindesmith, Alfred R., Anselm L. Strauss, and Norman K. Denzin
1975 Social Psychology. New York: Holt, Rinehart and Winston.
1977 Social Psychology. New York: Holt, Rinehart and Winston.
Lisansky, E. A.
1960 "The etiology of alcoholism: the role of psychological predisposition." Quarterly Journal of Studies on Alcohol 21: 314–324.
Lofland, John
1977 Doomsday Cult: A Study of Conversion, Proselytization, and Maintenance of Faith. New York: Irvington Publishers.
Lofland, John and Rodney Stark
1965 "Conversion to a deviant perspective." American Sociological Review 30: 862–875.
Lowry, Malcolm
1984 Under the Volcano. New York: New American Library. (originally published in 1947)
Ludwig, Arnold M.
1983 "Why do alcoholics drink?" pp. 197–214 in Benjamin Kissin and Henri Begleiter (eds.) The Biology of Alcoholism, Vol. 6. Psychosocial Factors. New York: Plenum.
Luft, J.
1961 "The Johari Window: A graphic model of awareness in interpersonal behavior." Human Relations Training News 5, 1: 6–7.
Lynch, R.
1982 "Play, creativity, and emotion," pp. 45–62 in N. K. Denzin (ed.) Studies in Symbolic Interaction, Vol. 4. Greenwich, Ct: JAI.
Lyotard, Jean-Grancois
1984 The Postmodern Condition: A Report on Knowledge. Minneapolis, MN: University of Minnesota Press.
MacAndrew, Craig and Robert B. Edgerton
1969 Drunken comportment: A Social Explanation. Chicago: Aldine.
MacAndrew, Craig and Harold Garfinkel
1962 "A consideration of changes attributed to intoxication as common-sense reasons for getting drunk." Quarterly Journal of Studies on Alcohol 23: 252–266.
Madsen, William
1974 The American Alcoholic: the Nature-Nurture Controversy in Alcoholic Research and Therapy. Springfield, IL: Charles C. Thomas.
Maisto, Stephen A. and Janice Boon McCollam
1980 "The use of multiple measures of life health to assess alcohol treatment outcome: a review and critique," pp. 15–76 in Linda Carter Sobell et al. (eds.) Evaluating Alcohol and Drug Abuse Treatment Effectiveness. New York: Pergamon.
Malinowski, B.
1962 Sex, Culture and Myth. New York: Harcourt (originally published in 1913)
Mandall, Wallace and Harold M. Ginzburg
1976 "Youthful alcohol use, abuse and alcoholism," pp. 167–204 in Benjamin

Kissin and Henri Begleiter (eds.) The Biology of Alcoholism, Vol. 4. Social Aspects of Alcoholism. New York: Plenum.

Mann, Marty
1968 New Primer on Alcoholism. New York: Holt, Rinehart and Winston.

Mark, V. H. and F. R. Ervin
1970 Violence and the Brain. New York: Harper & Row.

Marshall, Shelly
1978 Young, Sober and Free. Center City, MN: Hazelden Foundation.

Marx, G. T. and J. I. Wood
1975 "Strands of theory and research in collective behavior," pp. 363–428 in I. Inkeles et al. (eds.) Annual Review of Sociology, Vol. 1. Palo Alto, CA: Annual Reviews, Inc.

Marx, Karl
1983 "From the eighteenth Brumaire of Louis Bonaparte," in E. Kamenka (ed.) The Portable Karl Marx. New York: Penguin. (originally published in 1852)

Maxwell, Milton A.
1984 The Alcoholics Anonymous Experience: A Close-up View for Professionals. New York: McGraw-Hill.

McAuliffe, William E. and Robert A. Gordon
1974 "A test of Lindesmith's theory of addiction: the frequency of euphoria among long-term addicts." American Journal of Sociology 77: 795–840.

McCall, G. J. and J. Simmons
1978 Identities and Interactions. New York: Free Press.

McClearn, Gerald E.
1983 "Genetic factors in alcohol abuse: animal models," pp. 1–30 in Benjamin Kissin and Henri Begleiter (eds.) The Biology of Alcoholism, Vol. 7. Biological Factors. New York: Plenum.

McClelland, David C., William N. Davis, Rudolf Kalin, and Eric Wanner
1972 The Drinking Man. New York: The Free Press.

McCord, W., J. McCord, and J. H. Mendelson
1960 Origins of Alcoholism. Palo Alto, CA: Stanford University Press.

Mead, G. H.
1899 "The working hypothesis in social reform." American Journal of Sociology 5: 369–371.
1934 Mind, Self and Society. Chicago: University of Chicago Press.
1964 "A pragmatic theory of truth," pp. 320–344 in Andrew J. Reck (ed.) George Herbert Mead: Selected Writings. Indianapolis: The Bobbs-Merrill Company.

Mello, Nancy K.
1972 "Behavioral studies of alcoholism," pp. 219–292 in Benjamin Kissin and Henri Begleiter (eds.) The Biology of Alcoholism, Vol. 2. Physiology and Behavior. New York: Plenum.
1983 "A behavioral analysis of the reinforcing properties of alcohol and other drugs in man," pp. 133–198 in Benjamin Kissin and Henry Begleiter (eds.) The Biology of Alcoholism, Vol. 7. Biological Factors. New York: Plenum.

Meltzer, Bernard M.
1972 "Mead's social psychology," pp. 4–22 in J. G. Manis and B . N. Meltzer (eds.) *Symbolic Interaction: A Reader in Social Psychology.* Boston: Allyn and Bacon.

Menninger, Karl A.
1938 Man Against Himself. New York: Harcourt, Brace and World.

Merleau-Ponty, M.
1963 The Structure of Behavior. [A. L. Fisher, trans.]. Boston: Beacon. (originally published in 1942)
Merryman, Richard
1984 Broken Promises, Mended Dreams. Boston: Little, Brown.
Merton, Robert K.
1957 Social Theory and Social Structure. Glencoe, IL: Free Press.
Mills, C. W.
1940 "Situated actions and vocabularies of motive." American Sociological Review 5: 904–913.
1959 The Sociological Imagination. New York: Oxford University Press.
Mulford, Harold A.
1969 "Alcoholics," "Alcoholism," and "Problem Drinkers": Social Objects In-The-Making. Report to the National Center for Health Statistics, U.S. Department of Health, Education and Welfare, Washington, DC. (mimeo.)
1970 Meeting the Problems of Alcohol Abuse: A Testable Action Plan for Iowa. Cedar Rapids, IA: Iowa Alcoholism Foundation.
Mulford, Harold A. and Donald E. Miller
1964 "Measuring public acceptance of the alcoholic as a sick person." Quarterly Journal of Studies on Alcohol 25: 314–323.
Nathan P. E., N. A. Titler, L. A. Lowenstein, P. Solomon, and A. M. Rossi
1970 "Behavioral analysis of chronic alcoholism." Archives of General Psychiatry 22: 419–428.
Newsweek
1984a "Getting straight: how Americans are breaking the grip of drugs and alcohol." (June 4): 62–69.
1984b "Alcoholism and the recovering generation." (September 10): 71–80.
New York Times
1983 "Alcohol abuse in the United States." (October 23): 1.
Nietzsche, Friedrich
1887 A Geneology of Morals: Vol. 2. [William A. Hausemann, trans.]. New York: Macmillan.
O'Neill, Eugene
1955 Long Day's Journey into Night. New Haven, CT: Yale University Press.
Oscar-Berman, M.
1984 "Central nervous system disorders," pp. 190–191 in Raymond J. Corsini (ed.) Encyclopedia of Psychology, Vol. 1. New York: John Wiley.
Parsons, Talcott [ed.].
1978 "The sick role and the role of the physician reconsidered," pp. 11–16 in Action Theory and the Human Condition. New York: Free Press.
Pattison, E. Mansell
1966 "A critique of alcoholism treatment concepts." Quarterly Journal of Studies on Alcohol 27: 49–71.
Pattison, E. Mansell, E. B. Headley, G. C. Gleser, and L. A. Gottschalk
1968 "Abstinence and normal drinking: an assessment of changes in drinking patterns in alcoholics after treatment." Quarterly Journal of Studies on Alcohol 29: 610–633.
Pattison, E. Mansell, Mark B. Sobell, and Linda C. Sobell
1977 Emerging Concepts of Alcohol Dependence. New York: Springer.
Pendery, Mary L. Irving M. Maltzman, and L. Jolyon West
1982 "Controlled drinking by alcoholics: new findings and a reevaluation of a major affirmative study." Science 217: 169–175.

Pernanen, Kai
1976 "Alcohol and crimes of violence," pp. 351–444 in Benjamin Kissin and Henri Begleiter (eds.) *The Biology of Alcoholism, Vol. 4, Social Aspects of Alcoholism*. New York: Plenum.
Pittman, David
1967 "International overview: social and cultural factors and nonpathological," pp. 3–20 in David J. Pittman (ed.) Alcoholism. New York: Harper & Row.
Pittman, David J. and C. W. Gordon
1958 "Criminal careers of the chronic drunkenness offender." Quarterly Journal of Studies on Alcohol 19: 255–268.
Radcliffe-Brown, A. R.
1922 The Adaman Islanders. Glencoe, IL: Free Press.
Redd, William H., A. L. Porterfield, and Barbara L. Anderson
1979 Behavior modification: Behavioral Approaches to Human Problems. New York: Random House.
Robbins, Lee N.
1980 "Alcoholism and labelling theory," pp. 35–46 in W. R. Gove (ed.) The Labeling of Deviance: Evaluating a Perspective. Beverly Hills, CA: Sage.
Robinson, David
1979 Talking Out of Alcoholism: The Self-Help Process of Alcoholics Anonymous. Baltimore, MD: University Park Press.
Roebuck, Julian B. and R. G. Kessler
1972 The Etiology of Alcoholism: Constitutional, Psychological and Sociological Approaches. Springfield, IL: Charles C Thomas.
Roman, Paul M. and Harrison M. Trice
1976 "Alcohol abuse and work organization," pp. 445–519 in Benjamin Kissin and Henri Begleiter (eds.) The Biology of Alcoholism, Vol. 4. Social Aspects of Alcoholism. New York: Plenum.
Room, Robin
1982 "Alcohol, science and social control," pp. 371–384 in Edith L. Gomberg et al. (eds.) Alcohol, Science and Society Revisited. Ann Arbor: University of Michigan Press.
1983 "Region and urbanization as factors in drinking practices and problems," pp. 555–604 in Benjamin Kissin and Henri Begleiter (eds.) The Biology of Alcoholism, Vol. 6. Psychosocial Factors. New York: Plenum.
Roth, J.
1963 Timetables. Indianapolis, IN: Bobbs-Merrill.
Royce, James E.
1981 Alcoholic Problems and Alcoholism: A Comprehensive Survey. New York: Free Press.
Rubington, Earl
1977 "The role of the halfway house in the rehabilitation of alcoholics," pp. 351–384 in Benjamin Kissin and Henri Begleiter (eds.) The Biology of Alcoholism, Vol. 5: Treatment and Rehabilitation of the Chronic Alcoholic. New York: Plenum.
1973 Alcohol Problems and Social Control. Columbus, OH: Merrill.
Rudy, David
1986 Becoming an Alcoholic. Carbondale: Southern Illinois University.
Ryan, Christopher and Nelson Butters
1983 "Cognitive deficits in alcoholics," pp. 485–538 in Benjamin Kissin and Henri Begleiter (eds.) The Biology of Alcoholism, Vol. 7. Biological Factors. New York: Plenum.

Sagarin, E.
1969 Odd Man In: Societies of Deviants in America. Chicago: Quadrangle.
Sartre, Jean-Paul
1956 Being and Nothingness. New York: Philosophical Library. (originally published in 1943).
1976 Critique of Dialectical Reason. London: NLP. (originally published in 1960)
1981 The Family Idiot, Gustave Flaubert, Vol. I: 1821–1857. Chicago: University of Chicago Press.
Scheff, Thomas J.
1979 Catharsis in Healing, Ritual and Drama. Berkeley: University of California Press.
Schegloff, E. A., G. Jefferson, and H. Sacks
1977 "The preference for self-correction in the organization of repair in conversation." Language 53: 361–382.
Scheler, M.
1961 Ressentiment. [L. A. Coser, ed.; W. W. Holdeim, trans.]. New York: Free Press. (originally published in 1912)
1970 The Nature of Sympathy. [P. Heath, trans.] Hamden, CT: Archon books. (originally published in 1913).
1973 Formalism in Ethics and Non-Formal Ethics of Values: A New Attempt Toward the Foundation of an Ethical Personalism. Evanston, IL: Northwestern University Press. (originally published in 1916)
Schenkein, J. [ed.]
1978 Studies in the Organization of Conversational Interaction. New York: Academic Press.
Schuckit, Marc A. and Jane Duby
1983 "Alcoholism in women," pp. 215–242 in Benjamin Kissin and Henri Begleiter (eds.) The Biology of Alcoholism, Vol. 6. Psychosocial Factors. New York: Plenum.
Schutz, A.
1962 Collected Papers, Vol. I. The Problem of Social Reality. [M. Natanson, ed.]. The Hague: Martinus Nijhoff.
1964 Collected Papers, Vol. II. Studies in Social Theory [A. Brodersen, ed.]. The Hague: Martinus Nijhoff.
1967 The Phenomenology of the Social World. Evanston, IL: Northwestern University Press.
1968 Collected Papers, Vol. III. Studies in Phenomenological Philosophy [I. Schutz, ed.]. The Hague: Martinus Nijhoff.
Schutz A. and T. Luckman
1973 The Structures of the Life World. Evanston, IL: Northwestern University Press.
Scott, M. B. and S. M. Lyman
1968 "Accounts." American Sociological Review 33: 46–62.
Searle, John
1970 Speech Acts. Cambridge: Cambridge University Press.
Shils, E.
1976 Center and Periphery: Essays in Macrosociology. Chicago: University of Chicago Press.
Shott, Susan
1979 "Emotion and social life: a symbolic interactionist analysis." American Journal of Sociology 84: 1317–34.

Silkworth, William D.
1976 "The doctor's opinion," pp. xxiii–xiv in Alcoholic Anonymous. New York: A.A. World Services, Inc.
Skinner, B. F.
1953 Science and Human Behavior. New York: Macmillan.
Smith, Bernard B.
1957 "A friend looks at alcoholics anonymous," pp. 273–283 in Alcoholics Anonymous Comes of Age: A Brief History of A.A. New York: Alcoholics Anonymous World Services, Inc.
Snow, D. A. and C. L. Phillips
1980 "The Lofland-Stark conversion model: a critical reassessment." Social Problems 27: 430–447.
Sobell, Linda Carter, Mark B. Sobell, and Elliot Ward
1980 Evaluating Alcohol and Drug Abuse Treatment Effectiveness: Recent Advances. New York: Pergamon.
Sobell, Mark B. and Linda C. Sobell
1978 Behavioral Treatment of Alcohol Problems: Individualized Therapy and Controlled Drinking. New York: Plenum.
Solomon, Joel
1983 "Psychiatric characteristics of alcoholics," pp. 67–112 in Benjamin Kissin and Henri Begleiter (eds.) The Biology of Alcoholism, Vol. 6. Psychosocial Factors. New York: Plenum.
Spender, Stephen
1984 "Introduction," pp. xii–xxiii in Malcolm Lowry, Under the Volcano. New York: New American Library. (originally published in 1947)
Spinoza, Benedict
1888 The Ethics [R.H.M. Elwes, trans.]. London: George Bell and Sons.
Spradley, James P.
1970 You Owe Yourself a Drunk: An Ethnography of Urban Nomads. Boston: Little, Brown.
Stack, Carol
1974 All Our Kin: Strategies for Survival in a Black Community. New York: Harper.
Stark, R. and W. S. Bainbridge
1980 "Networks of faith: interpersonal bonds and recruitment to cults and sects." American Journal of Sociology 85: 1376–1395.
Steinglass, Peter
1977 "Family therapy in alcoholism," pp. 259–300 in Benjamin Kissin and Henri Begleiter (eds.) The Biology of Alcoholism, Vol. 5. Treatment and Rehabilitation of the Chronic Alcoholic. New York: Plenum.
Steinglass, Peter and Anne Robertson
1983 "The alcoholic family," pp. 243–307 in Benjamin Kissin and Henri Begleiter (eds.) The Pathogenesis of Alcoholism, Vol. 6. Psychosocial Factors. New York: Plenum.
Stivers, Richard
1976 A Hair of the Dog: Irish Drinking and American Stereotype. University Park, PA: Pennsylvania State University Press.
Stone, Gregory P.
1962 "Appearance and the self," pp. 86–118 in A. M. Rose (ed.) Human Nature and Social Process. Boston: Houghton Mifflin.
1976 "Personal acts." Symbolic Interaction 1: 1–16.

1981 "Appearance and the self: a slightly revised version," pp. 187–202 in Gregory P. Stone and Harvey A. Faberman (eds.) Social Psychology Through Symbolic Interaction. New York: John Wiley.

Straus, Robert
1974 Escape from Custody. New York: Harper & Row.

Strauss, A.
1959 Mirrors and Masks: The Search for Identity. New York: Free Press.
1978 "A social world perspective," pp. 119–128 in Norman K. Denzin (ed.) Studies in Symbolic Interaction, Vol. 1. Greenwich, CT: JAI.
1982 "Social worlds and legitimation processes," pp. 171–190 in Norman K. Denzin (ed.) Studies in Symbolic Interaction, Vol. 4. Greenwich, CT: JAI.

Stryker, Sheldon
1981 "Symbolic interactionism: themes and variations," pp. 3–29 in M. Rosenberg and R. Turner (eds.) Social Psychology: Sociological Perspectives. New York: Basic Books.

Sullivan, H. S.
1953 The Interpersonal Theory of Psychiatry. New York: Norton.

Sykes, G. M. and D. Matza
1959 "Techniques of neutralization: a theory of delinquency." American Sociological Review 22: 664–670.

Szasz, Thomas
1961 The Myth of Mental Illness. New York: Dell.
1975 Ceremonial Chemistry: The Ritual Persecution of Drugs, Addicts and Pushers. New York: Doubleday.

Thomas, W. I. and D. S. Thomas
1982 The Child in America. New York: Knopf.

Thorndike, E. L.
1913 The Psychology of Learning: Educational Psychology, Vol. 2. New York: Teacher's College Press of Columbia University.

Thune, Carl E.
1977 "Alcoholism, and the archetypical past: a phenomenological perspective on Alcoholics Anonymous." Quarterly Journal of Studies on Alcohol 38: 75–88.

Tiebout, Harry M.
1944 "Therapeutic mechanisms in Alcoholics Anonymous." American Journal of Psychiatry 100: 468–473.
1949 "The act of surrender in the therapeutic process with special reference to alcoholism." Quarterly Journal of Studies on Alcohol 10: 48–58.
1953 "Surrender versus compliance in therapy." Quarterly Journal of Studies on Alcohol 14: 58–68.
1954 "The ego factors in surrender in alcoholism." Quarterly Journal of Studies on Alcohol 15: 610–621.

Time Magazine
1985 "Cocktails '85: America's new drinking habits." (May 20): 68–73, 76–78.

Travisano, Richard
1981 "Alternation and conversion as qualitatively different transformations," pp. 237–248 in Gregory P. Stone and Harvey A. Faberman (eds.) Social Psychology Through Symbolic Interaction. New York: John Wiley.

Trice, Harrison M.
1957 "A study of the process of affiliation with Alcoholics Anonymous." Quarterly Journal of Studies in Alcohol 18: 39–43.

1966 Alcoholism in America. New York: McGraw-Hill.
1984 "Alcoholism in America revisited." Journal of Drug Issues 14: 109–123.
Trice, Harrison, M. and Paul M. Roman
1970 "Delabeling, relabeling and Alcoholics Anonymous." Social Problems 17: 468–480.
Ullman, Albert D.
1958 "Sociocultural backgrounds conducive to alcoholism." Annals of the American Academy of Political and Social Science 315: 48–55.
United States Government Printing Office
1976 Comprehensive Alcohol Abuse and Alcoholism Prevention, Treatment, and Rehabilitation Act Amendments of 1976. Washington, DC: Author.
Updike, John
1984 "Modernist, postmodernist, what will they think of next?" *New Yorker* (September 10): 136–137,140–142.
Urbina, S. P.
1984 "Amnesia," pp. 56–57 in Raymond J. Corsini (ed.) Encyclopedia of Psychology, Vol. 1. New York: John Wiley.
Valliant, George
1983 The Natural History of Alcoholism: Causes, Patterns and Paths to Recovery. Cambridge, MA: Harvard University Press.
Vander Mey, Brenda J. and Ronald L. Neff
1986 Incest as Child Abuse Research and Implications. New York: Praeger.
Victor, M.
1965 "Observations on the amnestic syndrome in man and its anatomical basis," pp. 311–340 in M.A.B. Brazier (ed.) Brain Functions: Vol. 2. Berkeley: University of California Press.
Vogel-Sprott, M.
1972 "Alcoholism and learning," pp. 485–509 in Benjamin Kissin and Henri Begleiter (eds.) The Biology of Alcoholism, Vol. 2: Physiology and Behavior. New York: Plenum.
Wallace, John
1982 "Alcoholism from the inside out: a phenomenological analysis," pp. 1–23 in Nada J. Estes and M. Edith Heinemann (eds.) Alcoholism: Development, Consequences and Interventions. St. Louis, MO: Mosby.
Wallace, P. M.
1984 "Aphasia," p. 80 in Raymond J. Corsini (ed.) Encyclopedia of Psychology, Vol. I. New York: John Wiley.
Warner, W. L.
1962 American Life: Dream and Reality. Chicago: University of Chicago Press.
Watson, J. B.
1913 "Psychology as the behaviorist sees it." Psychological Review 20: 158–177.
Watts, Thomas D. and Roosevelt Wright, Jr.
1983 Black Alcoholism: Toward Comprehensive Understanding. Springfield, IL: Charles C Thomas.
Weber, M.
1946 From Max Weber: Essays in Sociology [H. Gerth and C. W. Mills, eds.]. New York: Oxford University Press.
Weinstein, E. A. and P. Deutschberger
1962 "Some dimensions of altercasting." Sociometry 26: 454–466.
Wexberg, L. E.
1951 "Ursachen und Symptome der Arzneimittelsucht und des alkoholismus." Z. Psychother Stuttgart 1: 227–235.

White, R. W.
1956 The Abnormal Personality: New York: Ronald Press.
Whitney, Elizabeth D.
1865 The Lonely Sickness. Boston: Beacon Press.
Wholey, Dennis [ed.]
1984 The Courage to Change: Hope and Help for Alcoholics and Their Families. Personal Conversations with Dennis Wholey. Boston: Houghton Mifflin.
Wilden, Anthony
1968 "Lacan and the discourse of the other," pp. 86–222 in J. Lacan (ed.) Speech and Language in Psychoanalysis [A. Wilden, trans.]. Baltimore, MD: Johns Hopkins University Press.
Wiley, Norbert
1985 "Durkheim on religion: a revision." Unpublished manuscript, Department of Sociology, University of Illinois, Urbana.
Williams, Allan F.
1976 "The alcoholic personality," pp. 243–275 in Benjamin Kissin and Henri Begleiter (eds.) The Biology of Alcoholism, Vol. 4. Social Aspects of Alcoholism. New York: Plenum.
Wiseman, Jacqueline P.
1970 Stations of the Lost: The Treatment of Skid Row Alcoholics. Englewood Cliffs, NJ: Prentice-Hall.
Wittgenstein, L.
1954 Philosophical Investigations. London: Blackwell.
Woititz, Janet Geringer
1983 Adult Children of Alcoholics. Rutgers, NJ: Health Communications, Inc.
Zald, M. and R. Ash
1966 "Social movement organizations: growth, decay and change." Social Forces 44: 327–341.
Zurcher, Louis A. and David A. Snow
1981 "Collective behavior and social movements," pp. 447–482 in M. Rosenberg and R. H. Turner (eds.) Social Psychology: Sociological Perspectives. New York: Basic Books.
Zuriff, G. E.
1985 Behaviorism: A Conceptual Reconstruction. New York: Columbia University Press.
Zwerling, Israel and Milton Rosenbaum
1959 "Alcoholic addiction and personality," pp. 624–644 in S. Arieti (ed.) American Handbook of Psychiatry. New York: Basic Books.

Name Index

Subject Index

www.ingramcontent.com/pod-product-compliance
Lightning Source LLC
Chambersburg PA
CBHW050449051126
54379CB00003B/68
9781138534179